John Wallace

Carpet bag rule in Florida

The inside workings of the reconstruction of civil government in Florida

John Wallace

Carpet bag rule in Florida

The inside workings of the reconstruction of civil government in Florida

ISBN/EAN: 9783337221690

Printed in Europe, USA, Canada, Australia, Japan

Cover: Foto ©ninafisch / pixelio.de

More available books at **www.hansebooks.com**

THE INSIDE WORKINGS

OF THE

RECONSTRUCTION OF CIVIL GOVERNMENT
IN FLORIDA AFTER THE CLOSE
OF THE CIVIL WAR.

BY JOHN WALLACE.

Late Senator from Leon County.

———— —— —— ——

JACKSONVILLE, FLA.:
DA COSTA PRINTING AND PUBLISHING HOUSE,
1888.

PREFACE.

The author of this work was born in North Carolina and held as a slave until 1862, when he made his escape while General Burnside was operating with his army against the Confederacy in that State. He went to Washington, D. C., after which he entered the United States Army on the 14th of August, 1863, enlisting in the Second United States Colored Troops raised in that city, and served two years and six months in that regiment, which was engaged in the operations of the Federal forces in Florida in the year 1864, and the early part of 1865. Discharged from the service of the United States at Key West, January 1st, 1866, he returned to Tallahassee, where he has since resided up to this period. He had no education while a slave, and never had the benefit of any school before or since he was discharged from the army, and has acquired what knowledge he may have of letters from constant study at night, which studies he was compelled to relax on account of injury to his eyes by the explosion of a bomb shell, near his face, thrown by the enemy at the battle of Fort Myers, Florida. His physicians advised him that if he persisted in pursuing his studies it would result in total blindness. He has acquired the knowledge of facts upon which this work treats by being constantly in the midst of the actors of the theatre of this period. He was first appointed a messenger of the Constitutional Convention of 1868, and upon the adoption of the Constitution, was elected Constable for Leon County, the Capital of the State, serving for two years. Was elected twice to the lower branch of the Legislature, serving four years; and twice elected to the Senate, where he served for eight years.

In submitting this work to the public, the author does not attempt to present a work adorned with beauties of rhetoric, as he would desire, but has resorted, as far as his limited ability would permit, to such language in the construction of sentences as he judged would give the reader a fair conception of the transactions which took place during the period mentioned in the title of the work.

The design of this work is to correct the settled and erroneous impression that has gone out to the world that the former slaves, when enfranchised, had no conception of good government, and therefore their chief ambition was corruption and plunder; to prove that, although they had been for more than two hundred years deprived of that training calculated to fit a people for citizenship of a great republic like ours, yet their constant contact with a more enlightened race, though in the position of slaves, would have made them better citizens and more honest legislators if they had not been contaminated by strange white men who represented themselves to them as their saviours; that the laws of the State, passed with reference to the colored people in 1865, were not enacted as a whole to be enforced, but to deter the colored people from revenging any real or fancied wrongs that cruel masters may have inflicted while they were slaves; that these laws and the secret leagues, riveted the former slaves to these strangers, who explained them to be tenfold worse than they were; that it was white men, and not colored men, who originated corruption and enriched themselves from the earnings of the people of the State from the year 1868 to 1877; that the loss of the State to the National Republican Party was not due to any unfaithfulness of the colored people to that party, but to the corruption of these strange white leaders termed "carpet baggers;" that the colored people have done as well as any other people could have done under the same circumstances, if not better. This work is further intended to prove that notwithstanding the blunders of the ex-slaveholder towards the colored people, the deception and betrayal by the carpet baggers of the colored people into the hands of their former masters, yet they, like the thunder-riven oak, have defied the storm which has now spent its terrific force, and like a caravan of determined pioneers cutting out highways in a new country, the Negro is laying the foundation for a civilization that shall be fully equal in every respect to that of any other race or people; and that the ascendancy of the Democratic party to the State government in 1877, has proved a blessing in disguise to the colored people of Florida. Respectfully,

JOHN WALLACE.

CHAPTER I.

The Formation of Civil Government After the War. The Address and Proclamation of Provisional Governor Authorizing the Election of Delegates to Amend the Constitution. The Number of Delegates. Negroes Excluded from Voting by Governor's Proclamation. Election Held. Number of Votes Cast.

On July 13th, A. D. 1865, President Andrew Johnson appointed William Marvin, Esq., as Provisional Governor of Florida, to proceed to establish civil government. The President embodied in the commission of the Provisional Governor an injunction that no person should be allowed to vote for the delegates to any convention called by his authority who was not a qualified voter before the 10th of January, A. D. 1861—or, in plain words, that no negro should be allowed to vote at said election. It will be noticed hereafter that although there were hundreds of negro soldiers garrisoning different parts of the State, who had shared, in common with their white brethren, the fatigues, sufferings and dangers of war and the battle field, and a great many of those inhabitants and natives of Florida were enrolled and mustered into the service of the United States, had marched and fought side by side with the First and Second Florida Cavalry, two white Federal regiments raised in Florida, they were called upon and commanded by the President of the United States to aid, encourage and assist in establishing a government in Florida which excluded them from enjoying the same privileges that their white brothers enjoyed. The Provisional Governor carried out in letter and spirit the President's proclamation, and issued an address to the people of Florida setting forth his duties and the duties of the voters. The address and proclamation of the Provisional Governor are as follows:

To the People of Florida:

The civil authorities in this State having engaged in an organized rebellion against the Government of the United States, have, with the overthrow of the rebellion, ceased to exist, and the State, though in the Union, is without a civil government. The Constitution of the United States declares that the United States shall guarantee to every State in the Union a republican form of government, and shall protect each of these against invasion, insurrection and domestic violence.

"In order to fulfill this guaranty, and for the purpose of enabling the loyal people of the State to organize a State government, whereby justice may be established, domestic tranquillity insured and loyal citizens protected in all their rights of life, liberty and property, the President of the United States has appointed me Provisional Governor of the State, and made it my duty, at the earliest practicable moment, to prescribe such rules and regulations as may be necessary and proper for convening a convention composed of delegates to be chosen by that portion of the people of the State who are loyal to the United States, and no others, for the purpose of altering or amending the Constitution of the State, and with authority to exercise within the limits of the State all the powers necessary and proper to enable the loyal people of the State to restore it to its constitutional relations to the Federal Government, and to present such a republican form of State government as will entitle the State to the guaranty of the United States therefor, and its people to protection by the United States against invasion, insurrection and domestic violence.

"In the performance of the duty thus enjoined upon me by the President, I shall, as soon as the people of the State have had the opportunity to qualify themselves to become voters, appoint an election, to be held in the different counties of the State, of delegates to a State convention to be convened at a time and place to be hereafter named.

"The persons qualified to vote at such election of delegates, and the persons eligible as members of such convention, will be such persons as shall have previously taken and subscribed the oath of amnesty as set forth in the President's proclamation of May 29th, A. D. 1865, and as are also qualified as prescribed by the Constitution and laws of the State in force immediately before the 10th day of January, 1861, the date of the so-called ordinance of secession. Where the person is exempted from the benefits of the amnesty proclamation, he must also have been previously specially pardoned by the President before he can become a qualified voter or eligible as a member of the convention. This interpretation of the proclamation of the President I have received from himself in person, and also from the Attorney-General. The oath referred to may be administered by and taken and subscribed before any commissioned official, civil, military or naval, in the service of the United States, or any civil or military officer of a loyal State or Territory who, by the laws thereof, is qualified to administer oaths. The officer administering the oath is authorized and required to give to the person taking it certified copies thereof.

"In order to give the well disposed people of this State time and opportunity to qualify themselves to be voters for delegates to the convention, the election will not be held until a reasonable time has elapsed for them to take and subscribe the oath required, and to procure the special pardon, where such pardon is a prerequisite qualification. The election will be held immediately thereafter, and no allowance will be made for unreasonable delays in applying for pardons.

"Applications for pardon should be in writing, and addressed to the President of the United States, and state the grounds on which a special pardon is considered necessary. The application should have attached to it the original oath or affirmation contained in the proclamation of amnesty. In most cases, the application for pardon will not be acted upon by the President until it has received the recommendation of the Provisional Governor. It will save time, therefore, to seek his recommendation in the first instance. The application should then be sent to the office of the Attorney-General. I have been informed by the military authorities that a considerable number of Posts have already been established in the State, and others soon will be, with officers attached, authorized to administer the oath required, and to give certified copies thereof, so as thereby to give every facility for taking the oath, with little or no inconvenience or expense to applicants.

"In the meantime, and until the re-establishment of a State government, it is left to the military authorities to preserve peace and order, and protect the rights of persons and property. An understanding has been had with the Commander of the Department whereby persons occupying the offices of Judge of Probate may continue to take proof of wills and issue letters testamentary and of administration, and Clerks of Circuit Court may take proof or acknowledgment of deeds and mortgages, and record the same, as heretofore, and all persons occupying ministerial offices may continue to perform such duties and offices as are essential and convenient to the transaction of business. If any doubt should hereafter arise concerning the validity of their acts, such doubts can be removed by a legislative act of confirmation.

"By operation and results of the war, slavery has ceased to exist in the State. It cannot be revived. Every voter for delegates to the convention, in taking the amnesty oath, takes a solemn oath to support the freedom of the former slave. The freedom intended is the full, ample, and complete freedom of a citizen of the United States. This does not necessarily include the privilege of voting, but it does include the idea of future possession and quiet enjoyment. The question of his voting is an open question—a proper subject for discussion—and is to be decided as a question of sound policy by the convention to be called.

"On the establishment of a republican form of State government under the constitution which guarantees and secures liberty to all the inhabitants alike, without distinction of color, there will no longer exist any impediment in the way of restoring the State to its proper constitutional relations to the government of the United States, whereby the people will be entitled to protection by the United States against invasion, insurrection, and domestic violence.

"Dated at Jacksonville, Florida, this third day of August, 1865.

WILLIAM MARVIN,
Provisional Governor."

As the proclamation of the Governor authorizing the holding of the election for delegates contains but very little more than what appears in his address to the people of Florida, the author deemed it necessary to have only such parts of it contained in this work as do not appear in his address. The delegates were apportioned among the several counties as follows: Escambia, two; Santa Rosa, two; Walton, two; Holmes, one; Washington, one; Jackson, three; Calhoun, one; Franklin, one; Liberty, one; Gadsden, three; Leon, four; Jefferson, three; Madison, two; Taylor, one; Lafayette, one; Hamilton, two; Suwannee, one; Columbia, two; Baker, one; Bradford, one; Nassau, one; St. Johns, one; Duval, one; Clay, one; Putnam, one; Alachua, two; Marion, two; Levy, one; Hernando, one; Hillsborough, one; Manatee, one; Polk, one; Orange, one; Volusia, one; Brevard, one; Sumter, one; Monroe, one; and Dade, one. The proclamation set forth the qualification of voters as follows: "Free white soldiers, seamen and marines in the army or navy of the United States, who were qualified by their residence to vote in said State at the same time of their enlistment, and who shall have taken and subscribed the amnesty oath, shall be entitled to vote in the county where they respectively reside." "But no soldier, seaman or marine, not a resident of the State at the time of his enlistment shall be allowed to vote." "Every free white male person of the age of twenty-one years and upwards, and who shall be, at the time of offering to vote, a citizen of the United States, and who shall have resided and had his home in the State for one year next preceding the election, and for six months in the county in which he may offer to vote," and also take the oath prescribed by the President in his amnesty proclamation, were entitled to vote. The election was held in the several counties of the State on the 10th day of October, A. D., 1865, according to proclamation ordering said election, dated September 11th, 1865.

The Judges of Probate in the several counties, and the Clerks of Circuit Court, in case of the inability, absence, or other cause, the Probate Judges failing to act, were authorized to appoint the Inspectors of Election. The Clerk and County Judge were also authorized to call to their assistance two respectable inhabitants having the qualification of voters, and publicly count the votes cast, and to furnish to each person elected a certificate of his election, and also to forward a certificate of the election of each delegate to the Provisional Governor at Tallahassee. The Inspectors of Election were required to administer the amnesty oath to any person at the polls who could not exhibit a certificate of his having taken the oath previously.

The number of qualified voters up to the day of election was eight thousand five hundred and twelve. The number of votes cast for delegates was six thousand seven hundred and seven.

CHAPTER II.

The Assembling of the Convention. The Election of the Presiding Officer. Different Opinions of the Delegates as to the Negro Problem Before They Received the Governor's Message. The Governor's Message Solves and Settles the Problem. Negroes Testifying in Courts of Justice.

The convention met October 25th, 1865, and Hon. E. D. Tracy, of Nassau County, was called to the chair. A committee was appointed to wait upon the Provisional Governor and obtain from him a list of the delegates elected, which duty was promptly performed and the list of delegates forwarded to the convention by the Governor, namely:

Leon County—James L. Taylor, G. Troup Maxwell, Thomas Baltzell, David P. Hogue.

Gadsden County—George K. Walker, R. H. M. Davidson, Arthur J. Forman.

Jefferson County—W. M. Capers Bird, W. B. Cooper, Asa May.

Hamilton County—William J. J. Duncan, Alexander Bell.

Madison County—W. J. Hines, D. G. Livingston.

Wakulla County—James T. Magbee.

Liberty County—T. D. Nixon.

Jackson County—F. B. Calloway, Felix Leslie, Allen H. Bush.

Calhoun County—Jackson Richard.

Taylor County—Wiley W. Whidden.

Clay County—William Wilson.

Lafayette County—Moses Simmons.

Putnam County—Henry S. Teasdale.

St. Johns County—James A. Michler, Jr.

Levy County—William R. Coulter.

Duval County—S. L. Burritt.

Suwannee County—Silas Overstreet.

Columbia County—Silas L. Niblack, Thomas T. Long.

Nassau County—E. D. Tracy.
Baker County—Samuel N. Williams.
Bradford County—John C. Richard.
Hillsborough County—James Gettis.
Marion County—James A. Wiggins, Thomas J. Pasteur.
Hernando County—Samuel E. Hope.
Monroe County—Daniel H. Winterhurst.
Dade County—R. R. Fletcher.
Polk County—Francis A. Hendry.
Alachua County—W. Wash Scott, Samuel Spencer.
Escambia County—Benjamin D. Wright, W. W. J. Kelly.
Walton County—James M. Landrum, John Morrison.
Holmes County—James G. Owens.
Sumter County—James Love.
Washington County—Jesse B. Lassiter.
Orange County—William H. Holden.
Brevard County—James F. P. Johnson.
Santa Rosa County—Jesse McLellan, G. B. Dyens.
Volusia County—A. Richardson.

The following was the oath administered to the delegates-elect: "You and each of you do solemnly swear well and truly to discharge your respective duties and support the Constitution of the United States."

Thomas Baltzell, of Leon, and Benjamin D. Wright, of Escambia, were put in nomination for President of the convention. There were two ballots taken without an election, and on the third ballot Mr. G. Troup Maxwell, of Leon, withdrew the name of Baltzell, and the convention proceeded to ballot for Tracy and Wright, Mr. Tracy receiving twenty-four votes and Wright fifteen. Mr. Tracy was declared elected.

This convention, composed largely of men who had for four years worked and fought to sustain a cause which was finally lost, were willing to do anything honorable to show the government that they were acting in good faith, even if it were to sustain negro suffrage to a limited extent, had it not been for the sweeping message of Governor Marvin, the man appointed to carry out the policy of the President. Some of the gentlemen with whom I was acquainted expressed themselves to me that such a proposition would have been carried before the convention but for the opposition of Governor Marvin. The convention seems to have been entirely, or almost so, under the control and influence of the Provisional Governor and the military. It will be seen that they did but very little other than what was recommended to them by William Marvin, the President's agent. After reading carefully the message and recommendations of the Governor to this convention, and digesting the different subjects treated in the message, I leave the reader to draw his own conclusions as to any injustice done the negro by the convention; whether it was not in accordance strictly with the policy of President Johnson? Referring to the question of negro suffrage, the Governor says: "Shall the elective franchise be conferred upon the colored race, and if so upon what terms and qualifications?" "I am not advised that the President has expressed his views or wishes on this subject, and I know no more of the views or wishes of the members of Congress than is generally known." "I cannot think, however, that, if the convention shall abolish slavery and provide proper guaranties for the protection and security of the persons and property of the freedmen, the Congress will refuse to admit our Senators and Representatives to their seats because the freedmen are not allowed to vote at the State and other elections." "When the question of their admission shall arise, I think the main inquiry will be, not are the freedmen allowed to vote, but are they guaranteed in the Constitution protection and security for their persons and their property." "It does not appear to me that the public good of the State, or of the nation at large, would be promoted by conferring at the present time upon the freedmen the elective franchise." "Neither the white people nor the colored people are prepared for so radical a change in their social relations." "Nor have I any reason to believe that any considerable number of the freedmen desire to possess this privilege." The Governor was capable of reasoning from a very narrow standpoint when he asserted that no considerable number of freedmen desired the full panoply of citizenship, when two hundred thousand of their number had marched and fought under our national flag to assist in putting down the greatest rebellion known in the annals of history. The message of the Governor in reference to negro suffrage was still clinging to his conscience as a nightmare of injustice of which he could not rid himself, until he reached that point which brought him face to face with the question of the negro testifying in courts of justice. The Governor says: "Heretofore the negro, in a condition of slavery, was to a large extent under the power and protection of his master, who felt an interest in his welfare, not only because he was a dependent and had been raised, perhaps, in his family, but because he was his property." "Now he has no such protection, and unless he finds protection in the courts of justice he becomes the victim of every wicked, depraved and bad man, whose avarice may prompt him to refuse the payment of his just wages, and whose angry and revengeful passions may excite him to abuse and maltreat the helpless being placed by his freedom beyond the pale of protection of any kind." "Much sensitiveness is felt in this and other Southern States upon the subject of the admissibility of negro testimony in courts of justice for or against white persons. For myself, now that the negro is free, I do not feel any such sensitiveness. I do not perceive the philosophy or expediency of any rule of evidence which shuts out the truth from the hearing of the jury. It may be said that the intention of the rule is to shut out falsehood; but how can it be known to the jury whether the testimony be true or false until they have heard it and compared it with the other testimony in the case?" "The admission of negro testimony should not be regarded as a privilege granted to the negro, but as the right of the State, in all criminal prosecutions, to have his testimony, in connection with other testimony, to assist to establish the guilt of the accused, and it ought, reciprocally, to be the right of the accused to have such testimony to establish his innocence. But the question of the admissibility of negro testimony is merely incidental to the main subject, which is the duty of the State to protect the negro in the exercise and enjoyment of his rights of freedom. If this duty can be adequately performed, and the rights of the negro fully secured without his being allowed to make oath before the courts of the wrongs and injuries done him, then the interest of the State to have his testimony admitted will be so greatly lessened as to reduce the question to one of comparatively much less importance. If the colored race in this country can be fully and fairly protected in the exercise and enjoyment of their newly acquired rights of freedom, then, in my judgment, they will be a quiet and contented people, unambitious of any political privileges, or of any participation in the affairs of the government. Protected in their persons and property, they may be stimulated to be industrious and economical by a desire to acquire property in order to educate themselves and their children, and improve their physical, moral and intellectual condition." "What their condition as a race may be at the end of fifty or a hundred years, I do not think any person is wise enough to predict; but we may reasonably hope and believe that they will progress and improve in intelligence and civilization, and become, not many years hence, the best free agricultural peasantry, for our soil and climate, that the world has ever seen." "I think a clause may be so drawn as to accomplish this object and at the same time exclude the colored people from any participation in the affairs of the government."

"May Almighty God, in whose hands are the destinies of all the nations of the earth, and without whose blessing all your works will be in vain, enlighten your understandings so that you may see, and incline your wills so that you may do whatever will advance His glory and promote the peace, the happiness and the welfare of all the people of our beloved State.

"WILLIAM MARVIN,
"Provisional Governor."

The Governor should have known, from years of religious training, that the glory of God would not be advanced by excluding from the right of citizenship nearly one-half of the population of the State for no other crime than the color of their skins. Not quite half of the time has passed in which the Governor predicted that the colored people would only become the best agricultural peasantry the world ever saw, and yet he finds these very people occupying nearly all the industries, occupations and professions that are carried on by their white brothers, notwithstanding the great odds against them by reason of their former condition.

The convention adjourned after a session of twelve days, but the Constitution was not submitted to the people for ratification. There is no question that some of the best talent in the State was elected to the convention. Judge Burritt, of Duval, an able man and an intense loyalist, when advised of his election, was in New York city, and immediately embarked for Jacksonville on the ill-fated steamer "Mount," which was lost at sea with all on board. Had he been permitted to take part in the convention and the subsequent measures of reconstruction, it is quite probable that different results would have been reached. Judge Baltzell, also, was one of the most upright, able, clear-headed members of the convention, and had his life been spared he would have been a power for law, order and government. He was, without doubt, the ablest man in the convention, and thoroughly loyal to the restored civil government. George K. Walker was one of the purest and best men of the old *regime*. He was in very poor health, but he was most earnest in seeking to harmonize the conflicts growing out of the new condition of affairs, and to establish order, peace and civil law. On one occasion, when a member of the convention proposed some violent constitutional restrictions upon the freedmen, he in earnest and eloquent strains admonished the member and the convention to "remember that we are here only by the grace of the Federal government, and it is not becoming in us to deny to others the rights we claim for ourselves, and disregard the obligations we have assumed to the government through whose liberality we stand here free citizens of the Republic."

CHAPTER III.

The Election of the First Governor after the Civil War, and the Organization of the Legislature under the Constitution of 1865. The Remarks by Governor Marvin at the Inauguration. The Presence of Negro Troops Causes Great Sensitiveness. Extracts From Governor Walker's Message. Recommendations of Committee Appointed by Convention. Laws Passed by the General Assembly, and their Workings.

Twenty-two days after the making and the adoption of the Marvin Constitution, an election was held for Governor and other State officers. There seems to have been no opposition candidate for Governor, and no nominations were made for that office. The old line Whigs seem to have had an understanding that they would not vote for a Democrat, as they charged the Democrats with having brought on the war, and as D. S. Walker had figured so prominently in the politics of the State, having been elected one of the Judges of the Supreme Court, and one of the most popular leaders of the old Whig party, he became the candidate for Governor by general consent, Democrats being anxious to get back into the Union by the help of either friend or foe. The election was held on the 29th of December, and resulted in the election of D. S. Walker, he receiving five thousand eight hundred and seventy-three votes, with only eight votes cast against him. The Legislature met December 18th, 1865, and elected Joseph John Williams, of Leon County, Speaker, against G. Troup Maxwell, of Leon, by a vote of twenty to seventeen.

The two Houses, after the permanent organization, met in joint session and canvassed the vote for Governor, and declared Walker's election. W. W. J. Kelly, whose vote was only two thousand four hundred and seventy-three, was declared elected Lieutenant-Governor. After some preparations the Governor-elect came forward, accompanied by Governor Marvin, to be inaugurated. Governor Marvin addressed the Legislature, and recited to them the great difficulties he had to encounter, as Provisional Governor, in establishing a civil government, and how he found the State government overthrown and prostrated, with no money in the Treasury; and praising in the highest terms the work done by the convention, in incorporating in the Constitution that "neither slavery nor involuntary servitude shall in future exist in this State, except as a punishment for crime whereof the party shall have been convicted by the courts of this State, and that all the inhabitants of the State, without distinction of color, are free and shall enjoy the rights of person and property without distinction of color; and that in all criminal proceedings founded upon an injury to a colored person, and in all cases affecting the rights and remedies of colored persons, no person shall be incompetent to testify as a witness on account of color." He reminded them of the action of the convention in repudiating the State debt contracted in support of the rebellion, and of the ordinance nullifying secession. And further to assure them how heartily he endorsed the policy of the previous convention, pointed them to the fact that he had humbly obeyed the request of the convention that the civil officers of the Confederate State Government, who had been suspended at the surrender, by the military authority, had been directed by him to resume the exercise of their respective offices. The colored troops, which the convention had by resolution requested the Governor to exert himself to have removed from the interior of the State, he informed them had nearly all been removed to the seaboard by the General in command at that time. He recommended, among other things, that a law should be passed that where a laborer had entered into a contract in writing before the Judge of Probate or a Justice of the Peace, to labor upon a plantation for one year for wages, or a part of the crop, and the contract specified the wages to be paid, and the food to be given, that if the laborer abandoned the service of his employer, or was absent therefrom two days without the leave of his employer, or failed without just cause in other important particulars to perform his part of the contract, that then he may be arrested by the proper tribunal, and if found guilty on a hearing of the case, be sentenced to labor during the unexpired term, without pay, upon the higways, in a goverment workshop, or upon a government plantation to be rented or bought either by the State or by the different County Commissioners in their respective counties. He said that the faith of the nation was pledged for the protection of the freedmen, and those who had been loyal to the government during the rebellion. How the Governor could with any degree of reason conceive the idea that the Confederate State Government that had, during the war, hunted the Union men like the partridge on the mountains, and had denounced them as deserters and spies to the Confederate cause, and whose people had lost the services of that most valuable adjunct, the negro, whose stalwart arm had for years filled their homes with luxury, could deal justly with these two elements is beyond comprehension. After giving them all the advantages of religious training which inspires a sense of justice, yet it is not humane to have expected them at that period to be able to deal fairly and justly with those two classes of our population. It might be inferred from the attitude of the convention relative to the removal of the colored troops from the interior that the black soldiers stationed in the different parts of Florida at the close of the war were very overbearing in their conduct toward the ex-slaveholders, and incited the freedmen to lawlessness; but such was not the case. There were several colored regiments scattered through the interior; among them was the Second United States Colored Infantry, raised at Washington, D. C., two-thirds of its members being ex-slaves, and during the entire time they were stationed here I know of no complaint made against them of any misconduct toward the ex-slaveholders. In fact, when any of the white citizens were accused or arrested for any offense against the military authorities, they would always request the officer in command to have them arrested and guarded by the colored troops. They were spoken of by the whites in the very highest terms as to their conduct and general appearance, and thousands of whites would come out to witness their dress parade, and would often bring out their families, and not one word of insult was ever offered to them unless first insulted by the ex-slaveholder—who was always some low fellow who had shirked the Confederate army, and who imagined that such insults would palliate his shame. The reason why they desired the colored troops removed was that they believed the freedmen would be induced by the presence of these soldiers to be continually lying around their camps to the neglect of their crops, but these fears were unfounded; for the freedmen were seldom seen around the camps unless they came to exchange products for soldier clothes or for money.

After Governor Marvin had concluded his remarks, Hon. D. S. Walker, Governor-elect, came forward and took the oath of office, which was administered by the Hon. C. H. Dupont, Chief Justice. The Governor began his address by warning the Joint Assembly and the large audience against the bitterness of party strife, which four years previously had plunged the country into civil war. He said:

"By failing to regard the disinterested warnings of the Father of his country against the baneful effects of the spirit of party, and particularly when founded on geographical discrimination; by omitting, as he advised, to remember that the jealousy of a free people ought to be constantly awake against the insiduous wiles of foreign influence, and by neglecting, as he recommended, to frown indignantly upon the first dawning of every attempt to alienate any portion of our country from the rest, or to enfeeble the sacred ties which now link together the various parts, the people of the United States, nearly five years ago, became involved in the terrific civil strife which has but recently ended. We now hope that by a strict adherence to his advice, the unity of the government which constitutes us one people will again become dear to us."

The Governor then turned his attention to the subject of secession, which he attempted to defend in a very astute manner, well calculated to lead the youth of the State to believe that it was right. He said:

"During the late unhappy conflict, some of us were known as Union men; some as Constitutional Secessionists; and others as Revolutionists. A glorious opportunity is now afforded to fling away these names, and with them the strifes they have engendered, and to meet, as brethren ought to meet, upon the platform of the Constitution which our fathers made for us in 1787. If I shall be permitted to administer the government, I shall know no distinctions between citizens on account of past political differences. I will not condemn the Union man, because I know from experience how completely the love of the Union becomes a part of our very existence, and how it is endeared to us by a thousand glorious recollections and as many brilliant anticipations. I know that the heart of Florida's greatest and most renowned citizen was literally broken by the severance of the Union. Nor will I condemn the Constitutional Secessionist, because I know that, though he differed from me, his side of the question was supported by arguments, if not unanswerable, yet of great plausibility, and by the authority of many of the greatest names that this country has ever produced. Nor yet will I condemn the Revolutionist, for I know that he, though originally opposed to secession, went into the war, after the fact was done, upon the conviction that it was no longer an open question, and that it was the duty of every man to stand or fall with his own section. In fact, great questions connected with the integrity of the Union were, before the war, so unsettled, and the opinions of great men so varied, that it required a man greatly superior to myself to say with certainty who was right and who was wrong. Seeing the different luminaries which guided our people, I am not astonished that the very best men in our land were found arrayed in opposing ranks. I need not enumerate the host of great men who stood with the immortal Clay for the integrity of the Union and against the doctrine of secession. The logic of events has proved that they were right. But among those who held the contrary doctrine that a State might secede from the Union without infraction of the Federal Constitution, we find the names of such men as Mr. Rawle, a distinguished lawyer of Pennsylvania, to whom General Washington more than once tendered the office of Attorney-General of the United States; John Randolph, of Roanoke; Nathaniel Macon, of North Carolina; Mr. Calhoun, of South Carolina; P. P. Barbour, a late Justice of the Supreme Court of the United States; and Judge McKean, a late Chief Justice of the Supreme Court of Pennsylvania. Those who advocated the right of revolution quoted the remarks of Mr. Webster, that 'a bargain broken on one side was broken on all sides,' and that 'if the North should not obey the Constitution in regard to the rendition of fugitive slaves, the South would no longer be bound by the compact.' Mr. Greeley, then, as now, a great leader of

Northern sentiment, had said that 'he could not see how twenty millions of people could rightfully hold ten, or even five, in a Union with them by military force;' and again, 'if seven or eight States should send agents to Washington to say we want to get out of the Union, he should feel constrained by his devotion to human rights to say, let them go.' In this connection he also quoted the Declaration of Independence, that 'Governments are instituted for the benefit of the governed;' and that when any form of government becomes destructive of these ends, it is the right of the people to alter or abolish it, and to institute a new government. Mr. Lincoln, prior to his first election, had acknowledged this principle, with the addition, that not only a people, but any part of a people, being sufficient in numbers to make a respectable government, might set up for themselves. Mr. Tyler, a late President of the United States, held to the doctrine of secession, and Mr. Buchanan, the then President of the United States, said, just before the commencement of the war, that while he thought a State had no right to leave the Union, yet if she should leave it, the remaining States would have no right to coerce her to return. Amidst these various and conflicting views, all supported by the highest authority, it is no wonder that our people should have been bewildered, or that, being forbidden by the turn of events, to remain neutral, some should have adhered to the Union and others to the State."

The Governor next turned his attention to that problem which had perplexed the statesman, the philanthropist and the philosopher for more than half a century:—" What shall we do with the Negro?" He said:

"I think we are bound by every consideration of duty, gratitude and interest, to make these people as enlightened, prosperous and happy as their new situation will admit. For generations past they have been our faithful, contented and happy slaves. They have been attached to our persons and our fortunes, sharing with us all our feelings, rejoicing with us in our prosperity, mourning with us in our adversity. If there were exceptions to this general rule, they were only individual exceptions. Every Southern man who hears me knows that what I say is literally true in regard to the vast mass of our colored population. The world has never before seen such a body of slaves. For not only in peace, but in war, they have been faithful to us. During much of the time of the late unhappy difficulties, Florida had a greater number of men in the army beyond her limits than constituted her entire voting population. This of course stripped many districts of their entire arms-bearing inhabitants, and left our females and infant children almost exclusively to the protection of our slaves. They proved true to their trust. Not one instance of insult, outrage or indignity has ever come to my knowledge. They remained at home and made provisions for our army. Many of them went with our sons to the army, and there, too, proved their fidelity—attending them when well, nursing and caring for them when sick and wounded. We all know that many of them were willing, and some of them anxious, to take up arms in our cause. Although for several years within sound of the guns of the vessels of the United States, for six hundred miles along our seaboard, yet scarcely one in a thousand voluntarily left our agricultural service to take shelter and freedom under the flag of the Union. It is not their fault that they are free—they had nothing to do with it; that was brought about by the results and operations of the war. But they are free. They are no longer our contented and happy slaves, with an abundant supply of food and clothing for themselves and families, and the intelligence of a superior race to look ahead and make all necessary arrangements for their comfort. They are now a discontented and unhappy people, many of them houseless and homeless, roaming about in gangs over the land, not knowing one day where the supplies for the next are to come from; exposed to the ravages of disease and famine; exposed to the temptations of theft and robbery, by which they are often overcome; without the intelligence to provide for themselves when well, or to care for themselves when sick, and doomed to untold sufferings and ultimate extinction unless we intervene for their protection and preservation. Will we do it? I repeat, we are bound to do it, by every consideration of gratitude and interest."

The whites being to some extent exasperated about the freedom of the slaves, and not knowing what their conduct might be as free laborers, talk of the importation of white labor from

Germany, Ireland, Italy and other countries, was quite prevalent. As to this subject the Governor said:

"But let us always remember that we have a laboring class of our own which is entitled to the preference. It is not sufficient to say that white labor is cheaper. I trust we are not so far degraded as to consult interest alone. But interest alone would dictate that it is better to give these people employment and enable them to support themselves, than have them remain upon our hands as a pauper race; for here they are, and here, for weal or woe, they are obliged to stay. We must remember that these black people are natives of this country and have a pre-emption right to be recipients of whatever favors we may have to bestow. We must protect them, if not against the competition, at any rate against the exactions of white immigrants. They will expect our black laborers to do as much work in this climate as they have been accustomed to see white ones perform in more northern latitudes. We know that they cannot do it. They never did it for us as slaves, and the experience of the last six months shows that they will do no better as freedmen. Our fathers of 1783 knew that it takes five black men to do the work of three white ones, and consequently, in adjusting the apportionment of taxes upon the basis of labor and industry of the country, eleven of the thirteen States of the old confederation recommended that every five blacks be counted as only three. And if we can offer sufficient inducements, I am inclined to think that the black man, as a field laborer in our climate, will prove more efficient that the imported white."

Referring to the question of negro suffrage, the Governor said:

"We have been able to give an honest and conscientious assent to all that has been done, but each one of us knows that we could not give either an honest or conscientious assent to negro suffrage. There is not one of us that would not feel that he was doing wrong, and bartering his self-respect, his conscience and his duty to his country and to the Union itself, for the benefits he might hope to obtain by getting back into the Union. Much as I worshipped the Union, and much as I would rejoice to see my State once more recognized as a member thereof, yet it is better, a thousand times better, that she should remain out of the Union, even as one of her subjugated provinces, than go back 'eviscerated of her manhood,' despoiled of her honor, recreant to her duty, without her self-respect, and of course without the respect of the balance of mankind—a miserable thing, with seeds of moral and political death in herself, soon to be communicated to all her associates."

With the feelings that existed at that period among a goodly number of the whites with reference to the freedom of the negro, I must confess that it took a great deal of courage for the Governor to assert the negro's faithfulness to his master for generations past and during the war. Although the assertion was true, I have no doubt that a majority of the whites desired to see the negro prosperous, at least as a laborer, and to be fully protected in his person and property, if gratitude was to be measured to him as his faithfulness had been measured to his former master. As to their contentment, happiness, and being supplied with food and clothing, the Governor and others may have fed and clothed their slaves abundantly, but not enough so as to make them desirous of remaining slaves or to make them contented. If such was the case it would not have been necessary for the Legislature, anterior to the war, to pass a law punishing white persons for cruelty to slaves. In fact, it is absolutely necessary in order to govern a slave to punish him more severely than it would be necessary for the law to punish a freeman. I think "The Life and Times of the Hon. Frederick Douglass" is conclusive on this point. I am confident if all these slaves the Governor spoke of had been called up at that time they would have said to him that they felt quite happy, even while there were many who were destitute and had no home to go to. Yet most of these people were looked after by their former masters, as they had never left their premises. It was only those who had left the premises of, or those who had been driven away from, the places of their former masters, who were in danger of suffering. So the Governor was right in the abstract, but not in the concrete. The following poem fully expresses the feelings of the freedmen before and after their liberation. It was written and delivered by John Wallace at the celebration of the seven teenth anniversary of the Emancipation Proclamation, at Tallahassee. Florida:

Freedom, thou welcome spirit of Love,
   Whence and from where didst thou begin?
Thou from God's bosom as a dove
   Didst seek the earth to vanquish sin.
Before the land and skies were made
   Thy spirit hovered o'er the deep,
And when God earth's foundation laid,
   Did enter man when yet asleep.
As he arose from dust to flesh,
   Near him wast thou where e'er he went;
Though cast from Eden's garden fresh,
   Thou wast with him in sorrow bent.
And still wast thou all through
   Despotic ages past and gone,
And as a brother e'er proved true—
   Thy light 'mid darkness ever shone.
When Pharaoh Israel's children held
   Four hundred years abject, enslaved,
To free them Egypt was impelled,
   Though then was gained the land they craved.

America thought thee to evade,
   And to the South her slaves she sold;
But through power she was made
   To yield to thee this great stronghold.
Though here was called unto thy aid
   Grim war, the court of last appeal—
And North and South each other braved,
   Yet now they both thy blessings feel.
There were four million souls and more
   Of Africans in slavery bound,
They sought thy crown 'mid trials sore,
   Two hundred years, and then 'twas found.
Mankind has ne'er contented been
   Where slavery's cruel sway was held.

'Twas giant Freedom fought the sin
Till all its darkness was dispelled.
Go sound the trumpet, ring the bell!
Just seventeen years ago to-day
Sweet Freedom wrested us from hell
And put an end to slavery's sway.

The sagacious Governor, further to prove that the former slave was happy and contented, "maintained that it took five black men to do the same amount of work that three white men could do, and therefore the blacks should be protected against the exactions of white immigrants, as such immigrants would expect a black man to do the same amount of work as a white man." It is certainly true that a Northern man—or what the Southerners call a Yankee—will work a negro closer, harder and longer at a time than a Southern man will do, and will give him less, but as a general thing they will pay up regularly, of which I shall have more to say in another part of this work. I know of no rule or reason to prevent a colored man from doing the same amount of work that a white man can do if both have the same training. The same fatigue that overtakes the white man at the close of a day's labor, will overtake the negro, even though he is covered with a black skin. The only difference as to how much work one man can do more than another, depends upon his skill and his physical make-up. It rather looks as though the Governor was trying to show that the former slave did not work as hard as the Northern man did before the war, and therefore slavery was not a great hardship; but this will not stand scrutiny.

While the Governor's recommendations to the Legislature were not all that could be desired by the colored people, from a political standpoint, yet many features of them should forever commend him to the lasting gratitude of our race. Among these recommendations were the taking care of the indigent and decrepit of the former slaves, encouraging industry, virtue and education, which are the foundation of the up-building of any people.

The convention which made the constitution under which this Legislature assembled, had requested the Provisional Governor to appoint a commission of three gentlemen to prepare suitable laws for the government of the freedmen, and to report to the first Legislature that should assemble. The Governor appointed C. H. Dupont, of Gadsden County, A. J. Peeler and M. D. Papy, of Leon. Two days after the convening of the Legislature this Committee made the following report:

"The undersigned were appointed by the Provisional Governor, under a resolution of the recent State Convention, and charged with the duty of reporting to the General Assembly 'the changes and amendments to be made to the existing statutes, and the additions required thereto, so as to cause the same to conform to the requisitions of the amended constitution, and with reference especially to the altered condition of the colored race.'

"*First.* In entering upon the discharge of this duty, we are deeply impressed with the magnitude and importance of the task, and regret that the shortness of the time elapsing between the date of our appointment and the meeting of your honorable body has precluded the possibility of giving to the subject that thorough investigation which its importance demanded. Within the brief space allotted to us, however, we have endeavored to embody, in the form of bills upon various subjects, some suggestions which we trust may be found useful in directing your minds to such changes and modifications of the existing statutes and additions thereto as may be demanded by the recent alteration in the civil relations heretofore existing between the two races that constitute the inhabitants of the State. The constitutional provision declaring the abolition of negro slavery, suddenly removed from under the restraining and directing influence of the master nearly one full moiety of our population, and creates the necessity of bringing them more fully under the operation of municipal law. Heretofore there existed in each household a tribunal peculiarly adapted to the investigation and punishment of the great majority of the minor offenses to the commission of which this class of population was addicted. With the destruction of the institution of negro slavery that tribunal has become extinct, and hence the necessity of creating another in its stead, and of making such modifications in our legislation as shall give full efficiency to our criminal code. It is to the organization of such a tribunal, as of first importance, that we now desire to invite your attention. It must be manifest to every reflecting mind that the Circuit Court, as at present organized, extending as it does its jurisdiction over a large area of territory, embracing a dozen or more counties, and confined to the holding of stated terms, however efficient heretofore in the restraining of crime, is but illy adapted to the present exigency. In view of the great increase of minor offenses which may be reasonably anticipated from the emancipation of the former slaves, a wise forecast would seem to call imperatively for the erection of a criminal tribunal more local in its jurisdiction and of greater promptness in its administration of the penalties of the law. Such, eventually, was the design of the recent convention in extending the judicial power so as to embrace 'such other courts as the General Assembly may establish.' The constitutional provision granting this power to the General Assembly is as follows, to-wit: 'The judicial power of this State, both as to matters of law and equity, shall be vested in a Supreme Court, Courts of Chancery, Circuit Courts and Justices of the Peace; provided, the General Assembly may vest such civil or criminal jurisdiction as may be necessary in Corporation Courts and such other courts as the General Assembly may establish; but such jurisdiction shall not extend to capital cases.' With all the reflection that we have been able to bestow upon the subject, and aided by the light drawn from the legislation of other States, we have, nevertheless, found it extremely difficult to devise any plan of organization for the proposed courts which is entirely free from objection. We present, however, with great deference, for your consideration and action thereon, a bill entitled 'An Act to establish and organize a County Criminal Court,' which we think will be found, upon examination, to be as free from objection and as well adapted to the exigency growing out of the new order of things as can well be devised.

"*Second.* The next subject that claimed the attention of the Commission was the present state of our criminal laws as applicable to the two different races that constitute the population of the State. By reference to the statute book, it will be found that in most of the minor offenses, and a few of the more aggravated, a marked distinction is made between white persons and free negroes and slaves with regard to the commission of these offenses. After the maturest reflection upon the subject, we have come to the conclusion that a wise policy would dictate that, with a very few exceptional cases, this discrimination be abolished, as far as it may be done without impairing the efficiency of the prescribed penalties, and that both races be subjected to the same code. In making this recommendation, the undersigned would not be understood as favoring the idea that there exists, either in the Federal Constitution or in that of the State, any inhibition to control the authority of the General Assembly in making such discrimination, whenever the welfare of society or the safety of the community may demand it. This authority, however, is not to be exercised beyond the granting or restricting of what is usually denominated mere 'privileges,' in contradistinction to the absolute 'rights' of individuals. The enjoyment of the rights of person and property, together with means of redress, is, by our amended Constitution, guaranteed to all the inhabitants of the State, without distinction of color, and may not be invaded by the legislation of the General Assembly. With this limitation, the power to discriminate between the two races has always been exercised without stint by the respective States of the Union, not even excepting those of New England. Their statute books are replete with enactments confirmatory of the truth of this statement, nor is there any lack of judicial evidence on the point. In 1833 Connecticut passed a law which made it a penal offense to set up or establish any school in that State for the instruction of persons of the African race, not being inhabitants of the State, or to instruct or teach in any school or institution, or board or harbor for that purpose, any such person, without the previous consent in writing of the civil authority of the town in which such school or institution might be located. A case arose under this law, in which one of the points raised in defense was that the law was a violation of the Constitution of the United States, which guarantees 'that the citizens of each State shall be entitled to all privileges and immunities of citizens of the several States.' (Vide Crandall vs. the State, 10 Conn., Rep. 346.) In Kentucky the point has been repeatedly decided the same way; nor are we aware that its correctness has ever been judicially questioned in any State of the Union. Chancellor Kent, whose accuracy and research no one will question, states emphatically that in no part of the country, except Maine, did the African race in point of fact participate equally with the whites in the exercise of civil and political rights. (2 Kent's Com., 258, Note b.) But the right to exercise the power of discrimination does not rest alone upon the action of the States; it has, time and again, been sanctioned by every department of the Federal Government. In its legislation for the District of Columbia the Congress has never hesitated to recognize the difference that exists between the two races, both as it regards their social and political status. Such, too, has been universally the action of the executive department, backed by the official opinions of such men as William Wirt and Caleb Cushing, and endorsed by that giant of constitutional law, Daniel Webster, while acting as Secretary of State. Upon application to him for letters of protection to visit Europe, he refused to grant them, upon the distinctly stated ground that the applicants were not 'citizens' in the meaning of the word as used in the Constitution. But if there ever did exist any doubt upon this subject, it ought forever to be put at rest by the authoritative decision in the great case of Dred Scott vs. Sandford, reported in 19 Howard, S. C. Rep., 393. In the opinion delivered in that case, undoubtedly the greatest intellectual effort of the late Chief Justice Taney, it is expressly held that 'a free negro of the African race, whose ancestors were brought to this country and sold as slaves, is not a citizen within the meaning of the Constitution of the United States.' And it is strongly stated in the same opinion that it is not within the constitutional power of Congress to make him such. In commenting upon the legislation of Congress with reference to this race, the Chief Justice very forcibly and significantly remarks: 'This law, like the laws of the States, shows that this class of persons were governed by special legislation directed exclusively to them, and always connected with provisions for the government of slaves, and not with those for the government of white citizens.' And after such a uniform course of legislation as we have stated by the Colonies, by the States and by Congress, running through a period of more than a century, it would seem that to call persons thus marked and stigmatized 'citizens' of the United States —'fellow citizens'—a constituent part of the sovereignty, would be an abuse of terms, and not calculated to exalt the character of an American citizen in the eyes of other nations. This adjudication was rendered just four years prior to the commencement of the late revolution, and it may not be inappropriate to inquire whether any of the results of that revolution can be justly invoked to impair its authority as a just and enlightened exposition of the Constitution. It is true that one of the results was the abolition of African slavery; but it will hardly be seriously argued that the simple act of emancipation of itself worked any change in the social, legal or political status of such of the African race as were already free. Nor will it be insisted, we presume, that the emancipated slave technically denominated a 'freedman,' occupied any higher position in the scale of rights and privileges than did the 'free negro.' If these inferences be correct, then it results, as a logical conclusion, that all the arguments going to sustain the authority of the General Assembly to discriminate in the case of 'free negroes' equally apply to that of 'freedmen,' or emancipated slaves. But it is insisted by a certain class of radical theorists that the act of emancipation did not stop in its effect in merely severing the relation of master and slave, but that it extended further, and so operated as to exalt the entire race and placed them upon terms of perfect equality with the white man. These fanatics may be very sincere and honest in their convictions, but the result of the recent elections in Connecticut and Wisconsin shows very conclusively that such is not the sentiment of a majority of the so-called Free States. While we thus strenuously assert the authority of the General Assembly to exercise the power of discrimination within the limit before indicated, we would earnestly, but respectfully, recommend that it be exercised only in exceptional cases, and so far as may be necessary to promote the welfare of society and to insure the peace, good order and quiet of the entire community. Impressed with these views, and in furtherance of this end, we have prepared a bill to accompany this report entitled 'An Act Prescribing Additional Penalties for the Commission of Offences Against the State, and for other purposes.' The first section of the bill provides 'that whenever, in the criminal laws of this State heretofore enacted, the punishment of the offense is limited to fine and imprisonment, or to fine or imprisonment, there shall be superadded, as an alternative, the punishment of standing in the pillory for an hour, or whipping, not exceeding thirty-nine stripes on the bare back, or both, at the discretion of the jury.' By an examination of the respective codes, as applicable to the two classes of population, white and black, it will be found that they differ but little as to the nature of the offenses designated in each. The great mark of difference is to be found in the character of the punishments. There seems always to have existed in the minds of our legislators a repugnance to the infliction of corporeal punishment upon the white man, and hence the resort to fine and imprisonment for the punishment of offenses committed by him, while that mode of punishment is almost the only one applied to the colored man for the commission of any of the minor offenses. This discrimination, we think, is founded upon the soundest principles of State policy, growing out of the difference that exists in the social and political status of the two races. To degrade a white man by punishment is to make a bad member of society and a dangerous political agent. To fine and imprison a colored man in his present pecuniary condition, is to punish the State instead of the individual. The provision contained in the first section of the proposed bill is not designed to interfere with the discrimination above referred to, but only to give a wider range to the discretion of the jury in applying the punishment to the offense. The second section of the bill is deemed important to remedy a defect growing out of the extreme technicality of the common law with reference to the subject indicated. By the principles of that law, if the 'severance' from the freehold, and the felonious 'taking and carrying away,' be one and the same continued act, it would amount only to a 'trespass,' for which the injured party was remitted to his action for damages on the civil side of the court, but for which the perpetrator of the act could not be criminally punished. In view of the present condition of things, we think that this rule of the common law ought to be altered as is proposed to be done by the second section of this bill. The twelfth section restricts the privilege of the use of firearms by colored persons to such only as are of an 'orderly and peaceable character.'

The authority of the General Assembly to impose this restriction is beyond doubt. Neither the second article of the amendments to the Federal Constitution, nor the first section of the sixteenth article of the State Constitution, nor anything contained in either of said instruments, can by any fair interpretation be deemed to oppose any obstacle to the exercise of this authority. A reference to the legislation of the Northwestern States will show that they recognize the right to impose suitable restrictions upon this class of their population; and the section now under consideration is almost a literal transcript of the law of Indiana upon that subject. If the restriction is deemed important to the welfare of a community in which not one in a thousand is affected by it, how much more important with us, where nearly one full moiety of the population is of that class. The interests of the well disposed and peaceable colored man, whose right it is to enjoy the fruits of his honest industry, as well as the safety of the entire community, both white and black, imperatively demands that the privilege of bearing arms should be accorded only to such of the colored population as can be recommended for their orderly and peaceable character. It is needless to attempt to satisfy the exactions of the fanatical theorists. We have a duty to perform—the protection of our wives and children from threatened danger and the prevention of scenes which may cost the extinction of our entire race.

"Deeply impressed with the sense of the obligation that rests upon the white race, as the governing class, to do all that may lie in their power to improve the moral condition of the recently emancipated slaves, the undersigned most respectfully present for your consideration 'A Bill to be entitled An Act to Establish and Enforce the Marriage Relation Between Persons of Color.' Heretofore, from the very necessity of the case, this matter was left to be regulated by the moral sense of the master and the slave, and may in truth be said to have been the only inherent evil of the institution of slavery, as it existed in the Southern States. Now that the obstacle of compulsory separation is removed, and, as a Christian people, we should embrace the earliest opportunity to impress upon this class of our population, and, if need be, to enforce by appropriate penalties, the obligation to observe this first law of civilization and morality, chastity and the sanctity of the marriage relation.

"Next to the enactment of laws for the prevention of crime and the enforcement of the domestic relations, there is no subject so intimately connected with the permanent welfare and prosperity of a people as that of a well regulated labor system. Such a system we recently enjoyed under the influence of the benign but much abused and greatly misunderstood, institution of slavery. That has been swept away in the storm of revolution, and we are now remitted to the operation of an untried experiment. Whether we shall be successful in devising a plan to make the labor of the emancipated slave available is a problem of doubtful solution, and one in which he is vastly more interested than is his former master. This unfortunate class of our population, but recently constituting the happiest and best provided for laboring population in the world, by no act of theirs or voluntary concurrence of ours; with no prior training to prepare them for their new responsibilities, have been suddenly deprived of the fostering care and protection of their old masters, and are now to become, like so many children gamboling upon the brink of the yawning precipice, careless of the future and intent only on revelling in the present unrestricted enjoyment of the newly found bauble of freedom. Their condition is truly pitiable, and appeals to every generous bosom for aid and succor, and we have greatly mistaken the character of the Southern people if that appeal shall be made in vain. We are not responsible for this pitiable condition of the race, but we will, nevertheless, exert ourselves to save them from the ruin which inevitably awaits them if left to the 'tender mercy' of that canting hypocrisy and mockish sentimentality which has precipitated them to the realization of their present condition. If the effort to make the emancipated slave an efficient laborer shall fail, then, as a last alternative, resort must be had to the teeming population of overcrowded Europe. But let not this fearful alternative, pregnant as it is with the ruin and destruction of a helpless race, be adopted until we shall have given them a fair and patient trial. As the superior and governing class, we are bound to this by every principle of right and prompting of humanity, yea, by the obligation of gratitude. For where, in all the records of the past, does history present such an instance of steadfast devotion, unwavering attachment and constancy, as was exhibited by the slaves of the South throughout the fearful contest that has just ended? The country invaded, homes desolated, the master absent in the army or forced to seek safety in flight and leaves the mistress and her helpless infants unprotected; with every incitement to insubordination and instigation to rapine and murder, no instance of insurrection, and scarcely one of voluntary desertion has been recorded. This constancy and faithfulness on the part of the late slaves, while it has astonished Europe and stamped with falsehood the ravings of the heartless abolitionist, will forever commend them to the kindness and forbearance of their former masters. They will do all in their power to promote his welfare and to encourage and secure his moral and material improvement. While they confine him to his appropriate sphere of social and political inferiority, they will endeavor to stimulate him to all legitimate efforts at advancement, and by the exercise of kindness and justice towards him, teach him to value and appreciate the new condition in which he is placed. If, after all, their honest efforts shall prove unavailing, and this four millions of the human family but recently dragged up from barbarism, and through the influence of Southern masters elevated to the status of Christian men and women, shall be doomed by the inscrutable behest of a mysterious Providence to follow in the footsteps of the fast fading aborigines of this continent; and when the last man of the race shall be standing upon the crumbling brink of a people's grave, it will be some compensation to the descendants of the Southern master to catch the grateful and benignant recognition of this representative man, as he points his withered finger to the author of his ruin and exclaims, 'Thou didst it.'"

All of the recommendations made by this committee, so far as enactment of laws were concerned, were acted upon and passed into statutes. But the Legislature disregarded the committee's recommendation as to delaying the education of colored children, and passed a law taxing every colored male from the age of twenty-one to fifty, five dollars for the education of colored youth, and some good schools were established accordingly under the superintendency of Rev. E. B. Duncan, who was certainly an able and conscientious man, who worked hard to establish colored schools in every county. At that time railroad facilities were very poor, and I have known him to walk from county to county in South Florida to establish colored schools.

It is true, that some of the laws passed by the Legislature of 1865 seem to be very diabolical and oppressive to the freedmen, but when we consider the long established institution of slavery, and the danger to which the Southern whites imagined they might be subjected by reason of these people, who had always been subject only to the command of their old masters, we are of the opinion that any other people, under like circumstances, would have passed the same character of laws relative to the freedmen. Many of these laws we know, of our own knowledge, were passed only to deter the freedman from committing crime. For instance, the law prohibiting colored people handling arms of any kind without a license, was a dead letter, except in some cases where some of the freedmen would go around plantations hunting, with apparently no other occupation, such a person would be suspected of hunting something that did not belong to him and his arms would be taken away from him. We have often passed through the streets of Tallahassee with our gun upon our shoulder, without a license, and were never disturbed by any one during the time this law was in force.

The law in regard to contracts between the whites and freedmen was taken advantage of by some of the whites, and the freedmen did not get justice; but the great majority of the whites carried out their contracts to the letter, and the freedmen did as well as could be expected under the changed condition of things. These laws were taken advantage of by the carpet-baggers to marshal the freedmen to their support after the freedmen had been given the right to vote. We shall have more to say on this subject in a future chapter.

CHAPTER IV.

Governor Walker's Short-Lived Administration. Conduct of White Soldiers Toward Freedmen. The Freedmen Electing a Congressman, as They Thought. Stonelake's Fraudulent Land Certificate. The Freedman's Bureau and Its Agents. The Beginning of the Secret League. Preparation and Oath of League. "The Loyal League of America."

The administration of Governor Walker, which continued something over two years, by the existing military power, exercised under the Federal authority, and he was often perplexed to avoid conflict while in the legitimate exercise of civil authority. With the Freedman's Bureau, charged with the paternal care of the freedmen on the one side, and the United States army exercising a supervisory control over the general conduct, his administration was little more than a quasi civil government, yet all was done that was possible, within the restricted limits prescribed by the Federal power, to maintain law and order. The removal of colored troops from the interior of the State to the seaboard did not hasten the restoration of law and order, as contemplated by the resolution passed by the convention for that purpose. The white soldiery were stationed throughout the interior and finally superseded the colored troops, who were entirely removed from the State. The officers and soldiers of the regular army, many of whom did not stand very high in the estimation of our best Southern society, would abuse and maltreat the negro much worse than their former masters, who in many instances would have to interfere in his behalf, to save him from cruelty and injustice. Of course there were honorable exceptions; but a majority of the officers and men sent to this State to take the place of the colored troops, were unjust and sometimes cruel in their treatment of the freedmen—first from innate prejudice, and second in order to ingratiate themselves with their former masters, who were naturally irritated at the loss of their slaves. They, however, refused to countenance such conduct on the part of the soldiery, holding that however the negro might rejoice in his freedom, he had done nothing dishonorable to obtain it.

I can recall but few instances of brutal treatment of the freedmen by the Southern whites during Governor Walker's administration. I was personally cognizant of one case in the city of Tallahassee in the latter part of the year 1866, by the police, under Francis Epps, mayor. The mayor had enlisted from outside the city a dozen of what are generally termed "crackers," as policemen. They were of the class who had never owned a slave or dared to interfere with one while under the protection of the master, and they seemed to cherish an old grudge against the negro. They sought every opportunity to interfere in his exercise of his freedom, and would order him off the streets; and when two or three were assembled in conversation, would arrest them and beat them as long as they would submit. Under the advice of some of the more respectable of the white citizens, a party attempted one Sunday night to put a stop to this cruelty. They started around to the colored churches to summon the men to run these policemen out of town or put them to death. On their way to the churches they were met in the dark by the city marshal, Sam Quaile, who ordered them to halt. Thinking it was one of these "cracker" policemen, they discharged their guns in the direction of the voice, but inflicted no injury. The whites turned out and preserved the peace, and shortly after these "cracker" policemen were discharged and no further disturbance occurred. So far as the city of Tallahassee is concerned, the whites and blacks have lived on friendly terms.

Early in 1866 it was reported that the freedmen would be enfranchised, and many of them thinking the right had already accrued, called a secret meeting for the election of a Member of Congress. The meeting was held at the A. M. E. Church in Tallahassee, and Joseph Oats, formerly a slave of Governor Walker, was unanimously elected. The next step was to raise money to send the newly-elected Congressman to Washington. The money was forthcoming, as plenty of old men and women gave their last dollar to send one of their race to the National Congress. Several hundred dollars were thus raised and given to Oats, who shortly afterwards was "off to Congress." He remained away from Tallahassee until his money was gone, when he wrote back designating the time when he would return. The freedmen prepared a picnic at Houstoun's spring, about a mile from Tallahassee. Oats notified them that if they desired to know what he had done for them while in Congress, they must prepare to protect him, as the whites would kill him when they should learn what he had accomplished against them. The 20th of May, the day on which General McCook marched his troops into Tallahassee, and declared all the inhabitants to be free, was the day set apart for Oats to tell the freedmen the great work he had accomplished in Congress. At nine o'clock on that memorable 20th of May, the drums commenced beating and the freedmen to the number of two or three thousand formed in line and marched to Oats' dwelling and sent a committee armed with old cavalry swords and pistols to escort Oats to the place of destination. He was escorted to Houstoun's spring, when the committee, at his request, arranged that he should be surrounded by the freedmen and the whites kept from harming him or hearing what he said. The whites, however, did not know what was going on other than a celebration and picnic, and were not present. Oats' speech was, that he had seen the President, and they had true friends at Washington, etc. It was believed, however, that Oats did not go further than Savannah, where he had a good time, spent the freedmens' money, and returned home. After Oats had finished his story about the President, and his great labors in Congress, the crowd sent up their huzzas for half an hour and then sat down to a sumptuous dinner. Whisky was plentiful on the ground and was freely imbibed by the freedmen. A dispute arose among them as to where Oats had been, and the affair ended in a general knock down and drag out. Oats was a carpenter by trade, and before being set free had hired himself from his master; could read and write, and was therefore capable of hoodwinking the average freedman. He was a fine looking mulatto whose mother was said to be white.

During the years 1865–67 there was much speculation among the freedmen as to what the government intended to do for them in regard to farms; and as most of them had to work for a portion of the crop, it induced them to seek homes of their own.

One Stonelake, United States Land Register at Tallahassee, appointed soon after the surrender, knowing this fact, and taking advantage of the ignorance of the freedmen, issued to them thousands of land certificates purporting to convey thousands of acres of land. For each certificate the freedman was required to pay not less than five dollars, and as much more as Stonelake could extort from the more ignorant. He induced the most influential to make the first purchases, and, it was generally believed, gave them a portion of his fees to secure purchasers. The former masters warned our people against this fraud, but as Stonelake was one of the representatives of the paternal government, he was supposed by the freedmen to be incapable of fraud or deception. Many of them were led to believe that these lands consisted of their former masters' plantations, and that the certificates alone would oust the latter from possession. After showing the certificates around among his neighbors and exulting over the purchase of a plantation, he would eventually show it to his former master, who would explain the fraud, when he would rush back to Stonelake for his money, who would invent some new deception to quiet him, and explain that upon further examination of his books he found the lands were located further south. These explanations did not fully satisfy the freedmen, and they called a meeting and appointed several of their number to go down south and spy out the Promised Land. This committee expended the money raised by their confiding friends, and after an absence of several weeks in a pretended survey, reported that they saw some good lands, as well as bad, and advised the freedmen to occupy them, but as they were unable to locate the Promised Land, their advice was not followed, and the victims were left to vent their curses upon the swindler, Stonelake.

The Freedman's Bureau, an institution devised by Congress under the influence of the very best people of the Northern States, and intended as a means of protection of the freedmen, and preparing them for the new responsibilities and privileges conferred, in the hands of bad men proved, instead of a blessing, to be the worst curse of the race, as under it he was misled, debased and betrayed. The agents of this Bureau were stationed in all the cities and principal towns in the State. They overruled the local authorities with the arbitrary force of military power. Before it was definitely known that the Congress of the United States could confer the right of suffrage upon the negro the great majority of the agents were more oppressive of the freedmen than the local authorities, their former masters. The State having been impoverished by the war, the national government, realizing the condition of the people, and especially of the freedmen, who were set free with nothing but the scant clothing on their backs, sent provisions to the State to be distributed to such of the freedmen as were struggling, without means of subsistence, to make a crop. This meat and flour was placed in the hands of these agents for distribution, who appropriated it at their discretion, and frequently more largely for their own benefit than that of their wards. The Commissioner of the Bureau for the State, in company with a retired army officer, carried on a large plantation on the Apalachicola, until General Steadman was appointed to examine and report upon the condition of the Bureau affairs, when, in anticipation of his visit to the State his interest was suddenly transferred to his partner, who, after gathering and disposing of the cotton crop and all available stock on the place, gathered himself up and left without paying the rents. M. L. Stearns, a subordinate agent at Quincy, was publicly charged with the wholesale disposition of pork and flour, and evidence was produced to convict him of receiving and attempting to force collection of a mortgage for $750 received in payment for provisions; but the officers of the Federal Court refused to entertain the case. When he subsequently ran as the Republican candidate for Governor in 1878, he was publicly denounced in the newspapers and from the stump for having sold the freedmen's supplies to white farmers for his own benefit. His refusal to meet the charge lost him the support of the leading Republicans and a large class of the freedmen, so that with the entire control of the political machinery through the appointing power as acting Governor, he was defeated, while the State at the previous election, under Governor Reed's administration, with a weak and unpopular ticket, had been carried by over three thousand Republican majority. It was not a little remarkable that the Presidential ticket, ran several hundred ahead of the State ticket, and while Stearns was counted out Hayes was counted in,

As soon as the freedmen were enfranchised they began to receive better treatment at the hands of the Bureau agents. The contracts between them and the planters, which had heretofore been interpreted against them, were now more fairly construed in their interest. This latter action of Congress, too, was the gateway to the formation of the secret league of the freedmen.

Thomas W. Osborn, the Commissioner of the Bureau for Florida, stationed at Tallahassee, through his servant, a freedman, requested a meeting of three or four of the most influential colored men at the house of a colored man whose name I do not care to mention. He met them there and informed them that it was the desire of the government that they should form a secret league to prevent their being again returned to slavery. This was sufficient to bring out the old and young, the halt and the blind. In order to deceive and allay any apprehension in regard to the purpose of the gathering, they were instructed to answer any questions by saying that the assembly was for the purpose of forming a benevolent society. At the appointed time several hundred freedmen assembled, but only seventy-five or eighty were initiated the first night, as it was deemed wise to impress them with an air of deep solemnity and great formality.

In order to work the negro with greater facility in the interest of Osborn and his gang, this secret league was named the Lincoln Brotherhood, and T. W. Osborn made himself its president, and he became the grand head-centre of all the leagues and subordinate lodges subsequently formed throughout the country and State. Each member had to pay an initiation fee of from one to two dollars, and fifty cents per month thereafter. The subordinate lodges were organized by a deputy appointed by the president, T. W. Osborn. They were required to pay five or six dollars for their charter, which money went to swell the revenue of the parent lodge at Tallahassee, or of its grand chief. The lodge at Tallahassee became so large that it became necessary to remove from the private house where it was first organized to the lower colored Baptist church, in a part of the town seldom visited by the whites. The freedmen considered this league a great thing, and their meetings at the church were carefully guarded by armed sentinels, who halted any one who came into the vicinity of the church, requiring the countersign under penalty of the contents of the old musket. Auxiliary lodges were formed in every part of the county and throughout the State. The regular meetings of these lodges were held every Thursday night, in the most secret places to be secured. One who was ignorant of the purposes of these assemblies would be led to believe that the freedmen were preparing to massacre all the white inhabitants of the country. The rattling of the swords and handling of the muskets seemed to be the pride of these men. Many of them believed that the joining of the league made them brothers of the martyred Lincoln. The entrance to the lodge was protected by a double guard, called the inner and the outer sentinels. Whenever candidates for admission appeared the outer guard would have to vouch for their not being spies by giving two raps at the door. These were answered by the inner guard in like manner. The outer guard would then report the number present desirous of becoming members, and that he faithfully vouched for them. The inner guard would report to the President, who would order them to be conducted in, which was done by two persons called the Tylers of the Altar. These Tylers would lead the applicants in front of the altar, standing about two paces from the President's stand. Over the altar would be fixed two United States flags, hoisted in such manner as to reveal the full number of stripes and stars; three swords would be laid across the altar in an equilateral triangle, with a Bible in the centre. The candidates would be presented to the President by one of the Tylers; the President would salute them with the following words: "Brethren, what seek ye?" The Tylers would instruct them to respond—"Freedom and Equality." Then the President would say: "Signify your request by humbly kneeling at this altar." He would then descend from his stand and take his seat in front of the applicants at the altar, who were required to place their hands upon the Bible, when he would read the oath and require them to repeat after him as follows:

"I do solemnly swear that I will protect and defend the Constitution and government of the United States against all enemies, foreign and domestic; that I will bear true faith, loyalty and allegiance to the same; that I will go the rescue of a brother whenever I learn he is in trouble; that I will not vote for or assist, directly or indirectly, any person for any office who is not a brother of this league."

Later on, when the leading members of the Brotherhood learned that their secret work had been exposed by some of the more ignorant members, a new scheme was devised by O. Morgan, one of Osborn's representatives, to put an end to this exposure. A coffin was procured, a grave was robbed of some of its hidden treasures, and the skull of a man was brought forth to do the work. They now commenced holding their meetings in one of the basement rooms of the Capitol. The coffin would be hid away in the room with an old piece of canvas thrown over it to conceal it from view. The applicant would be brought in and made to take the usual oath, with the formalities before recited. The lights in the room would then be suddenly put out and the Tylers of the Altar would quietly place the coffin in front of the applicants; the skull would be placed on the top of the coffin in the middle of the triangle formed by the swords; the lights would be restored and the applicant told by the President of the lodge that this skull was that of a brother who had been recreant to his trust, had broken his oath and exposed the secrets of this league; that he had been found out by the brethren and put to death, and that such would be the fate of every one who ever exposed the secrets of the order. I do not think the coffin initiation ever went further than the towns, as it was thought it could not be carried on in the country without the whites finding it out. Some of those who were initiated with the coffin were frightened so much that they never returned, and they advised their friends not to join the lodge in Tallahassee for fear of being killed. So the Morgan plan was not very successful. This coffin and skull were found in the basement of the Capitol after the Democrats captured the State from the Republicans in 1876.

In May or June, 1867, the Republican National Committee sent to Florida William M. Saunders, colored, from Maryland, Daniel Richards, white, from Sterling, Ill., as speakers and organizers of the Republican party, as they claimed. They immediately joined in the hunt for plunder, and soon struck the trail of and came in contact with the preceding plunder hunters —Osborn and his Bureau agents, with the thousands of their Lincoln Brotherhood. How to circumvent this brotherhood, now so firmly established across their pathway, was a problem for grave consideration. Saunders, Richards and Liberty Billings, a former lieutenant-colonel of a colored regiment in the Union army and now located at Fernandina, held a consultation at Tallahassee, and with all the solemnity of a Methodist prayer meeting finally resolved to supplant the Lincoln Brotherhood by a new secret organization styled "The Loyal League of America." Here commenced the "tug of war" which subsequently culminated in two Republican factions in the State. Thus the "Union League," an institution formed and organized in November, 1862, in the city of Cleveland, Ohio, and which shortly after numbered its millions of membership, some of whom were in the rebel States and had the confidence of some of the warmest supporters of the Southern Confederacy, was prostituted to the forging of chains upon the souls of the confiding freedmen. Before they could be recognized as Republicans by Saunders, Richards and Billings, the freedmen were required to join the Loyal League of America. A new application had to be made, another five dollars initiation fee paid, with a monthly due of not less than ten cents, or whatever the President should require. In the Grand Council at Tallahassee, or at the office of Richards and Saunders, whenever an influential freedman applied for initiation, and they thought he could raise the money, they would charge him fifteen or twenty dollars to become a member of the league. Charters for the organization of lodges cost five dollars, and whenever the deputies could succeed in wringing it out of the people, they would charge them a greater sum. These fees were divided with the President of the League in Tallahassee, William M. Saunders, who constituted himself the Grand Council; and whenever he could make the deputies come up with the cash he would pocket the money. Grips, signs and passwords were given to the freedmen in these lodges, and they were told that they had received something beyond the reach and conception of their former masters, which led them to believe their late masters had no rights that they were bound to respect. This nefarious teaching made many of them very obnoxious and overbearing members of society. Thousands of dollars were wrung from the hands of our people by these devices. They were assured in these league meetings that the lands and all the property of their former masters would be equally divided among the former slaves, which led many to indolence. They were further instructed that the oath which they had taken in the League was of such a nature that they could not vote for any Southern white man for office; that to do so would cause their return into slavery. To rivet these teachings upon their consciences, violent speeches would be made in the lodge-rooms, and often in public, in denunciation of their former masters, who, in turn, had their hands full to explain and satisfy our misguided people, the best they could, that the men who were organizing them in secret lodges were mere demagogues for the sake of office and their worst enemies. This argument set some of our people to thinking, and but for this and the influence of the more sensible of the colored people, the property of the country would have in many instances been destroyed by the midnight torch. Although Saunders, Richards and Billings and their henchmen who organized the Loyal League were not altogether successful in putting to political death Osborn and his Bureau agents, yet their fight for the spoils had a great tendency to cripple them for life in many parts of the State. The whites at this time had become alarmed at these secret meetings and began to bestir themselves to find out the full secret of this league. Their first step was to get the negro into a good humor by delivering to him what he considered a fine present. If any whisky or brandy was about the white man would drop one or two drams into him, which would be the means of drawing him into conversation the more easily concerning the league. He would then start out by shaking hands with the freedman, telling him at the same time that this (placing his fingers into some curious form) is the secret grip of the league. This would please the freedman so well, to think that he knew something that the former master did not know, that he would undertake to instruct him as to the right grip, if he could recollect it. He felt grand at the idea that he was capable of teaching his former master something. Many of the grips, passwords and signs were exposed in this way; but the whites were yet kept in the dark as to the real intentions of the league. So insecure did the whites consider their lives and property that some of them were constrained to make application to become members of the league ; but this was refused. One gentleman, a wealthy planter in Leon County, to my personal knowledge made application to J. W. Toer, Esq., colored (who was a very good and polite old gentleman), and was admitted ; but the freedmen were told to watch him—that he was only a spy, and old man Toer was after that time looked upon by them as a traitor. This gentleman lived in a settlement where nine-tenths of the population were colored, and all of them were members of the league. He does not hesitate to declare that he was forced to join this league to save his property from destruction. There is no disputing the fact that the fears of the whites with reference to these leagues were well founded; for the men who controlled them had really nothing in view but public plunder. Notwithstanding the oath that had been taken by the freedmen as members of the Loyal League, and the violent speeches with promises made by its leaders to them, there was a sectional and natural feeling existing among most of them which was a resistless leaning toward those with whom they were better acquainted—their late masters. In 1867, some few months before the nomination of delegates to the Constitutional Convention of 1868, the freedmen called a public meeting in the courthouse in Leon County, and invited M. D. Papy, one of the most prominent lawyers in the State, Judge McIntosh, and other Southerners, to address them and give them some information as to their newly acquired duties as citizens. Those gentlemen and others attended the meeting and addressed the colored people. The meeting was largely attended and the addresses were well received; but Osborn and the rest of the plunder-hunters kicked furiously against this revolutionary movement on the part of the freedmen, while most of the whites looked upon the action of Papy and McIntosh as giving countenance to Osborn, Saunders and other carpetbaggers. If this action on the part of the blacks and whites had not been interfered with the State would have saved thousands of dollars. The freedmen in other parts of the State would have heard with gladness of the action of their former masters at the capital. They would have broken the chains of the league and looked up to those slaveholders of the State who had not in the days of slavery treated them cruelly. They felt confident that their rights would be absolutely secure in the hands of those men under the reconstruction acts of Congress. As a close observer of the times, and as one of the actors in the reconstruction theatre, I am certain, if the Southern whites could have taken in the situation, two-thirds of them would have been returned as delegates to the Constitutional Convention of 1868. This result would have enlisted two-thirds of the best white citizens of Florida in the ranks of the Republican party. But "to err is human." From this time up to the election of delegates to the Constitutional Convention of 1886 no further alliance was attempted between the whites and the freedmen. The whites, discouraged at the solidity of the freedmen against them, refused to take any part in the election of delegates to the convention. The two so-called Republican factions—one termed the Osborn Faction and the other The Mule Team (having acquired this name by the reason of Billings and Saunders using two mules to haul them around while perfecting their electioneering schemes), had everything their own way, with the military to back them.

CHAPTER V.

The Election of Delegates to the Constitutional Convention of 1868. Address of D. Richards, the First President. The Loyal League Overthrows the Lincoln Brotherhood. Notable Members of the Convention. The Richards Constitution. Re-capture of Convention. Minority of Non-resident Delegates. The Lincoln Brotherhood Ahead, and the Loyal Leaguers Rampant. Ratification of the Constitution and Election of Governor Reed.

Under militaty authority the State was divided into nineteen election districts, which were so arranged as to have the counties where the white population predominated attached to the counties having large colored majorities. There was but one polling place in each county, which necessitated the continuing the election for three days. The election was held on the 14th, 15th and 16th of November, 1867, under the formal supervison of the military. The question submitted was, For a Convention, or, Against a Convention; and for delagetes to the convention in case a majority of the votes cast were for the Constitution. Twenty-seven thousand one hundred and seventy-two registered voters were returned by the registering officers, of whom fourteen thousand five hundred and three were returned as having voted for a Constitution. All the districts returned delegates, and a full convention, forty-six in number, were elected. The following is a list of the delegates, as returned by military general orders No. 110:

First District—Escambia and Santa Rosa Counties—Geo. W. Walker, Geo. J. Alden, Lyman W. Rowley.

Second District—Walton, Washington and Holmes—John L. Campbell.

Third District—Jackson—W. J. Purman, L. C. Armistead, E. Fortune, H. Bryan.

Fourth District—Gadsen and Liberty—D. Richards, W. U. Sanders, Frederick Hill.

Fifth District—Franklin—J. W. Childs.

Sixth District—Leon—T. W. Osborn, Joseph E. Oats, C. H. Pearce, John Wyatt, Green Davidson, O. B. Armstrong.

Seventh District—Jefferson—John W. Powell, A. G. Bass, Robert Meacham, Anthony Mills.

Eighth District—Madison—Roland T. Rambauer, Major Johnson, William R. Cone.

Ninth District—Suwannee—Thomas Urquhart, Andrew Shuler.

Tenth District—Lafayette and Taylor—J. R. Krimminger.

Eleventh District—Alachua—Horatio Jenkins, Jr., William K. Cessna, Josiah T. Walls.

Twelfth District—Columbia—S. B. Conover, Abram Erwin.

Thirteenth District—Clay—B. M. McRae.

Fourteenth District—Duval and Nassau—L. Billings, N. C. Dennett, William Bradwell, J. C. Gibbs.

Fifteenth District—Marion—J. H. Goss, A. Chandler, W. Rogers, E. D. House.

Sixteenth District—Hernando—Samuel J. Pearce.

Seventeenth District—Hillsborough—C. R. Mobley.

Eighteenth District—Monroe—Eldridge L. Ware.

The convention met on Monday, January 20th, 1868, C. H. Pearce, colored, of Tallahassee, was elected temporary President, and H. Ford, of Baltimore, Md., also colored, was elected temporary Secretary, amid the shouts of hundreds of the newly enfranchised freedmen, who declared "the bottom rail on top," and "the year of jubilee am come." There were but twenty of the forty-six delegates present. The following Committee on Permanent Organization was appointed: Wm. M. Saunders, of Baltimore, chairman; Wm. R. Cone, S. B. Conover, Robert Meacham and O. B. Armstrong. This committee immediately reported—

1. For President, D. Richards, of Sterling, Ill., returned from Gadsden County (where he had spent but two days of his life) and W. H. Christy, of Jacksonville, for Secretary, with three assistants; a Chaplain, Sergeant-at-Arms, Postmaster, three doorkeepers and one financial agent—Paul Crippen, a stranger in the State.

2. Ten committee clerks, of whom Paul Crippen was one, and Henry Ford, the Postmaster, was another.

3. Nine pages and messengers.

The first section of the report was adopted, but as there was some objection to the others the appointments were devolved upon the President, who subsequently appointed the list recommended by the committee. The President-elect took the chair, and addressed the Convention as follows:

RICHARDS' ADDRESS.

"GENTLEMEN OF THE CONVENTION:

"For your kindness and partiality in electing me to preside over your deliberations, you have my sincere, heartfelt thanks. That the duties thus devolved upon me may be so discharged as to satisfy you that I am not entirely unworthy of this generous confidence, is now my greatest solicitude. From a sense of my own weakness, I have hesitated about whether I should accept this position of such high honor and trust; but relying on your charity, forbearance, and aid, I enter upon the performance of the duties with a prayer that the relations of friendship that now bind us together may continue to be the most cordial, and that our proceedings may be characterized by that spirit of kindness and generosity which the great events standing so close around us should inspire. Ours is the opportunity and privilege of elevating and benefiting humanity by forming for a whole State a fundamental law that should tend to promote patriotism, permanent peace and enduring prosperity with all our people. The age in which we live, generations that are to come after us, and the stern, uncompromising historian, will hold us to a rigid account for the manner in which we dispose of the great trust confided to us by an afflicted, unfortunate people. Permanent rules for the guidance of all in the development of the great resources of our State, and that are to control all the functions of government, are to be established by us, and may we heed the voice of humanity, and may a merciful Providence aid us in our counsels and direct us in our conclusions. With the mantle of charity we would cover the moral heresies, monstrous injustice and red-handed cruelty of the past, and with malice toward none and charity for all, and 'firmness in the right as God gives us light,' let us enter upon the majestic work of laying deep the foundations of a government that shall sacredly care for and protect the rights of all, and that shall deserve and receive the respect, love and confidence of all our citizens. Let no recollections of the bondage that was so long the withering disgrace of American civilization be impressed upon the Constitution we are about to form. Let it be not tinged with the blood-stains of a wicked rebellion and terrible war by presenting features of resentment, retaliation or revenge; but let it contain some cautious, jealous provisions that shall forever hereafter vigilantly guard, as with a two-edged sword, all approaches to the Temple of Liberty, Justice and Equal Rights to all; and it will stand as a proud monument to the wisdom of our times, and to the triumph of the principles of freedom and truth and a progressive humanity, over oppression, error, superstition and barbarism. Let us insure to all who have not forfeited their rights by treason or rebellion a common interest in our institutions, our laws and our government by religiously securing to them the right to vote and be voted for; and the consciousness that we are each a part of the government will soon induce a feeling of self-respect, manhood and pride in maintaining law and order and good government in society. We should provide for a system by which all may obtain homes of their own and a comfortable living, and also provide for schools in which all may be educated free of expense; clothe honest industry with respectability; inaugurate a public sentiment that shall crown the man with honors as the benefactor of his race who makes two blades of grass grow where one grew before, and prohibit all laws that are not equal and just to all within our State. And from out of the ashes of discord and strife, will arise the songs of gladness, thanksgiving and praise. Then the earth will respond to the gentle touch of scientific culture in bountiful harvests; the Land of Flowers will become the land of patriotism, peace and plenty; the hot wrath of wicked men will be restrained in their amazement at the great and wonderful transformation, and Florida will keep step to the grand music of the Union, and move forward in her career of glory as one of the States, and God in his infinite goodness will bless us in our basket and our store."

General Meade was notified of the organization, and being invited to attend, sent the following telegram:

"I regret that my public duties prevent my complying with your invitation to visit your convention. I have no communication to make beyond calling your attention to the remarks made to the Georgia Convention, and urging prompt action upon your part in the important duty assigned to you, and the earnest hope that you will speedily form a constitution and frame a civil government acceptable to the people of Florida and the Congress of the United States."

The Loyal League, headed by Richards, Billings and Saunders, all non-residents, had so far supplanted the Lincoln Brotherhood which Osborn had instituted, that it was only through the permission and courtesy of Elder C. H. Pearce, who held the colored vote of Leon County under control, that he was elected to the convention; and he was so tardy and cowardly in his movements that he had allowed the opposition to seize the organization of the convention before he could gather in his adherents, Richards was therefore master of the situation before Osborn had awaked to the fact that he was no longer dictator to the freedmen. But the representative from Illinois was not equal to the task he had assumed, and the insane greed for spoils soon lost him and his associates their hold. Billings and Saunders had the Loyal Leaguers, and William J. Purman was the accepted champion of the Lincoln Brotherhood.

The first effort of President Richards was to get control of the small sum in the State Treasury, for which purpose he gave an order upon the State Treasurer to pay over to Paul Crippen all money in his hands belonging to the State. The Treasurer, before responding to the order telegraphed General Meade, who immediately forbade any payment upon the requisition of the President of the convention without his special approval of each requisition. The five hundred dollars then in the Treasury was thus saved to meet the salaries of the existing State officers. These non-resident plunderers then determined to go directly to the property owners for their plunder, and by resolution of the convention President Richards and financial agent Crippen were authorized to issue script to the amount of fifty thousand dollars. Fifteen thousand was immediately issued on account of printing alone, and Col. W. M. Saunders retained ten thousand of the amount. The pay of pages and messengers was fixed at ten dollars per day, and that of clerks and other officers from fifteen to twenty dollars per day. As another illustration of the reckless disregard of interests of the State, J. T. Walls, delegate from Alachua County, about three hundred miles distant, was allowed $690; O. B. Armstrong, whose home was at the capital, $630; Wm. M. Saunders, delegate from Gadsden County, twenty miles distant, $649; F. Hill from the same district, with the same distance, $457; John Wyatt, from the same district as

Armstrong, with thirty-five miles to travel, $467. There were large amounts of script accredited to members and attaches of the convention who never saw a dollar of it; but the script was issued and retained by Paul Crippen and his co-conspirators.

At the time this script was issued the convention was sitting with a bare majority of the delegates returned as elected in attendance. As the convention filled up the struggle for supremacy waxed hot between the contending parties, and two weeks were wasted in the contest. Crowds of freedmen from the country would daily assemble around the capitol, and whenever Saunders and Billings were tired of scalping Purman and Osborn in the convention, they would address the freedmen in mass meeting in front of the capitol, relating to them that Purman, Osborn and their followers had gone over to the red-handed rebels, characterizing them as Lucifer and his rebellious angels disturbing and making war in Heaven, while the speakers described themselves as leading the Heavenly hosts and fighting to hurl the rebellious angels from the temple. The masses were thus kept excited in order to secure an influence over the colored delegates, who were quartered among the blacks, nine-tenths of whom adhered to the Billings faction. It would not have been safe for any of the delegates to have gone over to Purman. Many of the Democrats had been inclined to favor the Richards-Billings faction rather than that of Osborn, until the system of plunder was developed, when they became alarmed and gave their influence, with the military authorities, to prevent their success.

The Billings-Saunders delegates were quartered in a house under their control, which was characterized by Purman in debate as the Bull Pen. Saunders, in retort for thus stigmatizing his residence, would seize a chair to hurl at his head and this would require the interference of the Sergeant-at-Arms. Saunders was an eloquent and powerful speaker, good at repartee, an excellent parliamentarian and one of the shrewdest and most unscrupulous members of the convention. Richards was a less impassioned and more mild speaker—a sort of Uriah Heep specimen of the Northern carpet-bagger, of moderate ability and elastic conscience. Jesse H. Goss, of Marion County, a Southerner by birth, was identified with the Billings faction, but honest, upright and conscientious in seeking to protect the interests of the State and preserve the rights of the freedmen. C. R. Mobley, of Tampa, a Kansas refugee "border ruffian," identified himself with the Osborn faction; was a fair debater and opposed the extravagance of the Richards party. Jonathan C. Gibbs, colored, who was afterwards Secretary of State under Governor Reed, and Superintendent of Public Instruction under Governor Hart, was the best educated delegate in the convention, as well as the most conservative and polished speaker. He was a graduate of Harvard College. He adhered to the Billings faction, but labored hard and honestly to secure a constitution that should protect the property of the State as well as the rights of the freedmen. More than once he arose in the convention and denounced Billings of his own faction, who would wait until the lobby of the convention would be filled with freedmen, and make that the opportunity for delivering a fiery speech in denunciation of the former slaveholders. Although Mr. Gibbs was, through circumstances, inseparably allied to the Billings-Saunders faction, he was unqualifiedly opposed to the manner in which the convention started out in the extravagant expenditure of the people's money. Mr. Gibbs was not a politician, but an honest Republican, trying to lay the foundation for a respectable party in the State, and if the mass of the voters that composed the Republican party of Florida had possessed the intelligence to have followed his advice, the State would have been spared a great deal of bitterness between its black and white citizens, and some precious lives would have been preserved. E. Fortune, colored, identified with the Osborn-Purman faction, a native of Florida, had a fair education and was a forcible debater; and whenever he believed he was right, neither money nor promises could move him from his position. He opposed from first to last the conduct of the Billings-Saunders faction, and but for his unalterable opposition as one of the colored delegates, it is doubtful whether the Purman-Osborn faction would have succeeded. W. J. Purman, a full-fledged Northern carpet-bagger, who was believed by many to be an officer in the United States army at the time he was performing his duties as delegate, was a very persuasive and forcible speaker, but was not a match for Saunders. Purman was possessed of an indomitable will, which in most cases crowned him with success. Although in this fight he pretended to be opposed to the plunder system, his subsequent actions in the politics of the State showed him to be more unscrupulous and dangerous than Saunders, Billings or Richards. T. W. Osborn, also a carpet-bagger of the Purman type, was a man of considerable ability, but was no debater, and devoid of moral courage as of conscience. He was a good wire-puller, and that is the most that can be said of him. Col. Liberty Billings, who was a professed carpet-bagger, was at the time of his election a citizen of the State of New Hampshire. He was a man of powerful intellect, but his oratorical powers seemed to have been hid under a bushel, except when he was arraying the blacks against the whites. In fact, he never laughed or smiled, nor did he seem to be in his right element unless he was criticising in the most abusive language, the Southern whites. As to his financial policy in the convention, it was on the order of "hold what you have got and get all you can." Horatio Jenkins was a Northern man, an officer in the Union army. He had fine abilities, was a young man of fine personal character and popular address. Had he but had the courage to follow his own convictions instead of surrendering to the dictation of Osborn, he would have risen to high position in the State; but Osborn led him to ruin, and in after years he was compelled to leave the State in poverty and disgrace, one of the many victims of Osborn's vicious ambition. I shall record him better in a future chapter. Some of the lesser lights of the convention, who could neither read nor write, would be seen with both feet thrown across their desks smoking cigars, while the convention was in session, and would often address the President: "I ize to a pint off orter and deman that the pages and mess'gers put some jinal on my des." The President would draw a long sigh and order journals to be carried and laid upon the desks of these eminent statesmen, who would seize them up and go through the motions of reading them, perhaps upside down, saying at the same time: "I has not had a jinal to read for free or fo' days." The pages, indignant at this mockery, would exclaim to the President "that the delagates who called for the journals could not read them if printed in letters as large as the capitol." The modest President would order them to take their places and attend upon the gentlemen o the convention. Most of the pages of the convention could read and write.

If the convention, as then constituted, had been held in any of the New England States and had been guilty of the same conduct, nothing but a strong military guard could have secured their persons from violence. These ridiculous scenes continued for two weeks and more, when a portion of the members seceded, leaving the convention without a quorum. The sessions were continued, however, and in a few days adopted a constitution, which was said to have been prepared in Chicago and brought here by Richards to be forced upon the people of the State. (See Appendix A.)

Goss, the delegate from Marion County, was despatched with a copy of this constitution to Atlanta to procure the approval of the commanding General.

The convention took a recess February 8th, to wait the return of its messenger. During this time, Saunders and Billings, elated and more exultant over their supposed victory over Purman, Osborn and Company, called a mass meeting to assemble in the capitol square and addressed the freedmen, telling them that they had hurled the rebellious angels from the great Republican temple. After the speaking was over Saunders resolved the meeting into a nominating convention for the purpose of nominating State officers and also for members of the Legislature for Leon County. Liberty Billings was nominated for Governor, W. M. Saunders for Lieutenant-Governor, and Samuel Walker, for Congress. Leon County was allowed in this deal ten Representatives and one Senator. This apportionment does not appear in the Billings-Saunders constitution. In fact, all the officers of State were nominated by the mass meeting composed entirely of the Freedmen of Leon County. It looked as though there was office for all.

On Monday, February 10th, between twelve and one o'clock at night, the seceding delegates, or "rebellious angels," returned to Tallahassee in a body, broke into the capitol, recaptured the "celestial palace," and proceeded to reorganize the convention. The most amusing incident of the recapture of the convention was, that Saunders, although nominated for Lieutenant-Governor, was not satisfied to be on the tail of the ticket. Billings must come down from the head of the ticket and give place to Saunders. How to steer clear of the Billings breakers was a problem which quite puzzled his brain—but something must be done. As white and black masons did not affiliate at that time in the South, Saunders conceived the idea of organizing a colored lodge, and getting all the prominent colored men into it and then pledge them to demand the withdrawal of Billings as a candidate for Governor, while Saunders would pledge him his support for United States Senator. This was commenced on Monday night, February 10th. Several members had been initiated that night. Billings, filled with anxiety to know what was going on in the black camp, applied for admission and was refused. A disruption in the Billings-Saunders faction was now imminent. The lodge adjourned about midnight to meet the following night to complete its work. As its members entered the street they saw the capitol lighted up, heard the sound of voices, the earnest stamping of feet and clapping of hands. They were awe-stricken, and conveyed the intelligence to Saunders, who, startled at the scene, broke out with an oath that "Billings, the d—d traitor, has organized a convention against me and my friends." Saunders immediately sent messengers to the capitol to see what this strange thing really meant. When the messengers returned and informed him what had taken place, he said that his old familiar enemies were only holding a secret caucus. But "the end was not yet." The eighteen delegates who withdrew had now enlisted four new recruits to their standard, which swelled their number to twenty-two. They managed by some means to capture two of the colored delegates from the Billings-Saunders faction, which gave them a majority of two of all the delegates returned under general order No. 110. The freedmen undertook to mob these two delegates in the streets the next day, which resulted in one of the delegates named Shaler shooting one of the freedmen, but not fatally.

This convention now proceeded to vacate the seats of the non-resident delegates—Roberts, Saunders and Billings—elected Horatio Jenkins, Jr., President, Sherman Conant, Secretary, and other necessary officers, and immediately set to work to form the constitution which was finally adopted and became the organic law of the State. A squad of the Federal military, under direction of Governor Walker, was directed to guard the convention chamber against a threatened attempt of the ousted members to take violent possession. The freedmen seeing their supposed Lord and Saviour shut out from the capitol were excited to fever heat. The news went like wildfire through the adjoining counties. Large numbers of them assembled in Tallahassee, ready, as they thought, for battle. Each one had his club, about two feet long with a string through the end of it, so as to be fastened to his wrist. Their cry was that they wanted nothing but the blood of Osborn and Purman and their fellows. Nothing but the presence of the military prevented bloodshed. Some of the more ignorant of the freedmen were so carried away with Billings and Saunders that they wanted to attack the military guard at the door of the convention and attempt to drive them away and give Saunders and Billings possession of the hall. When it was definitely ascertained that Billings and Saunders could not get possession of the hall, some of the freedmen, who had said when the convention was first organized, "that the bottom rail was on top," began to mutter and to say that "the rail had again fallen to the bottom." General Mead, who had been appealed to by the minority faction, arrived in Tallahassee on the 17th day of February. Committees from each faction waited on him to learn his views on the situation. He finally ordered that all the delegates returned under the order of General Pope should go into the convention; the two contending Presidents to hand in their resignations to the Secretary, Sherman Conant, and the convention then reorganize, *de novo*, with the commanding General of the Division, General Sprague, presiding. This proposition was readily accepted by Jenkins, but Richards hesitated, as he saw in this action his political death staring him in the face. He finally consented under protest, and with palsied hand he wrote his resignation. On Tuesday, February 18th, at 3 o'clock, P. M., the convention met with all the delegates of both factions present. The Secretary, Conant, introduced to the convention Col. John T. Sprague, in full uniform, as its temporary chairman. A motion was then made that Horatio Jenkins, Jr., be elected President of the convention, which was carried by a vote of thirty-two to thirteen. Colonel Sprague then retired. The next step was a resolution declaring all the offices of the first convention vacant, but Sherman Conant was retained as the Secretary of this convention. This convention was not so liberal as the first in making offices for its followers. Its offices consisted of one secretary and an assistant secretary, one sergeant-at-arms, one doorkeeper, one chaplain, a printer and a financial agent. There was a marked difference in the last convention as to decorum.

Osborn and "the Brotherhood" having overcome the leaders of the Loyal League by recapturing the convention, were determined to pursue them to their death for future contingencies. To expel them from the convention would have the effect of killing their influence with the freedmen, and it was willed that they should go. Purman was appointed chairman of the Committee on Eligibility, and the day after the last convention was organized, made a report which was generally believed he had carried in his pocket from the time he entered the convention until he reported it, which was as follows:

"In the case of W. M. Saunders, returned as a delegate to this convention from the Fourth Election District, conclusive evidence is adduced that he is not a registered voter in nor an inhabitant of the district he claims to represent; that he is no citizen of Florida under the reconstruction laws.

"In the case of Liberty Billings, returned from the Fourteenth Election District, evidence is produced under the seal of the United States Court, that he, on the 12th day of August, 1867, in this State made oath that he is a citizen of the State of New Hampshire, and the official certificate of the Board of Registration is in proof that he is not a registered voter in the district he claims to represent.

"In the case of C. H. Pearce, returned from the Sixth Election District, the official certificate of the Board of Registration is in evidence that he is not a registered voter in the district that he claims to represent, that he was formerly a resident of Canada; that he there swore true faith and allegiance to the government of Great Britain.

"Your committee, in conclusion, beg leave to recommend the following resolution as the result and conviction of their unbiased investigation, uninfluenced by any sentiment or prejudice, either of a political or personal character.

Resolved, That W. M. Saunders, Liberty Billings and C. H. Pearce, returned as delegates to this convention from the Fourth,

Fourteenth and Sixth Election Districts, respectively, are hereby, for reasons stated in the foregoing report, declared ineligible to seats in this body."

In the case of Daniel Richards, from the Fourth Election District, the Committee reported that he was not an inhabitant nor registered voter of the district which he claimed to represent, and ineligible to a seat in the convention. These resolutions were adopted by a large majority, and this ended the Billings-Saunders reign in the Constitutional Convention of 1868.

It will be seen by the minutes of this convention, that its journal was not kept in such a way as to enable coming generations to know what had transpired throughout the whole proceedings. The following resolution is introduced as a witness to the insufficiency of the journal. It was offered by Mr. Alden:

Resolved, That the Journal of the Constitutional Convention of the State of Florida, from its organization until the third day of February, be recognized as the only Journal of the Convention to that date. Thereafter, that all the proceedings of this convention, except the meeting and adjournment of the convention, be expunged from the journal until the 18th of February, 3 P. M., from which time the journal shall be resumed and kept complete." (See Journal of the Proceedings of the Constitutional Convention of the State of Florida, page 48).

T. W. Osborn offered the following resolution, which was adopted under suspension of the rules:

"WHEREAS, It having come to the knowledge of this convention that D. S. Walker, Governor of the State of Florida, having his executive office in the capitol, and by virtue of his office as Governor, being in charge of the capitol and all the rooms therein, has in no manner been consulted or his assent asked by any officer or member of the convention for the use of the Assembly chamber or any other room in which to hold this convention, therefore,

Resolved, That we, as the Constitutional Convention of the State of Florida, sincerely regret that so great a discourtesy has been shown to the Governor of the State by this convention and by its former officers; and further that we request the President of this convention to wait upon Governor Walker and state to him the circumstances in the case, and ask the use of this room in which to hold the Constitutional Convention of the State of Florida."

Osborn offered another resolution, under suspension of the rules, that the Sergeant-at-Arms be instructed to inquire of Governor Walker the amount of wood that had been used by the convention, which wood had been purchased by the officers of the capitol, and used by the convention without consent from the Governor.

Although Osborn and Company, prior to the assembling of the convention, had been marshaling the freedmen against any respect for or recognition of the Walker administration, it seems that the struggle with the Billings-Saunders faction in the convention had resulted in making Osborn a special convert and forced him to at least a temporary membership of the Governor's political church; but Walker rather doubted the sincerity of the convert, and he never thereafter informed the deacons or other members of the congregation of this most sudden and remarkable conversion of this Saul of Tarsus.

The convention, as soon as it was organized, commenced reading a constitution which had been agreed upon by Osborn and Company, some time and at some place which are not definitely known, but was generally believed to have been made or agreed upon in the city of Monticello, whence these eighteen conspirators, after the manner of the Arabs, had folded their tents at the capitol and silently stolen away. The reading of the constitution would only be disturbed when some interlocutory decree of Osborn and Company had to be carried into effect. The following is a fair sample of some of these decrees: On the 20th of February, J. E. Davidson and M. L. Stearns, who received but a small fraction of the votes cast, were seated from the Fourth District, in place of Daniel Richards and W. M. Saunders; Richard Wells, who did not get twenty votes, was seated from the Sixth District in place of C. H. Pearce. O. B. Hart, who received the same number of votes as Wells, was seated from the Fourteenth District in place of Liberty Billings; John W. Butler, who made no contest, was seated from the First District in place of George Walker, who failed to attend the convention after being elected.

After passing a resolution declaring the script issued by the first convention void, the constitution was signed and the convention adjourned on the 25th day of February, subject to call of President, or any ten members, in case the President is out of the State. Nine members of the Billings-Richards faction signed the constitution under protest, as they were threatened that they should have no pay unless they did sign it.

Billings, now the candidate of his faction for Governor, began to stump the State against the adoption of the constitution. The freedmen were wrathy and began to raise money to end Richards and Saunders to Congress to protest against the admission of the State into the Union in case the constitution was adopted. Some four or five hundred dollars were raised and they went off to Washington. They had not been absent long before Richards sent back to the freedmen the following telegram: "Florida is safe; Congress is with us! Praise the Lord." For an hour the air was filled with shouts from the freedmen. One freedman while on his dying bed, and conscious of his approaching death, gave the only five dollars he had to be sent to Saunders and Richards at Washington. Saunders had not been there many days before the Osborn faction captured him and sent him back to the State to canvass for the adoption of the New Constitution. He came back but did not dare stop in Tallahassee for fear of being mobbed by the freedmen. Now that one of the trinity had deserted, Billings and Richards were left to conduct the canvass themselves with the assistance of C. H. Pearce, who had been ousted from the convention. Billings would hold his meetings on large plantations in the night time, so as to get all the old men and women out, as they generally controlled the younger class. In order to deeply impress the freedmen with the justness of his cause and of his unblemished Republicanism, he would have all the little colored children brought out to the meetings, and would ask the name of each, and then take them up and kiss them. A little soap and water would not have done some of them any harm. When he would kiss the children you could hear on all sides from the freedmen words like these: "I will vote ebery day for that man." "I will die for that man." "That man is a good 'publican." Billings hearing these words would shout to them, "Jesus Christ was a Republican." So attached were these people to Billings that they introduced a sign among themselves which was the given name of Billings. When one wanted to know how the other stood to Billings, he would say "Liberty," and if the other was a Billings man he would answer "Liberty."

On the Billings State Ticket was Sam. Walker, for Lieutenant-Governor, and D. Richards, for Congress, while the Republican party had nominated Harrison Reed for Governor, William H. Gleason for Lieutenant-Governor, and Charles Hamilton, for Congress. The Democrats, taking courage at the fight of the two Republican factions, nominated George W. Scott for the head of their ticket, and in conjunction with Billings, opposed the adoption of the constitution. The election was held on the 4th, 5th and 6th days of May, and resulted in the election of Governor Reed and Lieutenant-Governor Gleason, and the ratification of the constitution by five thousand majority. There is no question about the fact of Billings carrying Leon County against the constitution, though the vote as counted did not show it. Governor Reed was honestly elected, but a large majority of the votes cast in the above county were against the constitution but were for Harrison Reed, and the Legislative Ticket of Billings. The vote was more evenly balanced between Reed and Billings. The Billings Constitution was not put before the people to be voted on, as that could not be done without the indorsement of General Meade, and he refused to recognize that constitution for the reason that it was made without a majority of the delegates elected; but both constitutions were laid before Congress by the President of the United States.

One of the most noticeable traitorous features of the Osborn constitution was a clause to prohibit any person from being eligible to the office of Governor, Lieutenant-Governor, Member of Congress, or United States Senator, unless he had been nine years a citizen of the United States, two years a citizen of the State of Florida, and a registered voter. This was done to shut out such colored men as the educated and brilliant Gibbs, and other leading lights of the colored race in the State. They were handicapped, however, by the amendments of the Constitution of the United States, therefore their scheme did not work well; but the attempt to steal is bad morally, if not legally. This clause first took effect upon one of the schemers, William H. Gleason, who, not having been a citizen of Florida two years before the election, was ousted from the office of Lieutenant-Governor, by order of the court in proceedings instituted by Governor Reed in consequence of the attempt of Gleason and his co-conspirators to impeach and suspend Reed and inaugurate Gleason as Governor.

CHAPTER VI.

Memorial of Richards and Saunders to Congress Against the Osborn Constitution. Criticism on the Memorial.

After the re-assembling of the convention, which resulted in the utter defeat of Richards and Saunders, and the consequent setting aside of all the previous proceedings, the defeated parties carried the matter into the Congress of the United States, with the hope of preventing the admission of the State into the Union under the constitution made by the recognized body. They accordingly drew up the following memorial, which was laid before that body on the 23d of March, 1868:

FLORIDA CONSTITUTIONAL CONVENTION—ITS HISTORY.

Enclosed is the order of Major-General John Pope, commanding third military district, calling the Constitutional Convention of Florida, and his return of the delegates elected.

By the said order it will be seen that forty-six delegates were returned as elected.

On the 20th of January, when the convention was organized, thirty delegates were present, twenty-seven of whom voted for the officers elected, and two against them—one not voting, but who next day asked and obtained leave to have his vote recorded in favor of the organization.

Next day, 21st, standing rules were adopted by a unanimous vote. The convention was organized by electing to most of the offices radical republicans, and threats were openly made by the conservative Johnson office-holders and rebels that no constitution should be made, nor business done, until the organization of the convention was broken up. Conservative republicans, both in and out of the convention, began to caucus night and day, with the leading rebels freely admitted to their councils, to devise ways and means to overthrow the radicals. The principal hotel in the city was opened free to the delegates who would act with them, and who were all poor—many of them not money enough to pay board bills with. Whisky flowed free as water. Money was used in abundance to corrupt the delegates, which was like tendering bread to a starving man.

The unworthy, debasing influences brought to bear upon

the delegates would disgrace any other part of Christendom, if it does not Florida.

Like hungry wolves around a carcass, the Federal officeholders in the State congregated together there as with a common purpose, and that purpose to defeat reconstruction on a republican basis in that State. The caucuses of the organized lobby were held every night until nearly daylight, and money furnished by the Johnson office-holders, and every other influence was used to bring in delegates to join them.

Among those who took active part against the convention as oganized, and most of whom were almost constantly in caucus, were the following, viz: Harrison Reed, O. B. Hart, T. W. Osborn, Sherman Conant, Lemuel Wilson, A. A. Knight, O. Morgan, M. L. Stearns, E. D. Howse, W. J. Purman, S. B. Conover and E. K. Foster, all holding offices under the General Government.

Colonel John T. Sprague, commander of the State, previous to the organization, and during the convention, exercised his influence actively in the interest of .those who finally disrupted the convention. C. Thurston Chase and S. F. Dewy, both Federal office-holders, aided by their correspondence, counsels and advice the faction striving to gain the control of the convention or to break it up. E. M. Randall, brother of the Postmaster-General, was constantly in caucus with them, as was also Captain Dyke, editor of the Floridian, and keeper of Andersonville, where our Union soldiers were starved. Governor David S. Walker rendered them all the aid and comfort in his power, and after the convention was broken up and a new one organized, he was on the floor of the convention every day among the delegates and on one occasion made a speech to the convention.

Every effort to proceed with the business of the convention was violently resisted by this disorganizing faction in the body, aided by a powerful and thoroughly organized lobby, for two weeks. During this time only forty-one delegates had subscribed to the oath as required by the rules of the convention; the others having failed to appear and subscribe to the oath. The great struggle of the opposition was to turn enough delegates out or vote enough into the convention to give them control of it. At the end of two weeks' wrangling, the opposition were beaten on a close vote of twenty-one to twenty, and the combined conservative and rebel faction, to the number of eighteen, withdrew in a body to break up the convention. Other of the conservative delegates had previously gone home—one a Union man of such strong rebel proclivities that it was stated on the floor of the convention by his friends that he would not take the oath to support the Constitution of the United States and proclamations made thereunder. He had left some ten days previous.

When these last eighteen withdrew there were but twenty-two delegates left in the convention. These twenty-two delegates remaining in the convention diligently applied themselves to the object for which they came together during the following week. By taking the present Florida constitution, and making just such changes in it as the altered circumstances seemed to require, on the 8th day of February they finished their work, formed and signed a good constitution. They then adjourned for one week, in order to give time to lay the constitution before General Meade, and get his endorsement of the ordinance calling an election, as it could not be enforced without the general commanding the district gave validity to it by his endorsement.

When the seceding delegates withdrew, they immediately left the city of Tallahassee, fearing, probably, if they remained, some of their weaker members, who had been kept intoxicated all the time for two weeks, might get sober enough and be induced to go back into the convention, and thus make a quorum of all the delegates elected. They repaired to Monticello, some thirty miles distant, sent messengers and special trains, and money to try and gather together the fugitive delegates, who had previously gone home. They remained away from the capital an entire week, and until the convention had completed its labor, formed a constitution, signed it, and adjourned for a week to hear from General Meade. The convention adjourned on Saturday, February 8. The following Monday, February 10, the seceding delegates returned, *at midnight*, 22 strong. With the aid of the military furnished by Governor Walker, they broke into the State-house at dead of night. C. M. Hamilton, until very recently agent in the Freedman's Bureau, and believed by most of the delegates to be still in command, with power to enforce his orders, went and took from their beds two of the delegates who had already signed one constitution, took them to the State-house, and, between the hours of twelve and two o'clock in the night, they assumed to organize a convention, with the military standing guard around and in the State-house. A guard of soldiers, furnished by direction of Governor Walker, was stationed in the hall night and day.

On Tuesday, the 11th, this disorganizing organization went through with the performance of expelling four delegates who had not met with them at all, and then swore in five men who tried hard to be elected as delegates to the Constitutional Convention, but did not get votes enough, and consequently General Pope, although pressed hard for weeks to do so, did not return them as elected. They then telegraphed General Meade that they were organized as the Constitutional Convention of

Florida, and had a large majority of the delegates elected and returned. General Meade had hesitated to endorse the action of the adjourned convention of 22 delegates, for the reason that they had not a majority of the delegates elected to sign the constitution. A majority of those who had duly taken and subscribed to the oath, as required by the rules, had signed it. The general admitted to the messenger sent to confer with him that the convention, as first organized, was the only legal organization, and said if two more names could be procured to the constitution he would approve of it at once, and indorse the election ordinance.

The organization that held possession of the hall continued in session through the week, sending their published proceedings to General Meade, and their gross misrepresentations by telegraph through the Associated Press all over the country.

When the day arrived to which the regular convention stood adjourned, the delegates were confronted on their entrance to the hall with bayonets of United States soldiers. Application was then made to Governor D. S. Walker, as the chief executive civil officer in the State, to have all parties arrested and removed from the hall who were hindering the constitutional convention from assembling, and were thereby obstructing reconstruction in the State. He refused to take any action in the matter in behalf of the convention. Lieutenant Colonel F. F. Flint, commanding post of Tallahassee, was then informed that the civil authorities refused to aid in securing the hall to the convention, and was asked to assist the officers of the convention, with the military under his command, in entering upon the discharge of their duties. He declined to interfere, but kept up his guard around the concern then in the hall.

The correspondence upon this subject is enclosed; also, correspondence with General Meade, after he arrived at the capital. The communications are numbered 1, 2, 3, 4, 5, and 6, and especial attention is called to them. It will be noticed that Governor Walker says he shall use all the power he possesses to prevent one party ejecting the other from the hall, which, of course, means that he should protect the seceding revolutionary body, as he had helped them to the possession of the hall, and they were occupying it.

Thus it will be seen that, by the aid of Governor Walker and the military, the convention was prevented from assembling on the day that it was adjourned to and the illegal midnight assemblage was protected, receiving the high sanction of the civil and military authorities of the State. The correspondence with Governor Walker and Colonel Flint was on Saturday, February 15. On Monday, the 17th, General Meade arrived at Tallahassee. A committee of delegates from the convention waited upon him at once to learn his views. It was believed that if the legally organized convention were permitted to peaceably assemble in the hall where they were to meet, enough of those men in the hall would cheerfully join with the twenty-two delegates to make a majority of all elected. Indeed, many of the delegates in the hall said, "That as the ordinance providing for pay of the members had to be indorsed by the commanding General to render it valid, and as the authorities seemed to favor them, they thought it safer to remain with the organization than in the hall so long as they were sustained by the military.

The committee failing to get any satisfactory reply from the General, and understanding him to say that "the organization in the hall had no legal status, nor could get any," the President of the convention addressed the General a letter, marked No. 5, asking him to withdraw the forcible opposition to the assembling of the convention. No answer was returned; guard was continued in the hall and around the State-house after General Meade arrived there, with the concern he himself said had no legal status, in possession and in session.

The next day the General sent for the President and told him if he did not resign as President of the convention he should recognize the other body as the legal organization. Colonel Sprague also sought a number of interviews with the President and urged him to resign, saying if he did not the other body would be recognized, and then "you will have to take your chances of getting in there at all," (meaning the twenty-two delegates by you), while he (Colonel Sprague) with the whole military power was protecting the other organization in possession of the hall. The President desired General Meade to state his request that he resign in writing, which being complied with, the resignation was tendered under protest.

See letter from General Meade marked No. 6, and enclosed therein is the proposition to compromise to which he refers, and also the President's resignation.

At three o'clock, on Tuesday, February 18, delegates all met in the hall by request of General Meade. Colonel John T. Sprague took the president's chair. He called the meeting to order and made a speech to the delegates. He received and put motions, and decided questions, while two or three of his subordinate officers of his own regiment were sitting as delegates, and voting on motions put by their Colonel. S. B. Conover and W. J. Purman are both officers in Colonel Sprague's regiment,* and were sitting as delegates.

Horatio Jenkins was elected President. The standing rules,

---

*NOTE.—Purman was not an officer and Conover had only been a contract surgeon.

which had been unanimously adopted by the convention the second day after organizing, and which provided that said rules could not be amended nor changed without one day's notice, were all swept away by a resolution. By another motion the rules of Jefferson's Manual were adopted to govern the body, and within a half hour after the rules of the Florida House of Representatives were adopted under the operation of the previous question, without a word of debate. All the motions were made by the same delegate. All officers of the convention were summarily turned out by resolution, and all motions and resolutions were rushed through under the previous question without debate. The previous question was moved and ordered fourteen times within half an hour, and nine times in rapid succession by the same delegate, without yielding the floor. The journal next morning did not show that the previous question had been ordered at all the day previous, and omitted to give the yeas and nays on the most important resolution acted upon the day previous. It was ordered that the journal be corrected, but when it appeared again not more than half of the corrections had been made. After that, during the entire session, there were no minutes of proceedings ever read to the convention nor approved by it. It is a humiliating fact that not a single page of the journal, as published after the reorganization, is anything like a correct record of the proceedings.

On Wednesday, February 19, the day after the reorganization, the convention met and under the operation of the same inexorable previous question, expelled four delegates by a majority vote. They then swore in four others in their places, who had received but a small minority of the votes cast at the election, one receiving only *nine* votes, while the delegate turned out to give place to him had twenty-four hundred and twenty-four votes. They also swore in a Mr. J. W. Butler in place of George W. Walker, who had been returned as elected, but had not yet been in attendance. General Meade had said when in Tallahassee, that if the convention should swear any one in who was not returned as elected by General Pope's order, he should interfere. But Mr. John W. Butler, O. B. Hart, J. E. Davidson, M. L. Stearns, Mr. —— Wells, were all sworn in as soon as the General left the city, and acted with the convention until its close, and then signed the constitution.

Thus, with the aid of all the civil and military authorities, and a free use of money, whisky, and the previous question, the regular Constitutional Convention of Florida was broken up by the Johnson Federal office-holders, led on by Harrison Reed, United States mail agent, and David S. Walker, Governor of Florida.

After the adoption of the constitution an ordinance was

introduced and passed that any member who did not sign the constitution should be deprived of his pay for the entire session. See last day's proceedings.

The constitution provides that the Governor shall appoint the following State officers, viz: Secretary of State, attorney general, comptroller, treasurer, surveyor-general, superintendent of public institutions, adjutant general, commisioner of immigration, the Supreme Court judges *for life*, seven circuit judges, seven states attorneys, and all commissioned officers in the militia. Lieutenant Governor is elected. The Governor also appoints, with power to remove at pleasure, the following county officers in each county in the State, viz: An assessor, collector, treasurer, county surveyor, superintendent of schools, county judge, sheriff, clerk of Circuit Court, five county commissioners, and as many justices of the peace as he pleases, and *for life*. Constables are elected by the people.

By the appointment provided for in said constitution, less than one-fourth of the registered voters will elect a majority of the State Senate, and less than one-third will elect a majority of the Assembly; 6,700 voters in the rebel counties elect as many senators (twelve and one Indian) as 20,282 voters elect in Union counties. Seven senators are elected by 3,027 voters in rebel counties, and only *one* senator is elected by 3,181 in a Union county (Leon), and *twenty-three* voters elect *one* senator in a rebel district.

In the Assembly, 8,330 voters in rebel counties choose *twenty-seven* members and one Indian, while 18,652 voters in Union counties only choose *twenty-six* members. Madison county (Union), with 1,802 voters sends *two* representatives, while the rebel sent from Dade county has a constituency of *fifteen* voters, and the rebel from Brevard county represents a *bona fide* constituency of *eight* registered voters.

It grants suffrage to, and removes all disabilities from, the vilest rebels and haters of the government, and permits them to be elevated to places of power and trust, without regard to the reconstruction acts of Congress, and disfranchises thousands of the colored voters. All rebels are relieved from taking the registration oath that Congress has prescribed, and from taking the oath of office prescribed by the act of Congress and required of every officer under the General Government. It also assumes to regulate the eligibility of United States senators and members of Congress from that State.

The constitution having been formed in the manner above described, it is evident that means will be found to ratify it without regard to the number of votes actually cast for it, should the boards of registration be in any manner under the control of the men who broke up the convention.

The constitution formed by the legally organized convention before it was broken up extends the right of suffrage to just the class entitled to it under the reconstruction acts of Congress, and requires officers to take the same oath now prescribed for officers under the General Government, but authorizes the legislature by a vote of two-thirds to remove all disabilities imposed for having engaged in the rebellion. It apportions representatives in the Legislature upon the basis of registered voters; makes *all* State officers, except the judiciary, and many county officers, elective by the people, and jealously guards and protects the rights and interests of all classes in the State alike. Had the sanction of such high authority, both civil or military, been thrown around the legally organized convention, as seemed to be so eagerly extended to the midnight concern, there can be no question but what accessions would thus have been induced to their number, so that a very large majority of the convention would have cheerfully co-operated with the twenty-two delegates in forming and signing said constitution.

When we, with so much pride, recollect that General Meade is the hero of Gettysburg, it must not be forgotten that he is human, also, and fallible; and that he is more liable to make a mistake in dealing with civil affairs, when surrounded by designing, unscrupulous, intriguing politicians, than he is in his profession as a soldier. That he should not have sustained the organization he himself had before recognized as legal and regular, instead of breaking it up, was undoubtedly a great mistake.

Colonel Sprague, commander of the State, whose advice in relation to all local matters must necessarily have great weight with the General, is in thorough sympathy with the most conservative conservatives in the State. He has passed through three wars without being in either, having asked and obtained a position on Governor Seymour's staff during the last war, while his regiment was in the field.

For a truthful and more graphic account of the Florida convention see the letters of Solon Robinson, one of the editors, in the New York Tribune of the 8th, 10th and 12th of February last. Also see editorial in the Tribune of the 10th, fully sustaining and indorsing what Mr. Robinson had written.

Your memorialists pray that Congress may, in its wisdom and in view of all the facts set forth above, find that the constitution formed by the twenty-two delegates who remained and completed their work before the convention was broken up is the only one that should be submitted to the voters of that State for ratification.

D. RICHARDS,
W. U. SAUNDERS.

Governor Reed, although prominently spoken of for Governor by the most influential Republicans, was not attached to either faction of the convention, but gave his earnest efforts, while securing the rights of freedmen to prevent proscription of the whites on account of the rebellion; but the Osborn-Purman faction realized the fact that they could not succeed without his brain, and looked upon him as the only means by which they could hope to obtain success. They privately expressed fears that he would not be as pliant as they would desire in aiding their schemes of plunder, but could find no other alternative. The memorial, therefore, does not state what is true when it asserts that Harrison Reed took part in the canvass to defeat reconstruction on the republican basis. Both parties were bidding for Democratic support, which was finally knocked off to the Osborn faction. The Hon. Charles Summer vigorously opposed the admission of the State into the Union under this Osborn constitution. He declared upon the floor of the Senate that "Florida should not be admitted until she came with clean hands."

Governor Reed being the supposed candidate of the Osborn faction for the office of Governor, it was but natural that the Richards faction should attempt to place him in the most awkward position before Congress; hence his name heads the list with those whom they charge with defeating reconstruction on a repulican basis. There was some money spent, and many concessions made to the Democrats by the Osborn faction, to overthrow the Richards convention, as charged in the memorial. Reed was mainly instrumental in procuring those concessions, as he believed in the professions of future loyalty to the Union, and regarded it necessary to enlist the intelligent class in behalf of the reconstructed government to protect the State against misrule through the ignorance of the newly enfranchised freedmen. He favored an apportionment of the Legislature so as to secure the sparsely settled white counties against the domination of the populous black belt; he favored the admission of all to citizenship, with no test but that of allegiance to the amended constitution; he favored the appointing power of the Governor to general and local offices, temporarily, to save the State from a threatened war of races which would banish the whites from the old slave-holding counties and the freedmen from the white counties of South and West Florida. He was held responsible for these concessions, and was denounced by the radical leaders of the freedmen, and the colored vote of Duval, Nassau, Leon and Gadsden counties was mostly thrown against him and the constitution. It was only by these concessions that the conflicting elements could be at once harmonized and the State protected from violence and the necessity of military force. The result vindicated his judgment, and during the four and a half years of his administration no resort to force was necessary, and the freedmen were less proscribed than during the early stages of reconstruction in any other Southern State.

CHAPTER VII.

The Meeting of the Legislature of 1868. Inauguration of Governor Reed, and His Address. Ratification of the 13th and 14th Amendments to the Constitution of the United States. Election of United States Senators. Extracts from Reed's Message. Governor Reed's Cabinet. First Years of Reed's Administration. His Appointing Power a Source of Corruption. Corrupt Legislation. The Attitude of the Colored Members to These Measures. Osborn and the Federal Office-holders. Reed Calls on the Colored Voters for Support. Meeting of the Legislature November, 1868, and the Appointment of Electors. Attempt at Impeachment. The Ouster of Alden and the Appointment of Gibbs as Secretary of State. The Ouster of Gleason as Lieutenant-Governor.

The Legislature met and organized on the 8th day of June, 1868, under a constitution framed by the people of Florida in a convention assembled by the authority of what is known as the reconstruction acts of the Congress of the United States. On the 9th of June the joint Assembly repaired to the Supreme Court room to witness the inauguration of the first Governor of Florida, whose election had been secured by a majority of all the male inhabitants of the State, twenty-one years of age and upwards, without regard to color or previous condition of servitude. Governor Reed came forward and was sworn in as Governor of Florida by Judge Boynton, of the United States District Court amidst the shouts of thousands of glad people who now began to see the dawn of a new day. After taking the oath of office the Governor delivered the following

INAUGURAL ADDRESS.

FELLOW CITIZENS OF FLORIDA:

"In entering upon the high trust which your partiality has conferred, in deference to time-honored custom, it becomes my duty to briefly indicate the policy of my administration as chief magistrate of the State.

"In November, 1860, the constitutional rights of the people of Florida were subverted, and its civil government was overthrown. Since then the State has been without a constitutional government, and subject to military law. In March, 1867, the Congress of the United States, in obedience to its obligation to 'guarantee to every State a republican form of government,' prepared a plan by which the State could regain its forfeited rights and its people be restored to the benefits of the constitutional government. Under this plan, you have formed a government, which we are here to-day to inaugurate and prepare to make effective. You have formed and adopted a constitution based upon the great theory of American government, that *all men are by nature free and endowed with equal rights.* You have laid deep and broad the foundations of the State upon the principle of universal freedom. Bred to freedom and under republican institutions; believing slavery an unmitigated curse, as well as a violation of human rights—a moral, political and physical evil wherever tolerated, I most cordially congratulate you that it no longer exists to blight the fair heritage which God has given us here, and that the constitution which you have adopted contains no germ of despotism to generate future discord. I congratulate you also that no spirit of malevolence or bitterness, growing out of the wrongs and conflicts of the past, has been suffered to mar your organic law, but that in a spirit of magnanimity and forbearance worthy of the highest commendation, those who have forfeited their citizenship are welcomed back to the benefits and privileges of the government upon the sole condition of fealty and adherence to the constitution and laws.

"Amid the ruins of a government embodying antagonistic principles you have laid the foundation of a government insuring harmony, stability, security and peace. The conflicting elements and interests of the past now all unite in a homogeneous system, all yielding obedience to a common law, which respects alike the interests of all. Time alone can heal the social disorders and dissensions created by the disruption of society and the radical change in the system of government, consequent upon the war. We will patiently await its mollifying influences, interposing no obstacles to a speedy restoration.

"All classes of society and all the interests of the State demand peace and good government, and if the spirit of our constitution is appreciated and reciprocated, every citizen may realize these advantages, and the State may arise from its prostrate condition to a measure of prosperity unknown in the past, and become one of the brightest luminaries in the galaxy of our glorious Union.

"Fellow citizens, I accept the high responsibility of the chief magistracy under your new constitution, believing firmly in its principles, and unqualifiedly endorsing its policy and that of the Congress under whose clemency we are permitted to inaugurate anew a civil government for the State. I enter upon this high trust with the firm purpose of executing the laws in the spirit of liberality in which they are conceived, and in view of the highest interests of the State and the people. Relying upon your loyalty and patriotism, and the favor and guidance of that Divine Power which sways the destinies of all, I shall do what within me lies to render effective the government and to command for it the respect and obedience of all classes of our citizens."

After the inauguration of Governor Reed, the Legislature was notified by Colonel F. F. Flint that the Commanding General would not recognize the Governor-elect and Legislature until further orders from Congress. On the ninth of June the Legislature adopted the 13th and 14th Amendments to the Constitution of the United States. The Legislature on June 16th proceeded to the election of United States Senator for the term expiring March 3d, 1869. The cunning Osborn of the "Brotherhood" was a candidate for the short term, but it had already been determined by Purman and Company to give him the largest and longest slice of the public ham, so as to cover the entire term of Governor Reed, which would enable him to use his influence as Senator to fill the Federal offices with men antagonistic to the Governor should he refuse to give his signature to any subsequent legislation passed by the influence of Purman and Company to rob the State and its people. A. S. Welch was elected to fill the term expiring March 3d, 1869, and T. W. Osborn for the term ending March 3d, 1873. Osborn would have been elected for the term beginning March 4th, 1869, but it was thought by Purman and Company that it was important to have him in the Senate on the admission of the State into the Union so as to control the offices. Abijah Gilbert, an old gentleman of reputed wealth, resident at St. Augustine, was pitched upon on account of his money, he agreeing to cash $50,000 or $100,000 State bonds at 85 cents on the dollar, and for the further reason that he was very old and would always say "me too, Osborn," in any recommendations the latter would make for appointments to office. Gilbert was elected to fill the term ending March 3d, 1875. After the election of United

States Senators the Legislature adjourned until the 7th of July to await the action of Congress as to the admission of the State into the Union. On the 25th of June, Congress declared the State entitled to admission, and on the 30th day of the same month, Florida was represented in both branches of the National Legislature. The State having been admitted into the Union under the new Constitution, the Legislature now convened on the day appointed and received the message of Governor Reed. The Governor, after reciting the peculiar and extraordinary circumstances under which it assembled on the 8th of June—in a military district but without military sanction—said:

"After near eight years of defiant wandering and estrangement, during a portion of which time no peaceful citizen was safe from the demands of a lawless despotism, and life and property were at the mercy of usurpers, Florida has renewed her allegiance to the Federal Constitution and resumed her position in the union of States with a radical change in her fundamental law, which compels a corresponding change in our system of legislation."

In referring to the policy of the government conferring the right of suffrage upon the negro the Governor said: "The government could not, with honor, deny to the man who carried a musket in its defense a voice in its administration. To have required him in war to fight, and in peace to bear the burden of other citizens, and then deny him a voice in its administration, cannot be sustained by any argument based upon principles of justice or morals." Contrasting the Constitution of 1868 with the Amended Constitution of 1861, of the State of Florida, the Governor quoted from the latter the following: "No citizen of any of the States which are now at war with the Confederate States shall ever be admitted to the rights of citizenship in this State; no such person shall vote at elections, be eligible to office, hold real estate, exercise any profession or trade, be engaged in mechanical, manufacturing, commercial, banking, insurance or other business, under pain of confiscation to the use of the State of all property of such person as shall violate this clause of the constitution." With this he cotrasted the following from the new republican Constitution: "Every male person of the age of twenty-one years and upwards, of whatever race, color, nationality, or previous condition, who shall, at the time of offering to vote, be a citizen of the United States, or who shall have declared intention to become such in conformity to the laws of the United States, and who shall have resided and had his habitation, domicile, home, and place of permanent abode in Florida for one year, and in the county for six months, next preceding the election at which he shall offer to vote, shall in such county be deemed a qualified elector at all elections under this constitution." This message contained eighteen subjects, and showed great powers of thought and perception. All the varied phases of the State were discussed as though he had studied the subjects from boyhood, and any one who read it would be forced to the conclusion that it was his aim to administer an honest, and economical government for the State and its people.

The Cabinet of Governor Reed consisted of eight members. To show the Southern whites, who were greatly irritated at the turn of things, that he meant to give them an honest administration, he appointed Colonel Robert H. Gamble, Comptroller, the most important office of his Cabinet. Colonel Gamble was an ex-slaveholder and a Democrat. He also appointed James D. Westcott, Jr., Attorney-General, also a Democrat, who supported the slave power. From these appointments Governor Reed had a right to expect at least support from the Southern whites to give his administration a fair trial. No colored man was appointed in the Cabinet, although the Governor expressed his willingness to have negro representation in every department, and did send to the Senate the name of John C. Gibbs, for Secretary of State, whose right name was afterwards found to be Jonathan C. Gibbs, and his name was withdrawn. The Governor insisted on sending up the right name, but the Osborn-Purman faction threatened opposition to his administration if any negro was placed in the Cabinet. The Governor, not knowing what the end might be, for the moment refrained.

The administration of Governor Reed was contaminated with more agencies inimical to the establishment and maintenance of an honest civil government than the administration of any Governor of Florida since the State was first admitted into the Union. One of these agencies was the appointing power, where all the officers, both State and county, with the exception of constables, were appointed by the Governor, and nine-tenths of these officers had to be confirmed by the Senate. The Governor, unacquainted with the men in the different counties who were capable, honest, friendly, disposed to peace, order and good government, made it a rule to look to the Senators and Representatives from the counties to inform him of the fitness of the candidate for office. This, though in most instances unavoidable, opened the door to corruption and political treason to his administration. The carpetbag Senators and Representatives from the different counties would always manage to get the endorsement of some colored men whom they would represent to the Governor as having great influence and respectability in the county where they lived; and whenever an appointment was to be made in a Democratic county and one of these office-seekers wanted to secure the prize, but whose antecedents against the negro in the county where he lived was such that he could not get an endorsement, he would represent to the executive that he was the only man in the county that stood between the negro and his former master and prevented wholesale slaughter of his colored brothers. Whenever the executive could make opportunity without great delay to inquire into these representations, he would generally find them false, and would thereupon appoint a Democrat—when no honest Republican could be found—who was friendly to the just administration of these laws. Many of these offices were filled by men who held seats in the Legislature, and who had in their pockets plunder bills to be acted upon at the same session of the Legislature to give them a start. There were a few exceptions, among whom was Judge Goss, who resigned his position as Senator as soon as he was appointed Circuit Judge. The Governor, in several counties where it was held disreputable to hold office under a Republican Governor, had to appoint one man to fill two or three offices in order to get men friendly to the new administration. Men whose names came up in the Senate for confirmation, unless they were members of that body, would have to come down with the cash before they could pass through the gate of Purman and the other members of the carpetbag family in that body. The Governor was forced to appoint men as county judges and solicitors, some of whom it was very doubtful as to whether they had ever seen the inside of a law book. Many of the carpetbag office-holders, anterior to their advent in the South had been blatant Democrats at the North, but not even respectable cross-road politicians, yet who now claimed to be great men, and the proper leaders of the colored people of this State.

The second of these adverse agencies was the tendency of the Bureau carpetbag members of the Legislature to rush through corrupt legislation. These men, now secure in their offices for the several counties, but yet members of the Legislature, were in a position to dictate to the Governor as to legislation. They now began to feel the Governor's pulse. A bill was introduced in the Senate by A. A. Knight, an Osborn carpetbagger, while he was holding in his pocket a commission as circuit judge, "to incorporate the Florida Savings Bank." The bill was one granting extraordinary and indefinite powers without sufficient guaranties of protection to the public—rendering it lawful for public officers to deposit the funds of the State, and others to deposit trust funds, with no adequate security; giving a company with $20,000 cash capital the power to control an unlimited amount, and actually affording large facilities for obtaining money from the people, and by a breach of trust enriching the stockholders at the expense of the public. The managers and stockholders were, of course, to be the carpetbag office-holders. The bill was telegraphed from New York by L. D. Stickney, one of Secretary Chase's direct tax commissioners for Florida. A check for $500 was sent to Knight to secure its passage. It was passed in both Houses under suspension of the rules, within twenty-four hours after its receipt. It was taken to the Governor the same evening by Knight, who requested its immediate approval, so that he could send a certified copy to New York by the next mail. He vouched "on the honor of a Senator" for its freedom from any obnoxious features. The Governor held it for advisement over night; returned it with his veto, and, on its return, the Senate, with its swindling features exposed, did not dare to vote to pass it over the Governer's veto. Even Knight himself did not so vote. This was the first bill passed, and the first of the many vetoes by which Governor Reed sought to protect the State against fraud, corruption and villainy. This was a snug little place in which to deposit the people's money and cry out "broke" after making a division among the stockholders. The scheme was entered into to rob both negroes and whites, as well as to make away with the public funds.

This veto caused great consternation in the Osborn ring plotters, and from that time out they swore vengeance against Reed and his administration. Other infamous schemes were invented at the same session, which came to naught through the veto of the Governor. See "veto" journal of the Senate, page 224.

The Republican members of the Legislature who really represented true republican principles, were in the minority, and were, therefore, powerless to do much to arrest the disgrace which these corrupt practices were bringing to the party; and, as these schemes were adopted by a so-called Republican caucus, any member of the party voting against them in the caucus or otherwise was looked upon and denounced as voting against a party measure, and was accordingly set down as a traitor to the party. The most of the non-office-seeking and honest white Republicans were denounced as Democrats in those palmy days of corruption. J. H. Goss, J. E. A. Davidson in the Senate, and E. J. Harris in the Assembly were the typical white Republicans in the Florida Legislature at that session. They were Southern Republicans.

The "brothers in black," some of whom had heretofore followed the Billings-Richards faction, seemed to have been quite indifferent, either as to men or measures, since they had lost their supposed great leaders, while some of them, such as H. S. Harman and Richard H. Black, were men of education, and did all they could at that session to pass a school law for the education of the masses. Otherwise they seemed content to enjoy full citizenship. They knew nothing, it seemed, about stealing by legislation at that session, and had not the colored members been associated with their bad white leaders, they might have legislated for years before learning to steal by statute.

The Democrats at this session had very few members in

either branch of the Legislature, and amounted to but little. Among the most noted of them were Dr. J. L. Crawford, of the seventh district, now our able and courteous Secretary of State, A. L. McCaskill, of the second district, and George P. Raney, of the Assembly, from Franklin county, now one of the judges of the Supreme Court, and one of the most incessant workers in the legal profession that has ever adorned the bench. Mr. Raney was a pure and honest Democrat, whose advanced ideas the Democrats of the State may yet have to adopt to make the party a true Democratic party, and save it from overthrow.

The third of these agencies was the whites who had been excluded from office by the 14th amendment of the Constitution of the United States, who had previously taken an oath to support the Constitution of the United States by reason of holding certain offices and afterwards giving aid and comfort to the rebellion. The most of them had been politicians before and during the war, and had great influence in their several communities. They were now rampant, and when they would appear before their people would represent themselves as persecuted men. These men and their friends would seize on every corrupt measure or misstep of the carpetbag Legislature and carry it to their people as the result of their exclusion, and with the cry of "negro supremacy and domination" arouse the passions of their people to fever heat. The fact of their former slaves sitting in the Legislature, voting for an amendment to the Constitution which excluded them from the rights of citizenship, was a little more than human nature could have been expected to swallow without some protest, as did the negro protest who had carried a musket for nearly three years in defense of the Government, and was then excluded from the rights of citizenship. But if the carpet-baggers had gone in at the start for honest government these men would have had no material on which to feed and infuriate the people. Governor Reed would have been enabled to muster enough of the Southern whites to the support of the Republican administration in the State to have given it great strength and respectability. The Governor was, from the beginning, opposed to this wholesale plunder system, but the cry was, that it was carried on under his administration, and the odium was thrown upon his shoulders. *

This Legislature made radical changes in the criminal laws, as well as laws tending to protect the labor interests of the State. After memorializing Congress to remove the disability of those who had been excluded from citizenship by reason of participation in the rebellion, which was voted for by every ex-slave in the Legislature, both houses met in joint session and adjourned to meet in convention on the third day of November to appoint the Presidential Electors of the State.

T. W. Osborn, comfortably seated in the United States Senate for the term of four years, now began to reorganize his forces to resist the administration of Governor Reed. As United States Senator he was enabled to prevent the appointment of any one to a Federal office who would not agree to use his office in every possible way to cripple and retard the State administration. No officer was appointed with reference to his special fitness; but on the other hand the only qualification that seemed to have been necessary was that the applicant was a carpet-bagger, and that he would join him in his opposition to Governor Reed. Only two colored men were appointed to office by Osborn's indorsement, and these two positions were insignificant so far as the emoluments were concerned. Many of these Federal officeholders had been appointed by Governor Reed to fill the offices in the sev-

*NOTE.—Failing to either intimidate or subsidize the Governor for their purposes of plunder, as a last alternative, the Osborn ring, under the lead of Speaker Stearns, in the Assembly, and United States Marshal Wentworth in the Senate, determined to inaugurate a "war of races," and thus compel martial law, so that the Federal troops under the control of the marshal should have full sway. It was planned in secret counsel that before adjourning the Legislature bills should be passed to compel hotel keepers and railroad companies to receive and provide for negroes on the same terms as whites, and thus place the Governor between two fires. If he approved the bills the whites would be provoked to violence, and if he vetoed them the freedmen would all be arrayed against him, and his impeachment would be made certain. Accordingly, two bills were framed and passed in the Assembly, making it a penal offense to exclude persons from equal privileges in hotels or on railroad cars on account of color. To avoid difficulty, the Governor called the Republican Senators in council at the executive office and explained the impossibility of maintaining civil administration with such aggravating legislation, and finally he declared he could not sanction it. The only response was the immediate passage of the bill and its immediate veto by the Governor. It was near the last day of the session; and after the final adjournment the negro population had assembled in the rotunda of the Capitol and unitedly denounced Governor Reed as a traitor, and then the plan of impeachment was perfected, to be carried out at the next session, with Osborn to prepare the charges and Horatio Jenkins as prosecutor.

eral counties, but as the officers of the State and county had to receive their stealings and pay in State and county scrip at a discount—sometimes more than one-half—and the Federal officers were paid in greenbacks, it was an easy matter to get these spoilsmen to swear undying allegiance to Osborn. These Federal officers were appointed in every county, with instructions to resist every one, be he Republican or Democrat, who was friendly to the State administration, who should attempt to be elected to the Legislature; for it was here that Osborn proposed to block the wheels of the administration. Whenever, by reason of the scarcity of Osborn carpet-baggers in any county where Federal offices were to be filled and the duties were too multifarious for one or two persons, recruits would be sent from Washington to take the vacant places. Such persons needed no teaching on their arrival how to oppose Governor Reed, for that lesson had been taught them before they left Washington. These officers had great influence with the ignorant masses, who were taught by them that they had been sent by the Government to oppose Governor Reed. With this mode of warfare they would succeed in every election for members of the Legislature to either carry the Republican counties against the administration, divide the Legislative delegation, or elect a Democratic delegation. The latter was as great a victory to them as the former, as it tended to show the authorities at Washington that the Governor, though a Republican, was not backed up by his party, and enable Osborn to secure the appointment of all the applicants whom he recommended. To aid these officeholders to carry out the plans of Osborn, the freedmen were told that Governor Reed had gone over to the "Rebel Democracy." This of course alarmed the freedmen and for a time united the most of them against the Governor. In the meantime the Osborn-Purman faction began to subsidize such men as Goss, J. E. A. Davidson, E. M. Randall, and J. S. Adams, who were now sustaining Reed, and were in favor of straightforward, honest Republicanism, while most of the colored leaders were reluctant to give their full support to the Governor, from the fact of his not having put one of their race in his Cabinet. The Governor realizing this fact, and aware of the snare which Osborn had constructed for him, sent for C. H. Pearce, colored, who had been ousted from the Constitutional Convention by Osborn & Co., and who had now been elected to the Senate from the Eighth Senatorial District by a large majority; and had a consultation with him with reference to the conspiracy that Osborn and his officeholders had formed to resist his administration. Pearce was convinced that the Governor was sincere in trying to administer the government with honesty and pledged himself to do whatever he could to enlighten his people as to the true intention of the administration. Mr. Pearce was a minister of the A. M. E. Church, and had great influence with the colored people throughout the State. He was enlisted as an active agent and furnished with money to visit the various counties where trouble existed and quiet the apprehensions of the freedmen; and he rendered great service in Leon, Gadsden, Franklin, Hamilton and other counties, in allaying the fears of the colored masses, who were being constantly excited by appeals of the false leaders against the old white citizens and Governor Reed, who was charged with being their ally. This move on the part of Governor Reed had the effect of mustering the most of the colored ministers to his support. The ministers throughout the State began to teach their congregations that Reed was the embodiment of true Republicanism, while Osborn & Co. were mere tricksters and office-seekers, which in time united a large majority of the colored voters in favor of the administration of Reed. The Governor was determined to make no attack on the conspirators except when he would interpose his veto to corrupt measures; but he held himself in readiness for them to do their worst.

On the 3d day of November the members of the Legislature met in convention at Tallahassee to appoint the electors of President and Vice-President, the Legislature at its previous session having provided this mode of election. Of course the vote of the State was given to U. S. Grant. James D. Green, of Manatee County, was appointed as messenger to convey the result to Washington. A committee of the convention waited on Gov. Reed and notified him of their assembling and asked if he had any communication to make. He replied that he had none—that they were not sitting as a Legislature but as a convention for a specific purpose—that done they had only to adjourn. They claimed mileage and per diem, and proposed to appropriate

money for this purpose. The Governor reminded them that
they had drawn their salary for the year and could only claim
mileage, which he would accord to them from the executive
contingent fund. They unanimously demanded to be called in
special legislative session, ostensibly for the sole purpose of
appropriating pay. The Governor, although fully advised of
the purpose of Osborn and his satellites to suspend him by a
resolution of impeachment, thinking it best to have the fight
opened then and there, acceded to the demand of the convention and called them in special session for a specific purpose.
Osborn's gang immediately forced through the Assembly the
following resolution:

Resolved, That a committee of three be appointed to prepare
and report articles of impeachment against Harrison Reed, Governor of Florida, with power to send for persons, papers and
records, and to take testimony under oath.

H. S. Harmon, colored, Green of Manatee, and M. L.
Stearns were appointed this committee. The resolution was
reported to the Senate as though Governor Reed had been
impeached, but the Senate was sitting without a quorum, as the
Democrats were not in their seats, as were not some of the
Republicans; therefore their proceedings fell flat to the ground,
so far as it affected the right of Reed to act as Governor was
concerned. William H. Gleason, Lieutenant-Governor, and
George J. Alden, Reed's Secretary of State, interpreted this
action on the part of the Assembly a little differently from that
of Governor Reed and his friends, and different from all precedents of impeachment trials and investigations. The Constitution of the State making it the duty of the Lieutenant-Governor
to act as Governor in case of impeachment of the Governor, was
made to say that the fact of a resolution being passed by the
Assembly asking for articles of impeachment to be prepared was
equivalent to suspension, and therefore Gleason was Governor.
Alden, who before his appointment as secretary was frozen stiff
with poverty, had begun to pass through the process of thawing
from the genial influence of a good salary bestowed upon him by
the hand which he now attempts to bite. Gleason sets up his
claim as Governor at the old hotel in front of the Capitol, while

Governor Reed held the Capitol. Alden now deserts Reed and recognizes Gleason as Governor and steals the State seal out of the Secretary of State's office and attaches it to Gleason's documents. This went on for several days, during which time Reed's office was guarded night and day by armed police. Gleason becoming restless at not getting possession of Reed's stronghold, ventured one day to take possession by stratagem. He came into the executive office without saying anything to Governor Reed, and sat there for some time. George B. Carse, Adjutant-General, a very impulsive man, who understood the scheme of Gleason, at once ordered him out of the room. Gleason made answer that this was a public office and that he would not go out, whereupon Carse made a lunge at him with one hand with a revolver in the other. Gleason wore a fine beaver hat, which went one way while he went the other, he retreating in double quick time to the seat of his hotel government. The night following the day on which Gleason made his disgraceful retreat Governor Reed made up his mind to move on the works of the enemy. He commenced the attack by first using his pruning-knife in his Cabinet. He beheaded Alden and appointed Jonathan C. Gibbs, colored, as Secretary of State, and gave him possession of the office, and in a few minutes Gibbs was seated behind his desk receiving the congratulations of his friends. Numbers of freedmen were sent for from the country to witness and congratulate one of their race sitting in the Capitol as Secretary of State. These calls and congratulations went on until the next day, when Alden undertook to enter the door of the Secretary's office. He was at once ordered away by the Governor's police and the crowd of freedmen, who did not propose to see Mr. Gibbs disturbed. He was told by one of the freedmen that the scepter had forever departed from him, as he had sinned against Governor Reed. He remonstrated with them and told them, "All of us are true Republicans, my colored friends;" but the freedmen retorted, "You no 'publican if youse want to go in Mr. Gibbs' office." He was not long in finding out that it was safer for him to be somewhere else, and with trembling limbs made hasty steps away and reported to the wily Gleason what great disaster had befallen one of the gang. The appointment of Mr. Gibbs unquestionably added very material strength to

Governor Reed from the freedmen. They now saw that the man whom the carpetbag element had been denouncing as their enemy was more disposed to deal justly by them than were his traducers. Secret watchers were kept on the track of Gleason and Alden until Reed could sharpen his knife for the decapitation of Gleason. On the 9th of November Governor Reed, through his Attorney-General, Meek, assisted by J. P. Sanderson, M. D. Papy and A. J. Peeler, filed a petition in the Supreme Court of the State asking for a writ of quo warranto against W. H. Gleason, requiring him to show cause why he should not be ousted from the office of Lieutenant-Governor of the State of Florida, he not having been a citizen of the State two years, as required by the Constitution. D. S. Walker and Horatio Bisbee, Jr., appeared for the respondent. One of Gleason's pleas was that Governor Reed had solicited him to run for the office, which was untrue, for Reed had personally protested against his running, and offered him a Cabinet position if he would decline; another was that Governor Reed had instituted this suit in pursuance of a pledge made to Gleason that if he persisted in his effort to supplant him he would oust him by legal process. The proof was conclusive that he was holding office in violation of the Constitution, and he was, therefore, ousted from his place as Lieutenant-Governor of Florida. He appealed to the Supreme Court of the United States, so as to hold on in name, but not in fact, to the office until his term would expire. He knew, of course, that the Supreme Court of the United States had no jurisdiction of the case. The Osborn faction had by these two ousters learned something of the fighting qualities of Reed, and thereafter moved with more caution when they determined to attack him. The object of the Osborn gang was to get Reed out of the way and put Gleason in as Governor, and Horatio Jenkins was to be appointed Lieutenant-Governor, and he, being one of Osborn's henchmen, would not throw obstacles in the way of legislation that might be introduced to enrich the gang. The deposition of Alden and Gleason was a terrible blow to them and the balance of their companions; but the Legislature appropriated two thousand dollars to Gleason for attorney's fees and expenses in making the fight.

In view of the conduct of the Legislature and the consequent misapprehension and mutual distrust of the blacks and whites, the Governor determined to secure some armament for the State in case military force should become necessary. He visited Washington and sought the aid of the government by claiming from the Ordnance Department the issue of the arms due the State under a rule which had been suspended during the war. This was denied. He then called upon Governor Andrew of Massachusetts and Governor Fenton of New York for a loan of arms. This failing, he purchased through a personal friend in New York two thousand stands of muskets and Enfield rifles and four thousand rounds of ammunition on a credit of four months, giving notes for $21,000. The arms were shipped and delivered at Jacksonville, where they were received by the Adjutant-General, Carse, and General Houstoun, then president of the railroad company, and placed on board the cars to be delivered at Tallahassee. A guard of Federal soldiers had been placed by General Sprague at the control of the Governor, but fearing difficulty if a military force appeared on the cars, General Houstoun guaranteed their safe delivery if the guard could be withdrawn. The arms were on board and the train started at night with the Adjutant-General in charge. The railroad employees, without the knowledge of President Houstoun, introduced into the cars with the arms men engaged to throw them out when they should reach Madison County, where a company of Dickinson's guerillas was placed along the road to seize and destroy them. All the ammunition and all but eight hundred of the guns were thus thrown out and destroyed, or carried away to be used by the enemies of the government. The railroad company was responsible to the State for the loss, but the Osborn ring being implicated and in control of the Legislature, sought to involve Governor Reed and deprive him of the power and the means to pay the notes he had given, and the company was not called upon for the damages.

Thus ended the first year of Governor Reed's administration.

CHAPTER VIII.

The Meeting of the Legislature of 1869, and Another Attempt at Impeachment. Attempt to Bribe Members to Vote for Impeachment. Extracts from Governor Reed's Second Message. Gilbert Compelled to Pay for His Seat in the United States Senate. Reed's Vindication.

The second session of the Legislature under the Constitution of 1868, met on the fifth day of January, 1869, and organized by electing M. L. Stearns, of Gadsden County, of freedmen's provisions notoriety, as Speaker of Assembly, which placed the lower house of the Legislature in the absolute control of the Federal office-holders, the Senate being presided over by Gleason, who had appealed from the decision of ouster by the Supreme Court of the State to the Supreme Court of the United States. Samuel Walker, of the defunct Billings-Saunders faction—and elected to the Legislature from Leon County, now sought the opportunity to give active effect to his old prejudice against Governor Reed for being, as he said, instrumental in the overthrow of the Billings faction. Walker now renews the attack upon the Governor by reciting a resolution relative to impeachment passed at the November session. George P. Raney, Democratic representative from Franklin County, offered a substitute to the resolution, which reads as follows:

WHEREAS, It is known to this Assembly to be publicly alleged that Harrison Reed, Governor of Florida, has done and committed acts wrongful and unlawful, therefore, be it

Resolved, By the Assemby of the State of Florida, that a committee of five be appointed by the Speaker to inquire into and investigate the conduct, acts and doings of said Harrison Reed, Governor of Florida, and that the said committee be empowered and authorized to send for persons and papers, and take testimony upon oath in the premises; and that the said committee be required to report the result of its investigations at its earliest convenience during the present session; and that it accompany its report with the testimony taken in the said matter."

This resolution was adopted by a vote of thirty to five. Samuel Walker, who at first seemed to have been so anxious for investigation, voted against the adoption of the resolution for the reason that he thought to extort from the Governor the position of County Revenue Collector during the impeachment investigation. George P. Raney, a Democrat, was appointed chairman of the investigating committee, which placed Governor Reed between two fires. It was the purpose of the Democrats to show all the shortcomings and misconduct of the Republicans so as to break down anything like respectable government, while the plunder-hunting Republicans, by urging impeachment, expected either to get rid of Reed by impeachment or to compel him to seek safety under their wing by pledging himself to put his signature to all their corrupt legislation. To be driven to the plunderers would be certain disgrace and death to his administration and the Republican party of the State; and for him, a life-long Republican, to be driven to the Democratic party by these unprincipled men, would stigmatize him both politically and morally as a coward. Relying upon an Allwise Providence and the better judgment of fair-minded men of the Legislature, Governor Reed stood firm as the rock of Gibraltar to his Republican faith. While the committee was investigating the charges against the Governor it became evident to the plunderers that they would not be able to ham-string him without bribing some of the members of the Legislature. Their rooms in the hotels were the scene of caucuses every night, sometimes till near day. The great destroyer of the Divine promise of "peace on earth and good will toward men," with its demon-like redness and horrifying influence, was the chief attraction in these caucuses. Men could be seen staggering to and fro, breathing out curses against Harrison Reed. When conspirators were convinced that a member of the Legislature could not be beguiled by cigars and whisky, they would call him outside of the room to have a "private talk" with him. Convention scrip and greenbacks would be offered him to favor the impeachment of Harrison Reed. These night caucuses became so ridiculous and notorious that they brought forth the following resolution:

"WHEREAS, It is publicly charged that certain persons have received large sums of money and State scrip to induce said persons to use their influence to induce members of this Assembly to favor impeachment of His Excellency, Harrison Reed, Governor of this State; and whereas, It is publicly charged that said persons are so using their influence with said members; therefore, be it

Resolved, That the committee appointed by this Assembly to investigate the conduct and doings of His Excellency Harrison Reed, be and are hereby directed to investigate said charges and report the result of their investigation in the matter to this Assembly with their report in the matter of the affairs of His Excellency Harrison Reed; and the said committee are authorized to send for persons to enable them properly to investigate said charges."

The Assembly resolved itself into a committee of the whole on the resolution. They subsequently reported progress and asked leave to sit again. This resolution acted as a bomb shell in the camp of the conspirators, and from the time of its introduction until the termination of the investigation of the charges against Governor Reed, they had all they could manage to prevent being exposed and arrested for bribery. The original movers in this conspiracy were anxious that the resolution of investigation of the charges made against Governor Reed should be passed before his annual message was received. They expected that the Governor would refer to the charges against himself and would in that message lay down his express line of defense; but he, knowing what kind of men he had to deal with did not refer in any manner to his traducers, and many of them expressed themselves as being satisfied that they would force him to resign before the investigating committee reported; but little did they know yet the " staying " qualities of the Governor.

The two houses met in joint session on the 7th day of the month to receive the message of the Governor. The designation of the Lincoln Brotherhood had now been changed by those Republicans who desired good government to that of the Osborn Ring. The Governor came forward and delivered his message, which was clear and logical. Among other things he said: " With the election of America's great military chieftain to the highest office in the nation, the peace, welfare and prosperity of the Union is secured, upon the basis of freedom and equal rights. Thoughout our beloved State violent opposition to the Federal authority and republican government has ceased, and all classes of the people yield obedience to the laws. The last embers of the late rebellion are rapidly dying out, and our citizens, 'without distinction of race, color or previous condition,' are gradually uniting in behalf of common interests and mutual prosperity. The newly enfranchised citizen of color sits side by side with his white fellow-citizen without antagonism, in the cabinet, in the halls of legislation, the jury box, and on the boards of commissioners—occupies the magistrate's chair, and executes the decrees of court without exciting violence or occasioning asperity. The change since your last session is marvelous, and calls for grateful recognition." In referring to the organization of the militia, the Governor said: "Several volunteer companies of patriotic citizens, both white and colored, have been enrolled, and have selected their officers, but in the sensitive condition of the popular mind I have deemed it unwise to accept these organizations." The Legislature having passed a law at its first meeting in 1868 authorizing the election of a State Printer, the freebooters had no trouble to elect one of their number to that office. It had been pre-arranged before the meeting of the Legislature of 1868 what laws Osborn and his gang would enact to secure them the possession of the State for years to come. "Vandalize the State," was Osborn's order to Governor Reed. Immediately after the Governor had delivered his message, the ring had the Legislature to meet in joint session and elected E. M. Cheney, of Jacksonville—subsequently tainted with the notorious Yellow Bluff fraud—as State Printer. The ring now had both Senators and the Representative in Congress against the State administration, and the Jacksonville *Union*, a paper published in the interest of Osborn and Company, with E. M. Cheney, editor. The ring, elated at the success of electing Cheney for State Printer, and thinking that they had a large majority of the Legislature at their backs, went boldly to the friends of Reed and informed them unless Reed resigned his office as Governor within twenty-four hours after Cheney's election as printer, he should be impeached and utterly disgraced, and if the ring had to go to the trouble of impeaching and trying him before they could get clear of him, he should wind up in the penitentiary. These admonitions were carried to Governor Reed by the true friends of the Republican government, some of whom thought it best to let the government go into the hands of these men and go to pieces; but the Governor, like the brave Fitz James, said:

> "Come one, come all, this rock shall fly,
> From its firm base as soon as I."

The ring, now restless in spending so much money to impeach Harrison Reed, was determined to compel others to bear some of the burden. Abijah Gilbert, who had been elected United States Senator to fill the term commencing March 4, 1869, the gold of whose purse yet reflected in the faces of the spoilsmen of the last regular session of the Legislature, was pitched upon as the softest and most available man to fill and settle the whole bill. On the 19th of January a resolution was introduced reciting the fact that large sums of money had been used at the last session to secure the election of the said Gilbert, and that under such circumstances the election was unlawful and void. The Legislature thereupon went into an election of United States Senator. It was not the intention of the ring to elect another Senator, but this part of the game was only to make Gilbert come down with the cash. They said openly that Gilbert had not paid enough for his seat, and that this proceeding was the only way to make him fork up the coveted amount. Gilbert was on hand, and the old man was frightened nearly out of his breeches, and you could see notes flying from his room in the hotel to the Capitol to different members of the Legislature, requesting them to call at his room, as he desired to see them on special business. The members, who understood the whole game, would smile when receiving these messages from the old man, and would make haste to grant his request. After he had seen them they would come back to their seats entirely transformed relative to the election of United States Senator, and after one night-calling had passed, the next day a motion was made to indefinitely postpone the whole proceeding as to the election of Senator, which was adopted by a unanimous vote. Those who had been foremost in denouncing the election of Gilbert and declaring that he was elected by bribery, could now be heard to say that his election was fair and honest. They came near breaking the old man, and just before he left Tallahassee he said to one of his friends, "surely I have fallen into a den of thieves." Men who came to the capital with scarcely money enough to pay their fare on the railroad could now be seen with rolls of money, evidently extracted from Gilbert, and they were of that portion of the carpet-baggers who were interested in the impeachment of Harrison Reed.

The committee appointed to investigate the acts and doings of Governor Reed on the 26th day of January appeared at the bar of the House and made their report. There was a majority and a minority report. The first charge against Reed was that he had received five hundred dollars to appoint a person clerk of the court of Leon county, which the evidence showed was not true, but that the money was contributed to pay the indebtedness incurred by the central committee in the election campaign. The second charge was that a balance of six thousand nine hundred and forty-eight dollars and sixty-three cents in United States currency, proceeds of Virginia and other State bonds, sold under an act authorizing the Governor of the State to raise funds to pay the expenses of this session of the Legislature, had been used by the Governor and State scrip substituted for it. This scrip was receivable for all State dues, while the cash was absolutely necessary to carry on the State government then in its infancy and opposed by foes without and pretended friends within. The same witness who made the charge relative to the Leon county clerkship presented another to the committee that Governor Reed had, through a friend, offered to give him a contract to make a set of maps for the Surveyor-General's office if he would change his base and go in and work to prevent impeachment. This a portion of the committee treated as manufactured evidence, and consequently untrustworthy. The majority report of the committee did not make any recommendation. It was signed by George P. Raney, Democrat; F. N. B. Oliver, Democrat; John Varnum, Republican; Henry S. Harmon, Republican; and E. Fortune, Republican. The minority report was signed by E. J. Harris and Auburn Erwin, Republicans, and exonerated Governor Reed from the charges.

The Democrats were in doubt what to do; they did not want to commit themselves to Reed, nor did they want to help the plunderers, so they sat and watched the drift of things. Several resolutions and motions were made reflecting upon the character of the Governor. The ring worked long and hard, and at first thought they would succeed; but when they saw H. S. Harmon and E. Fortune, colored members, who had signed the majority report, voting to exonerate him, they gave up the sport. The following resolution was offered by Mr. E. Fortune, member of the investigating committee:

"WHEREAS, The committee appointed on the 6th day of January to inquire into and investigate the conduct, acts and doings of Harrison Reed, Governor of Florida, has, pursuant to instructions, reported the results of its investigations to this body, accompanied with the testimony taken in the said matter; therefore be it

"*Resolved by the Assembly of Florida*, That the said Assembly finds nothing in said report or testimony justifying an impeachment of Harrison Reed, Governor of Florida."

This resolution was adopted by a vote of forty-three to five, every member of the committee voting for it, and but one colored member voted in the negative. This committee was the creation of the ring, which shows how flimsy the testimony against the Governor was, and how desperate they were in their determination to remove him from between them and the people's money. Osborn, who had now come down from Washington, and was sitting in the hall when this vote was taken, swore vengeance against every Republican who voted to exonerate Reed; but his carpetbag friends gave him to understand that all the negroes and Democrats had agreed to exonerate the Governor, and that had they voted against him when they saw he would be exonerated, it would have had the effect of driving all the negroes to him and the Democrats, which action would have soon lifted them out of their fat places. The ring now called a caucus in the Senate chamber and pretended to make friends with the Governor and to support his administration. Chief Osborn was present and assured him that he was very sorry that this attempt at impeachment had been made, and that he was misled in the matter, and if the Governor would correspond with him in Washington no one should be appointed to a Federal office who was not friendly to his administration. Many speeches were made by the members of the ring, assuring the Governor that from that time forth Osborn and his friends would stand by him. Most of the carpet-baggers then in the Legislature were holding State offices by commission from Gov. Reed, and this agreement was made by Osborn and his followers so as to hold on to the State offices as well as the Federal offices which had been given them by the latter. This worked well for a time. Hon. C. H. Pearce, who had succeeded in rallying the colored members of the Legislature to the Governor, was very severe on the conspirators, and threatened to alienate the colored voters from the carpet-baggers if this persecution of Reed was continued. Reed appeared to be quite indifferent as to promises made by Osborn & Co., and asked the colored men in the caucus to stand by him if they believed he was trying to give the State an honest administration. After further assurances by the members of the ring that Reed should be supported, the caucus adjourned *sine die*.

CHAPTER IX.

Meeting of the Extraordinary Session of the Legislature of 1869. Governor Reed's Recommendations. The Four Millions of Bonds Scheme. Colored Meembers Playing Carpet-bagger. The Grand Jury Hunting Bribe-takers.

On the 17th of May, 1869, Governor Reed issued his proclamation convening the Legislature in extraordinary session for the following purposes, to-wit: "To maintain the credit of the State and provide for the means of defraying its current expenses. That the recent sale of the Pensacola and Georgia Railroad and the Tallahassee Railroad rendered immediate legislation necessary to protect the public interest and enable the purchasers to provide for the extension and completion of their roads and to enjoy the benefits of the Internal Improvement Laws of the State; and to ratify the Fifteenth Amendment to the Constitution of the United States."

In compliance with this proclamation, the two houses of the Legislature met at 12 o'clock M. on the 8th day of June and received the Governor's Message. The Governor recommended, among other things which were not mentioned in his proclamation, the passage of a proper quarantine law to protect our coast; a tenure of office law, so as to get rid of delinquent or unfaithful officers when the Senate was not in session, which officers could not then be removed without the consent of the Senate; and a law prohibiting common carriers from making distinction on acconnt of color. In conclusion, the Governor said:

"Allow me to congratulate you on the new era of prosperity which has opened upon our State, and the auspicious circumstances under which you now assemble. In all parts of the State, peace, security, harmony and prosperity prevail to a greater extent than at any time within the past ten years. Capital is more profitably invested; life and property are better protected. Let passion and prejudice give place to reason and judgment, and let wisdom and prudence control your counsels, while we render grateful homage to the great dispenser of all good for His innumerable blessings."

Several important acts were passed by this Legislature, among which were the law setting aside a homestead for each head of a family; an amendment of the school laws; important changes in the revenue laws; and the notorious act "To Perfect the Public Works of the State." From the presence of an unusual lobby it was apparent that some great catastrophe was to take place in the shape of a law. The carpetbag element seemed to be elated, and the hotels and boarding-houses in the city were filled with strangers. The poorest and the most shabby carpet-bagger could be seen drinking the sparkling champagne and wearing fine beavers. The famous Littlefield was too much engaged to walk, and his carriage was kept at the hotel in readiness to convey him to any part of the city to see the different members of the Legislature.

The Governor was privately advised that Osborn's United States Marshal, Senator Wentworth, had been furnished with a thousand dollars with which to secure votes for Littlefield. Alarmed at the prospect of corrupt legislation, he telegraphed Mr. Swepson, the purchaser of the railroads, and whom Littlefield represented, to come to Tallahassee. In reply, General Abbott, United States Senator from North Carolina, appeared for Swepson and pledged the Governor that no more money should be used, and no legislation but what was legitimate should be sought. He called in General Littlefield to witness the pledge, stating that the money to Wentworth was only for the furnishing a reception room at the hotel. After remaining a few days, General Abbott, still assuring the Governor that the company would act in good faith and allow no more money to be expended, then returned home; but, notwithstanding these assurances, and pledges, within ten days twenty-two thousand dollars were distributed by Littlefield as a corruption fund for the Osborn ring, to control the Legislature against Governor Reed, with a view of ultimately deposing him.

The bill was introduced in the Senate by Wentworth, of Escambia, and referred to a committee, which reported favorably on it. There were important amendments made to the bill by Senator John A. Henderson, of Hillsborough County. There were lots of members whom Littlefild had not "seen privately," and these would denounce the bill as a great swindle, but after a visit from him and a "private talk," they would either vote yes on every amendment or not vote at all, and would offer no further resistance to the scheme. The incorporators of this measure were General M. S. Littlefield, George W. Swepson, J. P. Sanderson, J. L. Requa, and William H. Hunt; the last a Senator from Dade County, and Gleason's partner. State aid was to be given at the rate of twelve thousand dollars per mile, which, according to the length of the route, would amount to four millions of dollars. This bill was passed by the Senate without a dissenting vote, some few members of the Senate being either absent or influenced from voting. In the Assembly the measure was passed with only three dissenting votes. As to bribery of any of the members to secure the passage of this measure, I shall only state what occurred and leave the reader to draw his own conclusions: A carpetbag Senator received a sight draft on the General the night before the passage of the bill. What that draft was for I am unable to say. The draft was presented to the General the next morning, who took it, read it, then tore it up, telling him at the same time, "This is all right, this is all right." The Senator undertook to insist on its payment, but the General began to talk so very loud about the matter that the Senator walked off cursing him, but in very low tones. The colored members of the Legislature who had heretofore been content with the salary which was provided by the Constitution as their pay now began to learn something of the meandering ways of their carpetbag leaders. They began to inquire how their white brethren could handle so much money, when they got no more pay than they did. Some of the Democrats who were not members of the Legislature informed them that their carpetbag friends from the different counties had traded on their votes in the Legislature ever since they had been permitted to sit in the Legislature as members. The colored members, from this information, began to hold separate caucuses, and finally they elected a permanent chairman of the caucus, and that chairman appointed a committee of three to ferret out all schemes which looked anything like money schemes. This committee was styled "the smelling committee." The duty of this committee was to visit the hotels and private rooms of the carpetbag members and ascertain, as best they could, whether there was anything or things, measure or measures before, or likely to come before the Legislature at that session which the carpetbag brother could make money from, and if so to report the same to the caucus. This committee was not to proceed in a body, but each man was to gather the facts as he could get them and report to the caucus in a body. The chairman of the caucus was empowered to inform any party or parties who were in need of votes in the Legislature to pass measures, the number of votes that could be had and the amount required to satisfy the members of the caucus. When any money was received from this source it was to be equally divided among the members. This plan worked for some time but no money was forthcoming. All information that could be gathered by the committee was reported to the chairman of the caucus, who would report what the measures sought to be passed were, and advised the members of the caucus to vote for them, yet he never reported any money. The members began to perceive that the chairman was getting very flush with money, and they naturally became suspicious that he was playing carpet-bagger on them. A meeting was called and charges presented against the chairman for not having paid over moneys received by him for the benefit of members of the caucus. He at first stubbornly denied having received any moneys for the caucus, but a party who had given him money for the caucus, finding his measure fought in the Legislature by members of the caucus, found fault with some of them, who said they had never received any money from the chairman. The note in which the complaint was conveyed was to the effect that he had made "the boys" a present of —— dollars which he had handed to Mr. S. The chairman having been convicted of the charge, now declared that the money was made a present to him individually, and refused to make a division. This broke up the caucus arrangement, and after that time each member struck out for himself. All the colored members of the Legislature did not belong to this caucus, but at least two-thirds of them did. This extra session adjourned on the 23d of June.

In the fall of 1869 the grand jury of Leon County attempted to inquire into the reported bribery of the members of the Legislature. It was believed that Littlefield, when he first arrived in the State deposited his money in the Freedman's Savings Bank in Jacksonville. The grand jury issued a *subpoena duces tecum* to the cashier of the Tallahassee Bank, which compelled him to appear before the jury and bring the books and papers belonging to that institution. The books and papers showed that a large number of the carpetbag members of the Legislature had received drafts from M. S. Littlefield, payable at this bank, which drafts had been collected. The drafts to the different members ran all the way up from two thousand to five and six thousand dollars to each member. No white man got less than two thousand dollars. The books further showed that only two colored members received drafts, and these two fell away down into the hundreds—receiving five hundred dollars each.

As the drafts did not show what this money was paid for it was thought by the prosecuting officer that indictments for bribery could not be sustained. Therefore, no true bills were found. See stub of blank draft book, Freedman's Savings Bank and Trust Company, Tallahassee, Fla.

Although no bills were found at this term, the Ring secured the indictment of C. H. Pearce, colored, a Senator from the Eighth Senatorial District, in the fall of 1876, by the grand jury of Leon County, for offering a bribe to Fred Hill, colored, of the Seventh Senatorial District. The circumstances of the case were as follows: Littlefield requested Pearce to inform Hill that he could get five hundred dollars to vote for Littlefield's four million bond bill. Pearce delivered the message, which, however, Littlefield did not intend to fulfill, as he had already secured a sufficient number of votes to pass the bill. Pearce afterwards denied having carried the message, but said that Hill had got the message from some carpet-bagger, and afterwards asked him about the matter, when he was told what Littlefield had said. The impeachers, who had grown fat from the lavish hand of Littlefield, deemed this a splendid opportunity to cripple Pearce for life, and insisted that Hill, who was one of Stearns' submissive tools, should report the matter to the grand jury. Harry Cruse, another submissive and obedient servant of Stearns, was pitched upon as a witness to the delivery of the message. No one ever believed (who understood the game) that Cruse knew anything about the matter until requested to testify, so as to get Pearce out of the way before the impeachment of Governor Reed, which was to take place at the earliest possible moment. The real bribe-takers, the men who had in their pockets five and six thousand dollars each of Littlefield's money, were now hiring men to swear away the liberty of Pearce, that his hold upon the colored voter might be broken. Littlefield, the man who offered the bribe, if it could be considered an attempt at bribery, was not arrested, nor did the grand jury which indicted Pearce for carrying the message, inquire into the conduct of Littlefield in the premises. Stearns, after the indictment was found, smiled as gracefully over the downfall of Pearce as he afterwards smiled over the consummation of various election frauds.

CHAPTER X.

The Purman-Hamilton Reign of Terror in Jackson County.

And here opens a scene of oppression and usurpation of power which is equally diabolical in many instances with the reign of "Bloody Mary." There was no portion of the State more disturbed by the operations of the reconstruction measures of 1868 than Jackson County. The two races became arrayed against each other in deadly hostility, which led to frequent occurrences of violence and bloodshed. This state of things was not due to the enmity of the whites to the blacks, nor their opposition to the new law enfranchising the latter—though they were opposed to it, of course—nor was it due to any natural bad temper or hatred of the whites on the part of the colored people, for under ordinary circumstances there are no more peaceable people in the world than the inhabitants of Jackson County, of both colors, and they would have passed through the ordeal of reconstruction without a jar or disturbance, had it not been for the evil influence of the very men who were delegated to preserve peace, to administer justice, and to promote good fellowship and kindly relations between the freedmen and their former owners.

Charles M. Hamilton and William J. Purman were sent to Marianna as agents of the Freedman's Bureau in 1866, and if the purpose of the head of that department of the government had been to establish a reign of terror over the people of that county he could not have selected more fitting instruments. Hamilton, though afterwards a member of Congress, was a man of very ordinary capacity, but possessed courage and will power in a high degree. Purman, as has been said, was a man of unusual ability—shrewd, eloquent and persuasive, and with perfect knowledge of the character and prejudices of the colored man at that time, and also with a hidden contempt for his ignorance. He directed all the operations of the Bureau and put Hamilton forward to do all the dirty or dangerous work. He played upon the weaknesses and impulses of the colored people and drew from them shouts of joy, and responses of applause and approval with the skill and ease a master organist brings out the great swells of music by a gentle touch of the key. These would occur when he was eloquently depicting to his eager listening audiences the horrors of slavery and the cruelty and oppression they had undergone. Every device was resorted to by these agents to embitter the colored man against the white man; and, with the powers they possessed, it is no wonder they succeeded upon material so easily mislead.

What incendiary harangues failed to accomplish they sought to do by exhibitions of their power over the whites, which they displayed in frequent acts of the grossest tyranny. They set at defiance the orders and decrees of the courts of justice when the matters involved were mere questions of right between two citizens, neither of whom were freedmen. They arrested and imprisoned peaceable citizens without any real cause, and refused to furnish them or their counsel with the charges upon which they were held. On one occasion they had brought before them two young ladies of the highest respectability on the charge of removing flowers from a Union soldier's grave, who protested their innocence and offered to prove it without the insult and humiliation of being arraigned at bureau headquarters, but their appeals were in vain, and they were forced to appear and stand up and unveil themselves in the presence of Hamilton to answer the charge, which no witness could be found to sustain.

Among their duties as agents of the Freedman's Bureau, was the supervising of labor contracts between the freedmen and their employers. For this service they charged each freedman twenty-five cents and the employer fifty cents. An enterprising and intelligent citizen of the county, happening in Washington, called upon General Howard, the head of the bureau, and inquired of him if his agents were allowed to do such things. The General informed him they were not, and requested him to furnish him with evidence of its being done in any case. Thereupon the gentleman prepared and posted notices requesting those who had receipts for moneys so paid to present them to him, or, in his absence, to a designated agent. This gentleman and his agent were immediately arrested and kept in confinement without charges being preferred against them until one of them was taken dangerously ill, when they were discharged out of fear of the consequences. Four young farmers, who worked a large number of freedmen under a contract approved and ratified by these agents, were arrested and imprisoned for doing what was provided in said contract, and without any charges or causes assigned, though the officers were repeatedly requested to furnish them. The men were discharged at the pleasure of the agents of the bureau. Many other minor acts might be mentioned showing a persistent determination to alienate the races and breed strife.

These deeds of tyranny and oppression were resorted to for the double purpose of demonstrating their power to the colored people and of humiliating the whites. Of course they bore their legitimate fruit and naturally awakened feelings of the bitterest hostility among the people who were the victims of such injustice and insult. While the colored people were not responsible for these misdeeds, they were inevitably drawn into the troubles which ensued and doubtless encouraged to commit the first act of bloodshed which opened that eventful chapter in the history of Jackson County.

In the fall of 1868 a man by the name of McGriff, residing near Port Jackson, had a difficulty with some of his colored employes and the matter in dispute, which became angry, was referred to the Bureau by McGriff; but he obtained no satisfaction. A few nights thereafter he was shot in his house and wounded. He left for Alabama and sent a man by the name of McDaniel to take charge of his place. In a short time McDaniel was called to the door at night and shot dead. These acts were traced directly to the failure of these agents of the Bureau to settle peaceably the trouble between McGriff and his employes.

One exasperation followed close on another, until the county was in a fever of irritation. In the spring of 1869, while Purman was going to his home in Marianna at night, in company with Dr. John Finlayson, they were fired into by parties in ambush, and the latter was instantly killed. Purman was shot through the neck, but not badly. A few days after that a man by the name of Colliter, who had made himself very obnoxious to the Bureau by his open and bitter denunciation of their conduct, was shot and killed in his house at night by unknown persons. From this time on, during the year 1869, the whole county was in a state of turmoil. The worst feelings existed between the races, and nothing but the tact and prudence of the older and wiser heads on both sides prevented general bloodshed.

In September of that year, while a party of colored people were holding a picnic near the Natural Bridge, they were fired upon by a party in ambush and one man and a child were killed. This was the occasion of arousing the blacks to the highest state of excitement and the bitterest feelings of revenge. On Friday night of the same week a party of white people were sitting on the piazza in front of the hotel in Marianna when a volley of shot was discharged at them from the cover of some trees near by, and the daughter of Colonel McClellan was instantly killed and the Colonel himself badly wounded. At once a large portion of the county was under arms. The greatest excitement prevailed, and a general massacre was threatened. Some of the parties implicated in the shooting fled for their lives, while others were taken and speedy vengeance visited upon them.

The Rev. Mr. Gilbert, a colored minister of the Methodist Episcopal Church, who was born and raised in Jackson County, informed me that Purman, in the League meetings, would advise the people to burn the gin houses and other property of the whites, and this teaching would be reported to the whites by some members of the League, and not many nights after this advice would be given the witness of a flaming gin house would tell that his advice had been followed. The shooting of McClellan and daughter was the last tragic scene in the drama of reconstruction; the last act of lawlessness that can be traced directly to the administration of the Freedman's Bureau in Jackson County. It is well to state that while these troubles were at their worst the great agitators, Hamilton and Purman, who had kindled the flames of discord and strife, absented themselves from the county and were sending incendiary messages from a safe distance.

Thus it was they plunged the colored people unnecessarily into a vortex of trouble and left them to work their way out the best way they could.

Governor Reed, whose administration, now reeling and

tottering from centre to circumference for want of confidence abroad to purchase the State securities, by reason of the repeated attempts at impeachment, was called upon by Purman and others who previously had joined with the Democrats to destroy the Republican administration, to declare martial law in Jackson County. The Governor informed them that if this was done it would be the end of Republican government in Florida, and refused peremptorily. First, because there were no circumstances that would justify it; and, second, there were no means provided by which to defray the expense. It was still insisted on, when the proposition was made that if Purman would take command a regiment should be raised. Of course he declined, as the Governor knew he would. The demand was then laid before the Republican State Executive Committee, who unanimously sustained it, and called the Governor into council at Jacksonville to enforce the decree. He demonstrated the impropriety of a resort to military force, as well as the utter impossibility of doing it for want of means, and pledged himself to maintain the peace of the State by the employment of a civil police under the existing law if they would pledge themselves to appropriate the amount necessary. He was finally pledged the support of the committee to procure a loan sufficient to defray the expense. On his own personal responsibility he raised $3,500 and appointed colored and white agencies to quiet the misapprehensions and allay the excitement. He sent as commissioners to Jackson County Dr. John Westcott and J. S. Adams, with authority to confer with the people and secure their co-operation in maintaining the civil law. These gentlemen immediately repaired to Jackson County, and after a thorough investigation reported that Purman and Hamilton were the cause of all the bloodshed that had occurred in the county. This state of affairs furnished the opportunity for the desperadoes—that can be generally found in all communities after the ravages of a war —to put in their work without hindrance. Dickinson was killed, it was generally believed, by the notorious Luke Lott, purely from an old grudge he had against him; but in those days every murder committed was swelled into a political murder, and under the then existing circumstances the true cause of a murder could not be justly ascribed. This was a trying time for the true friends of an honest Republican administration; and it was seriously doubted by Governor Reed and the friends of Republican government as to whether he would be able to maintain himself; but the Governor, faithful to the promise made in his inaugural address, stood his ground against fearful odds until the terrific storm of bitterness raised by Purman sullenly but gradually passed away.

Purman now, who had wooed a young lady of the people whom he had so terribly oppressed and whom he finally married, was anxious to return and reside in the county, after things had got quiet. He issued a circular to different leading Republicans asking them to attend a public meeting in Jackson County. Hon. J. C. Gibbs was invited and attended the meeting. Hamilton, the cats-paw of Purman, accompanied him. Large crowds of whites and blacks assembled, and any one who was present need not have been a close observer to discern "blood in the eyes" of that crowd. Purman attempted to speak and was howled down by the whites, with a good sprinkling of the blacks. Hamilton attempted to speak, but he was treated in the same manner. Mr. Gibbs was introduced, who spoke more than an hour, and was listened to with close attention by the people. He charged Purman and Hamilton, in their presence, and in the presence of the people, with having been responsible for the troubles in this county. Purman now saw that he had been caught in the trap which he had constructed with his own hands, and called upon the sheriff to guard, protect and give him safe deliverance from the county; and the very people whom he had oppressed accompanied him across the Chattahoochee river into Gadsden County. and he returned to Tallahassee as his city of refuge.

CHAPTER XI.

The Meeting of the Legislature of 1870. Extracts from the Governor's Message. Attempt to Force Old Man Gilbert, United States Senator, to Come Down With More Cash. Schemes of Plunder. The Third Attempt at Impeachment—its Incidents and Results. Bloxham Confronts the Ring. Carpetbaggers Teaching the Freedmen Their Idea of Free Citizenship. Bloxham Elected and Counted Out. Meeting of the Legislature of 1871.

The Legislature met on the fourth day of January, 1870, this being the third regular session under the Constitution of 1868. There being no quorum present the two Houses adjourned until next day, when they met and organized, and notified the Governor that they were ready to receive any communication he would be pleased to make. At 12 o'clock M. the two Houses met in joint session and received the Governor's message, which was admitted, even by his enemies, to be a very able one. A large crowd of lobbyists was on hand, as usual, to aid in getting through corrupt measures, they knowing what material they had to treat with in the Legislature. The Governor said that "during no period in the history of the State has there been more marked improvement and general prosperity than in the year just passed, and never have the laws been more generally and efficiently executed. In several counties organized bands of lawless men have combined to override the civil authorities, and many acts of violence have occurred; but these have been incidental to the State in all its past history, and arise less, perhaps, from special enmity to the present form of government than from opposition to the restraints of law in general. When we consider what has been accomplished towards the establishment of equal laws and the acknowledgment of equal rights within the brief time since Republican government has been inaugurated, I think we find little cause for complaint, and less cause to reflect upon either the form of government or its official exponent. The chief executive and judicial departments of the government have been tested in a manner unparalleled in the history of civil government, and have stood that trial in such a way as to afford assurance of future integrity and to command the respect of the people. Every weak point in the New Constitution has been taken advantage of, by parties who contributed to the formation of that instrument to bring dishonor upon the administration and the State. Conspiracies have been formed to secure the control of the financial and railroad policy of the State in the interest of corrupt men, and to render the government subservient to the pecuniary aggrandizement of a few at the expense of the best interests of the State and people. As the representatives of those interests, many of you, for the first time, are admitted to the rights of freemen. You have thus far resisted these extraordinary efforts to mislead, intimidate or subsidize you from the path of duty, and you have preserved the State from the incubus of a corrupt and corrupting power, which has fastened itself upon so many of the States now struggling to rise from the ruins of war. We received the high trust now held by us with the State desolated by seven years of anarchy and misrule, with an empty treasury, with six hundred thousand dollars acknowledged debt, and a much larger amount repudiated and hanging like a cloud upon our financial escutcheon, with bonds dishonored by years of neglected interest, with a school fund robbed of its last dollar to aid in a war upon the republic, with a railroad system half completed, bankrupted and at the mercy of an adjoining State; with revenue laws inadequate to the current expenses of the government, and which contemplated no payment of interest upon the State debt; with no schools or school system; no benevolent institutions, no alms-houses, no penitentiary, and scarcely a jail. Such was the inheritance bequeathed to us by the fortunes of war, and under such incumbrances we were required to establish and maintain a republican government, under which master and slave, whose relations had changed from the results of war, were to yield obedience to the same law and be entitled to the same privileges."

The Governor said that George J. Alden, late Secretary of State, stands indebted to the amount of $1,284 for commissions, as appears on record in the Secretary's office.

The Legislature had been in session some twelve or fifteen days, and money did not seem to be so plentiful as in the last session, so something must be done to make business brisk. John W. Butler, of Santa Rosa county, who was capable of leading any corrupt measure, was fixed upon as the proper man to face the public with an absurdity. A resolution was pushed through the Assembly for the election of United States Senator for the term commencing March 4, 1869. Old man Gilbert was telegraphed to as to what had transpired; but the old man, now secure in his seat, paid no attention to this money-making scheme. He had passed through the mill twice, and understood the game. The Senate refused to join the Assembly in this farce, which bothered the originators considerably; but they were equal to the occasion. The notorious Purman made his appearance in the Assembly and asked to be heard, but the speaker decided that he could not be heard without the consent of the body, the two Houses not being in joint session. Eight Democratic Senators were allowed to record their vote for O. B. Hart, Republican, and one Republican for David L. Yulee, whereupon Hart was declared elected United States Senator, and the Assembly adjourned until the next day. The Democrats had no faith in the election, but determined to make the thing as ridiculous as possible. Hart spent some money to secure his elective bauble, and at once proceeded to Washington to contest the seat of Gilbert, but the United States Senate refused to entertain his contest, and so he was caught out several hundred dollars by these plunder-hunters.

The Internal Improvement Board had disposed of one million one hundred thousand acres of land to the New York and Florida Lumber, Land and Improvement Company, for ten cents per acre, on condition of putting actual settlers for each half section and opening an immigration office in New York and establishing agencies in foreign countries. The plunderers believed this to be a rich company, and were determined to have a hand in the sale. While some of the members of the Legislature were honest, and desired to protect the interests of the people, the great majority of the so-called white Republicans made it an object to make money out of every measure that affected the public purse, and however corrupt a measure might be, and however damaging it might have been to tax-payers, it could be passed by the Legislature if sufficient money was paid to the leaders to appease their avarice. A resolution was introduced declaring the disposing of the lands of the board of Internal Improvement to be null and void, but it was postponed from day to day in the lower branch of the Legislature before it could be adopted for the sole purpose of extorting money from the company to whom the lands had been sold. It was finally adopted; but had the company thought the resolution was of sufficient importance to prevent its passage, it never would have been adopted. The company had its representatives on hand, who were confident that this matter was purely within the jurisdiction of the courts and not the Legislature, and they, therefore, paid no attention to the resolution. The Commissioner of Lands and Immigration reported the transactions of the board with reference to this sale in answer to the resolution passed by the Legislature, calling upon the board for an explanation, as will be seen by referring to Assembly journal, page 81. Schemes and counter schemes were introduced at this session, as in the sessions previous, to enrich the plunderers.

On January 21st James D. Green, of Manatee county, introduced a resolution authorizing a committee of five to be appointed to inquire into the acts and doings of Harrison Reed, Governor of Florida, which resolution was adopted. Governor Reed also sent a communication to the House requesting it to have an impartial committee appointed to investigate his official acts and the acts of several officers of the government. M. L. Stearns, speaker of the Assembly, appointed James D. Green, George P. Raney, John Simpson, H. H. Forward and William B. White as said committee. While the committee was engaged in its investigations the members of the Osborn ring were using large quantities of bad whisky, cigars and money to influence the colored members of the Legislature, regardless of testimony, to favor impeachment. They would call general caucuses, and those of the ring, not members of the Legislature, would be invited into the caucuses and allowed to vote. At these caucuses the silver-tongued, but tyrannical Purman, though a member of the Senate at the time, would appear and

" With smooth dissimulation skilled to grace
A devil's purpose, with an angel's face,"

he would tell the colored members how their own race had been murdered in Jackson county, and our Republican Governor, who stood at the head of the government, as a father stands at the head of his family, refused to declare martial law in that county and "hunt the hell-deserving rebels down." He would tell them that he demanded the impeachment of Harrison Reed in the name of the Republican party, in the name of all the negro blood that had been shed upon a thousand battle-fields in the late war. He would appeal to their passions in every way imaginable to secure their votes for the impeachment of Reed. These appeals did well for the moment, but they could not bear scrutiny. The most of these colored members had been forced to the opinion that if the Republican Government could be maintained in the State it could best be done by the man who was now at the head of the government, and that "it was not safe to swap horses while swimming the stream." They held a caucus and determined to await the report of the committee. Some of them were promised to be given so much money after they had voted for impeachment; but they preferred to have the money paid before-hand. The ring, fearing from the last attempt at impeachment, that the colored brother would not prove faithful, changed front and offered to place the money in the hands of third parties, to be delivered after the vote was cast; but the colored brother wanted no third party in this criminal matter. With doubting heart and palsied hand part of the amount agreed upon was paid to the colored brother, who now walks off and smiles to know that he has got the best of the man who so often sold his vote in the previous Legislatures. I shall tell more of the colored brother when I get to the report of the committee.

During the investigations in the acts and doings of Governor Reed he appointed E. C. Weeks as Lieutenant-Governor. This was denounced by the ring as usurpation of power, and a committee was appointed to inquire into the appointment, with the intention of making that one of the causes of impeachment. Weeks, on the next morning after his appointment, proceeded to the Senate and attempted to preside. Hon. John A. Henderson, from Hillsborough county, came to his seat in the Senate and saw Weeks in the president's chair. Henderson said nothing until the time arrived to call the Senate to order. Weeks seized the gavel and undertook to call the Senate to order. Henderson, who was aware that Weeks had been appointed, arose and inquired of the other Senators as to what that was in the president's chair? Weeks responded that he had been appointed Lieutenant-Governor by Governor Reed, which position authorized him to preside over the Senate. The Senator declared that the Senate would not recognize such appointment, which position was sustained by the Senate. Weeks retired in good order, and did not return. He some months after applied to the Comptroller for his pay as Lieutenant-Governor, but the Comptroller refused to pay the amount on the ground that he was not legally the Lieutenant-Governor. Weeks next applied to the Supreme Court for a mandamus, compelling the payment of the amount, and the Court ordered the amount paid, and thus affirmed the validity of his appointment.

The 4th day of January was set apart for the report of the committee of investigation. The author of this work deems it unwise to embody the whole of the evidence and the majority and minority reports, but will give only the strongest evidence against the Governor, suppressing entirely the testimony of the Governor himself. The strongest evidence is that of the letter, exhibit G, which is embodied in the majority report, and which testimony I have copied verbatim.

Sherman Conant sworn—Saw a letter in June, 1869, in possession of General Littlefield, at the City Hotel, in Tallahassee, Fla., addressed to Harrison Reed, Governor of Florida, purporting to have been written by George W. Swepson, a true copy of which is hereto annexed, marked Exhibit G. The letter was signed by George W. Swepson. I have never had any business transactions with Geo. W. Swepson, nor have I ever seen him sign his name. I saw in December this same duplicate original letter, and at the same time I saw an instrument of writing purporting to convey in real property in Florida, signed by George W.

Swepson to M. S. Littlefield, to which instrument was attached a certificate of acknowledgement, under seal, to the effect that George W. Swepson had acknowledged before such officer that he had executed such instrument. The signature to the letter above referred to and the signature to the instrument of writing last mentioned were in the same handwriting.

The committee conclude their report as follows:

"In regard to Governor Reed having received money as a consideration for calling the special session of the Legislature, which convened last June, we find that George W. Swepson wrote to Governor Reed in the following words and figures, to-wit:

(Confidential.)

"RALEIGH, N. C., May 31, 1869.

"HON. HARRISON REED, TALLAHASSEE, FLA.:

"DEAR SIR—I regret 'my inability to be in your city during the extra session of the Legislature. Had it been convened on the first of June, as at first contemplated, I could have come. As it is, I cannot. General Littlefield has the bill, etc., and will fully explain everything to you; we expect him to prevent any difficulty being made with you by Osborn's friends. I write hastily and to the point. You remember, when in New York, our agreement was this: You were to call the Legislature together, and use your influence to have our bills passed as drawn by us, and if you were successful in this you were to be paid twelve thousand five hundred dollars in cash, out of which amount was to be deducted the seventy-five hundred (7500) dollars you have heretofore received, leaving a balance of five thousand dollars to be paid at an early day.

"Should our bills as drawn pass, we want you to go to New York and sign and issue to us the State bonds, and receive the bonds of our road in exchange for them.

"Any arrangement General Littlefield may make in this matter, will be carried out in good faith.

"Very truly,
* (Signed) "GEORGE W. SWEPSON.

---

*NOTE.—It afterwards transpired that Osborn visited Swepson at Raleigh and prepared this letter, and pledged Swepson that if he would sign it he should have all the legislation he wanted, saying, "I control two-thirds of the members and unless you sign this you shall have nothing." Swepson had his private secretary, Rosenthal, to copy the letter in duplicate and handed one copy to Littlefield to take to Florida, where Conant was to take charge of its execution. At the same time Osborne received several thousand dollars from Swepson to insure success.

"This letter was sealed with private seal of Swepson, and was delivered by General Milton S. Littlefield to Governor Reed in Tallahassee, a day or two prior to the meeting of the Legislature in June. Governor Reed did not read this letter in General Littlefield's presence. No allusion to the letter was ever made by Governor Reed to General Littlefield, until in December, he said to him it was Mr. Swepson's duty to correct the vile slander of the Conant affidavit, and the newspaper articles upon it. We find that General Littlefield let Governor Reed have several sums of money during the session, but they were charged against him, and what has not been paid, is now held in account against him. He further states that he knows from Governor Reed's own acknowledgment that Mr. Swepson has let Governor Reed have seventy-five hundred dollars, $2,500 of which is secured by mortgage, and the balance is the $5,000 draft before alluded to. This is all we have been able to discover on this point, except that there was a duplicate original of the letter just recited, which was shown by General Littlefield to different parties at different times.

"In the matter of the printing of State bonds, we find there was material difference between the cost and that of other bonds subsequently printed at the same house in New York. We find no evidence of any fraud.

"Reluctantly it is that we have come to the conclusion we hold as to our duty; but in view of the circumstances, our duty is plain, and we therefore recommend that Harrison Reed, Governor of Florida, be impeached, and respectfully recommend the passage of the accompanying resolution."

JAMES D. GREEN, Chairman,
GEO. P. RANEY,
JOHN SIMPSON,
H. H. FORWARD,

Resolved by the Assembly, That Harrison Reed, Governor of Florida, be impeached of high crimes and misdemeanors, malfeasance and incompetency in office.

Mr. White, of Clay, from same committee, made the following minority report:

"After much time and labor given to taking of the testimony, still more time has been necessary to enable us to reach any satisfactory conclusions, and thus the report has been delayed. Looking back over the history of the State for the last ten years, so full of excitement, agitation, and turmoil, we are profoundly impressed with a sense of the value of the results of the reconstructive legislation of the National Government, and its subsequent result in the organization of our own State government. While we cannot claim that this legislation is absolutely perfect, or the results to be altogether those that may have been desired, yet knowing well the thousand difficulties that, from the peculiar situation and characteristics of the whole South would necessarily hang around and embarrass any attempt at adequate legislation at the hand of merely human law-givers, we believe that as a whole the legislation of reconstruction originated from patriotic motives, was framed in a friendly spirit, though some of its measures may seem harsh, and is as well fitted to promote the ultimate prosperity of the Southern States, and the wellbeing of their citizens, as could be hoped of any legislation that could have been expected under the circumstances.

"It has been, therefore, with no common regret that we have seen, as citizens, the strength of the State government impaired, its character tarnished, its credit injured, and its power for good diminished by the multitude of charges and accusations that, from whatever source coming, have actually been in circulation against the Executive of the State, and, as citizens, have felt that the best good of the State and people, the cause of truth and justice, and the private interests of the Executive, all alike demanded a full investigation into the truth of the charges made, and an impartial and fearless award of justice at whatever cost of private feeling or party pride.

"And it was with precisely such feelings that, when unexpectedly the duty of investigation devolved upon us, we entered into the examination of the charges made. We have made the examination with all fairness, justice and impartiality, and announce the consideration to which we have been irresistably led by the testimony that has been laid before us.

"From the nature of the charges made, and of evidence adduced to support them, the attention of the committee has been particularly directed towards the following transactions as especially requiring examination, and as indicating sinister motives, and involving criminality on the part of Governor Reed.

"1st. It was alleged that Governor Reed received from George W. Swepson five thousand dollars, which was supposed to have been improperly obtained for his own private use and advantage, upon the credit of the State.

"2d. It was charged that Governor Reed had received eleven hundred and fifty dollars from the Florida Railroad Company due the Sinking Fund, without authority from the Trustees of the Internal Improvement Fund, and had failed to account therefor to the Treasurer of the Fund, except in scrip.

"3d. It was alleged that Governor Reed had received

twelve thousand five hundred dollars for calling the extra session of the Legislature in June, 1869.

"4th. It was alleged that Governor Reed had received a balance due the State of some six thousand four hundred and ninety-eight dollars, upon the sale of bonds belonging to the State, in cash, and had accounted therefor in scrip.

"5th. It was alleged that Governor Reed had purchased a large quantity of arms for the use of the State, charging the State therefor a larger sum than he actually paid for them.

"6th. It was charged that Governor Reed had procured the printing or engraving of certain bonds for the State, and charged more for the same than he actually paid for the work.

"A large amount of evidence, both oral and written, was taken in reference to such of the different charges made, and full and mature consideration was given to the same. The testimony in full, as the same was taken by us, is herewith given, and made a part of this report, and in view of the conclusion ultimately reached, there seems to be no necessity of stating the particular findings separately in regard to the charges made.

"We give the charges made as presented, the evidence as received, and our own opinion upon the whole, leaving the final determination and judgment to the calm consideration of your honorable body, and the verdict of an enlightened public opinion.

"On entering upon the investigation, we determined that no bias of party feeling should induce us to shield the respondent if, from evidence, his corruption or criminality should clearly appear. On the other hand, realizing the confusion, disorder, and the manifold dangers that must necessarily follow an abrupt, if only partial disorganization of the government, we could not feel that our duty as citizens would warrant us in recommending impeachment for any light reasons, or a necessity appeared from the evidence of vindicating the character of our whole people and the cause of justice.

"As stated before, we have fully examined the evidence; have calmly considered it in the light of surrounding circumstances; and have heard the explanations of Governor Reed; and while we find instances of conduct on the part of the Governor that in our opinion are to some extent informal, irregular, and indiscreet, particularly in his connection with financial matters, we also find a lack of co-operation and accord existing between the Governor and a portion of his Cabinet, which indeed appears in their respective official reports, that goes far to palliate or perhaps excuse the irregularities referred to.

"With reference to a portion of the charges preferred, we find them in no wise substantiated by the evidence offered; and in regard to others, where seeming irregularity appears, and while entertaining grave doubts of the propriety of certain acts, we find that when taken in connection with the attending and difficult circumstances, there is absolutely no evidence of any criminal intention whatever on the part of Governor Reed.

"Before announcing our final conclusion, we desire to put far away any disposition to appeal in any degree to passion, prejudice, or party feeling, and if any such feeling unwittingly appears in our report, we desire most distinctly and solemnly to disclaim and disavow it.

"And on the other hand, when we look forward to the probable results that may reasonably, indeed almost certainly, be expected to follow in the present unsettled and excited state of the public mind upon any hasty and inconsiderate action at the present time, and before the final judgment of your honorable body, upon the results of this investigation as herein embodied, we ask for calm and considerate reflection in the name and for the sake of peace, order and obedience to law, appealing to that patriotic love of our common country, that universal desire to promote the general good, that conscientious regard for the precepts of justice and truth, which are the highest virtues in any legislative body, to sustain whatever action conscience and equity may demand.

"Before stating our conclusions, we feel bound in duty to call attention to the many difficulties and embarrassments, particularly of a financial description, with which, in the administration of a newly organized government, Governor Reed has found himself continually surrounded. Without sympathy, with scanty resources, without the support from a portion of his Cabinet, as it appears from the testimony and from official documents, called to fill a multitude of offices by the appointment of comparative strangers, he must have been seriously embarrassed and hampered on every hand.

"After deliberate consideration of the charges, the evidence, the surrounding and difficult circumstances, and in view of the results that may be expected to follow the action taken, we do not find the charges preferred to be so far sustained by the evidence given as to warrant us in recommending an impeachment, and accordingly offer as indicating the results of our investigation, the accompanying preamble and resolution.

"WM. B. WHITE."

WHEREAS, By resolution of this House, grave charges of incompetency, malfeasance and criminality were formally preferred against Harrison Reed, Governor of Florida, a committee of this House was duly commissioned to make investigation, and report in regard to the evidence upon which such charges were made; and,

WHEREAS, After full examination of the evidence adduced and due consideration given to the explanations of Governor Reed, said committee have reported that while there was evidence of irregular and indiscreet action on the part of Governor Reed, which may be considered reprehensible and not deserving of approval, yet that, taking into consideration the circumstances under which such action occurred, and the many difficulties encountered, no proof is found of any corrupt or criminal intention on the part of Governor Reed that warrants impeachment; therefore, be it

Resolved, That in view of the charges made, the evidence presented and the explanations offered, and in consideration of attending circumstances, no sufficient evidence appears to warrant the impeachment of Harrison Reed, Governor of Florida.

After the reading of the reports of the majority and minority of the committee had been concluded the Assembly resolved itself into committee of the whole on the subject. After some time spent the committee rose and reported the two reports back to the House and recommended the adoption of the majority report. Before this recommendation was acted upon it was ordered by the House that the whole testimony should be read. A motion was made to adopt the majority report, which was rejected by a vote of 29 to 21. John R. Scott, colored, of Duval County, moved the adoption of the minority report, which was adopted by a vote of 27 to 22. It will be seen that all the colored members, with the exception of Cox, of Leon, voted against impeachment. Hon. John R. Scott and H. S. Harmon, of Alachua, while debating upon the evidence, showed that the ring trying to impeach Harrison Reed would damn any State government if it once got thoroughly fixed in power. You might see during the roll-call the members of the ring watching the colored members whom they had both paid and promised money to vote for impeachment, frowning and trembling as the colored brother, who had spent the money, now forgetting the promise cast his vote to exonerate Reed.

There is an interesting incident connected with these reports which may properly appear here. Captain Green, after the investigation closed, called at the executive office and informed the Governor that they had agreed to report in his favor, and at the same time asked the appointment of Mobly, of Tampa, as judge in place of Magbee, who, he said, would resign if the Governor required. Judge Hart had been advised with in preparing the report for the chairman, Green, and he had also advised the Governor that it would sustain him. On the evening before the report was to be made D. Richards called upon the Governor and told him that unless five thousand dollars was paid before 8 o'clock the next morning the report would be against him. The Governor replied that nothing would be paid by him, and he would abide the consequences. Again, in the morning, the Governor was advised that Green and Simpson must have five thousand dollars or they would sign the report against him. Before roll-call in the Assembly, at 10 o'clock, Creen and Simpson had been shown a U. S. check for $6,000 payable to the U. S. marshal, which they were assured would be theirs if they signed the report against the Governor. Simpson afterwards publicly acknowledged that he was pledged $2,000 of the avails of the draft. They sought to suppress entirely the report prepared for the acquittal, but White was proof against their blandishments and alone presented the report through the clerk, Bynum. So certain were the conspirators now of full success that the clerk refused to read the report presented by White, and he was compelled to read it himself.

The most of the Democratic members voted for impeachment, but whether influenced by the testimony or from a party standpoint, I shall not attempt to say. [See Assembly Journal, 1870.] Osborn and his ring followers, now frustrated by the action of the Assembly sustaining Reed, immediately sued for a treaty of peace. A general caucus of all the leading Republicans was again called to meet in the Senate chamber the same night after Reed had been exonerated, and the Reed and anti-Reed men were present. The anti-Reed men were the first to speak, who made haste to acknowledge their wrong and beg pardon of the Governor and of their party for attempting to overthrow the Republican administration. Green, of Manatee, who offered the resolution of investigation, arose and pledged the Governor his future support, and wound up by saying that he felt like the little boy who got besmeared twenty miles from water. The famous Littlefield was on hand and made a speech congratulatory of the Governor. He said he felt like the old woman who sang " Hey, daddy's diddle, the cat's in the fiddle, and her tail flew out." A resolution was passed unanimously by the caucus to support the administration of Governor Reed, after which they adjourned.

All this time the administration was in a terrible muddle, and no one could conjecture what the end would be. Although the ring leaders of impeachment had pretended to ground their arms, it was apparent that they were still in deadly hostility. The Governor and his Cabinet could not co-operate, and a committee appointed by the Assembly to investigate the acts and doings of the several Cabinet officers reported the following:

"We have been painfully convinced of the want of that agreement and co-operation between the Governor and the Cabinet, which should prevail. Indeed, it appears from the evidence that the want of harmony has at times proceeded to the extent of actual opposition; and official colleagues at this time are not on speaking terms with the Governor. Such a condition of things ought not to continue; it impedes the transaction of public business; it tends to injure the State credit; it lessens the efficiency of the government and lowers it in the confidence of our citizens, and of the people without the State; and in full consideration of all the facts that appear, and of the importance of securing thorough co-operation between the State officers, and in due deference to the action of the Honorable Assembly, the committee find it to be their duty to conclude their report with the following suggestion:

"Without imputing special blame to any one, or entirely excusing any one, the committee desire to suggest to all the members of the Cabinet, the immediate resignation of the whole Cabinet and giving Governor Reed an opportunity, by and with the advice of the Senate, to select a Cabinet who could co-oper- with him."

A minority report requested Governor Reed to resign. Both reports were laid on the table.

In the summer of 1870 the Republicans of the State met in convention at Gainesville, to make nominations for Congressman and Lieutenant-Governor. The Osborn ring strove hard to re-nominate Charles Hamilton, of Jackson county notoriety, for Congress, but colored men who were delegates to the convention had made up their minds to have some representation on the State ticket, which resulted in the nomination of Josiah T.

Walls, of Alachua county, for Congress. So much were they elated in the nomination of Walls that they slept upon their success, and allowed the ring to nominate one of their number, Samuel T. Day, of Columbia county, for Lieutenant-Governor. The ring now organized to elect Day and defeat Walls. They sulked in their tents and refused to work for Walls' election. The Democrats nominated in that year Hon. S. L. Niblack, of Columbia county, for Congress, and Hon. William D. Bloxham, of Leon county, for Lieutenant-Governor. The ring was now for the first time confronted with a political giant, who was destined to overthrow the carpetbag dynasty of Florida. At this period no Democrat was anxious to receive the nomination for anything, and all of them looked upon Bloxham's canvass as a helpless one. With no money with which to make a canvass except that drawn from his own pocket; no State committee to organize the Democratic and conservative masses; with carpetbag postmasters and route agents to intercept his communications to the different counties, this man visited every county in the State and nearly every town, hamlet and cross-roads, and with the cry of carpetbag corruption and the reign of terror that had been inaugurated in Jackson county by Purman and Hamilton, which he so eloquently and truthfully depicted, he showed almost superhuman ability and success in reuniting and arousing the whites and the conservative elements in the State in solid phalanx against the plunder ring. The Democratic party in Florida, which had become disheartened and disorganized from repeated defeats, then began to show signs of vigorous life. Mr. Bloxham's record, shortly after the emancipation as an ex-slaveholder, in establishing the first colored school on his own plantation; taking the money from his own pocket to build the house, and paying the major portion of the money for a teacher, made him so very popular with the freedmen that the carpetbag leaders, with all their league oaths and false representations of re-enslavement of the freedmen, were utterly baffled in the attempt to divert a large portion of them from him. In fact, the Democratic party of Florida had no cohesiveness until Bloxham became its candidate in 1870, and it was Bloxham who rallied the masses against Stearns in 1876. Mr. Bloxham was not a member of the Constitutional Convention of 1865, nor did he labor under the heavy cloud of having been a member of the Legislature under the Andrew Johnson reconstruction, which had passed laws that enabled the carpet-baggers, in addition to the league obligation, to so frighten the freedmen as to rally them in support of the most unprincipled and corrupt men.

Osborn, who was anxious to be returned to the United States Senate, determined to leave no stone unturned to secure as many members of the State Senate as possible, preparatory to the expiration of his term. Duval county, as well as Leon, had heretofore opposed from the beginning of reconstruction Osborn and his whole gang. A Senator must be had from this county at all hazards, the will of the majority to the contrary notwithstanding, and this request of the chief was urgent and mandatory. The ring assembled in secret conclave in Jacksonville and discussed the probabilities and improbabilities of securing a nomination at the hands of the Republican nominating convention, by a free use of money and bad whisky; and if that should fail, the next step was to secure John R. Scott, colored, who was one of the leading lights among the colored men of that county, and have him to understand that they were in favor of him, in order that if he was nominated for the Senate they could more easily make a combination with the Democrats to defeat him and elect one after their own heart, Horatio Jenkins, Jr. Should they fail in this, or should the canvass look squally for them, then fraud upon the ballot-box was to be committed and Jenkins counted in; and should they fail in this, Jenkins was to contest the seat of Scott by making a combination with the Democrats in the Senate, touching the safety of their minority in the Senate, and thereby oust Scott and seat Jenkins. As to the true intention of the conspirators, Scott was unaware. Let us see if they were successful in any of these propositions.

John R. Scott, now ambitious for Senatorial honors, was worked up to fever heat to secure the prize. The convention met, and it was at once observed that W. H. Christy, white Republican, who did not belong to the Osborn gang, was the choice of the convention. The anti-ring delegates held a caucus, which was attended by Scott as one of them. Scott talked and advised with the other delegates, and assured them that he was with them for the nomination of Christy. He begged the caucus to make him chairman of the convention, which was done, and in a few minutes the convention was called to order. Scott, as pre-arranged, was made chairman. Christy was nominated by one of the anti-ring delegates, and instantly the carpetbaggers, Dockray, Jenkins and Cheney presented the name of Scott as Christy's opponent, as agreed upon before. The antiring delegates were astonished and rushed to Scott to have him withdraw his name, but he did not seem to understand what they meant. Ballotting commenced, and resulted in the nomination of Christy by a large majority, but Scott ruled that the resolution was unintelligible, and ordered a new ballot, which was had, and again Christy received a large majority. Some informalities which Scott contended compelled him to rule that the first ballot was unintelligible, happened this time all right, but he ruled just the opposite to what he did before, so that a third ballot was ordered, which again resulted in the nomination of Christy. The ring now gave up the ghost and abandoned their proposition. Scott and Dan McInnis were nominated for the Assembly.

The ring, expecting that they would have Scott to deal with, when it turned out that they had Christy, hesitated for a while to attempt to defraud him at the ballot box, and invented another plan, and that was to get Jenkins to the lower house, which would give him influence to be returned to the Legislature two years hence, and also to lead in the impeachment of Harrison Reed. Some days after the convention, while Christy was incidentally in the business place of Dan McInnis, W. M. Ledwith, who was at that time friendly with Osborn, came in, and said: "McInnis, I am authorized by Colonel Osborn to say to you that if you will simply withdraw from your place on the Legislative ticket and let Jenkins go on in your place, he will give you five thousand dollars, and give you also the regular pay; we do not ask you to take an active part in his favor." McInnis replied, "Ledwith, tell Osborn to go to h—l with his money; I have my trade to make my living from." Having failed to defeat the will of the majority in these two efforts, they resorted to the Democrats for success. They entered into an arrangement with H. H. Hoeg and Miles Price, who were ambitious for legislative honors, and members of the Democratic party.

Hoeg and Price being backed by a very small minority of the Democrats of the county, in the arrangement, to the effect that a ticket with Horatio Jenkins, Jr., for Senator, and H. H. Hoeg and Miles Price for the Assembly should be run in opposition to the regular Republican ticket, Hoeg and Price to furnish the money to run the campaign, except $1,000, which Jenkins was to contribute, which, according to the statement afterwards of Hoeg's accountant, they did to over $4,000. The Democrats on the day of election pretty much all voted for Christy, as did the Republicans; and according to the count, Christy, Scott and McInnis were elected by more than two-thirds vote of the county. The county board of canvassers (the clerk, judge of probate and a justice), after throwing out irregularities, etc., certified to the Secretary of State that the Christy ticket was elected by 825 majority. The day of election, the ring, with what following they could muster, went down to Yellow Bluff precinct, an obscure little village, to vote, thus laying the foundation for the fraud afterwards perpetrated. Yellow Bluff proper had about 80 votes, but the ring had invented a method by which a minority could be transformed into a majority without votes or the knowledge or consent of the voter. They waylaid the Inspector from this precinct, who had been entrusted with the ballot box to deliver at the County Clerk's office, and getting him drunk, broke it open, took out and destroyed the returns made by the Inspectors and substituted one of their own manufacture, with votes for the other ticket, to correspond with the return—the same being made to give Jenkins, Hoeg and Price small majorities. Resealing the box, it was conveyed to the Clerk's office, and the demand made for its count; but the canvassers failed to see it, and threw it out. At the time of the canvass, Governor Reed was in Jacksonville, and was appealed to personally by Cheney and Osborn to instruct the clerk and judge to canvass in Jenkins. He replied that he had never yet been a willing party to a fraud and immediately called upon the officers to discharge their duty under the law, regardless of the results. Osborn afterwards sent a note to the Governor apologizing for the request, and saying it was only because he wished to save the election of Walls. At the canvass of the vote by the State Board of Canvassers, Christy and his ticket were again declared elected. The ring now held another consultation meeting and determined to make their last desperate assault on Christy. They had an understanding among themselves to wait quietly until the meeting of the Legislature, and learn what Republicans were contesting the seats of Democratic Senators. Their henchman, Lieutenant-Governor Day, whose duty it was to preside over the Senate and appoint its committees, was to appoint the committee on privileges and elections exclusively from the members of the ring, with the exception of the two representatives of the Democratic party. This part of the programme was carried out to the letter, and the committee was accordingly appointed. The seats of several Democratic Senators were contested, and at the low estimate in which the ring held the voice of the people at that time it was not a question of honest votes cast for the candidates and contestants, but as to whether the ring could obtain votes enough in the Senate to seat or oust members in utter disregard of the Constitution, law, right or justice. They entered into an agreement with the Democratic Senators that if they would seat Jenkins in Christy's place, they, the ring members, would sustain Ross, Democrat, sitting member from Columbia County, whose seat was contested by Dr. E. G. Johnson, Republican. They also agreed to seat Allen, Democrat, from Hamilton, in place of the sitting member from that county, who was a Republican, and to seat Duncan, Democrat, from Lafayette and Taylor, in place of Krimminger, Republican. Christy did not occupy his seat more than three days. Senator Atkins, one of the two Democrats of the committee on privileges and elections, came to Mr. Christy just before the meeting of the Senate on the day he was ousted, and said: "Mr. Christy, in regard to this contest, we all know you and like you, and know you were elected. You have lived among us a long time, and we would prefer to keep you in your seat; but it becomes us as Democrats to make what capital we can out of these things, and if you will promise to do the same things for us that Jenkins and his friends have promised, we will keep you in your seat and send Jenkins home." Mr. Christy asked him what they had promised, and he said, "They promised to seat Allen, from Hamilton, to keep Charley Ross in from Columbia, and to unseat Krimminger." Christy's reply was—

"Mr. Atkins, I have fought as hard a battle for my seat in the Senate as any man ever fought, without compromising myself, and I don't propose to do so at this eleventh hour. I claim my seat as my right. I have no pledges to make to any man or any set of men." In a few minutes after this conversation the Senate resumed its session, the packed committee on privileges and elections, L. G. Dennis, W. J. Purman, and Fred Hill, reported Jenkins entitled to the seat of Christy. Eleven Democrats and four Republicans voted to oust Christy. The Republicans were Meacham, Wentworth, Hill and Dennis, and the only Democrat who voted yea was Ross.

Jenkins and his friends now had an opportunity to show whether the promise of a genuine carpet-bagger was worth anything, and whether such carpetbagger was worth a promise. A few days after the ouster of Christy, Ross, who had voted to unseat Christy, was ousted and Johnson seated, Allen was reported against, Krimminger was declared entitled to his seat, and every promise made by Jenkins and his ring friends was utterly disregarded and violated. The Democrats, who now saw that they had been outwitted by the carpet-baggers, went to Christy and solicited him to have his name associated with Ross to oust Jenkins, but he was not willing to have Ross who had voted against him now slid back on his shoulders. It would thus appear that the astute and unprincipled carpet-bagger was not only capable of misleading the negro, but the Southern whites as well, and that both were susceptible of being punished. Notwithstanding these men who were parties to the Yellow Bluff fraud stood before the public convicted of this glaring outrage upon the ballot box, which, if tolerated, would put an end to all republican government, yet they were allowed to hold the most important Federal offices, and to act as Chairmen and Secretaries of our State Republican committees. While Jenkins usurped the seat of Christy, Scott and McInnis were permitted to retain their seats from the same county. Ross, Duncan and Allen had received large majorities in their Senatorial districts, but were not permitted to occupy their seats. The freedmen had now begun to learn that the men who had been loudest in the denunciation of the Southern whites for openly opposing negro suffrage, were secretly engaged all over the State in nullifying that very suffrage when the exercise of it by them did not put a carpet-bagger in office.

Three or four days after the election of 1870 it became evident that Bloxham and Niblack were elected by good majorities, though the ring, through their newspapers, claimed the election of Day and Walls, whom they were confident had been defeated; and while they rejoiced in their hearts over the defeat of Walls, yet they could not hide their despondency over the defeat of Day. How to get Day in and count Walls out was a very difficult question to solve. The leaders of the ring and such other members as sat in the "amen corner" at once held a consultation to devise means to successfully behead Bloxham, the Democratic giant. It was proposed at first to count in Niblack for Congress and Day for Lieutenant-Governor, but this was objected to by some of the members on the ground that the returns from all the counties would not be so accessible as the returns from Yellow Bluff had been, and that such a step would cause the colored brother to kick through Walls, who was himself admitted to be very shrewd, and the whole fraud and the parties to it might be criminally exposed. They finally agreed to play the game of Yellow Bluff on a different and larger scale. In all the back Democratic counties which had Republican officers, who composed the county boards of canvassers, said officers were to delay the returns to the State Board of Canvassers a sufficient length of time so as not to be at the capital within the time prescribed by law, which was thirty days after the day of election. The Republican counties were mostly on the line of railroad and the returns from them could be got to the capital within three or four days. This proposition was to be kept very secret and sent to none but those who could be trusted as true sympathizers of the ring. All agreed that this was an excellent plan and the edict went forth, which was partially obeyed. The plan was made known by special couriers sent to the different counties in the garb of U. S. marshals, pretending to be hunting up election frauds committed by the Democrats. These marshals would arrest some Democrat on some frivolous charge and carry him to Jacksonville, put him under bond until court met, and then turn him loose. The next question was as to whether the ring could induce the Board of State Canvassers to act in accord with this plan. Reed, although not a member of the board, was yet sore about their repeated attempts at impeachment, and might hesitate to enter an alliance with his old enemies to carry out so critical a proposition, and would be hard to make understand their real plan; but Day *must* be counted in. Gibbs, Secretary of State and a member of the board, they feared could not be depended upon, as he was generally opposed to corruption in any shape. Gamble, the Comptroller, another member of the board, was a Democrat, and Meek, Attorney-General, was a Republican who, they feared, could not be relied upon for their purposes, though he was opposed to Governor Reed. E. M. Cheney, chairman of the so-called Republican State Committee, who was second in command of all the ring forces in Florida when Osborn was in the State, but in full command when he was in Washington or out of the State, had declared that the State had been carried by the Republicans, and must be so counted. The presence of Cheney, M. Martin, L. G. Dennis, the "Little Giant," and other leading lights of the ring, was an admonition to the shrewd Bloxham and the veteran editor of the *Floridian* that some political trick was imminent. Different ones of the ring approached Governor Reed and indirectly suggested the counting out of Bloxham and Niblack, but he informed them that if Bloxham was elected he ought to be so declared by the Board of Canvassers. The ring gave the Governor to understand that if Bloxham was counted in they would unite with the Democrats to impeach him, Reed, so as to make Bloxham Governor. Reed made them understand that he should not attempt to control the members of the board in the execution of their duty, but, whatever their action might be, he would have to submit. Gibbs was the next one besieged by the ring. The same whip of impeachment held over Reed was now successfully used on Gibbs. The counting-out process was demanded as a party necessity, while Gibbs himself was threatened with trumped-up charges relative to his office if he failed to do the bidding of the ring. In fact, the whole party influence was brought to bear on Gibbs, showing the necessity of the counting out of Bloxham. The Democrats had generally voted with the ring in the impeachment movements, and Gibbs, being between two fires, finally, but unwillingly, yielded to the tempters. Gibbs secured, the next victim to this outrage was Attorney-General Meek, who for some time stood in the doubtful column; but it was afterwards believed that he, too, yielded to the tempters, but proved faithful to them only for a little season. "The spirit was willing, but the flesh was weak." Although he had become alienated from the Governor and placed himself in official as well as personal antagonism, he hesitated to accede to the demands of the ring, but feared to oppose them. He claimed to have received an anonymous letter threatening violence if he assented to a false count. It was generally believed that the letter was written by himself. He returned to his home in Jacksonville, where he was taken dangerously ill and was unable to attend the final canvass. Mr. Adams, the Commissioner of Immigration, was authorized to present to the Governor his resignation upon condition that he would appoint Conant to serve until the assembling of the Legislature and then reappoint Meek or give him the judgeship of the Jacksonville circuit. The Governor, in order to get rid of an obnoxious Attorney-General, accepted the resignation of Meek, who was represented to him as in a dying condition, and appointed Conant to complete the canvass, upon the pledge that he would immediately vacate for a competent successor. The Governor discovered his mistake when, at the succeeding session of the Legislature, Conant sought to hold the office in defiance of him until the session ended his commission. He had got rid of Meek only to find a more bold, able and defiant corruptionist.

The board of canvassers met in the office of the Secretary of State on the 29th day of November and organized for the purpose of canvassing the returns from the different counties. Bloxham, in the meantime, had partially learned what trick was up and had his spies on hand. The board locked themselves in the Secretary's office and no one was allowed to enter but themselves. Col. Robert H. Gamble was the inside spirit, he being the Democratic member of the board, and Capt. C. E. Dyke standing at the key-hole on the outside waiting for a whisper from Gamble. When the returns were opened it was discovered that the special couriers sent to the different counties had done their work well. The counties of Brevard, Dade, Manatee, Calhoun, Lafayette, Sumter, Suwannee and Taylor were not in. It was evident to Gamble that the two members of the board were bent on counting the vote as then returned and to declare the result, which would have given Day a majority. Capt. Dyke, still at his post on the outside key-hole, had received several important dispatches from Col. Gamble as to the doings of the major members of the board, which he had conveyed to Bloxham. The information conveyed by these dispatches induced Bloxham to apply to Judge White, of the Second Judicial Circuit, for an injunction restraining the board from further canvass until the further order of the court. The Judge was holding court in the city of Monticello, about thirty miles away, and it took until the next day to receive the injunction. Dyke, not having heard from Col. Gamble for some time, wrote a note, which he shoved under the door, urging him to detain the board as long as possible, either by making motions, debating, conversation, or anything to kill time until the injunction should arrive. This dispatch fell into the wrong hands, as Gibbs was the first to see it, read it and then put it in a book in his office. Gamble went outside to carry another dispatch, when Dyke inquired whether he had received the one shoved under the door. He answered no, and rushed back into the office and asked who had received it. Meek wanted to know if Gamble imputed the stealing of the note to him, when Gibbs told him that he had picked up a note and laid it in a book. Gamble got very wrathy about the matter, but Gibbs informed him that he thought the note was of no consequence. The injunction was received the next day, the 30th, and was duly served on all the members of the board, and the board in a few days afterwards adjourned until the 26th day of December. When the injunction was served on the board the ring for a time thought all was lost. The board began to realize the fact that Bloxham was elected, but the ring having the United States Court in their hands rallied again, and assured the members of the board that White should be arrested for issuing the injunction, and begged them to remain faithful and steadfast. Meek failed to be comforted by these promises of security, and he resigned his position as Attorney-General on the day of the adjournment of the board to the 26th day of December. White was arrested and carried before the United States Court, charged with having violated the laws of the United States, and was kept under bond until the fraudulent count had been committed, and was then discharged.

The ring was determined to have some one whom they could control appointed Attorney-General and upon whom they could rely in carrying out the fraudulent count, as the fraud was so glaring that it took a man of great nerve to face the music. They were not long in finding that man. Major Sherman Conant, who at that time was one of the leaders of the ring, was selected to do the counting. Governor Reed was insisted upon to make this appointment, which he for some time refused to do; but the ring gave him to understand that Conant would resign as soon as the canvass was made, so as to let him appoint a man of his own choice to fill this important position. The Governor made the appointment as requested by the leaders of the ring and party, as it was then constituted, and the only thing the ring then feared was that Gibbs might falter. The interval between the time at which the injunction was served and the adjournment to the 26th of December was very interesting indeed to the members of the ring. Every night they met and discussed the question as to how to make this fraudulent count a success. It was suggested that Bloxham might go before the Supreme Court and compel an honest count by mandamus, which all agreed might be done. It was also suggested that the returns could be taken from the office of the Secretary of State and the Governor's office and destroyed, if those officers would avow that they had been stolen; but this plan was thought to be inexpedient. It was finally agreed that when the board adjourned it should adjourn to the Christmas week, at which time the Supreme Court could not be got together, and it would be near the meeting of the Legislature, and that body would then be called upon as accessory after the fact to give effect to the crime of counting out men who had been legally elected. The plan was only known to a few, and operated like clockwork.

The board met, as agreed, on the 27th of December, with the new Attorney-General and all the members of the board present. Conant and Gibbs, after the board had been called to order, withdrew from the Secretary's office, leaving the unsuspecting Gamble to await their return. It was charged that they went into the office of the Governor, but this was not true. When they returned they had made the canvass by throwing out the nine counties before mentioned, and declaring Day and Walls elected. A certificate of the result was carried to Gamble, who was informed by them that there was a little matter they had fixed up and signed, and they desired to get his signature to it. He looked at the paper and to his astonishment it purported to be the result of the canvass of the vote which they had met to make. He wanted to know when and where the canvass had been made, but received no answer. He refused to sign the certificate of the result of the canvass made by them, but this availed nothing. Day and Walls were declared elected, and the board adjourned *sine die*. The canvass was made in utter disregard of the injunction issued by Judge White, and said order was not dissolved until the 28th, the day after the canvass.

Bloxham, who had been outraged, as well as the people who had voted for him, now filed a petition in the Supreme Court of the State of Florida for an alternative writ of mandamus compelling the Board of Canvassers to reassemble and canvass the votes from the nine counties which they had thrown out. R. B. Hilton and S. J. Douglas appeared for the relator and J. B. C. Drew for the respondents. The petition showed that 2,582 votes were cast in the nine counties mentioned, and of these votes Bloxham had received 1,630, while 952 were cast for Day, showing a majority for Bloxham in these counties of 678 votes. The vote as cast in the whole State was as follows: Bloxham, 13,462; Day, 13,398; leaving Bloxham's majority 64. The answer to the writ was, First, that the court had no power to grant the writ in this case. Second, that the facts set up were not sufficient to entitle the relator to the relief demanded. Third, that the relator had not pursued the proper remedy.

The Legislature had been in session a few days, and pending the mandamus proceedings, it was brought to the attention of the court that the law which created the State Board of Canvassers had been repealed by the Legislature then in session. The court's attention was not called to the repeal of this act by the attorneys on either side; but the law repealing the act was accidently laid in front of the Chief Justice (Randall) while he and the other judges sat on the bench and were about to deliver an opinion that Bloxham should be counted in. It was very singular that the Chief Justice should take judicial notice of a paper when he did not know whether it was fictitious or genuine, especially when it involved the rights of all the people in the State. The court, after declaring its authority to grant a writ of mandamus directing the Board of State Canvassers to reassemble and complete a canvass of the returns of votes cast at a State election, where they have neglected to make a complete canvass of the returns in their possession, said, "Pending the proceedings by mandamus against the Board of Canvassers, the Legislature repealed the law creating such board, without saving proceedings or duties required by law to be performed by them and uncompleted. Held: That the power of the board to proceed was gone, and therefore the proceedings against them were dismissed." See 13th Florida Reports, p. 55. This act of the Legislature was very quietly and cautiously engineered through without being even suspected on the part of the Democrats.

The counting out of Bloxham and Niblack made Conant very popular among the members of the ring, and he was afterwards appointed United States Marshal for Florida. Gibbs received no credit from the ring, as the part he played in the matter was looked upon as being compulsory.

Thus the legislative branch of the government, instead of being the guardian of purity of the ballot box, was made the only loophole through which this fraud could escape to high places.

The meeting of the Legislature of 1871 was conspicuous for nothing except the election of a corrupt Chief Clerk of the Senate—the notorious Joseph Bowes, professed ballot-box stuffer; completing the Bloxham fraud; and the ousting of Democratic members who had been legally elected. There was no venture at impeachment, for the reason of the treaty of peace with reference to the counting out of Bloxham. The Governor's message was devoted chiefly to the finances of the State, but the Legislature refused to accept any measure recommended by the Governor, and after a session of twenty days it adjourned *sine die.*

CHAPTER XII.

The Meeting of the Legislature of 1872. Extracts from the Governor's Message. Corruptionists Hunting up and Investigating Charges of Corruption. The Blue Scrip Transaction. Colored Members Denouncing Corruption. Impeachment of Governor Reed. The First Articles of Impeachment. The Senate Takes Order, and Day Assumes the Office of Governor. The Assembly Withdraws Articles Fifth and Sixth and Presents Others. The Assembly Asking for Further Time to Prosecute the Impeachment. The High Court of Impeachment Refuses to Grant Further Time, and Adjourns. The Contrition of the Conspirators.

The Legislature met on the second day of January, 1872, and the Assembly, after electing its officers, informed the Senate of its organization, and the Senate sent the same information to the Assembly. Hamilton Jay, who was then clerk for S. B. Conover, State Treasurer, was elected chief clerk of the Assembly. Mr. Jay was a fresh carpet-bagger from the North, who had not tasted to any great extent the pap of the State, and he had not been in the State long enough to register. The leading carpet-baggers from all parts of the State were on hand in full force, and it was evident that something important regarding the interests of the ring was to be accomplished.

F. A. Dockray, who, from the first, had been Osborn's most active agent in all the efforts to override or remove Governor Reed, and who had been rewarded with the appointment of collector of the port of Jacksonville, came fresh from Washington and made demand for the appointment of Attorney-General, then temporarily held by J. B. C. Drew, a non-resident carpet-bagger, from Wisconsin. Drew demanded that his nomination for the position should be sent to the Senate. Dennis demanded the removal of all the county officers of Alachua and the appointment of W. K. Cessna as County Judge, with other corruptionists for the balance. W. J. Purman demanded the removal of all the county officers of Jackson county and the appointment of non-residents. All these demands were made upon the Governor under threat of impeachment if not complied with; and when Dennis repeated his demand and presented his alternative, the Governor is reported to so far have forgotten his church fealty as to reply: "Impeach and be d—d. I ask no favors of you or any of Osborn's corrupt crowd." These four combined immediately planned the suspension of Governor Reed, the installation of Lieutenant-Governor Day, the issue of two millions more of railroad bonds to Littlefield, one quarter of which was to be divided among members of the Legislature and the remainder distributed among the conspirators. Dockray and Drew furnished the evidence for the committee sitting in secret, made the report, based upon unsworn and unfounded testimony. Cessna, the tool of Dennis, from Alachua county, was the willing instrument to introduce the resolution, and Stearns, the Surveyor-General and Speaker; Jenkins, the clerk of the House and afterwards defaulting Collector of Internal Revenue; Purman, the United States Assessor of Internal Revenue; Wentworth, United States Marshal, then a defaulter for money used in the previous attempt to depose the Governor, holding seats and having control of the Senate under Osborn, were relied upon after suspending the Governor, to present a trial or even an examination of the testimony.

When the plan was all ready for execution the committee met, received the testimony and report prepared by Dockray and adopted them. Stearns called together all the more ignorant and prejudiced of the colored Assemblymen, pledging them to vote the next morning for a resolution of impeachment, assuring them that it would be proved that the Governor had appropriated the public funds, etc. Gillist, a Southern loyalist, from Putnam county, holding from Governor Reed the appointment of County Judge, was secured by promise of the position of Circuit Judge for the Fourth Circuit; Dukes, Democratic Assemblyman, from Columbia, was enlisted by the promise of a large share of the new bonds, of which, as chairman of the Railroad Committee, he had recommended the issue.

At nine o'clock at night twenty-four Republican Assemblymen were sworn by Stearns to vote for a resolution of impeachment, to be reported at the opening of the session next morning.

This done, ex-Governor Walker was waited upon by Stearns with a proposition that if he could furnish seventeen Democratic members to vote for a resolution of impeachment, the Governor would be suspended the next day. Governor Walker immediately secured a caucus of the Democrats, and induced them to rescind a resolution already adopted, pledging that they would abstain from further attempts to embarrass the Governor, and agree to vote for a resolution of impeachment the next morning. The first advice the Governor had of the consummation was from a Democratic member from Orange County who went to the executive office at nine o'clock and informed him that at eleven o'clock the night before he had been called from his bed to meet Governor Walker in caucus, and that he had induced the majority to "go back" on their previous action and vote a resolution of impeachment, and while he was thus engaged, he was summoned by the Sergeant-at-Arms under a call of the House to vote on a question of impeachment. Being thus advised that he would be immediately suspended, with no chance for investigation or trial, the Governor immediately asked friendly Senators an adjournment of the Senate until Monday, that being Friday, which was accorded, and the Governor immediately prepared to vacate the Executive office and return to his farm at Jacksonville to await results. The first signal of war against the administration was the following resolution, offered by one of the leading members of the ring from Alachua County, W. K. Cessna:

WHEREAS, There are many and grave charges afloat as to the mal-appropriation of the proceeds of the bonds issued by the State to aid in the construction of the J., P. & M. Railroad, and that the charter creating the company in charge of said road has not been complied with, either in spirit or letter; and that gross frauds have been committed upon the State; therefore,

Resolved, first, That a committee of five be appointed by the Speaker, whose duty it shall be to thoroughly and vigorously investigate the acts and doings of the J., P. & M. Railroad Company, and also that of the State officials in connection therewith, in every particular where the State is a party in interest, with a view to a speedy and vigorous prosecution of all offenders.

Resolved, second, That the said committee shall, with their report, recommend such measures for the action of the Legislature as will correct existing evils, and prevent loss to the State, and guard, as far as may be, against similar rascalites in the future.

Resolved, third, That the said committee shall have power to send for persons and papers, to employ assistance, and to do in the premises whatever else may be found necessary to a complete and successful elucidation and exhibition of the case, reporting daily all expenses incurred to this Assembly.

Resolved fourth, That the said committee shall report their progress weekly.

These resolutions were subsequently referred to a committee appointed at the last regular session to investigate the acts and doings of the said company.

The two Houses met in joint session on the second day of the session to receive the Governor's annual message. The Governor came forward at the appointed time and delivered his message, which was pronounced by all to be very able and interesting. He said:

GENTLEMEN OF THE LEGISLATURE:

For the last time during my official term have I the honor to meet you in session, to deliver my annual address as Chief Executive of the State; and while, since you last assembled, the State has passed a season of severe trial by flood and storm, yet, on the whole, it has kept a steady pace onward in population and in civil, political and industrial development.

Among the reconstructed States of the South none started upon a more truly conservative basis than Florida, and none have progressed more successfully in the scale of social, political and industrial improvement.

Florida, upon the whole, may be said to have been distinguished among the Southern States for general peace and quiet and obedience to law, notwithstanding reports to the contrary which have prevailed, much to the detriment of the State.

Still disturbances, breaches of the peace, infractions of the law, and scenes of fatal and disgraceful violence have occurred in many localities within our borders. This I have attempted to correct by the exercise of all the power vested in me by the Constitution, and by the use of all the means bestowed for that purpose by the Legislature. But at times all efforts have failed, and all the means at my command have seemed to be ineffective.

It is true that these same localities, being, to all intents, border sections, have from time immemorial been the resorts of lawless and reckless men, and in some of them, as in earlier periods of the existence of the Western and Southwestern

States, the law of Judge Lynch and the "Regulators" for years before the war, had been the only code of much efficacy.

I had hoped better results from the reorganization of government under Republican auspieces; but the bitterness resulting from the war, the noxious teachings of disappointed and defeated political opponents, assisted by the occasional lack of discretion on the part of injudicious political friends, succeeded for a long time in setting at naught the advice and the efforts of the better men of all classes, until improvement at times seemed to be hopeless; and I have been strongly and forcibly urged to the declaration of martial law.

But looking upon the suspension of the civil law as an experiment always full of danger and entirely opposed to all the principles of free popular government, I have hesitated and refused to take a step so fraught with manifold dangers, except as the very last resort, even at the risk of incurring the enmity and hospitality of my own political friends. And while my heart has bled for the violence and suffering inflicted upon the more helpless classes of the community, I have steadily relied upon the civil law and the good sense and latent patriotism of the general citizenship.

The power granted me in the detective law of 1868 was rendered almost nugatory through the restrictions and want of means imposed, I fear, by the jealousies and personal animosities of so-called political friends; I still have earnestly endeavored, through the aid of special detectives, employed at my own expense, to ferret out and bring to justice the perpetrators of violence and crime, for whose detection and punishment the ordinary enforcement of our criminal laws seemed inadequate. And at last these persistent efforts seem likely to be crowned with some measure of success. A large amount of useful information has thus been obtained, and a mass of testimony, the nature and extent of which it is improper to disclose till the entire safety of the witnesses is effectually secured, is at my disposal.

In the prosecution of this work, and in the absence of the proper legislative appropriation therefor, I have, of necessity, been forced to incur large expenses, accounts of which will be presented for adjustment at your present session.

RETRENCHMENT AND ECONOMY.

Much has been said within and without the Legislature about retrenching expenses and an economical administration of the government. All the measures heretofore adopted have been, for want of completeness, like saving at the spigot and losing at the bung.

A few salaries have been reduced, and the Constitution

and government weakened thereby, while the main sluiceways of extravagance and waste have been kept open.

This session brings direct instructions from the people that may not be disregarded with impunity. The plan heretofore adopted by the opposition of favoring every measure of extravagance in order that they may hold the dominant party responsible for lavish expenditure, must now be abandoned or the Representatives will violate their pledges to their constituents. The Republican members can no longer continue reckless, under penalty of political as well as personal condemnation.

Now is the time to inaugurate a system of true practical economy, and the Legislature should begin at its own doors, and thence through all departments of the government.

1st. Cut off all useless employes and supernumeraries and fix the per diem of members and officers upon a cash basis according to a business standard.

2d. Revise the fee bill and equalize the pay of county officers, reduce the fees of clerks of courts, compel the assessor to make his own roll without the additional charge, and reduce the percentage for the assessment and collection of the revenue. The sheriffs and county judges' fees are reduced to a proper standard, but in one of the circuits, at least, the judge has overruled the law, and the sheriffs charge 50 per cent. more than the law allows.

3d. Require all taxes paid in cash, and thus do away with the inducements to fraud in speculating in scrip, making false returns, etc., and at the same time reduce the aggregate expenses of the government 25 per cent.

4th. Require jurors and witnesses' fees to be adjusted by the counties. As now adjusted, there is no protection against duplicate and false certificates. At least 25 per cent. in amount would be saved by settlement of these accounts where they occur, instead of issuing certificates to be paid by the Comptroller.

The adoption of the amendments to the Constitution, which took effect on 15th May last, has reduced the salaries of the State officers so low that those who were not resident at the capital could not comply with the law of last session and transfer their residence. The combination of speculators and political gamblers to destroy the credit of the State reduced scrip so low that the heads of departments received only equivalent to $700 per annum, and the Governor $1,000. The judges' pay is at starvation point, and unless the cash system is at once adopted it will be impossible to sustain their position.

The change in the mode of pay of the members of the Legislature from a salary to per diem affords an opportunity for the Representives to show the sincerity of their professions by adopting a reasonable sum for their services. Take $5 per day as a basis, to be be paid in cash, and the aggregate pay of the members would be, for a sixty-day session, $22,500, being a saving of $15,000 for the session, and affording each member as much real value as when he received the larger amount in scrip. By establishing the pay of the clerks upon the same basis, and limiting the number to the real necessities of the Legislature, half as much more may be saved, making an aggregate saving of from $20,000 to $25,000 at each session.

Another source of great loss to the State is the hurried passage of the general appropriation bill, at the close of the session, when thousands of dollars are inserted of extra allowances and improper items, and lugged through because it is too late to correct and save the bill. This is an evil that must be remedied, and it is the duty of the members to see that the general appropriation bill is passed early in the session, and if extra pay or old claims are presented let each stand upon its merits. No appropriation bill yet passed has met strictly the requisitions of the constitution.

In 1870, under the act of the Legislature, $4,000,000 of bonds were issued to the Jacksonville, Pensacola and Mobile Railroad Company in exchange for the same amount of bonds of the company, bearing the same date and rate of interest.

I have no report of the company in relation to their condition and purposes, but they have not complied with the law in the extension of their road to the Chattahoochee by 1st of July, though I am unofficially informed that its completion to that point is now rapidly progressing, and will soon be consummated.

It appears that bonds were entrusted by the company to one of the firms of swindlers who abound in new York, which, by fraud and villainy, have diverted much of the proceeds from the work for which they were issued, and there remains but $1,200,000 for the purposes of extending the road beyond the river.

The last million of the four were delivered, and are held in trust to be disposed of when the amount of $300,000 balance due the Internal Improvement Fund is paid. This sum is still unpaid, and remains a lien upon that portion of the road between Lake City and Quincy.

The losses of the company in no way involve loss to the State, as the securities held by the State can at any time be converted for sufficient to redeem the State bonds.

I am advised that the interest on the bonds has been paid by the company up to, and including January, 1872, but the coupons have not been delivered at the Treasury, and the coupons upon the railroad bonds held by the State therefor remain uncancelled.

These bonds are included in the Comptroller's statement of the State debt, without note or comment, and the inference is left that no provisions are made for the interest or principal save from taxation. Now the State holds an equal amount of first mortgage bonds of $16,000 a mile on a completed road which has sufficient business to pay its running expenses, the interest on these bonds, and enough to constitute a sinking fund sufficient to discharge the bonds when due. This being the fact, it is unjust to the people of the State to seek to convey a different impression abroad, and it can only be excused on the ground assumed by the writer above quoted from the "Floridian" that their "only hope is in the utter financial bankruptcy of the State."*

RECAPITULATION.

Liabilities—
Bonded debt . . . . $ 747,945 08
Floating debt 563,704 89

Total $1,311,649 97
Resources—
Revenue uncollected 604,672 45
Amount due from United States . . 220,000 00
                                    ─────────
                                               $824,672 45

Total debt, Jan., 1872 . . . . $486,977 52

After discharging all the liabilities of the Internal Improvement Fund and meeting all the grants made to railroads, rivers, canals, etc., we shall have at least four million acres of lands remaining, as a final resource for any State liabilities.

COLLECTORS OF REVENUE AND TREASURERS.

The attention of the Legislature is particularly directed to the importance of more stringent laws to protect the counties

---

*NOTE.—"No greater calamity could befall the State of Florida, while under the rule of its present carpetbag, scalawag officials, than to be placed in good financial credit. * * * * * Our only hope is in the State's utter financial bankruptcy; and Heaven grant that that may speedily come! On the other hand, establish for the State financial credit on Wall Street, so that Florida bonds can be sold by Reed & Co., as fast as issued, and you give these foul harpies a life-tenure of these offices. * * * * * The temporal salvation of the tax payers is in having scrip low, so that they can buy it to pay taxes with, and in having the State's financial credit low so that Reed & Co. can't sell State bonds so as to raise money with which to perpetuate their hold on office."—FLORIDIAN Aug 1, 1871.

and State against embezzlement or losses from inadequate bonds of treasurers and revenue officers.

As the law now stands, it is claimed that when the security on a bond of one of these officers lapses by death or bankruptcy it does not authorize the demand for a new bond. If this be so, the defect should be immediately remedied, and the officer required to file a new bond within thirty days after notice, or his office declared vacant.

The provisions of the bill known as the "Funding Bill," of the last session, should be made to apply to all officers of the revenue, and a default to pay over the public moneys should be declared a felony. Bonds, however good, are not sufficient to protect the Treasury against loss from dishonesty and fraud.

With a statute rendering defaults a crime, and another compelling the payment of all the revenues in lawful currency, the frauds upon the Treasury, and speculation in public funds by revenue officers, will cease; as it now stands it is impossible to prevent them.

In every case of default now existing, I have uniformly instructed suits to be commenced; but the law officers have either been indulgent or found the law inadequate.

It has been held that I could not remove an officer in the absence of the Legislature, either for inadequacy of bond, fraud, neglect, or any other cause, so that when cases have been reported to me which called for immediate action, I have been compelled to forego a remedy. I early called the attention of the Legislature to this difficulty, but no action was taken and much loss has occurred in consequence.

RAILROAD POLICY.

In 1855 the State entered upon a plan for the construction of a system of railroads that was comprehensive and highly creditable to the intelligence and sagacity of its projectors, but which in its results has been ingeniously and almost imperceptibly expensive.

Few of the people understand that, besides the United States lands granted, these roads have cost the State over *three millions of dollars*, and have *never paid one cent of tax* either on their lands, their property, or their income; yet, so far as can be ascertained, from the records and sources of information left by the old government, such is the fact.

When this administration was inaugurated it found this state of things, viz:

The Florida road, 154 miles, sold by the board of trustees, in 1866, for $116,000, or $753 per mile, leaving $232,000 in mortgage bonds, the interest of which was guaranteed by the

State, with a large amount of accumulated interest, for the payment of which suits have been commenced;

The Central road (from Jacksonville to Lake City), 60 miles, sold by the board in 1868 for $111,000, or nearly $1,850 per mile, leaving an indefinite amount of unpaid interest for the State to meet;

The Pensacola and Georgia, and the Tallahassee roads, forfeited and liable to be sold by the board, with $1,424,300 bonds outstanding, upon which interest was accumulating against the State of $99,700 per annum.

These roads were immediately sold by the present board, for nearly the par value of the bonds, and sufficient to discharge them and leave no incumbrance for the State, except for unpaid interest.

Thus we find that the railroads cost the State through the Internal Improvement Fund, and the counties—

Lands conveyed for interest, 1,000,000 acres at $1.25	$1,250,000
Proceeds of lands sold since 1850 to 1868.	750,000
Accumulated interest and indebtedness now existing, probably	1,000,000
Amount of bonds given by counties	500,000
	$3,500,000

The Legislature of 1869 changed the plan for the completion of the roads, and offered bonds to the amount of $16,000 per mile in exchange for first mortgage bonds of the roads. While, individually, I was opposed to further involving the State in connection with the roads, yet the almost unanimous voice of the Legislature favoring State aid, as in most of the other States, I sanctioned the plan; and there would exist no valid objection had the issue been confined to the extension of the lines, instead of being issued on the road already built.

Under the new policy the State holds the roads as security for the payment of interest and principal, and will derive from $20,000 to $30,000 annual revenue from taxation of the lands and property and income of the road.

Under the old it had to pay from $100,000 to $150,000 annual interest, after donating all the State lands within six miles on each side of the road, and both lands and road were exempt from taxation.

LEGISLATIVE RECORDS.

I again invite you to provide a more stringent means of protecting the legislative records and papers from mutilation, fraudulent endorsement, or surreptitious removal or destruction. It should be made a felony for an officer or member of the Legislature, or any officer of the government to change, suppress, mutilate, purloin, or in any manner contribute to defraud the will of the majority. Clerks have been known to alter bills in engrossing and enrolling; journals have failed to give a correct record of proceedings; members have removed and suppressed bills during or on their passage, and after passage, before they could be signed by the presiding officers. Bills after passage and enrollment have been found deposited, months after adjournment, in the private desk of the secretary of one of the bodies.

GRAND JURORS.

Either the grand jury system should be altogether abolished and criminals arraigned directly before the magistrate or court, or proper safeguards should be placed around it so as to prevent its subversion to individual ends or malicious purposes, and thus made an engine of oppression rather than a bulwark of protection.

In the United States District Court, the discretion given to the District Attorney to apply or dispense with the "test oath" has placed it within the power of that individual, with the assistance of the United States Marshal, to mould the grand jurors at his will, and this power has been used to wrong and oppress citizens of the State, innocent of crime, and caused enormous unnecessary cost to the Federal Government.

In one of the circuits of this State (the second), also, I am advised, that, by overriding the law and imposing new tests not nominated therein, the judge and attorney have taken control of the selection of the grand jury, and in the same manner made it subject to their own will.

The propriety or impropriety of the test does not affect the case. It is the power to impose or dispense with it at will by the attorney or the judge, after the venire has been made up, that destroys the dignity, independence, and impartial character of the jury, and renders it a vehicle for personal malice and injustice.

I do not know that further legislation is necessary or can be made adequate to remove the difficulty; but if it cannot be corrected, the Constitution should be amended and the grand jury abolished altogether.

Every Legislature since the inauguration of Governor Reed had shown itself corrupt in the highest degree; but the colored members at this session began to show more manhood by openly denouncing the tricks of the carpet-baggers and refusing to be enslaved by caucus rule. In these caucuses the carpet-baggers had heretofore succeeded in carrying their points in many instances by telling the colored members that if this measure should pass the Democrats would be terribly outdone and would make no further opposition to the so-called Republican party of the State; but the ousting of Christy at the last session, and the attempted ouster of Scott, colored, at the same session for a Democrat who had not been elected, and the defeat of the Civil Rights bill in the Senate through the tricks of carpet-baggers, had a tendency to inaugurate a stronger opposition to these men than had ever existed before. The following resolution, introduced by Hon. Daniel McInnis, colored, of Duval county, will illustrate this fact :

"WHEREAS, It appears that after several attempts to have a Civil Rights bill, which gives to every citizen the same protection in the enjoyment of his liberties; and, whereas, it has become a painful fact from the action of Liberty Billings, acting president *pro tem.* of the Senate of the State of Florida, and others who are opposed to seeing the colored citizens of this State enjoy the same rights that he and his associates do, we again witness on to-day another defeat of the Civil Rights bill, caused by only those who profess to be our friends in connection with this great cause of civil rights; therefore,

"*Resolved*, That we, the colored members, and those who honestly sympathize with us, do unhesitatingly repudiate such friendship, and do now and henceforth withdraw from and decline from ever affiliating with, politically, or to aid in electing any such man or men who have so basely misrepresented our people."

This resolution was considered as open treason to the carpet-bag dynasty, and the mover and resolution must at once be gotten rid of for the reason that its success might cause other outbreaks. The resolution was ruled out of order by Speaker Stearns, of Freedman's Bureau notoriety. Stearns was third in command of the ring forces in Florida, and it would not have been well for him, politically, if chief Osborn had been informed that such treason had taken place, and had succeeded in his presence. McInnis was fought in his county by the ring because he denounced them for treachery to his people; and with the power of the Federal office-holders and the ambition of some of the more ignorant ones of his race. Mr. McInnis, one of the most faithful and honest representatives of the colored people, was prevented from being returned to the Legislature.

A resolution was offered by W. K. Cessna, which showed that a decree pro confesso had been entered in the United States Court in Savannah, Ga., before W. B. Woods in favor of Francis Vose vs. Harrison Reed, et al., Trustees of the Internal Improvement Fund. This decree was made at Chambers on the 16th day of December, 1871. The decree was made and entered without the consent of the board of the fund and against the protest of their attorney and solicitor of record, James B. C. Drew, truly made. Attorney-General Drew was instructed to enter a motion in the United States Court in the Northern District of Florida to set aside the decree. A committee of five was appointed to investigate and report to the Assembly without delay by what means and manner, and by whom such an extraordinary decree, disposing of the entire, or nearly the entire, domain of the State to a mischievous and bankrupt railroad corporation, without the knowledge or consent of a majority of the said board of trustees, as appeared by a resolution of said board. The resolution showed that Hon. John S. Adams, treasurer of the trustees of the Internal Improvement Fund, had made affidavit before a magistrate in the county of Leon, on the 6th day of January, 1862, that one George W. Swepson, as confidential financial agent of the board of trustees of the fund had received on or about the 4th day of April, 1869, the sum of $472,065, the proceeds of the sale of the Pensacola and Georgia and the Tallahassee railroads, for the purpose of paying the outstanding first mortgage bonds of said railroads. It appears by said affidavit that Swepson had neglected and refused to pay the said first mortgage bonds or to account for any moneys so received by him. The trustees were instructed to take such immediate steps as would best secure the payment of the said moneys, and to enter and vigorously prosecute such legal actions, civil and criminal, against Swepson as would best secure the said trustees against the loss of said large sum of money, and punish the said Swepson for his gross violation of trusts and embezzlement. (See Assembly journal, regular session of 1872, p. 77.)

On the 10th day of January a resolution was unanimously passed by the Assembly, declaring gigantic frauds to have been committed in diversion of the proceeds of bonds issued under the law of 1869, chapter 1,716, relative to the J., P. & M. Railroad, and the Governor was directed to issue no more bonds until the validity of the act had been decided by the courts. On February 1st a resolution was adopted ordering the arrest of M. S. Littlefield for his failure to appear before the special committee appointed to investigate the acts and doings of the J., P. & M. Railroad. Littlefield was not arrested, and the resolution was undoubtedly passed to extort money from him. The records are replete with such resolutions to deceive the public and extort money from individuals interested in any supposed public enterprise where the Legislature would be called upon to enable them to carry such enterprises into execution. The Legislature of 1871 passed a concurrent resolution, which emanated from Purman and his immediate carpetbag associates, authorizing the appointment of a committee of five, three from the Assembly and two from the Senate, to proceed to the office of the Treasurer of the State and "inspect, examine and compare the books, files and accounts and records of the same, and to cancel and destroy all Comptroller's warrants and Treasurer's certificates that may have been received and on file in said office, excepting warrants issued under the act approved February 18, 1870, known as greenback scrip." The committee was directed to make a full report to the Legislature of the accounts and condition of the Treasurer's office, and the numbers and amount of warrants and scrip that may have been cancelled and effectually destroyed by the authority of said resolution. This committee consumed twenty-one days after the adjournment of the Legislature of 1871 in a supposed searching examination to find corruption. They reported that their investigation was quite laborious and required deep scrutiny into figures, and that they had honestly obeyed the resolution passed at the last session of the Legislature, and had destroyed by fire $1,175,934.82. The committee commended very highly the manner in which the Treasurer's books were kept, but said nothing about the books of the Comptroller. The report of the committee was accepted in both Houses, and the committee discharged. It could be seen from the time of the report of this committee that the Treasurer, Conover, and Purman, the chairman of the committee, who had not been very intimate bedfellows, now became the best of friends.

Some time subsequent to the adoption of this report, it was discovered that some of the committee must have fallen asleep, as thirty thousand dollars, or thereabouts, of the certificates reported to have been cancelled and denominated as "blue scrip," found its way back into the Treasury and was again paid by the State. (See report of Senate committee, journal of 1872, p. 377.)

At this session of the Legislature rebellious outbreaks by the colored members were very frequent and disastrous to the carpet-bag plunder system. The delegation elected from Leon county, all colored, was elected against the deadly opposition of the ring, and stood opposed to the system of plunder, which had been inaugurated in almost every county of the State. The author of this work and John W. Wyatt had been fought very bitterly by the ring during their canvass in 1871 for the Legislature, and it was whispered that fraud would be committed to keep us out of our seats; but the whites in the county stood with us as against the ring, and therefore they were afraid to attempt it. One can imagine about how much love existed between the Leon county delegation and the ring. W. H. Gleason and other carpet-baggers, thinking to soon get rid of Reed by impeachment, commenced getting their schemes in readiness for transformation into laws. An infamous scheme was introduced by Gleason, of Dade, "to authorize corporations to change their names, consolidate their capital stock and merge their corporate powers." This measure was adopted by the caucus without any apparent opposition, the Leon delegation not voting for or against the measure in the caucus. This action on the part of the delegation led Gleason and the other members in the scheme to believe that all present were bound by the action of the caucus. The Democrats of the Assembly were notified as to the action of the caucus and agreed to hold themselves in readiness for a grand assault against the bill when it came up for consideration. When the measure came up for final consideration, Gleason, now confident that things were all right, led off in support of the bill. The Leon delegation followed in opposition, much to the surprise of Gleason and the other friends of the bill. Long faces could be discovered among the members of the ring as the Democrats would applaud John W. Wyatt, colored, as he thundered against the bill. This speech of Mr. Wyatt was the first ever ordered spread on the journal in the Legislature of Florida. The speech was as follows:

MR. SPEAKER:

There is to all appearances a dark and hidden meaning enveloped in the bill now before this Assembly, introduced by the honorable member from Dade, which I desire to call attention to. The title of this bill is to "authorize corporations to change their names, consolidate their capital stock, and merge their corporate powers."

We should ponder well over each sentence embraced in the title. In the first place why should corporations desire to consolidate unless by the unity and coalition thus formed they intended to become a vast and extended power, governing the people and exercising an influence, the magnitude of which would appall us? Then again, this consolidation of power would wield a powerful influence for good or evil, and experience and history furnishes proof that large, all-absorbing companies generally exert their influence in an evil direction. Such a consolidation would engender dissatisfaction and cause disorder and distress among corporations of less weight, and would be fraught with many disadvantages to parties desiring to invest a small amount of capital. Capital needs no legislation in order to provide for its use. Capital is strong enough to take care and provide for itself, but corporations are a dangerous power, especially large or consolidated corporations, and the American people fear them and view them with distrust. Take, for instance, the Pennsylvania Central Railroad, which has and is daily encircling with extended arms the smaller roads and railway corporations throughout the Union. As a result of such consolidations, look what a stretch of power and authority is placed within the hands of Thomas Scott, the president of that railroad. We, who are here in Florida, cannot conceive of the vastness of his schemes. We are too far removed from his field of operations, but I am credibly informed that, by means of the power that he and his board of directors possess, they carry everything desired throughout the State of Pennsylvania.

W want no *Tom Scotts*, *Jim Fisks* or *Vanderbilts* in this

State to govern us, by means of which they would influence legislation tending to advance personal interests.

The great curse of Florida has been dishonest corporations, rings and cliques, with an eye single to their central interest, and if this bill is suffered to pass this Assembly, in my opinion we may look for a continuation of abuses and a usurpation of the rights of citizens who may be opposed to the evil machinations such as are generally exerted by consolidated bodies.

The second clause in the title of this bill is to consolidate their capital stock. What a palpable farce! Look, gentlemen, thoroughly into this sentence. If such glaring opportunities for swindling, and forcing preconcerted measures, are fostered and encouraged by this Assembly, we would be denounced and aspersions of a foul nature be cast at our character, even by our constituents. They send us here to legislate wisely for the good of the people of this State, and not to favor jobs and schemes that emanate from the brain of political tricksters, and intriguing and designing parties.

We are here for a different purpose. We are assembled here to guard the interests of this State. Does this measure now before us tend to foster or enhance the condition of this State? No! It is plainly a coercive measure, intended to engulf the capital of minor corporations.

Were this bill to pass, men of limited means would be extremely cautious about investing in or giving aid to corporations, for fear their capital stock would be swallowed up by some tottering and unsound institution, and used to bolster up and furnish additional strength to a rotten corporation.

What assurance would be given to the minority of stockholders of a company, that had been merged into another and their capital stock consolidated, that would satisfy them that their rights would be safely protected after having been coerced into a scheme which they supposed to be fraudulent?

The last clause in this title is, "to merge their corporate powers." This sentence certainly needs careful examination, for I can readily see that it will prove a most dangerous combination of power, and it should be strenuously opposed by the whole strength of this Assembly.

Each corporation has certain powers and privileges embodied within its sphere of action, and it is now proposed to merge the powers of the different corporations and embrace them all in one strong and all-powerful combination.

The recent expose of the Tammany Ring in New York has satisfied all right thinking men that the power exercised by strong bodies, composed of many corporations, is the most dangerous to the public good and safety. Therefore it ill becomes us to pass a bill enveloped in darkness, as the title to this bill indicates it to be.

The gentleman who introduced this bill, it would seem, has a hobby for corporations. I am credibly informed that his signature is attached to no less than eight articles of association in this State. Doubtless the true intent of this bill is to consolidate these eight corporations, with their powers and capital stock, into one grand scheme for the controlling of future public works requiring State aid. As a sample of the magnitude and grandness of these schemes, I will here state that one of the eight corporations above mentioned declares its capital at ten millions of dollars. The shares are fixed at the low price of one hundred thousand dollars each. By referring to the Laws of 1868, Chapter 1,639, No. 15, I find an exhaustive law on corporations, which fully dictates their duties, powers and liabilities, etc., and I deem it imprudent to interfere with this law, because I find it fully answers all the requirements of a legal body corporate. Therefore, Mr. Speaker, as there is much doubt and uncertainty existing regarding the usefulness and effectiveness, in a right direction, of the powers which this bill would grant, I move that it be indefinitely postponed.

We now come to the last and most desperate attempt to get rid of Governor Reed by impeachment. This time the farce was not conducted with even the faint semblance of fairness which was displayed in the last attempt. The ring being outgeneraled in their former attempts, were determined to conduct things on the *ex parte* and Star Chamber plan. The resolution of investigation did not mention the name of Governor Reed, but State officials; and the less informed members of the Legislature did not know what was going on. During the investigation, Republican caucuses were held in the Assembly hall two and three times a week, and the state of the country and the Republican party were fully discussed. Cessna, the chairman of the Committee on Investigation, would be put forward to stir the blood of the colored brother by singing "John Brown's body lies mouldering in the clay," "Sherman's March through Georgia," etc. While singing these songs Cessna could imitate the plantation negro preacher in looks, voice and acts as no other carpet-bagger could, and in many instances could put to shame the best negro minstrel. These songs being considered old freedom songs, made Cessna very popular with most of the colored members. Nothing would be said in the caucus with reference to impeachment, but Purman would be on hand to denounce Reed and tell the colored brother "if God would take Reed out of the way it would be better for them and the Republican party." This argument, in connection with Cessna's songs, had great effect on many of the colored members and on the less informed whites as well. The most of the Democratic members at this session, as in the former session, were in favor of impeachment, not because they believed Reed's traducers were honest, but because they knew that every attempt at impeachment would strengthen them and imperil honest Republicanism.

On the 6th of February, Cessna's investigating committee made its report, which was loaded with numerous charges against Governor Reed. These charges sounded so very damaging that some of the Governor's most intimate friends were deceived by them and went to him and asked him to resign his office. The Governor said to them that if the Legislature would give him an half hour he would refute successfully every charge they had reported against him, and he felt perfectly confident that he would be clearly exonerated, if he were allowed a hearing before the High Court of Impeachment, in case he should be impeached by the Assembly. John R. Scott, of Duval County, spoke in favor of Governor Reed, but afterwards, as was prearranged, voted for the report for the usual consideration. The report was unanimously adopted, and Governor Reed stood suspended. The report was ordered spread on the journal, but it, with the alleged evidence, was suppressed, and even the order does not appear upon the journal. Governor Reed was never allowed to know what allegations were made. A committee of seven was appointed to immediately present articles of impeachment to the Senate. Another committee of three was appointed by the chair to go to the Senate and at the bar thereof, in the name of the Assembly and of all the people of Florida, to impeach Harrison Reed, Governor of Florida, of high crimes and misdemeanors in office, and that the committee demand that the Senate take order for the aforesaid Harrison Reed to answer to said impeachment. Boyd, Cessna and Duke were appointed as said committee. The committee performed its duty, and the Senate took order accordingly. A committee consisting of Cessna, Graham, of Manatee, Gibbs, Hires, Johnson, Osgood and Wallace, was appointed to prepare and report articles of impeachment against the Governor. As one of the members of the committee, I never saw the report of the investigating committee nor any other evidences upon which the subsequent articles of impeach- presented by the committee were based. Cessna pulled a roll of papers out of his pocket, which he said were the articles he would present. They had been prepared by Fred Dockray, Reed's old enemy, made so because the Governor had refused to appoint him Attorney-General. The following is the report of the committee appointed to prepare the articles of impeach- ment.

Hon. M. L. STEARNS, Speaker of the Assembly:

SIR—Your Special Committee appointed to prepare and re- port Articles of Impeachment against Harrison Reed, Governor, begleave to report for the action of this Assembly the accompany ing articles.

      W. K. CESSNA, Chairman,
      CHAS. F. HIERS,
      C. GILLIS,
      EDGAR M. GRAHAM,
      J. W. JOHNSON,
      J. WALLACE,
      ALFRED B. OSGOOD.

ARTICLES OF IMPEACHMENT

Exhibited by the Assembly of the State of Florida, in the name of themselves and of all the people of Florida, against Har- rison Reed, Goverrner of Florida, in maintenance and sup- port of their impeachment against him for high crimes and misdemeanors in office, for incompetency and malfeasance, and conduct detrimental to good morals:

ARTICLE I.

That said Harrison Reed, Governor of Florida, in the year of our Lord one thousand eight hundred and seventy, at Talla- hassee, in the State of Florida, unmindful of the high duties of his office, of his oath of office, and of the requirement of the Constitution that he shall see that the laws are faithfully executed, did unlawfully and in violation of the Constitution and laws of the State of Florida, cause to be issued, and did himself sign his official signature as Governor, to a large number of State bonds to the amount of five hundred and twenty-eight thousand ($528,000) dollars in excess of the amount of bonds authorized to be issued by the act of the Legislature of the State of Florida, entitled an act to alter and amend an act entitled an act to perfect the public works of the State, approved June 24, A. D. 1869, approved January 28, A. D. 1870, with intent then and there to violate the said act, whereby the said Harrison Reed, Governor of Florida, did then and there commit and was guilty of a high crime in office, of imcompetency and malfeasance.

ARTICLE II.

That in the year of our Lord one thousand eight hundred and seventy, at Tallahassee, in the State of Florida, said Harrison Reed, Governor of Florida, unmindful of the high duties of his office, of his oath of office, and in violation of the Constitution of the State of Florida, and contrary to the provisions of an act entitled an act to alter and amend an act entitled an act to perfect the public works of the State, approved June 24, A. D. 1869, approved January 28, 1870, did then and there, with intent to violate the Constitution of the State and the act aforesaid, and without authority of law, fraudulently conspire to issue State bonds to the amount of one million dollars ($1,000,000), for the purpose of purchasing the stock of the Florida, Atlantic and Gulf Central Railroad Company, for the use and benefit of persons and parties, and with full knowledge of and consent to said purpose, and in collusion with such persons and parties, for his and their pecuniary benefit, whereby said Harrison Reed, Governor of Florida, did then and there commit and was guilty of a high crime in office, and of incompetency and malfeasance.

ARTICLE III.

That said Harrison Reed, Governor of Florida, unmindful of the high duties of his office, and of his oath of office, in the year of our Lord one thousand eight hundred and seventy, at Tallahassee, in the State of Florida, did cause to be issued and did himself sign his official signature as Governor, to one million dollars of State Bonds, for the purpose of purchasing the stock of the Florida, Atlantic and Gulf Central Railroad Company for the use and benefit of persons and parties, contrary to and in violation of the Constitution of the State of Florida, and of the laws of the State of Florida, and especially in violation of an act of the Legislature of the State of Florida, entitled an act to alter and amend an act entitled an act to perfect the public works of the State, approved June 24, A. D. 1869, approved January 28, A. D. 1870, and with intent to violate the laws of the State of Florida, and especially said act, whereby the said Harrison Reed, Governor of the State of Florida, did then and there commit and was guilty of a high crime in office, and of incompetency and malfeasance.

ARTICLE IV.

That said Harrison Reed, Governor of Florida, in the year of our Lord one thousand eight hundred and seventy, at Tallahassee, in the State of Florida, unmindful of the high duties of his office, and of his oath of office, and in violation of the Constitution and laws of the State, and especially of an act entitled an act to alter and amend, etc., did cause to be issued, and did himself sign his official signature as Governor, to four million dollars of State bonds for the use and benefit of the Jacksonville, Pensacola and Mobile Railroad Company in the State of Florida, having full notice of the fraudulent title of said company to the property of the Pensacola and Georgia and Tallahassee railroads, and with intent to violate the Constitution and laws of the State of Florida, and especially of the act of the Legislature of the State of Florida entitled an act to alter and amend an act entitled an act to perfect the public works of the State approved June 24, A. D. 1869, approved January 28, A. D. 1870, whereby the said Harrison Reed, Governor, etc.

ARTICLE V.

That said Harrison Reed, Governor of Florida, in the year of our Lord one thousand eight hundred and seventy-one, at Tallahassee, in the State of Florida, unmindful of the high duties of his office, and of his oath of office, did unlawfully conspire with one David L. Yulee, and with other persons unknown, to issue bonds of the State of Florida, to the amount of one million dollars for the use and benefit of said Yulee and other persons, in violation of the Constitution and laws of the State, and especially of the provisions of the act of the Legislature of the State of Florida entitled an act to perfect the public works of the State, approved June 24, A. D. 1869, and with intent to violate and disregard the said acts, whereby the said Harrison Reed, Governor of Florida, did then and there commit and was guilty of a high crime in office and of incompetency and malfeasance.

ARTICLE VI.

That Harrison Reed, Governor of Florida, on or about the fifteenth day of November, A. D. 1871, at Tallahassee, in the State of Florida, and at divers other times, in the year of our Lord, one thousand eight hundred and seventy-one, at Tallahassee, in the State of Florida, and at New York city, unmindful of the high duties of his office, and of his oath of office, and in violation of the Constitution and laws of the State, and especially in violation of the provisions of the act of the Legislature of the State of Florida entitled an act to perfect the public works of the State, approved June 24, A. D. 1869, did cause to be issued, and did himself sign his official signature to one million of dollars of State bonds for the use and benefit of one David L. Yulee, and of other persons unknown, with intent to violate and disregard the provisions of said act, whereby the said Harrison Reed, Governor of Florida, did then and there commit and was guilty of a high crime in office and of incompetency and malfeasance.

ARTICLE VII.

That said Harrison Reed, Governor of Florida, in the year of our Lord one thousand eight hundred and sixty-nine, and in the year of our Lord one thousand eight hundred and seventy, in the city of New York, and at divers other times and places in said years, unmindful of the high duties of his office, and of his oath of office, and in violation of the Constitution and laws of the State of Florida, and especially the act of the Legislature of the State of Florida, entitled an act to fund the outstanding debt of the State, approved August 6, 1868, and an act entitled an act to fund the outstanding debt of the State, approved February 1, 1869, did fraudulently conspire with one Milton S. Littlefield, and with divers other persons, to embezzle the moneys received from the hypothecation of State bonds issued under and by authority of the aforesaid acts of the Legislature of the State of Florida, and did embezzle a large amount of the moneys received from the said bonds, to-wit, the amount of $22,000, with intent then and there to violate the laws of the State of Florida, and especially the said acts, whereby said Harrison Reed, Governor of Florida, did then and there commit and was guilty of a high crime in office, and of incompetency and malfeasance.

ARTICLE VIII.

That said Harrison Reed, Governor of Florida, in the year of our Lord one thousand eight hundred and seventy-one, a

Tallahassee, in the State of Florida, unmindful of the high duties of his office, and of his oath of office, and in violation of the Constitution and laws of the State, did receive from Milton S. Littlefield the sum of three thousand five hundred dollars as a consideration to influence his official action in sustaining the claim of the Jacksonville, Pensacola and Mobile Railroad Company to the title of the property of the Pensacola and Georgia and Tallahassee and Florida, Atlantic and Gulf Central Railroads, and as a further consideration to influence his official action in all matters between the State of Florida and the said Jacksonville, Pensacola and Mobile Railroad Company, whereby the said Harrison Reed, Governor, did commit and was guilty of a high crime in office, of incompetency and malfeasance, and of conduct detrimental to good morals.

ARTICLE IX.

That said Harrison Reed, Governor of Florida, in the year of our Lord one thousand eight hundred and sixty-eight, in the city of New York, and at divers other times and places in the year of our Lord one thousand eight hundred and sixty-nine, unmindful of the high duties of his office and of his oath of office, and in violation of the Constitution and laws of the State of Florida, and with intent then and there to violate and disregard the Constitution and laws of the State of Florida, did then and there conspire with one Charles Pond and with one E. B. Bulkley of the city of New York, to defraud the State of Florida of Fifteen Thousand Dollars ($15,000) of Bonds of the State of Florida, and in pursuance of said conspiracy did defraud the State of Florida of Fifteen Thousand Dollars of the Bonds of the State of Florida applied to the purchase of arms and equipments for the State of Florida, whereby the said Harrison Reed, Governor of Florida, did then and there commit and was guilty of a high crime in office and of incompetency and malfeasance.

ARTICLE X.

That said Harrison Reed, Governor of Florida, in the year of our Lord one thousand eight hundred and sixty-nine, at Tallahassee, in the State of Florida, unmindful of the high duties of his office and of his oath of office, and in violation of the Constitution and laws of the State of Florida, and especially of the act of the Legislature of the State of Florida, entitled an act to provide for and encourage a liberal system of Internal Improvements in this State, approved January 6, A. D. 1855, and with full intent to violate said act, did receive from one I. K. Roberts, Esq., in behalf of the Florida Railroad Company, a draft for the sum of Eleven Hundred and Forty Dollars ($1140) which was paid in currency of the United States to said Harrison Reed, Governor and Chairman of the Board of Trustees of the Internal Improvement Fund of the State of Florida, and did tender to the Treasurer of the State of Florida Scrip of the State in lieu of said currency, which was due to the Sinking Fund on account of said Florida Railroad Company, whereby the said Harrison Reed, Governor of Florida, was guilty of a high crime in office and of incompetency and malfeasance.

ARTICLE XI.

That said Harrison Reed, Governor of Florida, in the month of January of the year of our Lord one thousand eight hundred and seventy-two, at Tallahassee, in the State of Florida, unmindful of the high duties of his office and of the dignities and proprieties thereof, and of his oath of office, and in violation of the Constitution of the State and of the laws thereof, and with intent to violate and disregard his official duties and of the requirements of the Constitution and laws of the State of Florida, did conspire to influence one J. W. Toer, a Justice of the Peace, in the exercise of his judicial action upon a case pending before him, to-wit: "The case of the State of Florida against George W. Swepson," whereby the said Harrison Reed, Governor of Florida, did then and there commit and was guilty of a high crime and misdemeanor in office and of incompetency and malfeasance.

ARTICLE XII.

That Harrison Reed, Governor of Florida, in the year of our Lord one thousand eight hundred and seventy-one, at Jacksonville, in the State of Florida, in violation of the Constitution and laws of the State of Florida, of the high duties of his office and of his oath of office, and with full intent to violate and disregard the laws of the State of Florida, did unlawfully conspire with one Aaron Barnett to prostitute his official influence and position to the uses and purposes of the said Barnett, in receiving the sum of Ten Thousand Dollars ($10,000) from the said Barnett for his official sanction and signature to a contract for the conveyance of Internal Improvement lands to the said Barnett as assignee of said contract from the Jacksonville, Pensacola and Mobile Railroad Company, and did receive the said sum of Ten Thousand Dollars ($10,000) from the said Barnett for the reasons and purposes aforesaid, whereby the said Harrison Reed, Governor of Florida, did then and there commit and was guilty of a high crime and misdemeanor in office, of incompetency and malfeasance, and of conduct detrimental to good morals.

And the Assembly of the State of Florida, by protestation, saving to itself the liberty of exhibiting at any time hereafter any further Articles or other Accusations on Impeachment against the said Harrison Reed, Governor of Florida, and also of replying to his answers which he shall make unto the Articles herein preferred against him, and of offering proof to the same and every part thereof, and to all and every other Article, Accusation or Impeachment which shall be exhibited by them as the case shall require, do demand, that the said Harrison Reed may be put to answer the high crimes and misdemeanors in office herein charged against him, and that such proceedings, examinations, trials and judgments may be thereupon had and given as may be agreeable to law and justice.

After reading these articles, John W. Butler, of Santa Rosa County, offered a resolution that the Assembly resolve itself into a committee of the whole and attend the managers appointed by the Assembly to present the Articles of Impeachment exhibited by the Assembly against Harrison Reed, Governor of Florida; and at 5 o'clock P. M., the whole body, preceded by its chairman, supported by the clerks of the Assembly, followed the managers to the Senate chamber and presented the Articles. The Assembly, after a brief absence, returned and the committee rose. The following order was taken by the Senate:

Mr. Purman offered the following resolution:

WHEREAS, The Assembly, on this 10th day of February, 1872, by a committee of their members, at the bar of the Senate, impeached Harrison Reed, Governor, of high crimes and misdemeanors, incompetency, malfeasance in office, and conduct detrimental to good morals, and informed the Senate that the Assembly will in due time exhibit particular articles of impeachment against him, and make good the same, and likewise demanded that the Senate take order for the appearance of said Harrison Reed, Governor, to answer to said impeachment; Therefore,

Resolved, That the Senate will take proper order thereon, of which due notice shall be given to the Assembly;

Which was adopted.

Mr. Wentworth offered the following resolution:

WHEREAS, Harrison Reed, Governor, has been this day impeached by the Assembly of the State of Florida of high crimes and misdemeanors, incompetency, malfeasance in office, and conduct detrimental to good morals;

Resolved, That the President of the Senate be, and he is hereby, ordered to issue his warrant issuing to the Sergeant-at-Arms of the Senate, directing him to notify the said Harrison Reed, Governor, that he has this day been impeached by the Assembly of the State of Florida of high crimes and misdemeanors, incompetency, malfeasance in office, and conduct detrimental to good morals, and that he is deemed under arrest and disqualified from performing any of the duties of his office as Governor of Florida until acquitted by the Senate of Florida, and the Sergeant-at-Arms is hereby ordered and directed to make return to this body at once of his doing herein;

Which was adopted.

Mr. Henderson offered the following resolution:

Resolved by the Senate, That the Senate of the State of Florida will organize as a High Court of Impeachment for the purposes of the trial of His Excellency Harrison Reed, Governor of Florida, on Tuesday next, 13th, inst., at 12 o'clock M.

Mr. Jenkins offered the following as a substitute:

Resolved, That the Senate will proceed to organize as a High Court of Impeachment for the trial of Harrison Reed, Governor, on the 14th inst., at 12 o'clock M.

Resolved, further, That the Secretary of the Senate immediately notify the Assembly of the adoption of this resolution.

Mr. Henderson moved that the substitute be laid on the table.

The yeas and nays were called for, with the following result:

Those voting in the affirmative were—

Messrs. Adams, Atkins, Crawford, Ginn, Henderson, Kendrick, McKinnon, Moragne, McCaskill, Sutton and Weeks —11.

Those voting in the negative were—

Messrs. Billings, Dennis, Eagan, Hill, Hillyer, Jenkins, Johnson, Locke, Meacham, Pearce, Purman and Wentworth—12.

So it was not laid on the table.

The substitute was then adopted.

Mr. Henderson offered the following resolution:

Resolved by the Senate, That a committee of three be appointed to notify the Hon. E. M. Randall, Chief Justice of the State of Florida, that the House of Representatives of this State, have, through their committee, appeared at the bar of the

Senate, and impeached His Excellency Harrison Reed, Governor of Florida, of high crimes and misdemeanors, and that the Senate will organize as a High Court of Impeachment on Wednesday, the 14th inst., for the purpose of the trial of the said Harrison Reed, and that he be requested to be present to preside at the same.

Which was adopted.

Mr. Henderson offered the following resolution:

Resolved, That the Secretary of the Senate be instructed to notify His Excellency Harrison Reed, Governor of Florida, that a committee of the House of Representatives have this day appeared at the bar of the Senate, and in the name of all the people of the State of Florida, impeached him, the said Harrison Reed, Governor, etc., of high crimes and misdemeanors, and that the Senate have passed a resolution, of which the following is a copy:

Resolved, That the Senate will proceed to organize as a High Court of Impeachment for the trial of Harrison Reed, Governor, on the 14th inst, at 12 o'clock M.

Resolved, further, That the Secretary of the Senate immediately notify the Assembly of the adoption of this resolution:

Which was adopted.

Reed having been impeached, the conspirators were anxious, in case they were forced to try him, to secure beforehand all the votes they could for conviction, whether the evidence warranted it or not. They knew that Liberty Billings, who was of the defunct "mule team" faction, and then Senator from Nassau County, had no good blood for Purman and that gang, so they sought to secure his vote by electing him president *pro tem.* of the Senate, which placed him in position as Lieutenant-Governor. All the conspirators voted for him, and he was accordingly elected. The Sergeant-at-Arms returned and made return that he had duly complied with the order of the Senate, and had served a copy of his warrant upon His Excellency, Harrison Reed. A committee of three was appointed to attend the Lieutenant-Governor to the executive chamber to take the oath of office. Day now assumed the office of Governor by proclamation, but it is noticeable that the proclamation was not attested by any Secretary of State. The Democrats had by this time become very much dissatisfied in reference to Articles V and VI because they reflected upon the character of ex-United States Senator David L. Yulee. Some of them threatened to combine with

Governor Reed against the conspirators if those articles were not withdrawn, and in order to bridge over this threatened gulf midway, the conspirators planned the following resolution and additional articles, which were adopted:

Mr. Graham, of Manatee, was allowed to offer the following resolutions:

WHEREAS, The journals of this House incidentally reflect on the Hon. D. L. Yulee in the matter of the Articles of Impeachment against Harrison Reed; and, whereas, upon subsequent examination, we find that great injustice has been unintentionally done Mr. Yulee in the said articles; therefore,

Resolved, That the managers appointed by this House to present the aforesaid Articles of Impeachment to the Senate, sitting as a High Court of Impeachment, are hereby ordered and instructed to withdraw from the said Articles of Impeachment any matter which may in any manner reflect in a censurable manner upon the Hon. David L. Yulee, and for that purpose are hereby instructed to withdraw Articles V and VI of the said Articles of Impeachment for amendment; that a copy of this resolution be handed to the Hon. David L. Yulee by the Chief Clerk of the House, and that the same be spread on the journals thereof.

Resolved, That the managers be and are hereby instructed to present the following additional Articles of Impeachment against Harrison Reed, Governor of the State of Florida:

ADDITIONAL ARTICLES OF IMPEACHMENT AND REPLICATION TO THE PLEAS FILED BY HARRISON REED, GOVERNOR.

ARTICLE XIII.

That said Harrison Reed, Governor of Florida, unmindful of the high duties of his office, and of his oath of office, and in violation of the Constitution and laws of the State of Florida, between the 8th day of September, A. D. 1868, and the 1st day of July, A. D. 1869, in the city of New York, did unlawfully and improperly appropriate moneys belonging to the State of Florida, to-wit: The sum of $6,948.63, placed in his possession by James D. Westcott, Jr., and received by him as a Trustee—in this: That the said Harrison Reed, Governor, did substitute for said moneys certain securities of the State of Florida, purchased by him at a large discount, and did pay said securities into the Treasury of the State of Florida, and appropriate to his own personal use and benefit the difference arising from said speculation, and with intent then and there to defraud the State of the full value of said moneys in his hands as Trustee for the people of the State, whereby the said Harrison Reed, Governor of Florida, did then and there commit and was guilty of a high crime and misdemeanor in office, of incompetency and malfeasance.

ARTICLE XIV.

That said Harrison Reed, Governor of Florida, unmindful of the high duties of his office, of his oath of office, and in violation of the Constitution and laws of the State of Florida, at Tallahassee, in the State of Florida, on or about the 1st day of January, in the year of our Lord one thousand eight hundred and seventy, and on divers other days and times in said year, also on divers other days and times in the years of our Lord one thousand eight hundred and seventy-one and seventy-two, did embezzle moneys belonging to the State of Florida, to-wit: The sum of one thousand eight hundred and ninety-seven dollars and twenty-four cents ($1,897.24), in the possession of Jonathan C. Gibbs, Secretary of State, and did appropriate said moneys to his own use, benefit and purposes, then and there with intent to violate the Constitution and laws of the State of Florida, whereby said Harrison Reed, Governor of Florida, did then and there commit and was guilty of a high crime and misdemeanor in office, of incompetence and malfeasance in office.

ARTICLE XV.

That said Harrison Reed, Governor of Florida, unmindful of the high duties of his office, and of his oath of office, in violation of the Constitution and laws of the State of Florida on the 24th day of April, in the year of our Lord one thousand eight hundred and seventy-one, and on divers other days and times, in said year, at Tallahassee, in the State of Florida, did divert, misapply, and unlawfully and improperly appropriate the sum of eleven thousand dollars ($11,000), of the contingent fund appropriated by the Legislature of the State of Florida, and did appropriate and apply a large portion of said sum to his own personal use and benefit with full intent to violate the Constitution and laws of the State of Florida, whereby said Harrison Reed, Governor of Florida, did then and there commit and was guilty of a high crime and misdemeanor in office, of incompetency and of malfeasance.

ARTICLE XVI.

That said Harrison Reed, Governor of Florida, unmindful of the high duties of his office, of his oath of office and in violation of the Constitution and laws of the State of Florida, and of the dignities and proprieties of his high office, on the eighth day of ———, in the year of our Lord one thousand eight hundred and seventy, at Tallahassee, in the State of Florida, did wrongfully and maliciously misrepresent and fals fy his official acts and doings to one T. W. Brevard, with full intent thereby to misrepresent and falsify, for the purpose of affecting the interests of certain persons and parties, and to the detriment of the public interests and in violation of the express provisions of the Constitution of the State, whereby said Harrison Reed, Governor of Florida, did then and there commit and was guilty of a high crime and misdemeanor in office, of incompetency and malfeasance, and of conduct detrimental to good morals.

Resolved, That the managers and counsel presenting Articles of Impeachment against Harrison Reed, Governor, be instructed to file the following replication to the pleas of Harrison Reed, Governor, to said Articles of Impeachment:

In the Assembly of the State of Florida, February 16th, 1872.

The Assembly have considered the several pleas of Harrison Reed, Governor of Florida, to the several Articles of Impeachment against him exhibited by them in the name of themselves and all the people of the State of Florida, and reserving to themselves all advantages of exception to the insufficiency of his answer to each and all of the several Articles exhibited against said Harrison Reed, Governor, and for the replication to said pleas do say that the said Harrison Reed, Governor, is guilty of the high crimes, misdemeanors and malfeasance in office and conduct detrimental to good morals charged in said Articles, and that the Assembly are ready to prove the same.

The most singular feature of this whole impeachment scheme was that while the investigating committee could find sufficient witnesses in Florida upon whose evidence to base thirteen articles of impeachment, the board of managers could not find witnesses in the State to prove any one of those charges—for the proof of any one of them would have been sufficient.

The following is the resolution adopted asking for further time, offered by Mr. Graham, of Manatee:

WHEREAS, Additional time is necessarily required by the managers and counsel prosecuting articles of impeachment against Harrison Reed, Governor, before the Honorable Senate, to amend articles already presented, and to prepare and present others, and to procure the attendance of witnesses; and whereas, a large number of said witnesses reside out of the State and in remote parts of the United States, and their testimony is necessary to prove the various matters charged in said articles of impeachment, and without which testimony the Assembly, by its managers and counsel, cannot at this time safely proceed to the trial of the said Harrison Reed; therefore,

Resolved, That the managers be directed to proceed to the bar of the Senate and ask that necessary time be allowed the managers and counsel to amend articles presented, and to prepare and present others, and to procure the attendance of necessary witnesses to the trial.

The Assembly having appeared at the bar of the Senate on the 10th day of February and impeached Governor Reed, that body on the same day passed an order that the Senate notify the Assembly that the Senate would sit as a high court of impeachment on Wednesday, the 14th of February, for the trial of Gov. Reed. Immediately after the order had been passed a resolution was offered that the two houses adjourn *sine die* on February 19th. The resolution was postponed until the following Thursday. On the 14th of February a committee was appointed to escort Chief Justice Randall to the Senate Chamber. He arrived and was sworn by Associate Justice Westcott. The Chief Justice then swore in the Senators, when the Sergeant-at-Arms made the following proclamation:

"Hear ye! Hear ye! Hear ye! All persons are ordered to keep silence, under penalty of imprisonment, while the Senate of Florida is sitting for the trial of Harrison Reed, Governor of Florida, for high crimes and misdemeanors. God save the State of Florida and this honorable Senate!"

A short while after the court had organized it adjourned to await the report of the committee appointed to draft rules of procedure and practice for the guidance of the Senate while sitting as a high court of impeachment. On February 15th the court met and the Senate adopted rules for the government of the Senate while proceeding with the trial. (See Senate journal, page 304). A summons was made, returnable at 8 o'clock p. m. the same day. J. P. C. Emmons appeared at the bar of the Senate with authority from Governor Reed to act as his counsel, and he presented the following:

"In the matter of the impeachment of Harrison Reed, Governor of the State of Florida:

"I, Harrison Reed, Governor of the State of Florida, having been notified to appear before this honorable court sitting as a court of impeachment, to answer certain articles of impeachment found and presented against me by the honorable the Assembly of the State of Florida, do hereby appear by my counsel, J. P. C. Emmons, who has my warrant and authority therefor, and who is instructed by me to ask of this honorable court such time as may be necessary and reasonable for the preparation of my answer to said articles, and to conduct my defense thereto in all respects.

"Dated this 14th day of February, A. D. 1872.
"HARRISON REED."

Mr. Emmons, on behalf of Governor Reed, filed the following plea:

In the matter of the Impeachment of Harrison Reed, Governor of Florida, charged with high crimes and misdemeanors in office, incompetency and malfeasance, and conduct detrimental to good morals. Before the honorable, the Senate of the State of Florida, sitting as a Court of Impeachment.

And the said Harrison Reed, Governor of Florida, by his attorney, J. P. C. Emmons, comes here into court, and praying leave of the court to save and reserve to himself the same right of objection to all or any of the articles of impeachment against him preferred by the honorable the Assembly of said State, which he might or would have in case a demurrer to the same were here filed, and not confessing or admitting either the constitutional right of the honorable the Assembly in the premises, or the sufficiency in law of any of the said articles of impeachment for the purposes intended, says he is not guilty of the said supposed high crimes and misdemeanors in office, incompetency, and malfeasance, and conduct detrimental to good morals, or any of them, in manner or form as the honorable the Assembly aforesaid, in and by the said articles of impeachment has complained against him.

J. P. C. EMMONS, Attorney and of Counsel.
HARRISON REED, Governor of Florida.

Senator Hillyer offered the following order, which was agreed to:

Ordered that the answer of Harrison Reed, Governor, to the articles of impeachment exhibited against him be received and filed.

The counsel on behalf of the managers presented the following:

Mr. Chief Justice and Gentlemen of the Senate—
In behalf of the Assembly and as directed by the managers, I have the honor to request of the honorable Senate a copy of the answer filed by Harrison Reed, Governor of Florida, to the articles of impeachment exhibited against him by the Assembly.

Further than this:
Mr. Chief Justice—By instruction of the Assembly, the managers and counsel appointed to conduct this important trial of the impeachment of Harrison Reed, Governor, in view of the time necessary to consider the answer made by the respondent and to make replication thereto; in view also of the neccessity for proper time in which to procure the attendance of witnesses, who reside out of the State, whose testimony is necessary to prove the material matters and facts charged in the Articles of Impeachment, and without which the Assembly by its managers and counsel cannot with safety and deliberation and in justice to the respondent as well as to the people, proceed at this time to further trial, and also for the purpose of amending the Articles of Impeachment, already presented, and prepare and present other articles in addition thereto, to the honorable Senate, do therefore ask of this honorable Senate that necessary time be allowed the managers and counsel to procure the attendance of the witnesses, to make replication to the answer of Harrison Reed, and to present further Articles of Impeachment against him.

Mr. Chief Justice—We make this application with no purpose to interpose any extraordinary delay in the progress of this cause, other than that which of right we claim for ourselves, and in justice to the people and to the respondent.

We are approaching the latter days of the constitutional limit of time allowed for the regular session of the Legislature, and the managers and counsel are unitedly of the opinion that the presence of the necessary witnesses cannot possibly be obtained so as to enable the managers to join issue with the respondent before the sixty days have elapsed.

Now, in due respect of the position in which we present ourselves, Senators will understand that within the limits of the accusation we have made, and for further reason, because of the five additional articles which we propose to present, there must be a very considerable range of subjects and a great variety of practical considerations that will need to come under the responsible judgment and for the discreet and critical action of counsel.

We do not present a mere question of convenience, but we

show causes of substance; and in making this application we address ourselves to the sound discretion of the Senate.

There are other and very important considerations which urge our application, and those are the economy of time, and of great expense to the State, while we sit here with both Houses in session, engaged in dilatory proceedings, and waiting for the service of subpœnas upon witnesses in New York and New Jersey, and the production of documentary evidence existing out of the State. It may be urged by counsel for respondent that the time-honored right of the accused to a speedy and impartial trial is seriously jeopardized by a continuance; but we claim, Mr. Chief Justice and Senators, that the rights of the people in their collective capacity are as important to be preserved and to be guarded as jealously as those of the citizen in his individual character. We, too, are anxious for a speedy trial. But above all, we ask that justice shall be done — that by careful preparation and deliberate conduct, we shall divest ourselves of all the prejudice of personal differences, and of all the heat and hate which belongs to the political forum, that our case shall be properly and justly made up, and that if the respondent be found guilty on these charges and on the others which we shall present, it will not be charged to us that his accusers have acted hastily, unfairly, or unjustly, or with unseeming desire to add injury to misfortune.

In behalf of the managers, I ask that this statement may be placed upon the record:

WHEREAS, Additional time is necessarily required by the managers and counsel prosecuting Articles of Impeachment against Harrison Reed, Governor, before the honorable Senate, to amend articles already presented, and to prepare and present others, and to procure the attendance of witnesses; and, whereas, a large number of these witnesses reside out of this State, and in remote parts of the United States, and their testimony is necessary to prove the various matters charged in said Articles of Impeachment, and without which testimony this Assembly, by its managers and counsel, cannot at this time safely proceed to the trial of the said Harrison Reed, Governor; therefore,

Resolved, That the managers be directed to appear at the bar of the Senate and ask that further necessary time be allowed the managers and counsel to amend articles presented, and to prepare and present others, and to procure the attendance of the necessary witnesses upon the trial.

Mr. Jenkins moved that the further consideration of this subject by the managers be postponed till to-morrow, 12 o'clock noon.

Senator Henderson offered the following order:

That the managers make replication at 12 o'clock M. to-morrow, or show cause.

The yeas and nays were called for with the following result:

Those voting in the affirmative were:

Messrs. Adams, Atkins, Billings, Crawford, Dennis, Eagan, Ginn, Henderson, Hill, Hillyer, Jenkins, Johnson, Kendrick, Locke, McKinnon, Meacham, McCaskill, Pearce, Purman, Sutton, Weeks and Wentworth—22.

Nays—None.

So the order was adopted.

The court then adjourned till 12 o'clock to-morrow, at Senate chamber.

After presenting the application for continuance on the part of the managers the court adjourned to meet on the next day. After the adjournment of the court the resolution previously offered to adjourn *sine die* was taken up and passed by a vote of ten to nine—seven Republicans and three Democrats voting for adjournment. The High Court of Impeachment met on the 17th of February, at which time Governor Reed, through his counsel, presented the following:

In the matter of the Impeachment of Harrison Reed, Governor of the State of Florida.

To the High Court of Impeachment:

Harrison Reed, Governor of the State of Florida, respondent in said cause, by his counsel, comes and moves this honorable court to grant him, until Monday next, time to prepare answer to the Articles of Impeachment as originally filed and subsequently amended by leave of this court. This application is made in view of the concurrent action of the Senate and Assembly, fixing Monday next as the day of final adjournment, thereby precluding this respondent, unless by the voluntary action of the government, from making his defense before the expiration of his term of office, if ever. And this respondent confidently expects to make good his plea by such testimony as will be satisfactory to those who, from a hearing which was entirely ex parte, felt it their duty to make the charges and specifications filed against him.

This honorable court will take notice that at the time of filing his plea to the articles as first presented, this respondent reserved the right to file special answer to said articles severally upon the happening of a contingency, which has now transpired.

Mr. Henderson offered the following order:

Ordered, That the counsel of the respondent be allowed until Monday next, 9 A. M., to file his answer, amended answers, or plea to the Articles of Impeachment exhibited against him;

Which was adopted.

Mr. Wentworth moved that the Senate sitting as a High Court of Impeachment adjourn till 9 A. M. Monday;

Which was agreed to.

The Chief Justice then adjourned the court till Monday 9 A. M.

The High Court of Impeachment met February 19th, and the counsel for the respondent asked leave to file the following:

"And the said respondent, by his counsel comes and moves the court that the plea heretofore filed to the said articles of Impeachment be held and treated as the plea and answer to the said articles filed since then, the same as though said plea was this day filed."

"Very respectfully,
"J. P. C. EMMONS,
"Counsel for Respondent."

The request of the respondent was granted. The Board of Managers presented the following:

Resolved, That the managers and counsel prosecuting Articles of Impeachment against Harrison Reed, Governor, be empowered and instructed to prepare and file in the High Court of Impeachment the necessary replication to the answer and plea that Harrison Reed, Governor, has or may file to the said Articles of Impeachment.

Attest: M. L. STEARNS,
Speaker of the Assembly.
H. H. CLAY,
Clerk of the Assembly.

Which was agreed to.

The counsel for the Board of Managers of the Assembly offered a replication and asked that it should be filed.

The counsel for the respondent submitted the following, and asked that it be filed:

Counsel objects to the reception of the replication on the ground that it does not appear to be put in under the direction of the Assembly, nor the mode prescribed by law therefor.

The counsel for the managers then withdrew, and subsequently tendered the following replication:

In the Assembly and State of Florida, February 19, 1872.

Replication by the Assembly of the State of Florida to the pleas of Harrison Reed, Governor, to the Articles of Impeachment exhibited against him by the said Assembly.

And now comes the Assembly by its managers and counsel, and having considered the several pleas of Harrison Reed, Governor, to the several Articles of Impeachment exhibited against him in the name of the said Assembly, and of all the people of Florida, and reserving to the said Assembly all advantages of exception to the insufficiency of said pleas, to each and all the said several Articles of Impeachment, exhibited against said Harrison Reed, Governor, and for the replication to said pleas, do say that said Harrison Reed, Governor, is guilty of the high crimes and misdemeanors, of incompetency and malfeasance, and of conduct detrimental to good morals, and that the Assembly is ready to prove the same.

M. L. STEARNS,
Speaker of the Assembly.
H. H. CLAY,
Chief Clerk of Assembly.

Mr. Jenkins offered the following order:

Ordered, That the replication of the managers to the respondent's plea be received and filed.

Which was adopted.

Mr. Wentworth offered the following order:

Ordered, That the Senate sitting as a High Court of Impeachment do now adjourn in accordance with the concurrent resolution adopted by the Senate and the Assembly for the adjournment of the Legislature.

The yeas and nays were called for with the following result:

Those voting in the affirmative were:

Messrs. Adams, Dennis, Hill, Jenkins, Kendrick, Locke, Meacham, Purman and Wentworth—9.

Those voting in the negative were:

Messrs. Atkins, Billings, Crawford, Eagan, Ginn, Henderson, Hillyer, McKinnon, McCaskill, Pearce and Sutton—11.
So the order was not adopted.
Mr. Wentworth moved that the Senate room be cleared for deliberation;
Which was not agreed to.
The counsel for the respondent offered the following, and asked that it be filed:

In the matter of Harrison Reed, impeached for high crimes, misdemeanors, malfeasance in office and conduct detrimental to good morals.

I, Harrison Reed, Governor of the State of Florida, hereby by my counsel, J. P. C. Emmons, now come here into court and demand a trial of the charges aforesaid, embodied in the Articles of Impeachment, filed against me in this court, to which I have filed my plea verified by oath as required by the Constitution of this State.

And I now hereby solemnly protest, that, as I now make such demand and hereby declare myself ready for trial, further proceedings shall not be delayed or continued to an impossible day or time, within which my office as Governor aforesaid will have expired by constitutional limitation.

Ordered that the same be filed.
The counsel for the respondent offered the following:
Mr. Emmons, respondent, moved that the managers proceed with the evidence, or that he be acquitted and discharged.
Mr. Henderson moved that the Senate chamber be cleared for deliberation;
Which was agreed to.
Mr. Wentworth moved that the doors be now opened;
Which was agreed to.
The doors were opened.
Senator Jenkins offered the following order:

Ordered, That the High Court of Impeachment do now adjourn.

Mr. McCaskill offered the following as a substitute:

WHEREAS, Articles of Impeachment have been presented by the honorable Assembly of Florida against Harrison Reed, Governor, and whereas the respondent demands an immediate trial,

Ordered, therefore, That this court will continue to sit from day to day at 10 o'clock of each day, for the trial of Harrison

Reed, till adjourned by the limitations of the State Constitution, to-wit: Till the end of 60 days.

Mr. Purman offered the following order:

Ordered, That the Senate sitting in High Court of Impeachment do now adjourn.

The yeas and nays were called for with the following result:
Those voting in the affirmative were:
Messrs. Adams, Dennis, Ginn, Hill, Jenkins, Kendrick, Locke, Meacham, Purman and Wentworth—10.
Those voting in the negative were:
Messrs. Atkins, Crawford, Eagan, McKinnon, McCaskill and Pearce—6.
So the order was adopted.
The Chief Justice then declared the court adjourned in pursuance of the order of the Senate, and ordered the Sergeant-at-Arms to make the following proclamation:

Hear ye! Hear ye! Hear ye! The Senate of the State of Florida, sitting as a high Court of Impeachment, now stands adjourned. God save the State of Florida and this honorable court.

The Osborn conspirators made no hesitation in openly declaring, after the Governor had been impeached, that they did not intend to give him a trial. They only desired to get him suspended so that there would be no hindrance to the commission of fraud at the ensuing election, and the nomination and counting in of M. L. Stearns for Governor, while Day, the acting Governor, was to be nominated and counted in for Congress. Our next chapter will show how Governor Reed broke this slate and conspiracy.

CHAPTER XIII.

The Banquet of the Conspirators and the Handwriting on the Wall. Day's Proclamation and the Meeting of the Legislature. Extracts from Day's Proclamation. The Decision of the Supreme Court. The Conspirators Again Jubilant. The Conspirators Driven Into Court. Governor Reed Before The High Court of Impeachment. The Famous Argument of Judge Emmons. The Reply of the Managers. The Conspirators See Danger Ahead, and are Wrathy With Day. Honest Cessna Exposed. The Triumph of Governor Reed. Scenes Around the State House when Governor Reed was Discharged.

The Osborn conspirators having now deposed Governor Reed and, as they thought, buried him with his face downward, were jubilant and defiant. The strongest friends of the Governor grew weak, while the doubtful and faint-hearted of the conspirators grew strong. No one in the Republican party dared to utter a word in defense of Harrison Reed, under penalty of being read out of the party as a traitor. James W. Johnson, white carpet-bagger, one of the leading conspirators and a member of the board of managers of impeachment, was made private secretary of Governor Day, at a salary of $750 per annum. Not a speck of cloud could be seen by them in the political horizon to disturb their peaceful ten month's sail in the great ship of state to the verdant fields of plunder, which they so eagerly anticipated would be fully ripe and ready for wholesale harvest in the nomination, counting in and inauguration of M. L. Stearns, the Bureau agent, as Governor. Governor Reed, in the meantime, unassumingly contended that the adjournment of the court after issue had been joined and the Senators sworn to try the Articles of Impeachment, and the adjournment, after his arraignment without his consent and against his protest, operated as an acquittal. The Governor, in order to have the matter amicably settled as to who was the legal Governor, proceeded to the executive office and had an interview with Governor Day, and requested him to join with him, Reed, and ask the opinion of the Supreme Court as to the legal effect of the adjournment of the Senate without giving him a trial. Day, fearing that the court might decide that Reed was Governor, stubbornly refused to even countenance Reed's request, and laughed him to scorn. Judge Emmons, Reed's counsel, thought that he could get the matter before the court by a motion; but in this proposition Governor Reed showed himself to be a better lawyer than his counsel, for Reed contended that this could not be done without notice, if at all, which Emmons finally acknowledged was true. The conspirators had called a State convention to assemble in the city of Jacksonville, which met shortly after the adjournment of the Legislature. The convention being in session and Reed out of the way, no one dared to mar the occasion by opposing anything the conspirators attempted to put through. They elected a State Central Committee, which was in full accord with the conspirators. The convention was considered as a grand banquet given by them in honor of the overthrow of Governor Reed, and Cessna and Johnson figured as the great heroes. Day had left the seat of government at Tallahassee and was now in attendance at the banquet, partarking of its sweet felicities, and mirth and thanksgiving filled the hall.

As C. H. Pearce, the great leader of the freedmen of the State, and more especially of Leon County, had fallen a victim to the persecutions of the conspirators because he had stood by the administration of Governor Reed, was losing his grip upon the freedmen by reason of such persecution; and the conspirators desiring a colored leader who could bring the freedmen to their support, the author of this work, who had heretofore been Pearce's leading lieutenant, was counseled by Day to take his place. As Governor Reed was supposed to be dead and buried, this proposition was gladly accepted, and he was mustered in at the banquet with all the honors of one who had been brought up under this great leader and knew how to capture his most formidable political fortifications without injury to the conspirators, and was at once endorsed by the banquet as the next Republican candidate for Congress. This endorsement was never intended by the conspirators to be carried out in good faith, of which the author was well aware at the time, but only to hoodwink him and make him more zealous in bringing the freedmen to their support.

Governor Reed, taking advantage of the absence of Day from the seat of government, as well as the gathering of nearly all of the conspirators at the banquet, quietly proceeded from Jacksonville to Tallahassee, held a consultation with his true and tried secretary, Jonathan C. Gibbs, who stood as a wall of fire against the assaults made by the conspirators on the Governor, which consultation resulted in the Governor issuing a proclamation from the executive office declaring himself Chief Executive of the State, and commanding the people to give obedience thereto. The Governor also made several important appointments, among which were General William Birney to be Attorney-General, and F. I. Wheaton to be Judge of the Fourth Judicial Circuit. Secretary Gibbs recognized Reed as the legal Governor of Florida, and affixed the great seal of the State to this proclamation, and to the appointments. Reed also addressed a letter to the Judges of the Supreme Court of the State requesting their opinion as to the legal effect of the adjournment of the Senate without giving him a trial, and then returned to Jacksonville without the knowledge of the conspirators. The banquet was in the height of its glory when the handwriting on the wall was discovered by Day in the shape of Reed's proclamation that he had risen from the dead, and was still Governor of Florida. Day, with tremors which he attempted to conceal, cried: "Treason," while he summoned Johnson, his private secretary, to his side, apparently to give him comfort. Johnson obeyed the summons, and although haggard when he appeared, swore that he would go to Tallahassee and hang Governor Reed as high as Haman. Cessna mustered up a smile, which was barren of its usual fervor, and contended that the people would pay no attention to Reed's proclamation. Others suggested the calling of an extra session of the Legislature to impeach Secretary Gibbs for affixing the great seal of the State to Governor Reed's act, while all agreed that Day should call upon the General Government for troops if Reed could not be got rid of otherwise. The leading conspirators now proceeded to Tallahassee to assist Johnson in decapitating Governor Reed, who, having carried his point, had quietly returned to his home at Jacksonville. When the conspirators reached Tallahassee they found nothing to prevent their taking peaceable possession of the citadel; but the question as to who was the legal Governor was squarely placed before the Supreme Court.

The intention of Governor Reed was not to take forcible possession of the government, as the conspirators were in hopes he had done, so that they might invoke the aid of the General Government in their behalf, but to get possession by process of law. The appointment of Birney and Wheaton was intended to make a contest as to who was Governor. Day had appointed Judge Gillis of the same circuit as judge, and Reed thought Gillis would resort to the courts to establish his authority, thus involving the question as to the legality of Wheaton's appointment; but the Governor missed his aim in this, as Gillis made no resistance, and Wheaton had no trouble in exercising the duties of his office. The plan of issuing this proclamation and making these appointments, many thought was the work of Judge Emmons, but the judge, as well as Secretary Gibbs, often declared to the author afterwards that it was Reed's own invention. Reed's case now pending before the Supreme Court, the conspirators, like the builders of the tower of Babel, were confused, and no two of them could agree as to the best course to be pursued to prevent him from recapturing the citadel. They seemed to know beforehand what the opinion of Associate Justice Hart would be, but expressed themselves as being afraid of Chief Justice Randall and Associate Justice Westcott. Day insisted on calling a session of the Legislature for the double purpose of getting rid of Gibbs and of re-impeaching Reed if the court should discharge him. Day's proposition eventually prevailed, and the following proclamation was accordingly issued.

WHEREAS, The interests of the people of this State require the immediate assembling of the Legislature:

NOW, THEREFORE, I, SAMUEL T. DAY, Lieutenant-Governor, and, by virtue of said office, Acting Governor of the State of Florida, do hereby issue this my proclamation, convening the Legislature in Extraordinary Session at Tallahassee, the Capital, on Monday, the 22d day of April, A. D., 1872, at twelve meridian, at which time, in pursuance of the requirements of the Constitution, I will communicate to both branches of the Legislature the purpose for which they have been convened.

In testimony whereof, I have hereunto set my hand, and in lieu of affixing the great seal of the State, hereby proclaim that the same has been secreted or stolen.

Done at the Capitol, in Tallahassee, Florida, this seventeenth day of April in the year of our Lord one thousand eight hundred and seventy-two, and of the Independence of the United States of America the ninety-sixth.

SAMUEL T. DAY,
Acting Governor.

The Legislature met on the day designated in Day's proclamation, with only two members of the Senate and ten members of the Assembly. Both houses adjourned from day to day until a quorum was had. On the third day the Senate had a quorum, and on the fourth day there was a quorum in the Assembly. Both houses now notified Acting Governor Day of their organization and their readiness to receive any communication he might be pleased to make. In response Day sent a message from which we extract so much as relates to the contested case, as follows:

MESSAGE OF THE ACTING GOVERNOR.

Gentlemen of the Senate and of the Assembly:

I regret the occasion which has compelled me to assemble the Legislature at this season of the year, which is so important to many of you, who are engaged in agricultural labors.

The public necessity for certain legislative action has appeared to me to be so imperative, and my own earnest sense of the responsibility which devolves upon the Executive under the peculiar circumstances that have recently arisen, are considerations which have caused me to feel justified in calling you together at some sacrifice of your personal interests.

On the 10th day of February last, at the regular session of the Legislature, certain proceedings were had by both branches thereof, which impeached Harrison Reed, Governor of the State, of high crimes and misdemeanors in office, and in accordance with the constitutional requirements, Governor Reed was suspended from his official duties, pending the final determination of the Senate upon the charges against him, and as Lieutenant-Governor of the State the duties of the Executive devolved upon me.

On that day I occupied the Executive office, and assumed the authority and functions of Chief Magistrate of the State, not, however, without the embarrassment of finding the Governor's office stripped of all official records, papers, and documents properly belonging thereto, which had been secretly removed by Governor Reed himself, or by his direction.

The constitutional provision declaring the effect of an impeachment in relation to the rights of the person accused, is in the following expressed terms:

"An officer when impeached by the Assembly shall be deemed under arrest, and shall be disqualified from performing any of the duties of his office until acquitted by the Senate. But any officer so impeached and in arrest may demand his trial by the Senate within one year from the date of his impeachment." (Art. 16, Sec. 9.)

The Senate not having concluded the trial of Governor Reed, but having, on the contrary, continued the proceedings in the exercise of its judicial discretion, and having adopted a concurrent resolution expressive of the intention and purpose of both the prosecuting branch of the Legislature and of the Senate itself for a continuance, still holds in custody the person of the accused under its own warrant, and subject to its own rules and orders.

Such being the case, and Governor Reed having vacated the Executive office and removed his residence from the Capital to Jacksonville, did, on the 8th inst., by unlawful conspiracy with Jonathan C. Gibbs, Secretary of State, and in my temporary absence, clandestinely enter the Executive office, and unlawfully attempted to take possession thereof, and issued a so-called proclamation declaring himself still to be in the exercise of the Chief Executive duties of the State; the said Jonathan C. Gibbs confederating with him in this high-handed conspiracy, and affixing the Great Seal of the State to the so-called proclamation, attesting the same as Secretary of State.

In furtherance of this conspiracy to seize the State government, Governor Reed executed certain so-called appointments to office: one to William Birney, to be Attorney-General, and another to F. I. Wheaton, to be Judge of the Fourth Judicial Circuit; in which proceedings the Secretary of State co-operated and in all respects recognized the authority of Governor Reed.

Instead of seeking by legal and proper methods, and in accordance with the Constitution and Laws of the State, to reassume the duties of the Executive, Governor Reed and Secretary Gibbs, by a secret and artfully-planned conspiracy, seized the Great Seal of the State, together with important records and papers, being public property, and hastily removed the same to Jacksonville.

On being informed of these lawless and revolutionary proceedings, I repaired to the Executive office, and issued my proclamation, declaring the conduct of the conspirators "an attempted usurpation," and "revolutionary in its tendencies," and commanding obedience to the lawfully constituted authorities of the State.

In this action I have been almost universally sustained by the people, and have been offered every possible aid from all sections of the State in preserving the peace, order, and dignity of the government, and for the protection and support of my recognized Executive authority.

I have thus briefly laid before you the facts attending this most atrocious attempt by Governor Reed to seize the powers of the government, under color of a self-asserted right and in defiance of the judicial proceedings of a high constitutional forum, by which he was deprived of all authority whatever. It is true that this action has produced in some sections of the State confusion and distrust, and has made the exercise of official authority on the part of some State and county officers a matter of divided opinion, and afforded a plausible pretext for a class of political malcontents to obstruct and embarrass the adminstration of the laws.

But whatever may be the differences of opinion respecting the legal effects of the adjournment of the Legislature without the trial of the accused by the Senate, there can be no circumstances which justify or palliate a resort to force or to unlawful conspiracy on the part of any State officer or pretended official, in bold defiance of the determination of a judicial tribunal. Whether that decision be right or wrong, lawful or unlawful, it is not within the sphere of the recognized legal rights, nor within the proper exercise of the power to vindicate personal liberty, on the part of any citizen, be he high or low, rich or poor, to question or override, the validity or legal effect of any judicial proceeding, by attempting to subvert the laws, to defy the peace and good order of the State, and to incite rebellion and anarchy in the government.

Whatever may be the opinion of the supreme judicial authority of the State upon the question of the legal effect of the proceedings thus far held by the Senate in the suspension from office of Governor Reed, I do not deem it disrespectful, during the pendancy of the consideration of such opinion, to call your attention to the paramount necessity at all times of recognizing and abiding by the *de facto* Executive authority of the State. No department of the government is more essential for the preservation of the peace and order of the community. Its powers and agency are distributed over the State in larger proportion than those of any other branch of the government, and are brought more directly in contact with the people. It is the immediate representative of the sovereign will of the people, and upon its vigorous and discreet action the courts and all judicial authority rely for the ultimate vindication of justice and the security of good government. In this view of my own duty, I hold the conduct of Governor Reed and all his abettors as revolutionary and criminal, and in no manner justifying the countenance or support of any law-abiding citizen, *until* having been declared by a tribunal of competent jurisdiction entitled to resume his Executive functions. It is therefore that I feel bound by my oath, and by my sense of public duty, to compel obedience to my authority, and to use every power in me vested by law to suppress all attempts to subvert it.

I call your attention to these extraordinary facts, and suggest such legislation as in your wisdom the circumstances may seem to require.

On the 29th day of April the Senate and Assembly adjourned and proceeded to the Supreme Court room to hear the opinion delivered as to who was the legal Governor. The conspirators were in high spirits, as Hart had privately informed them that things were all right, and that the court would sustain Day. A. J. Peeler and George P. Raney appeared for Day, and Judge Emmons for Governor Reed. The arguments had been made several days before. While the court fully agreed that Governor Reed was entitled to a trial, yet a majority of the court, Associate Justices Westcott and Hart, decided that the Supreme Court had no jurisdiction to decide as to whether the adjournment of the Senate to an impossible day did or did not operate as an acquittal. The court further decided that Governor Reed being suspended, could not ask the opinion of the court as to any matter. Yet Reed was sufficiently Governor to get the court together on his case for the purpose of hearing arguments of counsel for and against his questions propounded to the court as Governor. Chief Justice Randall dissented, and delivered an opinion, which will be found elsewhere in this work. (See 14 Florida Reports, p. 308). The conspirators now had gotten over the scare which Governor Reed had first given them before the court, and thought themselves masters of the situation, and in the House the following resolution was adopted:

Resolved, by the Assembly, the Senate concurring, That this Legislature do adjourn on Friday, May 3d, at 12 M., until such time as the Acting Governor shall call them together again, on being informed by the Managers of Impeachment that they are ready to proceed with the trial of Harrison Reed.

Of course the managers were never to be ready, and Day would be the last man to call them together.

In addition to F. A. Dockray and Mr. Brevard, counsel for the Board of Managers, Governor D. S. Walker and Bolling Baker were employed. A resolution was offered by Mr. Oliveros, of St. Johns County, that the Board of Managers proceed at once with the trial of Governor Reed. This resolution was laid on the table.

After the Assembly had adopted its resolution to adjourn without giving Governor Reed a trial, the Senate, on the first day of May, proceeded by resolution to organize a High Court of Impeachment. This resolution was fought most bitterly by the conspirators in the Senate—Wentworth, Purman and others—while John A. Henderson and John L. Crawford, Democrats, battled for its passage. All manner of dilatory motions were made to prevent its passage, until the conspirators became exhausted and gave up the ghost, and the resolution was adopted. The conspirators in the Assembly, now forced into court by the action of the Senate, to make good their charges, passed a resolution on the 2d day of May, to send for persons and papers and to take testimony under oath. The High Court of Impeachment met May 2d, at five minutes to 12 A. M., the Chief Justice present. The Sergeant-at-Arms made his usual proclamation, and the Assembly was notified that the Senate was organized for the trial of Harrison Reed.

Committee of managers from the Assembly then came in with counsel.

Judge Emmons, counsel for Governor Reed, present.

The Chief Justice then announced that the Senate, as a High Court of Impeachment, was fully organized.

Counsel for respondent then asked leave to proceed with motions that he would present. The managers notified the court.

I desire to state that the managers are represented by T. W. Brevard and F. A. Dockray as counsel.

Judge Emmons, counsel for Governor Reed, then read the following paper as presenting his views:

In the matter of the Impeachment of Harrison Reed, Governor of Florida, before the High Court of Impeachment, organized by virtue of resolution passed the Senate May 1, 1872, at an extra session.

This matter came up for inquiry before a High Court of Impeachment, organized by the Senate, at the regular session of the Legislature of the State, at and during its session in February last.

At that time, and before the then court, Articles of Impeachment were filed in court; the respondent pleaded and the Assembly replied.

Issue was thereby joined.

On the application of the managers, the court acted upon and refused to continue the trial.

Respondent protested against any postponements or continuance, the effect of which would be to postpone his trial to an impossible day, claiming that the continuance of the trial to the next session of the Legislature would be to fix a time before the coming of which his term of office would expire by constitutional limitation, and that he announced himself ready for and demanded his trial. That the prosecution produce its evidence, or that the respondent be acquitted and discharged.

That a member of the court asked its body to proceed in the trial, and to sit from day to day therefor until such time as by constitutional limit the Legislature's session would cease. Without action, the court adjourned without day.

By operation of its own rule, adopted for its government, the Senate, sitting as a court, merged into the Senate proper in its sole legislative capacity. That such Senate thereafter adjourned *sine die*, the hour having arrived as fixed in a concurrent resolution, originating and passing both branches of the Legislature, after the commencement of impeachment proceedings and before the adjournment of said court.

This session of the Legislature was not provided for by the Constitution and laws of the State, neither was it contemplated in the mind of the court or of the acting Governor, when the adjournment before mentioned took place.

He by whom, by the Constitution, the duties of the office of Governor were to be performed, has exercised the constitutional prerogative belonging to the Executive of the State in calling an extra session of the Legislature, which is now in session. Among other acts of this body, this branch has, by its resolution, organized itself into a High Court of Impeachment to proceed in the trial of the respondent.

From the day of his impeachment to the present moment, the action of the Legislature has practically suspended this respondent from the powers, rights, privileges and immunities belonging to him under the Constitution and laws of the State.

And now Harrison Reed, Governor of the State, respondent herein, by J. P. C. Emmons, his counsel, comes here into this court, and asks and demands, in virtue of the proceedings had in the premises, that he, the respondent, be acquitted and discharged of and from all and singular said impeachment, as set forth in the Articles of Impeachment filed, and that he be discharged from arrest, and that he be relieved from any and all further attendance upon this court, or the Senate from which it was organized, growing out of the impeachment or the proceedings aforesaid.

Mr. Emmons then, after stating his motion to the above effect, asked some Senator to make the motion *pro forma*.

Mr. Henderson offered the following order:

Ordered, That the motion of the counsel of respondent be granted.

Without detaining the court to discuss how far, as a court, it is bound to apply a well-recognized principle in the very spirit of our institutions, that whenever it shall find in the detail of powers in fixing the distributive share which properly belongs to each branch of the government, a power inappropriately delegated to one which is in conflict with that which properly belongs to another, it will so construe that delegation as to make it belong where, by an antecedent delegation, it was intended, I will say, in support of my motion, and demand that by operation of law, when the court, at the last session, and the Senate, adjourned without day, the Constitution of the State of Florida fixed the day to which the Senate, as a legislative body adjourned as being the first Tuesday after the first Monday in January, 1873. And the High Court of Impeachment being composed of the members of that body, aside from its presidency, was not only the creation of, but dependent upon, the same authority for its existence. Thus the trial of the respondent, if it existed in continuance, was carried over until that day.

This to Harrison Reed, Governor, as aforesaid, was an impossible day.

For that the Governor's term of office is by the Constitution of the State terminated at the opening of the regular session of the Legislature in the year A. D. 1873, though the Constitution does not read that he shall continue in office until his successor shall be qualified, it was evidently intended so to read, and before then, in legal contemplation, a new Governor will have been elected and qualified. And, too, the Legislature can do no business, and certainly none in relation to the matter of this impeachment until after the happening of that event. And again, too, because the punishment provided for in the Constitution in the event of conviction cannot be meted out. And in language I have before used in the presentment of this matter elsewhere, I further say, that although the Constitution provides that upon extraordinary occasions a convention of the Legislature may be had, yet as controlling the effects of such adjournment the power comes neither within the legal or meritorious action of the Senate, because it depends upon the happenings of its contingencies which human foresight could not decide upon.

And again it would be a transfer of power over and control of the matter either to the Governor actual or acting, by enabling him to withold any communication to the Legislature in reference to the trial, or to the Legislature itself by enabling any member thereof by withholding his consent to destroy unanimity, whereby it could not act.

In support of my proposition as to the effect this extra session may have, I quote from a communication on this very subject from the pen of a gentleman whose well-earned reputation for legal sagacity and acumen entitles it to the very highest respect and consideration. He says: "The legal effect, if there be any, of the action of the Senate, is not overcome by the present extra session, convened at the call of the acting Governor, for if the effect attached, no subsequent action can avert it. The question then must be governed by what the law fixed at the time, whatever that was, either in favor or opposed to the position of Governor Reed, and no subsequent assemblage of the Legislature in extra session by call of the Governor can change it."

And as this communication is to my mind conclusive upon the status of this case, I read it in full, as a better presentation than I can originate:

THE DUTY OF THE SENATE IN THE IMPEACHMENT MATTER.

The question in regard to the legal effect of the action of the Senate upon the status of Governor Reed, propounded by him to the Judges of the Supreme Court, has excited no little interest in the public mind, and especially during the discussion of it before the Judges by the counsel on either side. The course of the arguments seemed to have been directed to sustain or to oppose the jurisdiction of the court in the first place, and secondly, the effect in law of the action of the Senate—that action being the adjournment of the Senate to a day beyond the official existence of Governor Reed. The discussion was an interesting one to us, and was conducted with much ability on both sides. With much anxiety was the opinion of the Judges awaited. The opinion has been given, and though the Judges differ, yet one thing has been settled by it, and that is that the question is one for the determination of the Senate alone. With all due deference to those who hold other views, we believe that the question does not turn upon technical ideas of "jurisdiction," for in all matters involving personal rights the courts have jurisdiction to investigate and inquire into them, as the court did in this case. There was no "case" before the court. An opinion as to the law was asked, and as propounded there *was* involved the question whether Governor Reed was restored to his official functions by the action of the Senate. The opinion of a majority of the Judges asserts that whatever may really in law be the effect of this action, the Senate alone is the tribunal to declare it. This proceeds from no want of jurisdiction in the Supreme Court to investigate the subject, but as a rule from a declared principle of law, that whilst one tribunal has a case pending before it, another court, although of concurrent jurisdiction, will not undertake to decide any question as to the effect of the action of the court having first acquired cognizance of the case until after final action, but leave the question to be decided by the court in which it originated. In the present case the rule of law is especially applicable according to the opinion of a majority, for the reason that the Senate has exclusive jurisdiction of impeachments.

Until the Senate shall finally decide, the court cannot interfere, but it is nowhere intimated that should the Senate transgress any of its powers, the court cannot so declare and give effect to its own judment in any given case.

Granting, then, that the Senate is the only tribunal to decide the legal effect of its own acts pending the impeachment and until they themselves decide or order affirmatively the final disposition of the case, the question still remains, what is the legal effect of their action in this case? We do not understand that the question rests upon the simple act of adjournment, nor was the argument of the counsel in behalf of Gov. Reed based on it, but on it coupled with the other and important facts, that the adjournment was without his consent and in opposition to his wishes and protest, and to a period beyond his official life, when no trial and no judgment of acquittal could restore him to his rights, even if by any stretch of ideas upon the subject there could by any *trial at all*. The question then still being one for the decision of the Senate, by what law, it may be inquired, is it to be governed? We say by the law of the land, controlling and governing all rights, private and official. The Senate (no more than any other tribunal vested with any judicial power) is not a law for themselves, with the right to decide according to their mere caprice; nor does there exist anything in what is called the usages and customs of parliament as contra-distinguished from the law appertaining to all cases, to justify a departure from legal rules and principles. In the celebrated case of Warren Hastings, Lord Thurlow, then Lord Chancellor, affirmed that the usages of parliament as contra-distinguished from the common law had no existence. "In times of barbarism," he said, "when to impeach a man was to ruin him by the strong hand of power, the usage of parliament was quoted in order to justify the most arbitrary proceedings." He added, "that the same rule of procedure and of evidence which obtain in courts below, he was sure would be rigidly followed." The House of Lords sustained this view, and during the trial all questions upon the admissibility of evidence were decided according to the rules of the common law as announced by the Judges. According to this, the principles and rules of the common law are to be invoked in the progress of the trial to determine all questions affecting the *rights* of the accused, for if it were otherwise there would be no rule by which the citizen could measure his actions and none by which his rights could be determined, for the usages of parliament furnish none. If, then, the rules and principles of the common law govern the court in the progress of the trial as the only law that exists, the same reason that affirms and maintains it is equally forcible to support the proposition that *all legal consequences* to the accused, resulting from the action of the court, are likewise to be ascertained and determined by the law of the land. These effects cannot rightfully be averted by resolution of the Senate alone, for by itself the Senate cannot change the law, but at most it can only rightfully prescribe rules to govern its own action, and regulate its own proceedings.

If the law pronounces that the action of the Senate in this case has the legal effect to discharge Governor Reed from the impeachment, then it is their duty so to declare, for the rule of law which requires it is as obligatory on the Senate as on all other courts or tribunals exercising judicial powers.

The inquiry naturally results, what is the law upon this subject? We have already said a simple adjournment by itself does not perhaps have the effect claimed, any more than the adjournment of a court does of itself so operate. But when a court pending a trial discharges the jury and adjourns against the consent of the accused, and without any reason which the law regards as *sufficient*, the authorities which were cited in the argument, as we understand them, affirm that as a rule of law the party is entitled to be discharged.

Now what are the facts here? The adjournment was not

the result of any necessity, either of law or of unanticipated occurrence. Governor Reed was arraigned; the Senate organized as a court; a plea was filed and issue made. The accused demanded a trial, as he had a right to do under the express terms of the Constitution. Without any reason declared, or so far as we know existing, the adjournment was ordered, and by the operation of the Constitution, *known to the Senate*, that adjournment carried the Senate over to next January, which was, *as also known to the Senate*, beyond the official life of the Governor. The deduction of fact, as well as of law, which we hold to follow from this is, that the adjournment of the Senate and the continuance of the impeachment before it, was not for the purpose of a trial, but that there should be no trial; and we hold it to be against any principle of law, that a party arraigned can be held to prevent a trial instead of to give him a trial, and that natural justice at least requires that in all such cases the effect should be a discharge; and any and all courts should, when the question properly comes before it, so declare. And why? Simply because, as it seems to us, the spirit of the law which gives power in order to try is violated, and the spirit of justice requires that the party should be held discharged, for he is presumed to be innocent until the contrary is proved, and, as in such case, no chance to prove him guilty exists, he is entitled to the practical benefit of the principle applicable in his behalf.

The legal effect, if there be any, of the action of the Senate, is not overcome by the present extra session, convened at the call of the acting Governor, for if the effect attached, no subsequent event can avert it. The question then must be governed by what the law fixed at that time, whatever that was, either in favor or opposed to the position of Governor Reed, and no subsequent assemblage of the Legislature in extra session by call of the Governor can change it.

If these views be correct, the Senate will not only be doing justice to itself, but to the body of the people, not to mention Governor Reed himself, by at once ordering the discharge of the impeachment. Any other course will afford a proof that the tactics of party, assuming the guise of public good, are of more potent control than the law, which it is the highest interest of Senates, courts and people to have administered.

In the able appeal made by Messrs. Peeler & Raney, they more particularly relied upon the question of the jurisdiction of the Supreme Court to pass upon the legal effect of the action of this court. And as to this question alone, did the majority of the court confirm itself, so far as any disagreement was concerned? And while Justice Westcott, who delivered the opinion of the court too plainly to be misunderstood, conceded what would have been the unanimous opinion of the court in the event of the question coming before the court in other circumstances, he held that the court was by the comity of courts estopped from taking such jurisdiction in this case as would call for a full declaration of the rights of this respondent.

But as to what constituted an acquittal within the meaning of the Constitution, he fully agrees with Chief Justice Randall when he says that, and I here quote from his opinion:

"What is the true intent and meaning of the word acquittal as here used in the Constitution? The court does not differ as to the proper definition of the term as here used. It is our unanimous opinion that it is not restricted to an actual judgment of acquittal after a vote upon full evidence failing to convict by the requisite two-thirds of the members of an organized Senate.

"We think its true signification to be *any* affirmative final action by a legal Senate *other* than a conviction, by which it dismisses or discontinues the prosecution. Any final disposition of the impeachment matter by the Senate, *other* than a conviction, is therefore an acquittal, *for the purpose of removing the disqualification from performing the duties of the office.*"

Judge Westcott fully agrees with the Chief Justice in all but the question of jurisdiction. And I shall, therefore, read the opinion of Chief Justice Randall as the opinion of the Supreme Court, on the question now here presented for the determination of this the High Court of Impeachment.

As to jurisdiction now or hereafter, Judge W. says: "Our power in the matter of this impeachment is limited and circumscribed by the fact that it is a matter beyond our jurisdiction entirely. After an impeachment perfected according to the Constitution the whole matter is with the Senate, and it has the exclusive right of determining all questions which may arise in the case. If its action is unconstitutional we have the right and power to declare its nullity, and in a proper case before us of any party to enforce the right of which it proposed to deprive him.

Particularly was there no difference of opinion, as to the total want of analogy between the jurisdiction, power and final action of the Parliament of Great Britain, and that of the Senate of a State in this country. And while this was true it was conceded beyond controversy that the action of this forum would and must be that of a court, one in which questions of law and evidence are to be viewed and passed upon with the same governing principles that regulate inquiries into analogous subjects; matter in all judicial tribunals proper.

And the doctrine that in an impeachment "the same rules of evidence, the same legal motions of crimes and punishments prevail; for impeachments are not framed to alter the law, but to carry it into more effectual execution. The judgments and action must therefore be such as is warranted by legal principles and precedents," as fully sustained by the authorities cited, was recognized in all their force, as applicable, and but for the want of jurisdiction, would have received the judgments of that court in sustaining that for which the respondent contended.

This doctrine is fully laid down in Webster in the Prescott case, by Woodeson in his lectures, 4 Black. Com., Chit. Crim. Law, and other authorities cited and read in that argument. And, too, Selden in his works, more particularly at 1651-2, fully indorses this rule, and the necessity and propriety of its application. See, too, Lord Winston's case—motion in arrest of judgment, where the Lords entertained the motion and decided it.

And then, in reference to the general practice in courts of law, when the issue is joined and the jury is empanelled and sworn, and the cause is continued without the consent of the defendant, either on motion and the discharge of the jury, or by the withdrawal of one juror, by the consent of the court, the defendant is thereby discharged and acquitted.

Before I cite in the argument any authorities to this well settled point, I add, that in this case the court was the court and jury. The Senators were sworn to try, etc., and having been so sworn, should have returned a verdict; and not having done so and the court having adjourned, and particularly as no day was given, respondent was entitled to an acquittal and discharge as asked for.

To this rule, see the People vs. Barrett and Ward, 2 Cairns Report 304.

Reynolds vs. State, 3 Kelley (Ga.), Report Sup. C., 53, citing State vs. McKee, 1 Bailey, 651, where the court say: Taking then our own decisions, and those of the United States Courts of New York and England together, we are enabled to say that a jury after they are charged can be discharged, and the prisoner tried a second time, for the following causes only:

Consent of the prisoner; illness of one of the jury, the prisoner or the court; absence of one of the jurymen; the impossibility of their agreeing on a verdict. Beyond these I apprehend the court has no right to go.

See, too, Mount vs. State of Ohio, 14 Ohio, 295.

Hawkins' plea of the Crown, title Discontinuance, 243.

Mr. Emmons then read the opinion of Judge Randall.

OPINION OF JUDGE RANDALL.

The communication of Governor Reed states a case purporting to be the case made by the record of proceedings of the Senate organized for the trial of his impeachment.

The case as found in the journal of the Senate does not differ essentially in any legal aspect from that stated by him.

The question presented is, what is the effect of the action taken by the Senate and the Assembly upon the honorable, the Assembly, which was lately pending before the Senate upon the personal and political rights of Governor Reed, and the political rights of the Legislature and the people.

The office and purpose of the process of impeachment, as was well stated by one of the counsel who appeared in behalf of the Lieutenant-Governor, is to provide that the State may not be degraded by a delinquent officer; and as well, as was stated by other counsel, that in this process neither the State nor any citizen should be deprived of any lawful right by the action of any branch of the government.

It was well urged that this court had no authority to sit in review of or to reverse or nullify the action or proceedings of the Senate. But it was not well said, in a legal sense, that the Senate was a body having a superier jurisdiction, because its powers comprehend a broader and more elevated plane, untrammeled by the severe rules and axioms of the common or statute law. If this be true, the modern theories of government and the forms of civil governments framed in the later periods, are but solemn complicated frauds, machines for the amusement and the impoverishment of the people. If all political and judicial supervisory power is lodged in any one body of men, notwithstanding the establishment which all people love so reverently, organized under written constitutions, which in terms divide the powers of government into several departments of magistracy, supposed to be created to perform the offices of correctives and balances, then are such several departments mere cheats and shams, baubles and playthings invented to delude and ensnare.

If this be so, what need of any other department than a single body of men, or indeed a single human being covered with tinsel, whose "ambrosial locks" and imperious nod may dispense all power and all justice and command the obedience of all other men; a government fashioned after that of heaven itself, but whose Mentor is a mere piece of crumbling pottery?

On the other hand, the Senate, created by the written law of the people, like any other department or fraction, has such authority as is conferred by law. It has not been supposed to be a tribunal higher than the executive or judicial branches of government. As a judicial body it can act only upon the request of another branch called the Assembly. It has judicial jurisdiction of but a single proceeding. It cannot reverse or set aside the judgement of the Supreme Court, or of a Justice of the Peace. It may, if the Assembly complain and prove, dismiss our members for violation of law, but it cannot prescribe our judgments. Neither department is utterly independent of or "above" the other. The Legislature, by the repeal of a law, may take from the courts the power to act in a given case depending upon the existence of the repealed act, but it cannot deprive the courts of the power to administer the existing law. It may pass an unconstitutional act, and no power can prevent its action, but it cannot enforce it, nor will the courts permit its enforcement; nor can the Legislature enforce any law without the aid of the judicial tribunals—neither is superior, neither is inferior.

The remarks addressed to the court by counsel concerning the higher or supervisory character of the branches of the Legislature, as judicial tribunals of which the courts may stand in peculiar awe, cannot be considered otherwise than as an argument that the proceedings of the Senate in such capacity were beyond the *control* of any other tribunal. This is not a question in the consideration of the matter now under examination.

The simple question is, what is the necessary legal effect and result of the action of the Senate and Assembly upon the impeachment and trial of the Governor. I may further remark that the proceedings of the Senate in this matter are, unquestionably, beyond the control of this court, even as the proceedings of the court are beyond the control of the Senate. The respect which each body owes to itself precludes the possibility of any interference by it with the action of the other, or any invasion by either with the jurisdiction of the other. The final action of the Senate is to be examined only for the purpose of ascertaining what action it has taken and what results legally flow from such action, to the end that such results may be declared. And I venture to declare that this final action must be examined with reference to the law governing the powers of the actor, for, so far as the rights of others are concerned, even a legislative or judicial body cannot violate the law so as to deprive the people or any one of them of rights intended to be secured by law, without abrogating the principle underlying the whole fabric of Republican institutions, that governments are instituted among men for the protection of men's rights; and the courts are organized as integral parts of the government for the purpose of enforcing this protection.

The house of Assembly impeached the Governor, and by virtue of the Constitution he stood bereft at once of the Executive function which at once devolved upon the Lieutenant-Governor. The Governor yielded, and pleaded to the charges.

The Senate by its first rule, its law adopted for the purposes of the trial, resolved to "continue in session from day to day, Sundays, excepted until final judgment shall be rendered."

The Assembly declared itself not ready to prove the charges by reason of the absence of testimony and witnesses.

The Senate by a vote of eleven in the negative, to nine in the affirmative, rejected an order proposed by one of its members "that the Senate sitting as a High Court of Impeachment do now adjourn in accordance with the concurrent resolution adopted by the Senate and Assembly for the adjournment of the Legislature.

The Senate thus refused to postpone the trial as was requested by the Assembly, and thus practically repeated or reaffirmed the rule to proceed from day to day until final judgment.

The Governor demanded a trial and protested that the trial should not be postponed to a time beyond the expiration of his term of office, and insisted that such postponement not only would deprive him of his right to trial and his right to be heard in his defense, which was secured to him by the terms of the Constitution, but would deprive the Senate of the power to try him, as he would be out of office by the constitutional limitation of his term before the next meeting of the Legislature, and the power of the Senate, therefore, to give judgment would be gone; such postponement would leave nothing upon which a judgment could operate. Whereupon the Assembly, not proceeding with the trial, the Senate sitting for the trial, adjourned, and the Senate and Assembly forthwith adjourned without day.

Now the sole question is, what is the legal result and the legal effect upon the rights of all the parties affected. I cannot avoid the questions by declining to answer, upon the ground that the court cannot determine the regularity or review the action of the Senate in its judicial capacity. I would decline such interference whenever it should be demanded from any source. Has the Senate taken such action that as to itself, and to Governor Reed, and to the proceeding, it must necessarily take any further action in the case to bring it to termination. Is its power over the case exhausted? If I understand the majority of the court, they decline to interpret this action of the Senate; and then, I think, they do proceed to construe it, differing with me as to our duty to declare our opinion of its legal effect.

They conclude that the proceedings had by the Senate were not final until so declared by that body, while my conclusions are that the action taken was final as to result and effect; and if the Senate consider the matter again it should come to the same conclusion, uninfluenced, however, by our opinions in the matter of its duty, of which it alone will judge.

I have neither time nor inclination, nor is it material in my judgment, to comment upon the various authorities, legal and historical, relating to impeachment proceedings, upon the legal effect of the prorogation or dissolution of the British Parliament, for, according to the view I take of the case, I may agree consistently with the argument of the learned counsel who responded to the counsel of Governor Reed. I deal only with the case presented and its peculiar circumstances.

I conceive that the analogy between the qualities and organization and powers of the House of Lords, and those of the Senate of this State, is utterly wanting in at least two important particulars. The points of departure may be discovered in the following statement:

1. The Senate in conjunction with the Assembly may adjourn and thus dissolve their session, and may thus cease to act, and deprive themselves of the power to act in a legislative or judicial capacity, *of their own volition.*

The House of Lords is a court in its fundamental existence, having all the incidents and jurisdiction of a judicial tribunal at the common law; having power to try not only political but other offenses, and to review the judgments and proceedings of all other courts; its judicial existence cannot be divested or destroyed by its own action; it cannot dispose of cases before it by its dissolution or adjournment; it cannot dissolve itself; like all common-law courts, its cases remain before it until it takes affirmative action; it cannot terminate its own sessions by adjournment, but only by the command of the sovereign, and the sovereign cannot dismiss causes from its jurisdiction. Hence, the prorogation or dissolution of the Parliament, being done in virtue of the royal command, a power not to be resisted in that respect, does not divest it of jurisdiction over pending causes, and an impeachment, being a proceeding against *the person*, survives every accident save the death of the accused. (I understand this to be the law of England, and I think the death of the accused destroys from that moment all jurisdiction of the House of Lords or other criminal courts over the proceeding, and that such proceedings as were pending are from that moment abated).

2. The impeachment before the House of Lords is a proceeding against the citizen and peer in his individual capacity for offenses committed either in his official or personal capacity. The trial is the trial of an offender, and the judgment is that of a court, the highest in the kingdom, whose process issues to enforce its judgments, even to the taking of the life of the per-

son convicted. It tries and convicts of murder and of larceny upon an impeachment, and as an appellate court it tries the rights of liberty and property, and pronounces and enforces its judgments and decrees at law and in equity.

The Senate can judicially try only upon impeachment, and it can try, not the citizen for committing crime, but only an officer, as such, for the sole purpose of deposition from his office and eligibility. Its judgments can be enforced only by means of judicial process from the courts of law, construing and acting upon the judgment of the Senate as upon a law of the State.

One deposed from office by the judgment of the Senate may be kept from office only by the courts, the power of the Senate being exhausted by the rendition of its judgment. But the judgment of the Senate even will not be enforced by the courts, if the judgment be not authorized by the law of the land, of which the courts cannot refuse to determine.

The Senate must have jurisdiction of the officer or it cannot try him. If the Senate postpone the trial to a day when the officer ceases to exist, it doth forthwith postpone and divest itself of jurisdiction over the matter charged, of power over the officer, of the power to render a judgment, and there is no other logical sequence, in my judgment, than that it postpones the case out of its jurisdiction, and so there is nothing further upon which the Senate or court can operate. In other words, the case is dismissed, gone out of existence so effectually that it cannot breathe again, no power can restore it, and the accused discharged from the custody of the court.

It cannot be said with any degree of plausibility that the constitutional provision, that the officer impeached shall be "deemed under arrest and disqualified from performing any of the duties of the office *until acquitted* by the Senate," contemplates an acquittal only by a vote of "not guilty."

An *acquittal*, as I understand it, is a discharge by virtue of any action of the Senate whereby it refuses expressly or otherwise further to entertain the case or act upon it, or which places the cause beyond its reach, and by which it has no longer any power or authority to render a judgment upon the guilt or innocence of the officer.

This Senate has already established this as the correct interpretation, in the case of the impeachment of a high judicial officer of this State, by its vote that the prosecution be discontinued and the case dismissed. Upon this the officer resumed, without question, the duties of his office. If the constitutional provision referred to contemplates a vote of "not guilty" or any judgment upon the merits of the charges, then is the judge of the Sixth Circuit still suspended, and incalculable mischief and wrong done to the people by his subsequent unauthorized action. I am of the opinion, and I submit that any action of the tribunal in question which precludes a further proceeding in the case pending before it, necessarily terminates the case as effectually as though it were dismissed in express words. It puts an end to the case absolutely, and necessarily discharges the party from the arrest.

The right to a trial on the part of the accused is as sacred as the right to try on the part of the accuser.

The power to suspend and postpone the trial and to resume it, depends upon the jurisdiction. The right to arrest and suspend from office depend upon the power to give a trial and to convict or acquit. The Constitution contemplates a trial, and the power to try, once gone, all the consequences of the accusation cease. A refusal to try is a refusal to convict.

Without denying the power claimed on the part of the House of Lords to proceed at its next session after a dissolution of the Parliament and to conclude any business begun and not concluded, and not denying the power of the Senate to adjourn and postpone the trial of an impeachment to a day when it may proceed to try the officer accused, it is my judgment that the postponement to a day when it will have no jurisdiction of the officer is an absolute dismissal of the matter from the further consideration of the Senate, and a discharge of the accused must follow as a matter of law.

So, concluding upon the premises stated, I must upon my convictions of duty, say that, in my opinion, Governor Reed had the right officially to solicit the opinion of the court, whenever, after the adjournment of the Legislature, he saw fit to do so; that he had a lawful right after such adjournment to resume the power and proceed to the discharge of the duties pertaining to the Executive Department whenever he saw fit. Yet it was wise to address the constitutional advisers of the Executive upon the matter before resorting to any measure which would have disturbed the peace of the community.

As my brethren have come to other conclusions as to their duty; have formed other opinions as to the status of the proceeding in question, or that the Senate alone can determine the effect of its action by an express declaration, while I regret to be obliged to differ from them, I am equally obliged, out of respect to the law, to cheerfully acknowledge that my conclusions are not legitimate, for so the court decides. And I respect its opinions, as all good citizens should, notwithstanding any differences of private judgment.

The counsel for the Managers read and filed the following:

Resolved, That the Assembly proceed this day at 12 M. with the prosecution of the trial of Harrison Reed, and that the Managers and counsel on the part of the Assembly take such proceedings to secure the immediate attendance of State witnesses as are necessary and proper to do in the premises.

Adopted by the Assembly May 2, 1862.

M. H. CLAY,
Clerk of the Assembly.

Mr. Wentworth moved that the Senate as a High Court of Impeachment for the trial of Harrison Reed do now adjourn until to-morrow at 12 M.

Which was agreed to.

And the Senate as a High Court adjourned.

The conspirators now fully realizing the predicament into which Day had got them, by calling an extra session of the Legislature, began to cast all sorts of epithets upon his devoted head. As a common-place observation, Reed had killed two birds with one stone. The issuance of his proclamation declaring himself Governor had not only put his case before the court, but had so frightened Day as to induce him to call the Legislature together. If the Legislature had not been called together the conspirators would have succeeded, and Governor Reed would have remained suspended until the expiration of his term of office. A second caucus was held in the hotel, and Cessna, Johnson, Stearns, Purman, Wentworth and several others, as well as the author of this work, were present, and a concurrent resolution was agreed upon to be rushed through the Legislature at all hazards. This resolution was to be presented as having passed both Houses at the regular session of the Legislature, and was invented as a complete answer to Judge Emmons' argument before the High Court of Impeachment, that the Senate having adjourned to an "impossible day," such adjournment operated as Reed's acquittal. On May 3d, the day on which the High Court of Impeachment was to meet, this resolution was presented by Cessna in the Assembly, and passed without a dissenting vote. The resolution was immediately reported to the Senate. Shortly after the resolution was reported the High Court of Impeachment, after several feeling-shots by test votes as to how the Senators would probably vote on Emmons' motion, the court adjourned until 5 o'clock P. M. As soon as the court adjourned the astute Purman, chairman of the Judiciary Committee, knowing this resolution to be such a glaring fraud, did not dare report it as an important matter, but reported it among several others as lost bills, the resolution being the last in the enumeration. These bills and resolutions were objected to by John A. Henderson and McCaskill, Democrats. Henderson looked at Purman and smiled, and then rose and moved that the resolution be laid on the table, which was unanimously carried. The following is the resolution:

Be it Resolved by the Assembly, the Senate concurring, That the journal of the Assembly for the 12th day of February, 1872, be corrected by inserting the following concurrent resolution which passed this House on that day but was by mistake omitted from the journal; also that the Senate journal of the 16th day of February be corrected in like manner by the insertion of the said joint resolution, which reads as follows, viz:

Resolved by the Assembly, the Senate concurring, That the present session of the Legislature shall be adjourned *sine die* on Monday, the 19th instant, at 12 o'clock, meridian, and the presiding officers of both houses shall at that hour declare their respective Houses so adjourned.

Resolved, further, That should the present session of the Legislature adjourn *sine die* before the trial of Harrison Reed, Governor, is completed, the acting Governor is requested to call a special session for the purpose of proceeding with said trial, whenever the managers on the part of the Assembly and Harrison Reed, Governor, shall notify the Secretary of State, in writing that they are ready for trial, or as soon thereafter as possible.

After the exposition of this resolution the Democratic members of the Senate thought it expedient to investigate the acts and doings of honest Cessna. John A. Henderson had moved a resolution to the effect, and as the discharge of Governor Reed waxed hot on the part of the conspirators he thought the time had arrived when the Democrats should know what was in store for them in case Day should remain Governor. The following reflected the policy of Day and his followers:

SENATE CHAMBER,
TALLAHASSEE, FLA., May 4, 1872.

To the Senate:

Your committee, appointed under a resolution of the Senate, of date the 2d instant, in words as follows:

Mr. Henderson moves the appointment of a special committee of three, who shall examine the pay rolls of the Senate and Assembly of the last session, and also the statements, returns and pay rolls of the several committees of the Senate and Assembly which have been returned to the Comptroller's office, and report upon the various refusals to allow pay in every case, and upon the cases of suspended pay in every case, and who made a verbal report of the same day, desire to submit the folfowing report:

That the appropriation to W. E. Burleigh, for pay as clerk of the Investigating Committee of the last session, appointed to enquire into the sales of the Pensacola, Georgia and Tallahassee Railroad; of Hamilton Jay, as clerk of the Assembly Judiciary Committee, and of Leroy D. Ball, as clerk of the Assembly Committee, to examine the books of the State Treasurer and Comptroller, were disallowed by the Speaker of the Assembly, on the pay rolls as made out, because "the services of such clerks for these committees were not authorized by the Assembly."

That the janitors of the last session were not borne on the pay rolls, and consequently were not paid, because these attaches were not by name included in the Appropriation Bill, and consequently could not be paid.

We are satisfied that the janitors were in regular attendance with the knowledge of each House, and ought to have been paid.

We are further satisfied that the clerks aforesaid, or some of them, did serve, but how much we cannot say. On this subject we cannot omit to say that in addition to the application of W. E. Burleigh, for pay as clerk of the Railroad Investigating Committee, $260 has also been paid to Mr. Bowes for like services, and the sum of $270 has been paid to F. A. Dockray for same services.

The multiplicity of clerks about the capitol during the session, as well as in vacation, who are emyloyed without authority of law, and who press for recognition and payment by appropriation of the Legislature is a growing evil, and calls for our unqualified disapprobation.

Your committee have found one suspended claim in the office of the Comptroller, coming within the scope of our resolution, as follows: In a "statement of expenses incurred by the Assembly Committee appointed to investigate the sale of the

Pensacola and Georgia and Tallahassee Railroad, January session, 1872, between January 12 and February 8, 27 days," are the following items: To F. A. Dockray, clerk, 27 days, at $10 per day, $270; to F. A. Dockray, witness, 4 days, at $3 per day, $12; mileage, $18; actual expenses allowed in lieu of mileage, $30; to F. A. Dockray, 14 days at $20, expenses incurred in Washington and New York investigating testimony produced before the committee preliminary to session of the Legislature, $240; United States currency, $280, which was certified "correct," by order of committeee, and signed W. K. Cessna, chairman. The last item in this bill had been suspended by the Comptroller, because it was not expenses incurred by authority of the Legislature or of either branch, and not covered or included by the appropriation.

It would be injustice to fail to say, that while this committee were making their investigations, Mr. Cessna called at the office of the Comptroller, and having obtained leave of the Comptroller, withdrew this statement and cancelled this last item, stating that his approval was not intended to certify its payment, but that it was his idea that the voucher would be the certificate of correctness upon which payment would be made, and that he had declined to sign such voucher.

Very respectfully,
JOHN A. HENDERSON,
ROBERT MEACHAM.

Osborn and his conspirators now exposed, outgeneraled and utterly confounded, could be seen, night and day flying from Democrat to Democrat, beseeching them most solemnly to enter into a combination with them to save them and their chief from disaster and disgrace, and in consideration of their support the conspirators were to divide all the offices of the State equally with them. The Democrats, remembering the Ross-Johnson-Christy trick, contemptuously declined. The Democrats and Governor Reed's Republican friends granted them only one request, which was to adjourn the High Court of Impeachment from day to day so as to give the conspirators ample time to prepare for death—for it was a dreadful thing for them to die by Harrison Reed ascending the throne. The following proceedings of the court will show how the conspiracy was crushed out, and the rightful Governor sustained:

HIGH COURT OF IMPEACHMENT, FOUR O'CLOCK P. M.

High Court of Impeachment met pursuant to adjournment.

The Chief Justice in the chair.

The roll was called and the following Senators answered to their names:

Messrs. Adams, Atkins, Crawford, Dennis, Eagan, Henderson, Hill, Hunt, Johnson, Kendrick, McKinnon, Meacham, McCaskill, Purman, Sutton, Weeks and Wentworth—17.

A quorum present.

The Sergeant-at-Arms made proclamation.

The managers, with counsel, and the counsel for respondent, appeared in court.

The argument of counsel was concluded.

Mr. Dennis offered the following as a substitute for the order of Mr. Henderson:

Ordered, That the Assembly is hereby notified that the Senate will continue to sit as a High Court of Impeachment for the trial of Harrison Reed, Governor, and that the managers are hereby required to proceed with the prosecution of the Articles of Impeachment presented by them.

Mr. Billings moved to lay the order of Mr. Dennis on the table.

The yeas and nays were called for with the following result:

Those voting in the affirmative were:

Messrs. Billings Crawford, Eagan, Henderson, Hunt, Johnson, Kendrick, McKinnon, McCaskill and Sutton—10.

Those voting in the negative were:

Messrs. Adams, Atkins, Dennis, Hill, Meacham, Purman, Weeks and Wentworth—8.

So the motion was laid upon the table.

Mr. Purman moved that the room be cleared for the purpose of deliberation.

The yeas and nays were called for with the following result.

Those voting in the affirmative were:

Messrs. Adams, Atkins, Dennis, Hill, Meacham, Purman, Weeks and Wentworth—8.

Those voting in the negative were:

Messrs. Billings, Crawford, Eagan, Henderson, Hunt, Johnson, Kendrick, McKinnon, McCaskill and Sutton—10.

So the motion was not agreed to.

Mr. Dennis offered the following order:

HARRISON REED.

Ordered, That further consideration of the motion be posponed until Monday at 12 o'clock.

Mr. McCaskill moved that the motion be laid upon the table.

The yeas and nays were called for, with the following result:

Those voting in the affirmitive were:

Messrs. Adams, Atkins, Billings, Crawford, Eagan, Henderson, Hill, Hunt, Johnson, Kendrick, McKinnon, Meacham, McCaskill, Sutton Weeks and Wentworth—16.

Mr. Dennis voting in the negative.

So the motion was laid upon the table.

Upon the original order of Mr. Henderson,

The yeas and nays were called for with the following result:

Those voting in the affirmative were:

Messrs. Billings, Crawford, Eagan, Henderson, Hunt, Johnson, Kendrick, McKinnon, McCaskill and Sutton—10.

Those voting in the negative were:

Messrs. Adams, Atkins, Hill, Meacham, Purman Weeks and Wentworth—7.

So the order was adopted.

The Chief Justice then declared, as a legal consequence of the adoption of said order, Harrison Reed, Governor, discharged from custody.

The Senate chamber was packed to overflowing, both with the excited friends of Governor Reed and those of the conspirators during the roll-call on the motion to discharge the Governor, and the casual spectator could readily distinguish the contending factions by their demeanor as the roll was proceeded with. Whenever a Senator would answer yea, as his name was called, the conspirators and their friends would flinch and dodge as though they were engaged in a stiff skirmish line of battle with Reed and his friends, and each contending foe was not firing at the advancing column, but at his individual man. When the name of Dennis Eagan, of Madison, was reached, and he answered *yea*, Cessna, the chairman of the Board of Manageer, threw his hands across his head and wrung them as though he was suffering the most excruciating pains. Purman ran to prevent the Secretary from returning the vote as recorded, but the Chief Justice paid no attention to him, and ordered the vote to be returned. When the Chief Justice announced that Governor Reed was discharged, men could be seen in every direction running and shouting at the top of their voices that Reed was again Governor of Florida. The Board of Managers looked around for its chairman to lead them back to the Assembly hall, but he could not be found, so the balance of the managers deem it wise to get away the best they can, and they retreat in confusion, the counsel for the managers leading the retreat. Governor Reed marched into the Executive office and took possession. While the Senate was struggling to get a final vote on the motion to discharge, Day, now filled with anguish, was pacing back and forth, first to the door of the Executive chamber and peeping out for his messenger, and then back into the office. When the messenger came running with the dreadful intelligence which was the end of his career as Governor, so anxious was he to know the result that he did not wait his arrival, but ran to meet him and asked: "How is it?" "Reed's discharged." He turned his back on the messenger and wept.

At this session of the Legislature, C. H. Pearce, the great colored leader, who had been convicted by the conspirators on a trumped up charge of offering a bribe, was turned out of the Senate. Bolling Baker and J. B. C. Drew, who defended him, instead of making the point that the carrying of a message for another was no crime, made the point that the indictment read "the jurors," instead of "the grand jurors." This point was properly overruled by the court below and affirmed by the Supreme Court. When the vote was taken to declare Pearce's seat vacant, Purman, who expected to come before the freedmen again for office, and fearing Pearce would remind them as to how he voted, left the Senate to avoid his name appearing as one of those who voted to turn Pearce out, and the Senate passed a resolution stating that fact. (See Senate journal, p. 20).

Nothing of importance was transacted by either branch of the Legislature at this extra session, after the discharge of Governor Reed, but the appointment of J. P. C. Emmons Attorney-General. Both Houses adjourned *sine die* May 6th.

CHAPTER XIV.

The Supplicant Conspirators. The Conspirators Capture the Republican Convention of 1872, but Completely Exonerate Governor Reed. Bloxham Nominated for Governor by the Democrats, and the Ring Desperate. The Election of Hart and the Canvass of the Vote.

Governor Reed, who had been slandered, persecuted, pursued and hunted like the partridge upon the mountain by the Osborn conspirators, because he had interrupted their systematized plan for wholesale plunder, was now at the head of the government, with all the appointing power in his hands, in which situation he could have had himself re-elected, or could have turned the State over to the Democrats if he had possessed the weakness of nine-tenths of humanity to avenge themselves for wrongs perpetrated upon them whenever opportunity offered; but the Governor, following the teachings of the good book, which declares "vengeance is mine, I will repay," was determined to pass the scepter of the State into the hands of a decent Republican if possible. The conspirators were well aware that Reed stood with flaming sword in hand between the gubernatorial chair and the Bureau-agent, M. L. Stearns, now began to beseech him humbly for quarter. Day, the fraudulent Lieutenant, Governor, was the first to do him reverence. He appeared at the Executive Office Nicodemus-like in the night, subsequent to the day Governor Reed was discharged, confessed his sins and asked forgiveness of the Governor. He informed him that he was misled by the other conspirators, and that he knew from the first that the Articles of Impeachment were only fabrications invented by Dockray, Osborn and Company, that he was forced to play his part for fear that the conspirators, who were instrumental in counting him in, might assist Bloxham in getting him out. Governor Reed, with much vehemence, said: "Then you were willing to disgrace me, who was elected by the people, with falsehood, to sustain a corrupt ring, and yourself, when you knew that you never were elected Lieutenant-Governor. Your days as Lieutenant-Governor are numbered." Day saw that the Governor was not quite disposed to shield him from the proceedings then pending before the Supreme Court in regard to his title as Lieutenant-Governor, retired from the Executive Office in dispair. Chief Osborn was the next to offer supplication. His term of office would expire at the end of Governor Reed's administration, and he did not see his way clear, as all of Governor Reed's troubles had originated from him. He suggested to the Governor the proposition of going in with him from henceforth, the honor and spoils to be equally divided between them. Governor Reed made this the occasion of opening the door of the pent up prison house of his thought, and with quivering voice he said: "Go in with you, who have so often attempted to disgrace me and my adminissration! Go in with you, who have brought dishonor on the Republican party of Florida, so that it is a stink in the nostrils of decent people! Go in with you, and your gang of plunderers and freebooters, who, except for the intervention of the Executive would have bankrupted the State for generations unborn! Go in with you, whose conduct, even since you were elected to the Senate of the United States, has been one continued effort to breed a conflict between the two races! Go in with you, who have caused me to be bankrupt in trying to allay the excitement which you and your Federal office holders have aroused among the freedmen! Palsied be my tongue should it sanction such an agreement, and withered be my hands if they should be used to carry out any agreement entered into by me with such an unprincipled wretch as you." Osborn, who now saw that Governor Reed could not be brought to his support, under any consideration, took leave of him and invented another scheme.

The Osborn conspirators, now thoroughly convinced that Reed was a very dangerous animal to deal with, invented a second plan to get control of the State Government. Although they had heretofore warned the freedmen against trusting any Southern man, be he Republican or Democrat, and had driven some of the Southern Republicans to the Democrats, some to sympathize with the Democrats, some on the half-way ground, and a majority in the dangerous attitude of silent lookers-on, they now made a complete change of front, and pitched upon O. B. Hart, a Southern Loyalist, an ex-slaveholder, a native of Florida, who was to be incidentally spoken of by them as a probable nominee for Governor on the Republican ticket of that year. This was to be done to mislead Governor Reed and the friends of honest government. Hart was only to be nominated in case of emergency and as a last resort. M. L. Stearns was their man, to be nominated if they could succeed in alienating the freedmen from Reed and uniting them on Stearns. The agreement was that they would go into the convention with plenty of money and bad whisky, to be used on such of the freedmen as were hungry, and with a great flourish of trumpets declare Stearns nominated whether nominated or not; and if a general break up was imminent, then Stearns was to rise in the convention, thank them for the high honor they had conferred upon him and tell them he now withdrew for the sake of harmony in the great Republican party. Such action would naturally draw the sympathies of the average freedman to him, two-thirds of whom would be as innocent as to his true intentions as so many children playing with a rattlesnake for pretty calico. After his withdrawal, Hart was to be immediately nominated as the candidate for the whole party, thereby apparently showing that the ring had been whipped out. Stearns, after withdrawing from this so-called nomination, was next to be nominated Lieutenant-Governor for his generous act of withdrawing from the head of the ticket to save the party. Was the plot successful? It was evident to the best informed anti-ring men in the party that chief Osborn had issued some important orders to be carried out in all the counties in selecting delegates to the nominating convention; but just what those orders were it was difficult to surmise for some time. Some of Governor Reed's old friends who had sworn allegiance to the ring during the Governor's suspension from office, were yet understood to continue their allegiance, but it had really ceased the very instant he was discharged by the Senate, though the ring was unaware of that fact. By this means Governor Reed was informed as to what the ring intended to carry out. A call for a Republican State Convention was issued by E. M. Cheney, to meet at Tallahassee, which convention met in July or August of 1872. Congress having passed a law allowing Florida two representatives, the convention had to nominate candidates for Governor, Lieutenant-Governor and two Members of Congress. The convention met, and it was not long before the fact was developed that the ring had put in some good work in all the counties to get possession of the State Government. Money was used lavishly by the ring, with whisky to back it up, and the average colored brother, who was of course now hungry, must be abundantly fed at once or his vote would be cast against the ring, who had taught them that selling their votes was true citizenship. Money was so much in demand by the colored brother that the members of the ring attempted to teach him a second lesson, that he should vote for a man on principle and not for money; but the colored brother refused to learn the esson, and insisted on that first taught him, which was money and not principle, and that this money must be forthcoming without debate. His demand was at once complied with, and the coffers of the colored brother were agreeably filled, though the ring doubted his fidelity to them. Had he not been contaminated with whisky and money at this convention, and a free and fair expression of the will of honest Republicans been had, Governor Reed would have been the choice of the convention for Governor. There was an intense feeling against Stearns and other members of the ring, and they had their hands full running to and fro in the convention trying to keep him in line of battle until a decided victory was won. As the roll call was proceeded with it disclosed the fact that the colored brother, who had now worked the ring for all it was worth, was deserting its standard in large numbers and joining the anti-ring element in the convention. The ring, who had captured the organization of the convention in the outset and elected secretaries whom they could rely upon in any emergency, began to see that they had lost their money and whisky, and without bold work, immediate work, and effective work, would lose all. They began to dispute the result of the roll call which had left Stearns behind. A recount was demanded by them, which was had, and Stearns was declared nominated. At once a rush was made by a majority of the delegates to the Senate chamber for the purpose of holding another convention. The ring observing this determination of the delegates, were prematurely forced to play their second card, but which worked out with as much precision as a mathematical problem. They rushed to Stearns and informed him that now was the time to save the day, to play the withdrawal card. Stearns, who was awaiting the signal, after partially restoring order in the convention, arose and said that he had been fairly nominated by the Republicans of the State as their standard bearer, but for the sake of harmony in the Republican party he preferred fighting in the ranks as a private soldier until victory should be won. This had the desired effect, as great applause followed it. O. B. Hart was now put in nomination and was declared the nominee of the party for Governor. Immediately a member of the ring was upon his feet eulogizing Stearns as the martyr of the Republican party of Florida and the embodiment of republicanism, and winding up by nominating him for Lieutenant Governor, and he was accordingly nominated. It will thus be seen that the ring, though beaten in their first game, were successful in their second. W. J. Purman, who had fled from Jackson County, and who was now playing between S. B. Conover, State Treasurer, and the ring, was nominated for Congress, and J. T. Walls was renominated in the Second Congressional District. The ring, now fearing that Governor Reed would take the stump in vindication of himself before the people, of the oft repeated calumnies which had been heaped upon him, by Articles of Impeachment and otherwise, from the very inception of his administration to the last year thereof, dreaded the consequences, as they had no evidence which would stand the test, even of an insignificant cross-examination. In open convention, and in the face of all the charges they had made against the Governor, they declared themselves to be the enemies of safe and honest government, and to mankind generally. A resolution was introduced by a one of the conspirators and unanimously adopted, endorsing in every shape the administration of Governor Reed as an honest and upright administration; and as a token of their sincerity a resolution was also unanimously adopted pledging the support of the party to Governor Reed as the next United States Senator for the term beginning March 4, 1873, and ending March 4, 1879. This, they claimed, would only be a just reward for their unwarranted persecution of him for four years.

The Democrats met in convention that year and nominated the valiant Bloxham for Governor, and Colonel Bullock, of Marion County, for Lieutenant-Governor. General Barnes, of Jackson Coutny, was nominated for Congress in the First District, and S. L. Niblack, of Columbia County, in the Second District. The Democrats, encouraged at the success of Bloxham in 1870, this year took a lively interest in the canvass all over the State, and if Governor Bloxham had been spared from his friends, whose speeches drove the votes of the freedmen from him, he would have been elected. These indecent and blatant politicians went all over the State, not canvassing for votes, but denouncing "niggers," so as to become more prominent before the Democratic party than Bloxham. Indeed, some of the older politicians in that party desired Bloxham's defeat to make room for themselves as the leaders of the party. There was a considerable number of the better class of white Republicans who met in convention at Jacksonville, styled the Liberal Republican Convention, and endorsed Bloxham for Governor and Horace Greeley for President, and the road looked clear for Bloxham until his so-called friends took the stump. This canvass was a very bitter one, and the ring was driven to desperation. Another weight that Bloxham had to carry was that he was viewed by the freedmen as being in opposition to General Grant, who was at the time the nominee of the National Republican party, and the average freedman looked upon him as their only Lord and Saviour.

The ring, after stultifying themselves by the indorsement of Governor Reed's administration, received orders from Chief Osborn from Washington, that a persistent fight must be made in every county to elect men to the Legislature, and none others, who would support him for the United States Senate. The Federal office-holders set to work to carry out these orders to the very letter. The most ignorant of the freedmen were taught that they were as competent for the Legisluture as the most intelligent among them, which teachings were received by many of them with "Hurrah for Osborn!" This teaching was protested against by the most intelligent freedmen, which brought about two Republican tickets in some counties. The ring, or Federal office-holders, of course furnished them all the money necessary to elect the ticket or count it in. What money, whisky and promises failed to accomplish the United States Deputy Marshals would make up for by intimidation at the public meetings and on the day of election at the polls. Osborn was not to be known in this fight as opposing Governor Reed's election to the United States Senate until after the State election had been held and the canvass of the vote by the State board.

S. B. Conover, who had proved treacherous to Governor Reed, and who was an aspirant at the convention for Gubernatorial honors, now turned his face to the United States Senate, in a kind of three-cornered fight. He made a fight in the county convention of Leon, but failed to secure the nomination for the Legislature on account of his unpopularity with the freedmen. This unpopularity was caused by his having come to the Constitutional Convention of 1868, adhering to the "mule team" faction, and then suddenly deserting his banner and going to the Osborn faction, and because of his treachery to Governor Reed. The ring would not trust him, therefore he was forced to treat with Governor Reed's friends to have any political standing at all. The author of this work and several others of Governor Reed's friends were sent for to have a consultation with him. The meeting was held in the office of the State Treasurer. Conover proposed to have the author withdraw from the Republican Legislative ticket and have himself put on the ticket in consideration of the pay allowed a member. This proposition was rejected. He then proposed that John Whyatt, colored, who had been nominated at the same time the author was, withdraw for the same consideration, which was accepted by Wyatt. Conover wanted Wyatt to wait the result of the election, but Wyatt informed him that the cash must be paid before the election, as he could wait for contingencies. The money was paid and Wyatt withdrew. The Republican majority of two-thirds at the beginning of the reconstruction had by the plundering conduct of the ring dwindled to a bare majority in both branches of the Legislature, and the ring was hard pushed; they therefore suggested to Governor Reed the propriety of bringing in the colored troops from Georgia to carry such counties as they could conveniently be imported into, and swell the vote for Governor, but he declined favoring such a proposition, and informed them that he had promised the people to give them a fair election as far as his power as Governor could be extended, and that he would countenance no steps looking to the defeat of the will of the people, and that the will of the people ought and should be obeyed. Notwithstanding Governor Reed's dissent from this proposition, it was attempted to be carried out in Leon and other counties. All necessary arrangements were made with Joseph Bowes, a carpetbag professional ballot box stuffer, to bring them in on the day of election in Leon County at all precincts bordering on the Georgia line. The Southern outrage mill was to grind fine enough to bring to their aid at the polls the United States troops on the day of election and overawe the whites and prevent them from interfering with the illegal voters from Georgia. This attempt at fraud proved abortive, as the ring's over-anxiety to secure votes for the head of the ticket and also to secure the legislative delegation from this county for their chief, Osborn, nominated a ticket outside the Republican organization in oppositon to the regular ticket headed by C. H. Pearce for the Senate, who had been convicted of bribery and ousted from the Senate by these same conspirators, but who were now seeking the endorsement of his people by re-election. The alien voters were to cast their ballots for the ring legislative ticket, as well as for Governor. This scheme was discovered by Pearce through the information of Governor Reed, who suspected the ring would attempt what they had before suggested to him. This scheme was made known to whites through Pearce and his friends, which brought a union between the anti-ring legislative ticket and the whites in this county as against fraud. This scheme was denounced in such severe terms on the stump both by the Democrats and anti-ring Republicans as to force the ring into a denial of the plot; yet, those who were acquainted with the character of these men, know they still meditated fraud. The soldiers were placed at each polling precinct. Governor Reed, in the meantime, had confidentially instructed those sheriffs of the different counties that he could rely on, to arrest and imprison any one who came from Georgia and voted or attempted to vote. Bowes, who had the management of the whole affair, was dubious in carrying out this plan, as he was convinced that it could not be done without bloodshed, as the whites as well as the anti-ring freedmen had sworn that his should be the first blood shed. The colored troops from Georgia hearing of the threats made by the whites and anti-ring freedmen, failed to appear on the day of election, although the United States Deputy Marshals and soldiers were there to protect them. So an anti-ring delegation was elected; but had it not been for the aid of the whites the ring would have counted in its delegation, though they had not got a vote. The ulterior object of the conspirators in making O. B. Hart the last resort for the nomination for Governor was that he was decrepit, and that a round or two in the canvass would bring a speedy termination of his life, and leave Stearns Governor of the State. Governor Reed seems to have been cognizant of all their tricks, and informed Hart that this was their object; but the old man was so very anxious to become Governor that he paid no attention to the warning. Hart was now pushed into the canvass as though he was a young and healthy man, and when the campaign closed it was patent to all that the old man was not long for this world.

The State was carried for the Republicans by between four and five thousand majority, but the Legislature was very close. The rains in South Florida prevented many Democrats from going to the polls—for this is where Bloxham must look for his success. The ring again attempted to force the Returning Board to count out the legally elected Democrats to the Legislature and count in a large majority for the Republicans. They informed Governor Reed that it was to his interest to count in a large majority of Republicans, as he had been endorsed by the Republican Convention as the next United States Senator. He gave them to understand that he did not want the senatorship unless a majority of the legally elected members of the Legislature should say so by their votes. J. C. Gibbs, Secretary of State, was besought to do some fradulent counting, and the Osborn conspirators promised to make him the next Member of

Congress if he would count to suit them, but Gibbs informed them that he had been there before. Before the vote of the State was canvassed by the Board, Governor Reed discovered, in looking over the returns sent to his office, that the returns from Jackson, Gadsden and Jefferson Counties had been opened and the returns altered. These returns gave the Democratic ticket large majorities and converted Hart's majority into a minority. The real party who altered the returns was one Burleigh, a carpet-bagger who was a clerk in Secretary Gibbs' office at the time, and Governor Reed had often warned the Secretary that he believed him to be a spy; but Gibbs thought him to be honest, and had the utmost confidence in him. The conspirators, knowing they had carried the State and had a small majority of Republicans in the Legislature, felt confident that with a free use of money, and with Governor Reed out of the way they could re-elect Osborn to the United States Senate. They had endorsed the Governor for the Senate, and all honest Republicans of course would demand his election in case the Legislature was carried by the Republicans. Something must be done to weaken Reed in the estimation of the Republicans before the meeting of the Legislature. It is believed, though I am not certain in this, that they actually hired Burleigh to alter these returns so as to implicate Governor Reed and give themselves some data and excuse upon which to base oposition to the Governor's election, and secure the election of Osborn. The author of this work was personally acquainted with Burleigh, and after the fraud had been discovered, and Burleigh was about to leave the State for fear of an indictment, he inquired of him as to who induced him to commit the fraud, and he unhesitatingly declared that neither Governor Reed nor his friends nor any Democrat had anything to do with it, but that it was done for the benefit of the party. The conspirators constituted themselves the party, as they had captured the party organization. Before the State Board commenced the canvass Governor Reed requested them to put off the canvass for a day or two, as he had something very important to lay before them. He did not even inform Gibbs what had been done, and Gibbs was as ignorant as to the alteration of these returns as an animal without reason.

The Governor privately secured new returns from Jefferson and Gadsden, and attempted to send a messenger to Jackson, but was betrayed, and then for the first time he revealed confidentially to Adams, one of the state board of canvassers, the fact of the altered returns from Jackson and asked delay in opening the convass until he could procure a true return. The delay was refused by Mr. Adams, who claimed that they had a correct copy, which would be substituted, Again opening the canvass, the board secretly sent Col. M. Martin to procure a new return and to exposed the mutilated copy so as to sustain a charge against the Secretary of State, Gibbs, and Gov. Reed, of attempted fraud in the interest of the Democrats, This would dispose of Reed for the Senate, and as Gibbs would almost certainly be endorsed by the colored brother as one of the members of Hart's cabinet—he being a man of unquestioned ability—this would end his aspirations and his place would be filled by a carpet-bagger. The canvass was commenced after the return of Martin, and all the leading chiefs were on hand. The fraudulent returns from the counties named were thrown out and the true returns handed in by Martin were counted, which elected the State ticket by a good majority, but the lower branch of the Legislature was very close. The ring now commenced the war upon Governor Reed again by industriously circulating among the freedmen that he attempted to sell out the Republican party, but that Colonel Osborn and the members of his ring had caught him and Gibbs in the act and saved the freedmen from utter destruction. This false accusation had great weight, not only with the mass of the freedmen, but with some of the more intelligent, who believed that Governor Reed was the guilty party, and he was denounced by the members of the ring whenever they met a member of the Legislature whom they suspected would support him for the Senate, and the freedmen were instructed to brand every man as traitor who dare talk of voting for Harrison Reed for United States Senator. Adams, who had promised, on his honor, to return the fraudulent returns to Governor Reed after the canvass, and conscious of the innocence of the Governor, now handed the returns to some of the members of the ring to be used against him in the future politics of the State, and more especially at his home in Duval County. Though Colonel Bisbee and all the chiefs were fully advised that Governor Reed was the first to expose this fraud, yet those very returns were used in Duval County against him, and they were kept on hand by some member of the ring and read to the freedmen to prevent his having any influence with them in his own county. Abram Grant, for instance, who, we have no doubt, believed what he heard the members of the ring assert, said that he believed that Governor Reed attempted this fraud. Grant, a freedman himself, and knowing very little about the dark doings of these conspirators, although a citizen of the Governor's county, was allowed, while advocating the nomination of Colonel Bisbee, to declare from the stump that the Governor attempted to sell out the party by means of these fraudulent returns. Grant was never corrected in this statement by Bisbee or any of these conspirators, on the stump or in the newspapers. Was this "edifying to the old or hope-inspiring to the young," to have our fellowman slandered in this wise and refuse to raise our voice against it? This slander could not with propriety be denied by these men because they were accessory before the fact.

A week before the meeting of the Legislature of 1873, Chief Osborn, anticipating the great opposition to his re-election to the United States Senate, evacuated Washington and hastened to establish his headquarters at Tallahassee in the old City Hotel, at which place his retinue of Federal officeholders soon gathered to do the bidding of their chief. Governor Reed, at the same time watching the manoeuvres of the ring, set to work a counter plan to head them off. He proposed to Hart, the Governor-elect, to allow him the privilege of delivering the annual message to the Legislature. To this proposition the ring demurred, and of course Hart sustained the objection. They finally decided to allow the Governor five minutes only to address the Legislature. They knew he could strike some heavy blows and that he had them in store for the ring, and if he was permitted to deliver a message that would most probably review the conduct of the ring from his inauguration to his exit, it would certainly cause disaster and defeat to the chief and the election of the Governor to the Senate. He, however, had to accept the short time allowed him, and as a Christain gentlemen, attempted to make the inauguration of Hart as imposing as possible. He hired a fine team and himself and family proceeded to the Tallahassee depot to receive Governor Hart. When the train arrived with Hart, who was accompanied by a number of the members of the ring, Governor Reed left the carriage and went to the car which bore the distinguished guest, and after greeting him by a friendly shake of the hand, offered to assist him in getting his traps from the cars. Hart, whom Governor Reed had appointed at the beginning of his administration one of the judges of the Supreme Court, now haughtily turned away from him, saying that he had other matters to attend to. Hart and his ring friends then got out of the car and actually took possession of the Governor's carriage, filled it with himself and the ring managers, without so much as saying "by your leave," and drove off to the city, leaving Governor Reed and his family to get away the best way they could. Osborn and his officeholders now met in secret conclave and arranged plans to capture the organization of the lower branch of the Legislature. It was well known by them that at least three members of the Leon County delegation, Wallace, Proctor and Conover, would not, under any circumstances, vote for a member of the ring for Speaker, and that none of the delegation could be brought to the support of Osborn unless they were actually bought; and they could not elect the Speaker with Republican votes without this delegation. They must resort to strategy to secure the election of one of their number. Colonel M. Martin, who had also received great favors from the hands of Governor Reed, being appointed by him warden of the State prison, when he was near starvation, was agreed upon as the man who must save the sinking ship. John R. Scott was again made the pliant tool of the ring, though he professed to be opposed to them. They agreed that Scott should be put in nomination for Speaker by the Republican caucus, and that Martin should be held in reserve for the Democrats to vote for, as they knew that the whites had naturally rather have a white man to preside over them than one of their fomer slaves. Scott, as usual, was silly enough to believe that the ring favored him for Speaker.

Scott was to be put forward because he was black, thus compelling the representatives from Leon County to vote for him or to suffer violence from the freedmen, who would be told that the Leon delegation had voted against one of their own color for Speaker. This delegation being thus forced to vote for Scott, some carpet-bagger would nominate Martin and the other carpet-baggers, violating the caucus obligation, were to follow after the Democrats had given votes enough to elect with the carpet-bag vote thrown to them. The friends of Governor Reed were not united as to the best course to pursue, and he had no white friend among the carpet-baggers in the Legislature upon whom he could depend. This division among the Governor's friends caused some of the anti-ring members to ally themselves with S. B. Conover, the Governor's State Treasurer, and support him for the Speakership, not because they had any special confidence in him, but because they believed him to be the most available man against Martin, whom the Democrats had agreed to support in case there was any chance of Scott's election. Conover was reported to have voted for Bloxham when he ran for Lieutenant-Governor in 1870, and unless he falsified his own word, he voted for Bloxham this year when he ran for Governor. The object of the ring in attempting to secure the Speakership was that they had instituted several contests for Democratic seats so as to turn enough of them out of the Legislature to elect Osborn without the aid of the Leon County delegation, who were pledged to the whites of that county never to vote for Osborn. In our next chapter we shall see how they succeeded.

CHAPTER XV.

Governor Hart's Administration. The Ring Makes preparation to Capture the Organization of the Lower House of the Legislature. The Meeting of the Legislature of 1874, and Carpetbag Treachery to the Negro. Extracts from Governor Hart's Message. Protest of the European Bondholders Against the Neglect of the State of Florida. The Protests of Bondholders Gotten up to Cover Stearn's Tracks. The Assembly Investigating the Stealing Statutes. The Attempted Sale of West Florida. M. Martin and the State Prison. Governor Reed Attempts to Head off Stearns' Railroad Steal. Governor Reed's Memorial as to His Claim Against the State, and the Appointment of a Joint Committee. A Scramble for the Agricultural College Money. Varnum Trips up Cowgill.

The administration of Governor Hart, though he was the first native Governor of Florida, was full of vacillation and uncertainty as to a real line of policy. His administration lasted for fifteen months, the most of which time he spent at the North in the fruitless attempt to rebuild his health, which he had wrecked beyond hope of recovery by being forced into the canvass of 1872 by the members of the Ring for the express purpose of incapacitating him for the exercise of his official authority if elected. The Ring, now further to humiliate Governor Reed, had Hart appoint him a member of the Board of County Commissioners of Duval County, thinking that he would spurn the idea of accepting so inferior a position after having been Governor of the State. He, however, took them by surprise and accepted the position, and it was not long before he began to investigate and stir up the carpetbag scrip ring in Jacksonville, and after having struck one blow at a fradulent scrip grab, in which he beat them out of a couple of thousand dollars, his removal was demanded by the Ring, and he was at once decapitated by Hart. Hart went to the North after the adjournment of the Legislature of 1873, and M. L. Stearns, Lieutenant-Governor, assumed the head of the government. His first step was to lay wires by which to force the State to aid him to secure the nomination for Governor three years hence. William Archer Cocke, the Attorney-General, refused to be used for that purpose, and Stearns was driven to the alternative of employing outside counsel to bring suit in the United States Supreme Court, pretending to protect the interest of the State, but for the real purpose of getting possession of the Jacksonville, Pensacola and Mobile Railroad, the earnings of which were to be exclusively used, as far as possible to force his election to the United States Senate at the next meeting of the Legislature; but failing in that to compel his nomination for Governor by intimidating and buying out those freedmen who so bitterly opposed him. He began to interfere with the local school boards of the different counties, and whenever he could influence its members, no one in the black belt counties could get a school unless he was in favor of Stearns' and Hart's so-called administration. This administration inaugurated a most alarming proposition among the freedmen, which came near precipitating them into a war among themselves with reference to the representation in the Legislature from the colored Methodist and Baptist churches. The freedmen prior to the emancipation knew nothing of any other churches than the Missionary Baptist, Primitive or footwashing Baptist, and the Methodist Episcopal; but at the close of the war the A. M. E. Church sent ministers from the North, the most of whom were men of intelligence, and these men enlisted some of the most intelligent of the freedmen under their banner as ministers. These ministers, discerning the scarcity of leaders among the freedmen, went into politics. A large number of them, previous to this year, had been repeatedly elected to the Legislature and had been fighting the Ring under the leadership of Governor Reed, which had alienated them permanently from that faction. The freedmen who belonged to the Baptist churches were taught that the members of the Methodist churches were cheating them out of a just representation and of their share of the offices; and that the Ring would see to it that the Baptist members should be elected to the Legislature. This teaching created church jealousy and great prejudice, which, in some counties, caused frequent rows, and but for the foresight and better judgment of the more intelligent ones in the churches, a general outbreak and bloodshed would have been the result among the colored churches. There were some vacancies to be filled in the Legislature of that year, caused by resignations, some of the members being appointed to Federal offices by Walls, Purman and Conover, or through their recommendation. In one county two Baptist ministers were put up for the Legislature without a regular nomination, one of them could neither read nor write, and when called upon to make a speech said to his auditors that if elected he would do whatever Governor "Starns" told him to do. This was an old colored Baptist preacher in Leon County, named Henry Griffin. Acting Governor Stearns and C. A. Cowgill, Comptroller, took the stump for this intelligent candidate, and brought to bear the whole power of the so-called administration in his behalf. Griffin was a Primitive or foot-washing Baptist, and the other candidate was a minister of the Missionary Baptist Church, whose name was John N. Stokes. The white Democrats and the freedmen united and defeated Griffin and Stokes, but Stokes was counted in by one majority.

The Ring having been defeated in the attempt to re-elect Osborn, turned their attention to M. L. Stearns to save the day. Conover, who had been elected to the United States Senate, now began, with the assistance of Purman and Walls, the Congressmen, to appoint some of the most influential colored men to some of the most important Federal offices, with, also, a good sprinkling of Democrats. These appointments alarmed Stearns and his followers, as the masses of the freedmen now saw, for the first time in the history of the State, their own color filling Federal offices that had heretofore been held by some of the most inferior members of the carpetbag ring. There was an agreement among the members of the Ring to go on no bond of any freedman appointed by Conover, Purman & Co. The white Democrats in many portions of the State did not hesitate to endorse these appointments, as they preferred an honest colored man in a Federal office rather than have the State infested with strangers whose sole purpose in the state was to fatten at the expense of those whose interests were identified with the soil; and the Osborn carpet-baggers who had grown rich from plunder, Federal and State offices, absolutely refused to go on these colored men's bonds until forced to do so when discovering that the Southern whites were only waiting for them to refuse so as to give them an opportunity of going on the bonds themselves, hereby proving to the freedmen what they had repeatedly asserted, that the carpet-baggers cared nothing for the interest of the negro, but to secure his vote to place them in office. This administration witnessed the inauguration of the packing of juries for political purposes, of which we shall treat in a future chapter.

The Ring, desiring to recover their lost ground in the lower branch of the Legislature, and being unwilling to trust any one of the members of the Ring as candidate for the Speakership on account of the anti-ring sentiment among the Republicans in that body, determined to capture the Assembly by stratagem. The night previous to the meeting of the Legislature the Ring members of the Legislature called a caucus meeting of all the Rep blican members to settle upon some one as the Republican nominee for Speaker. They had arranged secretly with the Democrats to elect M. Martin, warden of the State prison, for Speaker. The Democrats did not desire to vote for Martin, and any considerable number of them could not be brought to his support unless the Ring could show that a very incompetent Republican would be nominated by the caucus. So the Ring set to work among the colored members and advocated the election of Alfred B. Osgood, of Madison County, colored, who had always supported the Ring, not because he endorsed their action, but because he feared their power. The better informed colored members warned Osgood that the Ring was only putting him up as man of straw to be knocked down; but he, being ambitous, heeded not the warning, and was nominated for Speaker of the Assembly by the unanimous voice of the Republican caucus. While Osgood was a good fellow, he was not competent to act as Speaker. The Ring, however, had now carried their point, and went to the Democrats complaining, saying they were willing to do almost anything to prevent a negro being elected Speaker.

If Osgood had been better posted in parliamentary law the Democrats would have preferred him to Martin, and he would have been elected. The author of this work and the whole delegation from Leon County, while they were confident that Osgood would be slaughtered in the house of his friends—as was intended when John R. Scott was nominated for Speaker—supported him in good faith, prepared for the defeat which awaited him. Both branches of the Legislature met January 6th, 1874. Before swearing in any of the new members of the Assembly, McKinnon, Democrat, made a motion, which was carried, that M. Martin take the chair in the temporary organization. This motion was voted for by all the members of the Ring and all the Democrats, which showed that the secret work of the Ring had been well performed. The Assembly then adjourned until the following day. During this time the Ring members employed their time in encouraging the colored members to stand by Osgood and they would elect him on the following day, while at the same time they were telling the Democrats that they would do all they could to defeat him. The next morning the members-elect were sworn in and the Assembly proceeded to elect its Speaker. Several ballots were taken before a result was reached, the most of the Democrats who had voted for Conover for United States Senator hesitating at first to vote for Martin, and many of them voted for Swearengen, Democrat, from Wakulla County, who had voted for Conover for United States Senator; and, had the anti-ring Republicans not been intimidated by the freedmen and feared losing their influence with them, Swearengen would have been elected, as he should have been, to beat the treacherous members of the Ring. The colored brother got wrathy at the action of the carpet-baggers in voting against Osgood, but this availed nothing, as the bargain had been signed and sealed, and the goods must be delivered. Martin was finally elected. Bryant, of Polk, and Hardee, of Brevard, would never consent to vote for Martin, and if the other Democratic members had followed the same course Martin would have been defeated, and a Democrat elected Speaker. In the Senate the same sharp skirmishing relative to the swearing in of the newly elected members, four in number, took place. These were three

Republicans and one Independent or Conservative Republican, the Hon. Samuel Spearing, from Duval County, colored, who had been elected by the assistance of the most respectable Democrats in the county. Before the Senators-elect were sworn in a resolution was offered by John A. Henderson that the seat of Sturtevant, from the Twenty-first Senatorial District, be declared illegally held by him, and that Israel M. Stewart be declared the rightful Senator. Of course the Ring was not prepared to allow so damaging a resolution to pass, which would nearly transfer the Senate into the hands of the Democrats before Stearns could assume the reins of government, which the Ring so ferverently prayed might not be long in coming. After considerable wrangling the Senators-elect were sworn in and the Senate organized, with a full set of Republican officers. On the 9th of January Governor Hart addressed his message to both branches of the Legislature, in which he said:

"It is also very gratifying to know that the spirit of political hatred and bitterness, which was the fruit of that great rebellion, is well nigh extinguished, and the people of all parties are more united and harmonized than they have been for many years. Indeed, an era of good feeling and political toleration seems to have dawned throughout the State. Political antagonisms still exist, but that peculiar acerbity and rankling animosity that once characterized political opposition, has given place to the ordinary antagonisms that are legitimate and founded upon reasonable differences of opinions.

"That spirit of lawlessness which at one time threatened the peace of the Commonwealth, and which broke out in disgraceful outrages, disturbing the peace of society, and throwing some counties into a state of violent agitation, has, under the management of prudent and determined local officers, subsided, and is now obedient to the wholesome restraints of the law.

"From my standpoint of observation as Chief Executive, viewing as I do our past political history, the present condition of the State and reasonable expectations that the immediate future holds out, I have strong reasons for entertaining the hope that our beloved State has passed through the severest fires of its affliction, and that henceforth, by the united will and purpose of our whole people, peace and good government will be secured, and the people become prosperous and happy. I have reasonable assurances for this hope, in the fact that all political parties seem united to this end. God has given to us a goodly heritage. The bright skies, balmy and healthful atmosphere, and genial and fruitful soil of Florida is now largely attracting the attention of the people of the North. A good government, with wise and wholesome laws and a quiet and industrious and law-abiding citizenship is all that is required to make Florida, at no distant day, a prosperous and happy Commonwealth.

"The condition of my health has been such that my physicians thought it advisable for me to spend the summer North. During my absence from the State the Lieutenant-Governor constitutionally became the acting Governor, and I am happy to say that in his administration of the affairs of the government he has proven that the confidence placed in him by the people at the last general election was not misplaced.

FINANCIAL.

"Your wise financial policy for reaching a condition of cash payments established at the last session by the new law for the collection of the revenue and the act known as the Funding Bill started well and is progressing hopefully. We have encountered many difficulties in obtaining assessors who will dillgently assess all the taxable property, and collectors of revenue who will faithfully collect and pay over but, have generally succeeded in obtaining better men to hold those offices than many who have heretofore held them, and now under the wise provisions of your new tax law the revenew is being better assessed, collected and paid in than ever before in the history of our State. This fact, working together hand in hand with an earnest economy everywhere urged and practiced by the Comptroller, and infact by every department of the administration, has already lessened the volum of scrip afloat and issuing every day, and eased the treasurer some in regard to expenses that must be paid in cash. Shortly after the passage of the funding law we obtained the implied promise of the Board of Trustees of the Agricultural College Fund to invest the proceeds of the sale of their scrip with the Comptroller for new bonds, in order that the treasury of the State might have the benefit of that much cash to help along the benificent policy of the funding law. The first effect of this promise was the appreciation of the price of scrip and of the credit of the State to a noticeable extent. While under said law the Comptroller was diligently at work disposing of bonds, and with the proceeds redeeming old bonds that had been hypothecated in New York, the said promise was frequently, with apparent hearty ceherfulness, creating the most perfect confidence, renewed by the said board through its treasurer, when at the moment of highest expectation of fulfillment and immediate relief of the credit and finances of the State, it turned out to our astonishment and consternation that the said board was deceiving us all the while, and had invested their money in bonds which the Comptroller had sold in New York while redeeming said hypothecated bonds, thus leaving the money in New York instead of bringing it to Florida. This great dissapointment gave a check to the progress of our good work, and the violation of the promise has otherwise wrought mischief to the State. But this unwise act of the said board towards Florida cannot efiect the real value of our new bonds. They are and will necessarily remain among the best of securities, and as soon as the late universal business panic shall have subsdied we may confidently expect them to find sale at the price fixed, and the policy of the funding law to be in a reasonable time a fair triumph for Florida. I hold the board responsible because of its emphatic endorsment of the action of its treasurer. The only excuse that I have herd is that in June the treasurer of the board saw a contract made by the Governor and Comptroller giving the entire control of all these bonds to the New York man. I have reason to believe that the investment with him was virtually made before said treasurer saw the contract to which he refers. That contract will be found in the report of the Comptroller, and it will be seen that no reasonable and fair construction can torture it into such a meaning. The Comptroller was in frequent, almost daily, communication with said treasurer, urging the performance of said promise, and was as often assured that it would soon be done, that there was some difficulty in obtaining said proceeds from the purchasers of said scrip, but that it would soon be done all right. The said treasurer well knew that all of said bonds that had not been disposed of in New York were in the Comptroller's possession, in Tallahassee. I cannot imagine any good reason why we should thus have been deceived and said money left in New York instead of being brought to Florida, and I recommend an investigation with the view of ascertaining what was the inducement, provided it can be done without expense to the treasury."

During this year arose a difficulty between Governor Hart and Attorney-General Cocke, growing out of the very troublesome Vose claim against the State, which led to the Governor's asking Cocke to resign. The following extracts from the message give the Governor's version of the case and the Attorney-Genral's reply to the request to resign.

"It may be seen that the suit brought in the United States

Circuit Court by F. Vose against the Board of Truestees of the Internal Improvement Fund, holding all the swamp and overflowed lands in trust for the purposes of the Internal Improvement act of 1855, was not defended by the former board, but was wholly neglected and allowed to go to decree *pro confesso* against that board and to subsequent interlocutory decrees, without any attempt to set before the court the equities of the board and of the State therein. That the present board has deplored that neglect and intended to make every effort possible in order to get these defenses set forth before the court; that it employed the Attorney-General, himself a member of the board, as its attorney to accomplish it if possible, fully believing that if the court could be informed of the purposes and efforts and acts of this board, the court would not interpose to hinder it in any way. At the last term of said court, and after the Circuit Judge who rendered the decree had left Florida, this board (the Attorney-General being absent at Jacksonville, in attendance on said court on said case) learned with astonishment and consternation that a consent decree had been rendered, placing the board in the humiliating condition of virtually admitting openly in court on the records thereof all the allegations and charges made in the plaintiff's bill of complaint, and thereby admitting its own total incompetency and unfitness for administering the said trusts as required by law, and that the court ought to appoint and authorize other persons to do so in its stead. I have not yet been able to learn that any attempt was made by said attorney to have said decree *pro confesso* opened or to file any answer setting forth said defenses before said court. The board have consequently settled with its said attorney to employ another to still make now the almost hopeless effort to get all of said interlocutory decrees opened so that said defenses can be filed and brought to the attention of the court. For this, and for reasons arising from our railroad complications, as I have elsewhere stated them, of course the Attorney-General must see the great embarrassment of his remaining in the Cabinet, and a quiet suggestion of my desire for his resignation was made to him by me personally without going into any statements or discussion of the reasons. He suggested me to address him a letter and he would answer it. I then wrote my request, and he declined on the ground that I had not assigned my reasons.

"I sent him the following letter, viz.:

"EXECUTIVE OFFICE,
"TALLAHASSEE, FLA., January 2, 1874.

"*Hon. William Archer Cocke, Attorney-General of Florida, Tallahassee, Fla.:*

"DEAR SIR—Your answer of yesterday declining to resign

because I had assigned no reasons for my request, is at hand. I regret this because I did not expect it of you, even if there had been nothing special between us on the subject. If I remember rightly, from the first you voluntarily informed me, quite as a matter of course, that if at any time I should desire a change a very slight mention of it would produce your resignation promptly. Your course of non-action in the Anderson case, after fully understanding the course which the administration thought it best to pursue, and, though expressing your difference of opinion on one point only, yet promising official co-operation, and a reasonable certainty of success in getting the decree *pro confesso* against us opened so as to let in the defenses of the State; and the effects and consequences of that course to the State; your letter read in the Supreme Court of the United States, your letter in the newspaper implying a charge agains, the administration, and your consent decree in the Vose caset furnish me with my reasons for desiring your resignation.

When you think calmly for a moment upon these things, and upon the subsequent action of the Board of Trustees of the Internal Improvement Fund on the subject of said consent decree, and of its attorney, which action you have reason to know that I approve, you cannot help but see that you have placed yourself in antagonism, and that you and the administration cannot any longer work together in confidence and harmony, which the public interests so much require.

"I am, very respectfully, your obedient servant.
"OSSIAN B. HART,
"Governor of Florida.

"In answer to which letter I have received the following reply, viz.:

"ATTORNEY-GENERAL'S OFFICE,
"TALLAHASSEE, FLA., January 2, 1874.

"*To His Excellency, O. B. Hart, Governor State of Florida:*

"SIR—Your letter of this date is received. I consider that in the discharge of my official duties I have followed the law and my solemn conviction of right. I hope to act in harmony with the administration, but as the Attorney-General of the State I must pursue such course as the law indicates and I conceive for the best interests of the State. The reasons assigned by you not being sufficient, I therefore respectfully refuse to resign the office of Attorney-General.

"Most respectfully, your obedient servant,
"WILLIAM ARCHER COCKE,
"Attorney-General of the State of Florida.

"It may be seen that the "Cabinet of administrative officers," who, the Constitution provides, shall aid the Governor, is required, by this refusal, to endure the presence in it of an Attorney-General in whose abilities as a lawyer, and diligence in attending to his important duties in the courts, the Governor has lost all confidence. Believing that the interests of the State require it, I recommend action by the Legislature in the matter."

At this time the holders of certain bonds of the State issued in aid of the Jacksonville, Pensacola & Mobile Railroad, known as the Dutch Bondholders, through their attorneys made the following protest, which was laid before the Legislature by the Governor:

To the Governor of the State of Florida :

The undersigned respectfully represents that he is the duly authorized agent in this country of Geo. M. Boisevain, Joseph Zadacks, Adrian Stoop, Adrian J. Milders, N. J. deu Tex and many other persons residing in the Kingdom of Holland and elsewhere, *bona fide* purchasers and holders to a very large amount, to-wit: to the amount of more than three million dollars of the bonds of the State of Florida, issued by the said State in aid of the Jacksonville, Pensacola & Mobile Railroad Company, and bearing date the first day of January, A. D. 1870, payable on the first day of January, A. D. 1900, and which bonds were issued by the said State under and in pursuance of an act of the Legislature thereof, passed June 24, 1869, and the several amendments thereto, in which act and amendments it was and is among other things, provided, and in exchange for the bonds so issued by the said State, the company should execute and deliver to the said State its own first mortgage bonds, embracing all and singular its railroad property and appurtenances, and which latter bonds were so issued and delivered to the State, in compliance with the laws aforesaid, and are now held by the State as a trustee for the benefit of the purchasers of the said State bonds as a further security of the same. The undersigned further represents that it was the duty of the State of Florida to defend and protect the lien of the bonds of the said Railroad Company so issued as aforesaid, for the benefit of all concerned in the preservation of such lien, and for this purpose through its agents and officers to exercise all due diligence to prevent the success of any and all attempts to impair the said lien by legal proceedings or otherwise.

The undersigned further represents that there is now pending in the Circuit Court of the United States of the Fifth Circuit and Northern District of the State of Florida, an action, in which Edward C. Anderson, Jr., and others are plaintiffs, and the Jacksonville, Pensacola and Mobile Railroad Company and others are defendants, in which action the bill of complaint was filed on or about the 24th day of July, 1872, and which action has for its object the foreclosure of a pretended mortgage lien upon those parts of the line of the Jacksonville, Pensacola and Mobile Railroad Company heretofore known as the Pensacola and Georgia Railroad and the Tallahassee Railroad. The undersigned further represents that the State of Florida, through its Governor, Attorney-General, and proper officers, had due notice to appear and defend the said suit, and were requested to do so on behalf of the bondholders, whom the undersigned now represents, but refused to appear or take any action in the same, and wholly and entirely neglected their duty in the premises, and permitted a judgment and decree to be taken by default in favor of the plaintiffs in the said action, notwithstanding the fact, which the plaintiff is informed and believes to be true, that the pretended mortgage lien, asserted by the plaintiffs in the said action, had and have no existence whatever. It has been constantly represented on behalf of the said State by its officers, including the Governor, that the bonds of the Jacksonville, Pensacola and Mobile Railroad Company delivered to the State were a first lien upon the entire line of the said Company, and that fact has been so declared in the opinion of lawyers of the State of Florida, from time to time consulted on that subject, and es the undersigned believes in a judicial decision of the highest court of that State, and the bondholders, whom the undersigned represents, purchased the bonds of the State of Florida upon the faith of such representations and such opinions. The undersigned is informed that in and by the decree in the cause referred to, it is directed that that part of the line of road referred to shall be sold on the fifth day of January proximo.

The undersigned, on behalf and by the direction of the purchasers and holders of the State bonds referred to, and whom he represents as hereinbefore stated, hereby protests against the action of the State of Florida in the premises as wanting in good faith to the *bona fide* purchasers of its bonds. And further protests against the said judicial decree and the action of the State of Florida in permitting the same to be rendered; and particularly protests against the proposed sale of the said Railroad, or any part thereof thereunder; and against any and all proceedings taken, or to be taken, in the said cause, as against good faith, contrary to law and of no validity against the bondholders, on whose behalf this protest is made, and on whose behalf such proceedings will hereafter be taken in the premises as they may be advised are necessary for the full protection of their rights.

The undersigned further protests, in the names, and on behalf of the said holders of the said bonds of the State of Florida, against the failure of the State of Florida to pay the interest thereon at maturity, according to the tenor of its obligations, as an act of bad faith not only unjust to the said bondholders, but unlawful in itself, and an act of repudiation destructive to the credit of the State of Florida, rendering her promises and obligations worthless in the markets of the world.

The undersigned, in the name and on behalf of the said holders of the bonds of the State of Florida, demands that the State of Florida shall, with all due diligence, take whatever steps may be necessary to prevent the sale of any part of the line of the said Jacksonville, Pensacola and Mobile Railroad under the said decree, or under any other proceeding of whatsoever kind, which can in any way impair or affect the lien of the bonds of the said Jacksonville, Pensacola and Mobile Railroad as a first and prior lien now held by the State as aforesaid for the security of its obligations to the State and through the State as a Trustee for the security of the holders and purchasers of the State bonds. The undersigned, in the name and on behalf of the said holders of the bonds of the State of Florida, also demands that the State of Florida shall make provision for the prompt payment of the outstanding and over-due coupons of its bonds, hereinbefore referred to, and give due and public notice of the time and place of such payment, in order that such coupons may be duly presented at the time and place designated for payment.

(Signed) ROBERT H. HARDAWAY,
Attorney for M. K. Jesup & Company, of the City and State of New York, who are lawful Attorneys for George M. Bocsevain, Joseph Zadack, Adrian Stoop, Adrian J. Milders, and N. J. deu Tex.

Witness—EDWARD M. WEST,
Justice of the Peace.

This protest, while looking plausible on paper, was conceived in sin and born in iniquity. The Democratic papers throughout the State were denouncing the action of the Acting Governor Stearns is employing, without authority of law, counsel to bring suit in the United States Supreme Court to saddle the four million fraudulent Littlefield bonds upon the people of Florida, and he, fearing an anti-administration Legislature, instigated this protest to cover his foot-prints. It will be seen by the message of Governor Hart, Assembly Journal of 1874, p. 29, that the suit was commenced in the summer of 1873, and the protest of the bondholders was not filed until the 29th of December of that year. The administration afterwards furnished another glaring bit of testimony showing the utter insincerity of its action. D. P. Holland, who claimed that he had bought the Jacksonville, Pensacola and Mobile Railroad, by virtue of an execution issued out of the United States Circuit Court, Northern District of Florida, and held a deed thereunder, was importuned by the members of the Ring to offer to sell his interest to the State, which he acceded to. The condition on which he offered to sell the road to the State and put it in possession was that there should be paid to him sixty-two thousand five hundred and thirty-three dollars, together with costs and interest, the State assuming the amount then due on account of the operating expenses and repaying the sums of cash that he had borrowed to improve the property, and he to take his pay in the six per cent. bonds of the State at the price fixed by law. This proposition was equally acceptable to the ring, and a bill was introduced in the Legislature to carry the proposition into effect. The Ring now called a Republican caucus, and James Johnson, carpet-bagger, and M. L. Stearns, Lieutenant-Governor, appeared before it in advocacy of the passage of the bill as a strictly party measure. They said in their speeches before the caucus that if this measure was passed, "Old Dyke" and the Democratic party would be utterly outgeneraled and as mad the "fretful porcupine." Attorney-General Cocke had explained this scheme to the members of the Legislature, who did not understand it before, and the colored members from the counties of Leon and Alachua, with the assistance of part of the delegation from Duval, had an understanding with the whites to defeat the measure. The Leon and Alachua delegations and honest Dan McInnis from Duval County. gave the ring to understand that they would vote for the bill, though they did not tell them so. These delegations made no resistance in the caucus, therefore the Ring thought they were all right. Attorney-General Cocke prepared some telling points and placed them in the hands of some of the colored members to be used in the attack.

The bill was called up, and the Ring was happy in the assurance that they would hear no opposition from any of the Republican members, while some of the Democrats, who did not know that enough colored men had been secured to defeat the bill, had blood in their eyes and were howling "fraud, fraud, fraud!" The author of this work led the fight, which took the ring by surprise. Hon. H. H. Mitchell, of Hillsborough County, Democrat, followed; the members from Alachua, Gass, and Washington, colored, followed, and Dan McInnis, from Duval County, brought up the rear. The fraud was so glaring that before the discussion ended the most of the carpet-baggers left the hall and did not dare to vote for the measure, and it was defeated by a large majority. The bill as defeated in the Assembly, was to pay Holland one hundred thousand dollars in State bonds bearing six per cent. interest, and it was generally believed that the bonds were to be divided among the getters-up of the scheme. The colored members were jubilant over the defeat of this measure because they thought they had got partially square with the carpet-baggers for their treachery to Osgood, and the carpet-baggers were given to understand that bolting the solemn action of caucuses was a game they could play too.

The Ring, at the beginning of their ravages in the State, had secured the passage of a law which had worked great injury and inconvenience to the people all over the State, that all legal advertisements should be made in papers designated by the Secretary of State. This law was enacted to support carpetbag papers, which were so unpopular in the communities in which they existed that they could not sustain themselves. The people were compelled to advertise in them, and there was no limit designated by law as to their charges, and enormous prices were charged for such advertisements, which the people had to pay. The Democratic press had, from the beginning, denounced this law, and continued their denunciation from year to year until the anti-ring Republicans acknowledged the justness of their cause. At the session 1873 this law was repealed by the united action of the anti-ring Republicans and the Democrats and was signed by the presiding officers of the respective houses, but was stolen either before or after it reached the Governor. This was not the only statute that was stolen at this and previous sessions, as statute stealing had become an active industry among the carpetbag statesmen. The following is the resolution passed in reference to this statute and the appointment and report of a committee thereunder:

WHEREAS, That the last regular session of the Legislature passed an act repealing the legal advertising act; and whereas, said act or bill was stolen by some unknown party or parties; thefore

"*Resolved*, That a committee of three be elected by this Assembly to find out the party or parties who stole said bill, and said committee shall have power to send for persons and papers, and that this committee endeavor to find all bills which were lost or misplaced last session."

Messrs. Wallace, Swearingen and McInnis were elected said committee, who made the following report:

"That inasmuch as statute stealing has come to be somewhat systematized in Florida, the committee made a most patient and persistent effort to uncover the thief in question. The testimony in the case is not sufficient, in the opinion of the committee, to convict the thief. The chief clerk of the Assembly, however, testified most unqualifiedly that he delivered the bill to the then private secretary of the Governor, but the Governor's secretary testifies with equal clearness that he did not receive it; and with this discrepent testimony the committee would respectfully submit the case for the consideration of the Assembly."

During this year an attempt was made by the State of Alabama to acquire that portion of the territory of Florida lying west of the Apalachicola River, and sent three commsssioners to Tallahassee to conduct the negotiations to that end on behalf of that State. The following resolutions and reports give a full hisrory of this affair:

ANNEXATION OF WEST FLORIDA.

To the HON. M. MARTIN,
Speaker of the Assembly:

WHEREAS, We the undersigned, were appointed a Joint Committee on the part of the Senate and Assembly to consult with the Commissioners appointed by the State of Alabama, in relation to the Annexation of West Florida to Alabama, find, upon investigation, that a former Commission was appointed by that State for the same purpose, and that upon representations made by them, the following Joint Resolution was passed by the Legislature of this State, and approved by the Governor on the 24th day of January, A. D. 1869, to-wit:

JOINT RESOLUTION relative to the Alabama Commissioners.

WHEREAS, The State of Alabama has appointed a Commission to visit the State of Florida for the purpose of procuring the annexation of all that portion of Florida lying west of the Apalachicola River; AND, WHEREAS, It is the desire to promote the best interest of all the people of our State; therefore, be it

Resolved, That the Governor of the State be and he is hereby authorized and directed to appoint a committee of three to confer with the Commission appointed by the State of Alabama; and the said Commission are authorized to go to Montgomery and there confer with the Commission and authorities of the State of Alabama; and the said committee are appointed the duly accredited agents of this State to negotiate for the said transfer; and they shall report at the next session of the Legislature by bill or otherwise.

Be it further resolved, That between this time and the time of the next meeting of the Legislature, the Governor shall issue his proclamation for an election in the district proposed to be annexed, to be held and conducted in the manner of a special election as prescribed by law; and at such election the qualified electors in said district shall vote for annexation or against annexation.

Be it further resolved, That prior to the aforesaid election the Commissions appointed by the respective States shall agree upon the terms and conditions of transfer; and in the proclamation of election the aforesaid terms and conditions shall be set forth for the information of the electors; and in making returns of the election in the county of Holmes, the returns of votes on the east and west side of the Choctawhatchie river shall be kept separate and apart, in order to get a correct expression of the people on the east and west side of that river.

Be it further resolved, That the aforesaid election shall not be final or binding until the Legislature or people of the State of Florida, and the Congress of the United States, shall consent to the transfer of said territory.

Approved January 27, 1869.

In conformity with said Joint Resolution, the Governor of the State of Florida appointed a Commission consisting of the Hon. W. J. Purman, Charles E. Dyke and N. H. Moragne, who visited Montgomery in conformity with the provisions of that resolution, and they entered into an agreement and stipulation with the duly constituted authorities of the State of Alabama, a copy of which is hereunto attached, and reported their doings to the then Governor of Florida. The Governor then, in accordance with the said Joint Resolution, issued his proclamation for an election in West Florida, and a majority of the votes cast at that election were in favor of the annexation of West Florida to Alabama, and it is quite evident to your Committee that a large majority of the people of West Florida are still in favor of annexation. The Governor of the State of Florida in his next annual message after the election presented to the Legislature the report and doings of the Commission; since that time there has been no further legislation upon the part of Florida in relation to that matter.

The Legislature of the State of Alabama passed an act which was approved by the Governor of that State on the 27th day of March, A. D. 1873, a copy of which is hereunto annexed, and in accordance with the provisions of said act, the Governor of Alabama has appointed the Hons. R. W. Cobb, J. C. Goodloe and ex-Governor Parsons, to confer with the proper authorities of the State of Florida, with full power to carry out the provisions of that act. These gentlemen are now in the city. In view of these facts, your committee are of the opinion that the matter is of sufficient importance to warrant some decided action upon the part of this Legislature. We therefore recommend the passage of the following concurrent resolution:

Resolved, That the Hons. R. W. Cobb, J. C. Goodloe and ex-Governor Parsons, Commissioners appointed by the Governor of Alabama to confer with the properly constituted authorities of the State of Florida in relation to the cession of West Florida to Alabama, be invited to address the Senate and Assembly in joint convention in the Assembly Hall at 10 o'clock A. M. on Tuesday the 27th inst.

A. L. McCASKILL,
L. G. DENNIS,
    Senate Committee.
JNO. L. McKINNON,
J. W. MENARD,
W. H. GLEASON,
    Assembly Committee.

AN ACT to provide for the annexation of West Florida to the State of Alabama with the assent of the State of Florida and Congress of the United States.

SECTION 1. *Be it enacted by the General Assembly of Alabama,* That the sum of one million dollars in coupon bonds of the State of Alabama, of not less than one thousand dollars each, payable in thirty years after the date thereof, bearing eight per cent. interest per annum, payable semi-annually at the office of the State Treasurer in the city of Montgomery, be and the same is hereby appropriated and is to be paid to the lawfully constituted authorities of the State of Florida as a consideration and compensation to said State for the cession by said State to the State of Alabama, of all the soil and jurisdiction now held by the State of Florida into and over that portion of the territory of the State of Florida lying and being west of the thread of the Chattahoochee and Apalachicola Rivers, and west of a line running due south from the thread of the mouth of the Apalachicola, bending west so as to pass between the Islands of St. George and St. Vincent, known and called West Florida, including the lands belonging to and heretofore owned by the State of Florida, within the district of country above described, whether of seminary, school, sixteenth sections, internal improvement, swamp and overflowed, together with the five per cent. arising from the sales of the United States land, lying west of the rivers above mentioned, accruing after the cession of said territory, and guaranteeing to the State of Alabama full and complete title thereto, with indemnity for all loss the State of Alabama may sustain growing out of any adverse claim or claims which may be set up thereto, provided that this sum shall be paid by this State and accepted by the State of Florida in full satisfaction of the share or proportion falling to West Florida of the public debt of the State of Florida, and the State of Alabama shall in no wise nor to any extent be responsible for any portion of said public debt of the State of Florida by reason of said purchase.

SECTION 2. *Be it further enacted,* That the Governor be and he is hereby authorized and empowered to appoint three commissioners on behalf of the State of Alabama to tender to the lawful authorities of the State of Florida the aforesaid bonds of this State in consideration of the cession aforesaid, and that the said commissioners be and they are hereby authorized and empowered on behalf of this State to make the tender aforesaid, and to do and perform all the acts and things which may be requisite and necessary to perfect and consummate the cession of the territory aforesaid by the State of Florida to the State of

Alabama, and the delivery by the State of Alabama to the State of Florida of the bonds aforesaid in compensation for said cession: *Provided*, That said commissioners be and they are hereby limited and restricted to the tender of the sum of one million dollars in the first section of this act mentioned and set forth: *And provided further*, That upon the acceptance by the State of Florida of the tender aforesaid, and the ratification by the Congress of the United States of the act of cession as aforesaid, the cession herein provided for shall be complete, and the bonds of the State hereinbefore mentioned shall be executed and delivered by the authorities of the State of Alabama to the authorities of the State of Florida in full satisfaction and compensation of the cession of the territory aforesaid.

SECTION 3. *Be it further enacted*, That the sum of three thousand dollars, or as much thereof as may be necessary, be and the same is hereby appropriated to pay the expenses of said commission, to be paid out of the treasury on the warrant of the Auditor, to be issued on the order of the Governor.

Approved March 27, 1873.

DAVID P. LEWIS, *Governor*.

ARTICLES OF AGREEMENT

Between the Commissioners of the two States for the Cession of West Florida to Alabama.

An agreement entered into this 17th day of May, A. D. 1869, between W. J. Purman, C. E. Dyke and N. H Moragne, Commissioners on the part of the State of Florida, appointed under joint resolutions on the 25th of January, 1869 and Messrs. J. L. Pennington, A. J. Walker and Charles A. Miller, Commissioners on the part of the State of Alabama, appointed under joint resolution approved December 31, 1868, witnesseth as follows:

First. The State of Florida cedes to the State of Alabama that portion of Florida lying west of the thread of the Chattahoochee and Apalachicola Rivers, and west of a line running due south from the thread of the mouth of the Apalachicola, bending west so as to pass between the Islands of St. George and St. Vincent, which territory so ceded is called in this Agreement West Florida.

Second. The State of Florida bargains, sells, grants and conveys to the State of Alabama all the lands heretofore acquired by the State of Florida, and situated within the district of country above described, which may be undisposed of at the date of the consummation of this agreement, whether of Seminary, School, or Sixteenth Sections, Internal Improvement, Swamp and Overflowed, and the five per cent. arising from the sale of the United States lands lying West of the rivers above mentioned, accruing from and after the date of the consummation of this agreement, and guaranteeing to Alabama full and complete title thereto for the purposes hereinafter specified, and agreeing to indemnify the said State of Alabama for all loss she may sustain growing out of any adverse claims which may be set up thereto. *Provided*, that the State of Florida, pending the consummation of this agreement, shall dispose of none of the lands above mentioned, either by sale, donation or otherwise, except in accordance with the laws in force in said State at the date of the signing of these presents and for the benefit of West Florida.

Third. The State of Alabama takes the said lands subject to the trusts imposed by the acts of Congress granting the same.

Fourth. That immediately after the assent of the Congress of the United States to this Agreement between the State of Florida and the State of Alabama, it shall be the duties of the Governors of Florida and Alabama to issue their respective proclamations, naming a day within sixty days after such assent of Congress shall be obtained, when the jurisdiction of Florida shall cease, and when the officers and people of the territory of West Florida shall be subject to the jurisdiction of the State of Alabama in accordance with and under the laws and Constitution of same.

Fifth. That all judicial and other local officers in the territory of West Florida shall continue to exercise the functions of their several offices, after the said transfer shall have been consummated, for the full terms for which they were elected or appointed; and all such judicial and all other proceedings of such officers shall be in accordance with the Constitution and laws of Alabama.

Sixth. That the several counties in West Florida shall compose one Judicial Circuit of the State of Alabama, and the Judge of the Court of the First Judicial District of Florida shall be the Judge of the Circuit Court of the State of Alabama, for a circuit composed of said counties, until his term as Judge of the District Court of Florida shall terminate, and the said counties shall compose a Chancery District of the Southern Chancery Division of the State of Alabama, and the Chancellor of such Division shall be the Chancellor of the said Chancery District, and the terms thereof shall be held at times and a place to be prescribed by such Chancellor, and all Chancery causes pending in the District or Circuit Court of said counties, shall, with all the papers and records of the proceedings therein, certified by the several Clerks of the said Distrtct or Circuit Court, be transferred to the said Chancery Court, and be therein cognizable, and the said Chancellor shall appoint a Register for such Court.

Seventh. And the County Judges of the respective counties above named shall be Judges of Probate under the laws of the State of Alabama until their respective terms, for which they were elected or appointed under the laws of Florida, shall terminate. And the Board of County Commissioners of the said respective counties shall be the County Commissioners in their several counties for the terms for which they were elected or appointed. And the Sheriffs, Coroners, Justices of the Peace, Clerks of the Circuit or District Court, by whichever name they may be called, County Treasurers, Collectors of Revenue and Assessors of Taxes, shall fill the corresponding offices under the laws of the State of Alabama to the end of the terms for which they were respectively elected or appointed. And the several Clerks of the Circuit or District Court shall be the Clerks of the Circuit Court under the laws of the State of Alabama; and the said Circuit Court shall have jurisdiction of all cases in the District or Circuit Court of the said counties, except that the Chancery causes shall be transferred to the Chancery Court as hereinbefore stated. And the said Judges of the County Court shall be Probate Judges, and have jurisdiction of the causes in their respective County Courts, and be Probate Judges under the laws of the State of Alabama. And the said County Commissioners and County Judges shall execute all the powers of County Commissioners and Probate Judges under the laws of Alabama.

Eighth. The State of Alabama, in consideration of the cession by thè State of Florida hereinbefore mentioned, shall pay to the said State, within ninety days after the consummation of the annexation of West Florida to the State of Alabama, the sum of one million of dollars in bonds, bearing interest at the rate of eight per cent. per annum, redeemable at the Treasury of the State of Alabama in thirty years from the date thereof, the interest to be payable semi-annually in the City of New York. The said sum of one million of dollars shall be in compensation to the State of Florida for the proportion of the debt of said State, which the amount of taxes paid by the several counties embraced in the district of country ceded to Alabama may bear to the taxes paid by the remaining portion of the said State of Florida; and the balance of the said sum of one million of dollars shall be in full payment for the Seminary, Sixteenth Section, Internal Improvement, Swamp and Overflowed lands ceded to the State of Alabama, the title to which is guaranteed by the State of Florida as hereinbefore mentioned, which said balance shall be for the use and purposes contemplated in the grants of the said lands by the Congress of the United States, and as provided for by the laws of the State of Florida in force at the date of this agreement.

Ninth. That the counties respectively in the territory of West Florida shall be allowed, and by this stipulation have authority to retain the State taxes assessed and collected for the first year under the revenue laws of the State of Alabama, and the amounts so retained shall be appropriated by the County Commissioners to the improvement and erection of court-houses and other public buildings in their respective counties.

Tenth. The benefit of the indorsement laws of the State of Alabama, to the extent of sixteen thousand dollars per mile, shall apply to the construction of a railroad from the point of junction with the Pensacola and Georgia Railroad of Florida, on the Apalachicola River, in the direction of Quincy, to the waters of Escambia Bay, or to a junction with the Pensacola and Louisville Railroad in Florida, or the Alabama and Florida Railroad in Alabama, and to the Pensacola and Louisville Railroad, and to no other railroad, for the period of three years from the date of the consummation of this Agreement; and the charter of the Pensacola and Georgia Railroad of Florida, with the amendments thereto, shall be in force in the district of country embraced in the first Article of this Agreement, for the purposes specified in said charter and amendments, and the Pensacola and Georgia Railroad Company shall be entitled to construct their roads and shall be entitled to all the benefits of the indorsement laws of Alabama, as hereinbefore expressed, the same as if their said charter and amendments had been granted by the State of Alabama; and the State of Alabama, neither under any general act of incorporation now in force, nor by any special act of legislation heretofore or hereafter to be adopted, shall authorize the construction of any railroad from the Chattahoochee or Apalachicola Rivers through the district of country before mentioned, in the direction of the waters of Escambia Bay, or to a junction with the Pensacola and Louisville Railroad, for the period of three years from the date of the Agreement hereinbefore set forth.

Eleventh. Until otherwise provided, the counties as now constituted lying west of the line mentioned in the first Article of this Agreement, shall be entitled to the same representation in the General Assembly of Alabama that they are now entitled to in the Legislature of Florida; and that portion of Franklin County embraced within and lying west of said line shall be known as the county of Franklin, and shall be entitled to at least one Representative in the General Assembly of Alabama, and the Senators and Representatives of the above counties shall hold their offices for the full term for which they were elected.

Twelfth. The solvent taxes returned from the district of country agreed to be annexed, unpaid at the time such annexation shall be consummated, shall be the property of the State of Florida, and shall be assumed by the State of Alabama and paid in money. The amonnt so due and unpaid shall be ascertained from the tax returns made to the Comptroller of the State of Florida.

Thirteenth. This agreement shall not be of force until the same shall be ratified and approved by the States of Florida and Alabama in a legal manner, and by the legal and proper authorities, and the Congress of the United States has given its assent thereto.

(Signed)   W. J. PURMAN,
           N. H. MORAGNE,
           J. L. PENNINGTON,
           A. J. WALKER,
           CHAS. A. MILLER,
                    Commissioners.

For the sole purpose of bringing the matter contemplated in the Resolutions of the State of Florida before the people thereof, I assent, as a Commissioner on the part of said State, to the above, reserving to myself as a citizen the right to judge of the expediency or inexpediency of accepting *any terms* for ceding to a foreign and alien jurisdiction any part or portion of the people and Territory of Florida.

C. E. DYKE.

The Alabama Commissioners met the two houses in joint session, and in their address strongly urged the annexation scheme; but the matter went no further because of the exhorbitant demands of the Ring that the commissioners should "talk turkey" before any legislative action should be taken.

Mr. Martin, who was Warden of the State prison while Speaker of the Assembly, in which situation he was able to so shape appropriation bills as to give him a good margin after scantily feeding and clothing the prisoners, was determined that the inside workings of that institution should be known to no one but himself and the inmates. Heretofore the committee appointed to visit and inspect the institution went rather on a frolic than for the purpose of a real inspection, and of course he would make it doubly pleasant for them, especially when his conduct in the management was reported by many to be very questionable. A committee was elected to visit the prison and report to the Assembly. The anti-ring Republicans and the Democrats assisted in getting Dan McInnis, colored, of Duval, and T. C. Gass, colored, of Alachua, on the committee. Martin, suspecting mischief in McInnis and Gass, as they did not take much to carpetbag conduct, had a special train prepared with wines, whiskies and cigars on board for the comfort of the visiting guests. He gave Gass and McInnis to understand that the train would start at a designated hour, but to the astonishment of his colored guests the train left just two hours sooner than the time designated and the colored brother was left behind. McInnis was a very energetic and determined representative, and by other means he and Gass were on the ground in time to see Martin out, who pretended that they had misunderstood him as to the time. Martin at once set out his liquors and cigars, which Gass and McInnis refused to partake of, but went about their investigation. Martin had been working the prisoners on his own private farm or vineyard while pretending to be cultivating grapes for wine-making for the State, and he made thousands of dollars for himself out of the prisoners while the State lost thousands by his management. This conduct, and his cruelty to the prisoners, had been whispered around among colored members by the Democrats, and McInnis was disposed to give the matter a thorough sifting, as far as in him lay. In his tour of inspection he came to an apartment where there were a number of prisoners chained down flat on their backs. Martin, who had lost sight of McInnis, started on his trail, and finally found him standing over the chained convicts, interrogating them as to their treatment. Martin out with an oath, saying, " Get out of here, you son of a b—." McInnis refused to depart. Martin then called his guard and had the drum corps play the "rogue's march" and marched Gass and McInnis off the premises at the point of the bayonet. This action on the part of Martin was reported to the Legislature, and an investigation was ordered under the following resolution, introduced by Mr. Proctor:

WHEREAS, It is reported that two of the members appointed by the Assembly to visit and inspect the State prison were, without any cause, forcibly ejected from the prison by order of the Warden, who is Speaker of the Assembly; therefore
"*Be it Resolved*, That the Assembly inquire into the conduct of the Speaker-warden on the occasion of the visit of said members of the Assembly to said prison, that the Assembly may take such action in the premises as may be deemed necessary."

On motion of Mr. Wallace, a committee of five was elected by the Assembly, under the resolution above recited, to investigate the conduct of the warden of the State prison; namely, Messrs. Swearingen, Wallace, Chadwick, Mitchell and Washington. This committee, after making a thorough investigation into this outrage, reported to the Assembly concerning Martin's conduct, after which the following resolution was adpoted; but owing to the early adjournment he was spared from exposure and disgrace:

Resolved, That a committee of two on the part of the Assembly and one on the part of the Senate, be elected to inspect the State Penitentiary, to proceed immediately to thoroughly inspect the condition of the State prison; and said committees be instructed to ascertain, if possible, the quantity and quality of food and clothing furnished to convicts the past year, and the disposition made of the labor of said convicts, and that said committee be authorized to summon, swear and examine witnesses, and books and papers properly belonging to the State Penitentiary.

While the members of the Ring were looking anxiously for the death of Governor Hart, and desiring the possession of the railroad to assist them in the gigantic fraud which they had already planned to retain possession of the State, this proposition was left at the adjournment of the Legislature as unfinished business, having been referred to the Committee on Railroads, where it was strangled.

At this time Gov. Reed, desiring to get rid of the complications growing out of the unsatisfactory condition of the railroads and to if possiable place them on a sound and healthy basis, made to Gov. Hart, and through him to the Legislature a proposition to buy the roads and retire the outstandings bonds. The offer was coldly received and was not acted upon.

TALLAHASSEE, February 9, 1874.
His Excellency, OSSIAN B. HART,
Governor of Florida :

SIR: In view of the present complication of affairs in connection with the Jacksonville, Pensacola and Mobile Railroad and the efforts to involve the State in further embarrassment in relation to it, as well as to injure its credit, I beg to submit the following proposition for the consideration of yourself and the two houses of the Legislature, viz: If the State will make a clear and full title to the Road from Jacksonville to the Chattahoochee, with its branches and all its franchises, rolling stock and property, I will agree within ninety days to find a responsible party to purchase the same and pay three hundred thousand dollars, ($300,000) return the outstanding State bonds issued to the Company and guarantee the construction of the road from the Chattahoochee to the State line within five years from the date of the transfer.

     I have the honor to be,
      With great respect,
       Your obedient servant,
        HARRISON REED.

At this session also, Governor Reed made an attempt to get a settlement of his claims against the State for moneys expended by him while in the discharge of his duties as Governor of the State. The following memorial shows the nature and extent of his claim:

The memorial of the undersigned respectfully represents—
That from June 8th, 1868, until January 8th, 1873, he was the Governor of Florida, elected by the people in accordance with the Constitution of the State and the Laws of the United States;

That as such Governor he was charged with extraordinary responsibilities and complicated duties, involving the rights and liberties of the people, the peace and order of society, and the integrity and honor of the State;

That it became necessary, in carrying out the laws of the State without money in the Treasury or credit abroad, for him to borrow large sums of money on his own personal responsibility, to discharge his duties efficiently and save the State from disorder, and resist successfully the efforts to disorganize and overthrow the Government;

That he was subjected to expenditures of more than ten thousand dollars for attorney fees and expenses in defence against unjust charges in impeachment, and resisting revolutionary schemes calculated to bring the State under martial law; and for which he has never received remuneration nor presented any claim;

That his extraordinary expenditures for the maintenance of civil government and constitutional rights, and to meet the (sometimes unreasonable) exactions of the people under the laws, amount to over thirty thousand dollars, for which he has received no compensation; and but for these expenditures the State would have been remitted to military government and a condition of anarchy and bloodshed, as well as almost irretrievable bankruptcy, as other reconstructed States, under far more favorable circumstances, have been;

That the accounts of your memorialist for the expenditures were examined and allowed by a committee of the Legislature in 1871 to the amount of sixteen thousand dollars, and again in 1873 to the amount of twenty-four thousand dollars;

That he is now largely indebted and his property encumbered, on account of these expenditures, and he is now subject to a heavy interest which, if not speedily arrested, will absorb the accumulation of years of frugal industry.

And your memorialist further represents—

That while it is contrary to his desire as a private citizen to array himself in hostility with or question the veracity of any State officer, and especialy one in whom he had formerly placed implicit confidence, yet justice to himself and to the State, whose high trust he has executed, requires that he should deny in detail and in extenso each and every allegation of the report of the State Comptroller in relation to the action of your memorialist in connection with the hypothecation of bonds in New York, and that he state unqualifiedly that, while Governor he never at any time received money on account of the State, nor in any manner ever bound the State, nor attempted to bind the State, nor ever pledged its bonds for any money for which he has not accounted to the Treasury and the Legislature;

That it is not true that your memorialist hypothecated any bonds with the New York Warehouse and Security Company, nor increased the rate of interest on loans made by others from that company; but that he did procure the extension of a loan previously made from that company for three months upon the same terms as the loan previously carried, which were unconscionable and unreasonable, and which he would never have consented to as an origional proposition;

That there was no such claim—legal or equitable—against the remaining bonds of the State in the hands of Bayne & Co. as that which the Comptroller claims to have allowed and paid;

That the Comptroller nor any other person has seen or holds any receipt, note or obligation executed by your memorialist on account of the State of Florida, by which the bonds could be charged with any such sum as he has allowed and claims to have paid;

That your memorialist, when called upon by the Comptroller, publicly stated in the Senate Chamber that all that was properly and legally chargeable against said bonds was the amount set forth in his report to the Legislature, and that when the Senate was prepared to pay that amount he would guarantee the return of the bonds; and that subsequently he presented that report to the Comptroller in his office and renewed the pledge to procure the return of the bonds upon paymen in accordance therewith; and on another occasion he repeated the statement, and finally, in a letter, set forth in the Comptroller's report, called attention to that report as correct;

That he offered his personal services, gratuitously, and all official information, to assist in the settlement upon the basis of his statement aforesaid; and all overtures were repelled with what your memorialist regarded as indignity and arrogance;

That the representative ot Bayne & Co., then in attendance here, said to your memorialist that they would surrender the bonds upon payment in cash of what your memorialist admitted to be due, and said at the same time that they held additional collaterals from General Littlefield of near five hundred thousand dollars;

That the statement of account of Bayne & Co. against General Littlefield and now in his hands, and which your memorialist is imformed was laid before the Comptroller, showed that these bonds were held as collateral for only about eighty-three thousand dollars.

Your memorialist, therefore, in view of the public interest involved as well as his own, most respectfully and urgently request that your honorable body will appoint a joint committee to examine and investigate thoroughly and impartially all matters touching the charges of the Comptroller referred to, and everything in connection with the hypothecation and redemption of the State bonds in question; and that your committee also examine and adjust the claims of your memorialist,

And as in duty bound will ever pray, &c.,

HARRISON REED.

TALLAHASSEE, January 16, 1874.

Mr. Sturtevant offered the following joint resolution in the Senate, which was adopted:

Resolved, By the Senate, the Assembly concurring, That a joint commit ffive, two members of the Senate and three from the Assembly, be appointed to take into consideration the memorial of Ex-Governor Harrison Reed, and to report as soon as practicable to the Legislature all matters pertaining thereto.

In pursuance of this resolution, John L. Crawford and E. C. Howe, on the part of the Senate, and E. R. Chadwick, J. B. Browne, and John E. Proctor, on the part of the Assembly, were appointed a committee to investigate and report upon the accounts of Governor Reed as prayed for in the memorial. On the 14th of February, 1874, the committee reported as follows:

The committee to whom was referred the memorial of ex-Governor Harrison Reed, ask leave to make the following report:

The amounts claimed by ex-Governor Reed are as follows:

Expenditures under act of the Legislature of 1868,	$22,603.19
General contingent expenses	6,067.30
Balance on Executive contingent expenses	5,245.85
House rent and interest on same	5,690.00
Total	$39,606.34

Of this amount, $32,900.06 is the principal of the account, and $6,706.28 is interest, reckoned at 7 per cent.

Vouchers were presented for $20,070.25, leaving a balance for which there are no vouchers, save the official statement of Governor Reed, of $12,820.81.

Evidence taken before the committee went to show that Governor Reed had borrowed	$24,136.29
Which amount the State had paid and holds a receipt for the same. From this amount, however, should be taken the amount Governor Reed paid Warehouse and Security Company, New York, charges on hypothecated bonds	1,587.15
Leaving a balance of	$22,549.14

which should be deducted from the amount due him from the State.

The committee are of the opinion that at most Governor Reed can only claim $500 per year for house rent. Allowing this, would leave the principal of his account at $29,460.06
From which deduct 22,549.14

Leaving a balance of . . . . $ 6,910.02
in his favor.

As Governor Reed claims three years' interest at 7 per cent. on whatever sum may be due him, and as the committee desire to present his claim in full, in order that each member of the Legislature may know the extent and particulars of the claim, we add to the above three years' interest at 7 per cent $1,451.28

Making a total of $8,362.20
Governor Reed also claims that he paid $2,000.00
interest on bonds in New York, but the coupons he claims to have paid have not been returned to the State, but are still in New York. If he should secure the return of those coupons and that amount is allowed him, and all the other items of his accounts are allowed also, then the grand total of his account against the State would be $10,362.20

It is proper for the committee to state that most of the expenditures claimed to have been made by Governor Reed were incurred under the head of secret service, and under the provisions of chapter 1,660, Laws of Florida. As to the necessity or propriety for those expenditures, each member of the Legislature can judge as well as your committee.

If Governor Reed should only be allowed the amount for which he presented vouchers, he would then stand in debt to the State, but the committee think that large latitude should be allowed him in the consideration of his claim, and in view of all the circumstances under which the expenditures were made, the committee recommend that the Legislature should treat the claim of the ex-Governor with the utmost generosity consistent with the interests of the State.

In the Senate the report of the committee was not acted upon at this session, the Lieutenant-Governor, M. L. Stearns, using his influence quietly against its consideration.

At the session of 1873, an act had been passed authorizing the issue of one million dollars of State bonds, to bear six per cent. interest in gold, and payable in thirty years. These bonds were to be sold for not less than eighty cents on the dollar. Thousands of dollars of State scrip had been issued to run the State government, and as soon as the bill became a law a scrip ring was formed about the capitol among some of the cabinet officers, for the purpose of converting the scrip into these bonds. As, at this time, scrip was selling for thirty-five and forty cents on the dollar, these industrious gentlemen were able to drive quite a profitable trade.

The Agricultural College scrip, amounting to about one hundred thousand dollars, was soon to be received from the general government. It would sell for about eighty thousand dollars. While Cowgill, Hart, Stearns and Company were smacking their greedy mouths over this expected prey, Varnum slipped to New York and purchased State bonds from Bayne & Co., already held by them against the State. Cowgill intimates in his report that something was rotten in this transaction of Varnum's, but whatever may have induced him to make the purchase, he did at least one righteous act while treasurer of the Agricultural College, by beating these vultures out of eighty thousand dollars. The following is Cowgill's lamentation to Hart on this matter:

"While I know that much has been accomplished by this settlement, yet the reasonable expectations which were entertained of selling all the bonds have not been realized.

"To this end I attempted to have the money arising from the sale of the Agricultural College scrip invested in these bonds, so that the money might come into the Treasury.

"Assurances had been given by several of the Trustees of their approval of this investment.

"To induce them to do so, I addressed to them the following letter:

TALLAHASSEE, May 17, 1873.

GENTLEMAN: I have the honor to request that you will invest the money belonging to the Agricultural College in the new bonds of the State of Florida.

I would not make this application did I not feel assured, both as a citizen and as Comptroller, knowing the resources of the State, that the investment will be perfectly secure, and more advantageous to the College than any likely to be made.

These bonds are sold at 80 cents, and bear interest payable semi-annually at six per cent. in gold; thus for $800 you get a bond for $1000, and when U. S. currency and gold are equal in value the interest is 7½ per cent. on your investment, and with gold at 14 per cent. premium (at or about which rate it will probably continue for some time), the investment yields a trifle over 8½ per cent.

I enclose copy of a letter I sent to Bayne & Co., of New York, with whom I am successfully negotiating in reference to the return of the old hypothecated bonds of 1868 and 1869, and also refer you to a statement published in the last Sentinel concerning the receipts and expenditures of the State since 1st of January, as evidences of our return to a healthful condition financially.

If those interested in the future of our State, (and who is not?) will cordially unite in assisting to restore our finances, we will soon be on a cash basis; and I regard the expression of your confidence in this progressive prosperity of our State, as will be evidenced by this investment, as a very important, and perhaps essential auxiliary.

I am leaving for New York on business, and I hope to hear from you formally, so that I can show to bankers the confidence your board reposes in the recuperative energy of our State.

Very respectfully,

C. A. COWGILL, *Comptroller.*

Trustees of the Florida Agricultural College.

A favorable response to this request was personally solicited from the Trustees by Lieutenant-Governor Stearns and other gentlemen. The board met May 22d, and after their adjournment, Lieutenant-Governor Stearns was informed by members that the investment was directed to be made in the new bonds and so telegraphed to me in New York. General Varnum, Treasurer of the Agricultural Board, came to New York and informed me that the Trustees had come to no definite conclusion, but had left the whole matter of investment in his hands. Obtaining from him no satisfactory information, and snpposing that he was for some unknown reason delaying the action and yet never doubting that in the end and at the time when the State most needed the money, the purchase would be made from the State, I returned to Florida.

It was not until October that I suspected that General Varnum might have invested in the bonds belonging to Bayne

& Co., and October 15th I addressed a letter to them, asking if General Varnum had purchased bonds from them. In reply to this letter I received a telegram and a letter as follows:

NEW YORK, October 27, 1873.

DR. COWGILL:

My Dear Sir:—We dispatched to you a few days ago in reply to your favor of the 15th inst., as follows: "Varnum alone can give the information."

I answered thus, at the instance of General Varnum who proposed to see you in person with reference to the subject matter of your note.

This is the first time that you have put a direct question to me, as to whether or not Varnum, Treasurer, had bought bonds from us. If you had done so, under *restrictions* placed upon me, I should have declined to answer you, but in so doing that of itself would have given rise to suspicion upon your part, that probably some such transaction had taken place.

You would have then sought and obtained the information from the party or parties who *alone* had the right to communicate it.

I never could see myself any good reason for not conversing freely with you upon the subject, yet I *assure you* we are *not* at *liberty* to do so. It is proper to say that the resolution of the Board of Trustees, confirming the purchase of the bonds from us made early in *last* June, and indeed the preliminaries of the negotiations, dating *very much* earlier than that, with some of the Trustees exacts of Treasurer *positively secrecy* as to the purchase and sale referred to, until the matter was consummated and ordered *officially* to be given to the public.

My relations with you warrant me in withholding no information from you, when sought, and by consent of Varnum I write this. Yours truly,

L. P. BAYNE.

P. S.—The transaction was one of pure business. Varnum wanted to buy, and we certainly wanted to sell.

In this letter Mr. Bayne says truly that it was the first time I "had ever put a direct question to him as to whether or not Varnum, Treasurer, had bought bonds," and it is equally true that I had never put an *indirect* question upon the subject, as the possibility of either General Varnum purchasing for, or of Mr. Bayne selling to the College, had never crossed my mind until October.

I then addressed to the Trustees of the Agricultural College two communications, as follows:

OFFICE OF COMPTROLLER,
TALLAHASSEE, FLA., November 10, 1873.

To the Trustees of the Florida Agricultural College:

GENTLEMEN—Section 17 of the act entitled an act to establish the Florida Agricultural College, approved February 18, 1870, says the "Trustees shall report to the Comptroller annually on the first day of October" their action in reference to the sale of land or land scrip, and the disposition of the proceeds of said sale, in such form as he may direct. This seems to make it the duty of the Comptroller to indicate to the Trustees the form in which this report shall be made.

I therefore request the report to be made in the form of full and explicit answers to the following questions:

1st. Was the land or land scrip sold?

2d. At what time was the sale made?

3d. Upon what terms, whether for cash or upon credit, and if for credit, mention manner and date of payment.

4th. To whom was the sale made, and by whom as the agent of the board?

5th. Have the terms of sale been strictly complied with: if not, mention the date and place and mode of actual payment.

6th. To whom was the money paid as the agent of the Trustees?

7th. What disposition was made of this money—was it at once invested permanently, or was it placed on temporary deposit? If so, at what rate of interest?

8th. What permanent investments have been made, date of purchase of bonds or other securities, description of bonds, from whom purchased and at what price?

9th. By whom such investments were made as the agent of the Trustees, and by what authority?

10th. An itemized account of all necessary expenses incurred in these transactions.

Very respectfully,
C. A. COWGILL, *Comptroller.*

COMPTROLLER'S OFFICE,
TALLAHASSEE, FLA., Nov. 10, 1873.

To the Trustees of the Florida Agricultural College.

GENTLEMAN—In May last, I addressed you a communication which was designed to place before you the propriety of investing the fund, derived from the sale of the lands given by Congress to the College, in the new six per cent. gold bonds of the State of Florida.

Believing then as I do now, that it would be to the advantage of the College if the Trustees would invest this money so as to benefit the State by placing funds in the Treasury, thereby assisting materially in restoring the State to a cash basis, I urged them to do so, saying that I considerid the endorsement of the State's credit by this action of the Trustees almost essential to such restoration.

No formal reply was given to this communication, but Lieutenant-Governor Stearns was distinctly told by some of the Trustees that they had directed the investment to be made in Florida bonds, and that it was clearly understood that these bonds should be the bonds of 1873, so that the purchase money would come into the Treasury. This assurance Lieutenant-Governor Stearns telegraphed to me, according to an arrangement made between us previous to my departure for New York, where I was then engaged in redeeming the hypothecated bonds of 1868-9, and the information thus conveyed to me was used by me officially while endeavoring to place the bonds upon the Stock Exchange of New York.

A day or two after I had received the telegram from Lieutenant-Governor Stearns, General Varnum, as the Tresurer and Agent of the Board, appeared in New York and informed me that the action of the Trustees in reference to this investment was a secrect; that the whole matter was left in his hands to be acted upon at his discretion, and that Lieutenant-Governor Stearns could have had no authority for giving me the information. That he was not prepared to say what he would do—that he desired to do the best thing for the College, and he wished to prevent speculators from taking advantage of the opportunity to sell their bonds.

After my return to Florida, which occurred on the 6th of July, General Varnum, in other conversations, by saying "that all would be right," that he "had authority to invest, but could not say when he would do so, but that all would be right," and by using similar expressions to myself and other Cabinet Officers, induced us to rest perfectly confident in the belief that the investment was to be made in the bonds of 1873, and that the money would go into the State Treasury. We could place no other construction upon the expression "that all would be right," as we were thinking and talking in this connection of nothing but the means of appreciating the State's financial condition.

I never was more greatly surprised and grieved than when I learned by a letter from Mr. Bayne, of New York (a copy of which is herewith enclosed), that the money had been invested by General Varnum in the purchase of bonds held and owned by him (Mr. Bayne) as his own private property, and to-day I am informed that while General Varnum was in New York in June, he then purchased 50 bonds for $40,000 from Bayne & Co., and contracted to purchase 50 more when there mainder of the Agricultural College Scrip money should be paid by Mr. Lewis, while at this time in New York, and afterwards in Tallahassee, he informed me that " he did not know what he should do, but must keep all a secret until his mind was made up," etc.

I can perfectly understand why the Trustees might feel it to be their duty to say to the Comptroller in answer to his letter, " we would like to purchase the bonds from the State so as to benefit the State Treasury, but we must purchase from those who will sell the cheapest, therefore we will buy in the open market after advertising for proposals, but I cannot understand why, after an apparently studied reticence on the part of your agent, every departure from which only misled me and other State officers, whether so intended or not, the money should have been invested in bonds owned by a private individual—no one hearing of the transaction until its consummation, and no other parties having a chance to make a lower offer.

I think I may with propriety, and therefore do ask: Was not the State of Florida deserving of some consideration in this transaction? She has acted liberally by providing that all necessary expenses of obtaining and investing this money shall be paid from the State Treasury (Sec. 11 of Chap. 1766), and I think she was entitled to a prompt, courteous and candid reply to the communication made by the Comptroller. I have the honor to ask if the money has been thus invested, and if there remains no chance for the State to receive any benefit from the Agricultural Fund.

Very respectfully,
C. A. COWGILL, *Comptroller.*

On the 12th of November, the Trustees acknowledged the reception of these letters, promising a speedy answer, and requested that I would furnish them with a copy of the contract made with Bayne & Co., with which request I promptly complied.

The following letter from the President of the Board of Trustees was sent to me on December 10th.

OFFICE SUPERINTENDENT OF PUBLIC INSTRUCTION,
TALLAHASSEE, FLA., December 10, 1873.

C. A. COWGILL, ESQ., *Comptroller:*

SIR—Your communications to the Trustees of the Agricultural College bearing date November 10th, were received, and I have been directed by the Board of Trustees to place in your hands the entire action of the Board in relation to the subject of your communications, which you will find in the annual report of Trustees to His Excellency, O. B. Hart, a copy of which I will furnish you at an early day.

Yours respectfully,
JONATHAN C. GIBBS,
President Board of Trustees.

On the 17th of December, a proof of this report to the Governor was furnished me. In it I look in vain for even an *allusion* to my second letter of November 10th, in which I state how the proposals made by me to General Varnum to purchase bonds from the State were received, and also ask why the purchase was not made according to my request, although a copy of the contract with Bayne & Co. *furnished to them by me* in response to their wishes is printed as part of General Varnum's report with other matter equally irrelevant.

I am surprised to find no assertion that the Trustees intended to purchase from the State, as I had always supposed such to have been their intention, as their order to invest in the 1873 bonds was given in response to my letter of May 17th, strengthened by the personal solicitation of yourself and others, and quite recently most of the Trustees have informed me that they had so intended and supposed the bonds had been purchased from the State.

General Varnum, as agent of the Trustees, went to New York, and while there refused confidential communication with me and when the State daily asked him, through the Comptroller, who, by your permission, held exclusive charge of the bonds, to buy her bonds, gave no direct reply, and certainly gave not the slightest intimation that he was then buying or had bought from Bayne & Co. as the supposed agents of the State.

In his report to the Trustees of the College, General Varnum says "that Messrs. Bayne & Co. by contract with the Comptroller had been authorized to make exclusive sale of the new bonds until October first," and further that "Bayne & Co. having in their possession all of the new bonds which had been issued or ready for sale under the contract with the Comptroller of the State," etc.

Both of these assertions I deny most positively. The third paragraph of the agreement made by your Excellency and myself with Bayne & Co. gives them no control of the bonds. Its only force is a *moral* obligation resting on Bayne & Co. to aid and assist us in selling the State bonds, and by reference to Mr. Bayne's letter to me of October 27, it will be seen that there is no claim on his part that he was acting for the State; on the contrary, he asserts that secrecy was an essential part of the agreement between General Varnum and their firm, that the transaction was not to be made known to me, and of course not to the State. Who ever before heard of any one purchasing from an agent and making it a condition of the sale that the agent should not inform his principal of what had been done?

Again, Mr. Bayne did not have in his possession all the bonds that were for sale. He had only the "bonds" sold to him. If General Varnum had read article 3 of the agreement referred to, *before* he purchased the bonds, he would have seen that if Bayne & Co. sold any bonds for the State they must be paid for in Tallahassee before delivery, and a glance at the numbers of the bonds delivered to him in June by Bayne & Co., being 1 to 5 and 126 to 170, must have shown that they were part of the two hundred and fifty bonds sold to Bayne & Co.

A circular is presented by General Varnum as part of his report and called by him "the circular of Bayne & Co. as State Agents for sale of bonds."

This circular is not dated (perhaps purposely), and contains no assertion that it was issued by Bayne & Co. as State Agents. I knew nothing of it until a copy was sent to me in August or September, two or three months after the purchase of Bayne & Co.'s own bonds by the Trustees.

Mr. Bloxham says in his report to the Trustees detailing the sale of the Land Scrip, "one-half of the money, the first payment, amounting to 40,500, *was paid down* and deposited to the order of the Trustees." This being the case, the reason of the difficulty in collecting this money in June spoken of by General Varnum is not apparent, and it appears strange that General Varnum did not collect it himself when in Cleveland for that purpose.

Mr. Bloxham has told me there was no necessity that General Varnum should have gone to New York to collect it, as his check sent through our bankers in Tallahassee would have brought the money here, where the bonds of 1873, belonging to the State, could have been obtained.

Even in October, the last instalment of $40,000 might have

been given to the State, for there was not the slightest necessity to give Bayne & Co. the money and a large bonus in addition in order to save it, as the financial panic could not affect the *land scrip* belonging to the College, which had not passed out of the control of the Trustees, for Mr. Bloxham says in his report that the "scrip unpaid for is deposited in the name of the Trustees in the Merchants National Bank of Cleveland, a government depository, and to be *delivered to Mr. Lewis only upon his paying the purchase money* for the same. In other words, we hold possession of the property, the very best security."

The facts thus stated force me to the conclusion that the *agent* of the Trustees never intended to purchase the bonds from the State, and if the Trustees desired to do so, it is difficult to understand why they passed a vote of thanks " for the faithful and efficient manner in which he had carried out the instructions of the Board."

"I do not consider that the report of the Trustees of the Agricultural College to the Governor contains full and satisfactory answers to my communications."

CHAPTER XVI.

The Meeting of the Legislature of 1873. An Extract from Gov. Hart's Message. His Cabinet. The Election of United States Senator, and Acts of Bribery. The Exposure of the Littlefield Fraud by Attorney-General Cocke. The State's Ungratefulness to Gov. Reed. Miscellaneous.

Both branches of the Legislature met Tuesday, January 7, 1873. In the Senate there were twenty-three of the twenty-four members present—ten Democrats and thirteen Republicans, one Republican coming in next day, which made the Senate ten Democrats and fourteen Republicans. The Senate, after swearing in the newly elected Senators, adjourned until the next day. The next morning the Senate elected its officers, who were all Republicans, and notified the House of its organization. The great struggle for the supremacy of the ring was made in the House, where they resorted to every artifice imaginable to secure the Speakership. Colored men were brought from counties where the ring had great influence, for the purpose of exciting the masses of the freedmen around Tallahassee, and they were actually advised to commit violence on any member of the Legislature who would not abide by the caucus nominee. Notwithstanding the threatened violence, five Republican members refused to attend the caucus. These members were Bush, of Columbia, white; Lee, of Sumter, white; both Southern Republicans; Wallace and Proctor, of Leon, colored, and Thompson, of Columbia, colored. The ring men began to see danger ahead, and word was sent to the freedmen in the surrounding country that the Leon county delegation had sold out to the Democrats. The freedmen were at the State-house next morning in large numbers denouncing the delegation if they should dare vote against a colored man for Speaker, and caused one of the members of the delegation, Mr. W. G. Stewart, colored, to hesitate and vote for John R. Scott. The House was called to order by W. H. Gleason, ex-Lieutenant-Governor, and now a member from Dade. The Assembly consisted of twenty-eight Republicans and twenty-five Democrats, with two Democrats and one Republican absent. The ring members, now reeling and tottering for fear, nominated John R. Scott, of Duval, colored, for the Speakership. The author of this work, amid hisses and threats of violence, nominated S. B. Conover as against Scott. Conover received twenty-eight votes—the solid Democratic vote being cast for him and the five Republican votes who refused to attend the caucus. Scott received twenty votes, and Conover was therefore declared elected. The scene in the House, among the members of the ring, and anti-ring members, was almost indescribable. The members of the ring were swearing and denouncing the Leon delegation while with bowed heads they carried the news of the disaster to their chief. The anti-ring members and the Democrats, both in and outside the Legislature, were jubilant, and stood around in little knots defying the misguided freedmen, who wanted nothing but the blood of the Leon county delegation. In fact, the author of this work was menaced by a mob of the freedmen, who had been taught that they had been sold out by him, and but for his having been armed and ready for this, his life would have been taken. The Assembly adjourned until next day, and then perfected its organization by electing a full Republican set of officers. The ring being satisfied that the election of Conover Speaker meant to turn no member out of the Legislature who had been legally elected, held a consultation to have the Committee on Privileges and Elections elected by the Assembly in place of by appointment of the Speaker, but the expediency of this proposition was doubted by Osborn, as it would only exasperate the anti-ring element and probably cause them to vote for a Democrat for the Senate rather than for him. So this proposition was abandoned, and Osborn proposed to await the appointment of the Committee on Privileges and Elections, and then capture it by money. Before the committee was appointed several petitions giving notice of contests were presented in favor of Republicans, looking to unseat Democratic members. Conover, who, knowing that great pressure would be brought to bear on the Republican members of the committee to unseat Democrats, and that the unseating of Democratic members would defeat himself for the Senate, and elect Osborn, was much perplexed as to whom to rely upon among the Republicans who would withstand Osborn's money and vote with the Democratic minority of the committee. He finally approached the author of this work, and said to him that he had made up his mind to appoint him chairman of the Committee on Privileges and Elections, and that he hoped he would not vote to unseat any member of the Legislature who had been honestly elected. The author gave him to understand that neither money nor promises would cause him to swerve from the path of duty. Poor Conover gave a long sigh and departed On the 10th of January the Assembly met at its usual hour, and the standing committees were announced by the speaker. The Committee on Privileges and Elections was Wallace, of Leon, chairman; Montgomery, of Madison; McKinnon, of Washington; Hannah and Elijah—three Republicans and two Democrats. The Democrats were well pleased with the appointment of the committees, they having the chairmanship of the Judiciary Committee—H. L. Mitchell, of Hillsborough. The ring now saw that there was work ahead to be done, and they went about it with a will. Nothing of interest was done for several days, the Legislature awaiting the message from the Governor.

The message of Governor Hart was received eight days after the meeting of the Legislature, and every one looked for a very able paper, more especially on account of such delay. The message, when received, to the utter astonishment of those who believed Hart to be an able man, was the poorest and most sickly State paper that had ever been delivered to the Legislature by any Governor of Florida. The most important subject in the message was his reference to the scrip that a former Legislature had ordered to be destroyed, some of which found its way back into the State treasury and was again paid. He said: "I am informed that there is an uncertain amount of old State scrip out that has been paid, but is being brought in and paid again. Why it was not cancelled, when paid, how it got out of the treasury again, and how much there is of it out—whether $10,000, or $300,000, or $400,000—is uncertain. It is known that some old scrip that was in the office has been destroyed by burning, but I am not informed how much."

The ring, though defeated in the election of speaker of the Assembly, lost no time in arranging Hart's Cabinet. They insisted that no colored man was fit for a Cabinet position but Jonathan C. Gibbs, and he, they insisted as pre-arranged, had attempted to count in Bloxham, a Democrat, as against Hart, a Republican; and while some of the more ignorant of the colored brothers were loud in denunciation of Gibbs for this supposed treachery, they contended that if Gibbs was the only colored man qualified for a position in the Cabinet, he should be appointed by Hart and then watched. Hart and the ring protested against this proposition until the colored brother held a caucus and demanded Gibbs' appointment, with a threat that the colored members would combine with the Democrats and clog the wheels of the administration. The colored of both branches of the Legislature went to Hart in a body and intimated their intention, whereupon Hart became frightened and conceded their demand, and Gibbs was appointed Superintendent of Public Instruction of the State. The yielding of this point by Hart and the ring was a signal for the colored brother to be defiant as to Hart's threat, thereafter made, that he would use the whole power of his administration against any member of the Legislature, for any office or for re-election to the Legislature, who should dare to vote for any one for United States Senator whom he, Hart, considered not in full accord with his administration, which was then wholly controlled by Osborn and his ring. The balance of the Cabinet consisted of Samuel B. McLin, Secretary of State; Charles Foster, Treasurer; C. A. Cowgill, Comptroller; William Archer Cocke, Attorney-General; Dennis Eagan, Commissioner of Lands and Immigration, and John Varnum, Adjutant-General. The Cabinet was a very fair one, with the exception of McLin, who was a deserter from the rebel army, and being self-condemned for his own treachery for having volunteered in the Confederate service and then deserted before he smelled gunpowder, he was satisfied that neither the Democrats nor the carpetbaggers cared to trust him, and he was therefore the tool of the most rabid and unprincipled members of the carpetbag dynasty of the State.

Osborn and his ring followers, convinced by the independent action of the colored members of the Legislature in demanding the appointment of Gibbs, that they would have hard work to secure permanently any considerable number of them to vote for Osborn, began open bribery to carry their project through. There were three caucuses held every night until the Senator was elected. Osborn and his bribe offerers assembled nightly at the old City Hotel, and reported to each other what progress was being made to secure votes for the chief, and to devise other plans that might be a sort of auxiliary to the main plan of bribery. S. B. Conover and his followers held nightly caucuses over the old bar room once run by Scott, while spies were sent to the Osborn den who reported nightly what was done and said in the Osborn caucuses. The Democrats held nightly caucuses in the Capitol, and some of them reported nightly to Conover and his caucus what had taken place and what was said by the Democrats. The Osborn managers having convicted C. H. Pearce for bribery, and expecting that Pearce would make this the opportunity to get even with them, contrived a new plan of bribery in which they could not be detected. Before the voting for Senator commenced some of Osborn's leading strikers would place in the hands of such colored members as they thought money could control, an envelope sealed, saying at the same time, "Take this, I know it will do you some good." After the recipient had had a reasonable time to open the envelope and count the money, the fellow who gave it would have occasion to run on him again and engage in the praise of Osborn, winding up by expressing the hope that the recipient would vote for him when it became necessary to secure his election. These sealed envelopes generally contained from two hundred and fifty to three hundred dollars. If the member was very influential this dose of two hundred and fifty would be repeated, and if that did not get the patient in such condition as to enable him to talk Osborn, a third dose was given sufficiently large to double the other two. This would enable the patient to vote for and talk Osborn for some considerable time; but it will be seen hereafter that these double doses did not effect a permanent restoration to Osborn. Conover and the notorious Fred Dockray had entered into an agreement that one or the other should be elected to the Senate. Dockray had lots of the Government money, which he had stolen while Collector of Customs at the port of Jacksonville, which he was using lavishly to secure the election of himself or Conover, and Osborn had all he could do for some time to hold the colored members whom he had secured through conquest of money in the different counties. After Dockray saw there was really no chance for himself he told Conover he must hold up as he saw no way of getting his money back. This was a gala time for the colored brother, and those of Osborn's strikers whose pockets had suffered famine for want of fat Federal offices. The first Senatorial caucus held by the ring revealed the fact that Osborn had been "weighed in the balance and found wanting." and that those whom he had confidently relied upon to support him were voting for some one else. Another discouraging feature of the general caucus was the absence of some Republican members who would never attend the Osborn or general caucus. The ring, after failing in their attempt to force these Republican members into the caucus, turned their attention to the Committee on Privileges and Elections. They planned to turn seven Democrats out of the lower branch of the Legislature and put in seven men—be they Democrats or Republicans—whether elected or not, who would promise to vote for Osborn first and last after being seated. They set the masses of the colored men around Tallahassee at work to intimidate those Republican members of the Committee who were not inclined to unseat members of the Legislature to secure the election of Osborn. The freedmen were told that the Democrats whose seats were contested were "Ku-Klux" and held their seats at the price of innocence of negroes, and that any negro who would refuse to unseat them ought to be mobbed or secretly murdered. A band of freedmen was regularly employed to follow, watch and browbeat the chairman of the committee, who, at every meeting of the committee, had voted with the two Democrats to postpone the report until after the Senatorial contest. The committee had examined the testimony in each contest and found that there was no testimony on which to base a real contest; that the contests had been gotten up solely in the interest of Osborn. The chairman of the committee deemed it advisable to be accompanied by friends in going to and from the Conover caucuses at night, and often passed the employed band of freedmen, who uttered curses and threatenings against him for not having unseated Democrats and put in "'Publicans." The Osborn jacobins at this juncture were desperate, and seemed willing to commit almost any crime to secure the election of their chief; and they now having exhausted all the fury of threats and intimidation on the chairman of the Committee on Privileges and Elections to no advantage concluded to change the base of operations and to attack him with moral suasion—promises of money and property. Honest W. K. Cessna, of impeachment notoriety, was appointed by Osborn to use money and promises, and O. Morgan was appointed to use property. W. H. Gleason had specific work laid out for him. Under the Osborn Constitution the Seminole Indians in the Southern part of the State were entitled to one representative in each branch of the Legislature. As the Seminoles reside mostly in the counties of Dade and Monroe, and as Gleason was then a member from the county of Dade, and was supposed to know many of the members of the tribe, he was to bring a man from somewhere, with high cheek bones, tall and dark-skinned, and represent him as belonging to the Indian tribe.

At the proper time the man was brought before the committee and introduced by Gleason as J. King, one of the Seminole Indians from the everglades. It was very amusing to see this fellow trying to act, look and talk Indian. The committee could not understand anything he said, but Gleason talked for him. It was evident to the committee that the fellow was either a cracker from some of the southern counties, or that he was picked up about Jacksonville to be used for the purpose and was well paid for his attempt to simulate an Indian. It was some few days before the committee reported on the case of the Indian, and he seemed to be very anxious for admission. This white Indian one day approached the chairman of the committee and said to him in good English that he would give him twenty dollars to report in his favor. The chairman thereupon inquired of him could he not talk more English.

He said "No, that would be known." The chairman gave him to understand that he cared nothing for his twenty dollars, but that the committee would report in a few days. Of course the committee reported against him, and sent him home. Up to this time the chairman of the committee had not been directly approached on the subject of unseating Democrats for money. Honest Cessna now goes about his work. The contest for Senator was waxing warm, and the ring saw no way to steer clear of defeat. John E. Proctor, one of the rebellious members from Leon county was given seven hundred dollars by one of the Osborn managers to be used to influence the chairman to report in favor of the contestants. Proctor took the money and bought two mules for his farm and requested the chairman to stand his ground. Cessna, thinking that the seven hundred had somewhat softened the heart of the chairman, waited until the Lord's day to make his last grand effort to elect Osborn to the Senate. He quietly repaired to the residence of the chairman and requested a private interview. He presented the following proposition: That the Republican members of the committee should unseat William Peeler, of Clay county, Democrat, and seat Henry Brown, a Republican; unseat W. W. Harkins, of Lafayette county, Democrat, and seat William D. Sears, Republican; unseat Joshua H. Lee, of Hamilton county, Democrat, and seat James Burnan, Republican; unseat Emory Vann, of Taylor county, Democrat, and seat Mark Richardson, Republican; unseat Samuel Hope, of Hernando county, Democrat, and seat Authur St. Clair, Republican; and seat J. King, the Seminole Indian. If this proposition was consented to by the chairman, he was to receive one thousand dollars, which amount was counted out to him by Cessna in hundred dollar packages and shaken in his face, with the promise of any office that he should desire. This amount of money to a poor man was very hard to refuse; but the chairman, remembering the promise he had made to the white friends who had prevented his being swindled out of his election, informed Cessna that the testimony in these cases would not sustain such action on the part of the committee. Cessna also informed the chairman that O. Morgan desired to see him Monday morning. Before the meeting of the Legislature on Monday, Morgan met the chairman and wanted to know whether he had seen Mr. Cessna or not, and was answered in the affirmative. Morgan asked if their meeting was satisfactory, and if so, he desired to say that the large house just behind the City Hotel was his property, and that he would give him clear title to the same. The chairman had now become threadbare, and he informed Morgan that neither money nor property would change his opinion as to those contests. The house and lot which was thrown into the attempted bargain was valued at three thousand dollars. Conover, who had learned of these negotiations, became very much alarmed, and from that time to the end of the contest the chairman, for the most of his time when he was not asleep, was honored with the presence of the vigilant doctor. At one stage of the contest a false alarm got out that the chairman had yielded to the tempter, and Conover came rushing to him almost with tears in his eyes, and said: "My whole fortune is in your hands, and if you go back on me by turning Democrats out of the Legislature, who were legally elected, it will be looked upon as my act, as you are my friend, which will drive every Democrat from me. Do you want any money?" The chairman told him if he had any money to spend to go and buy those who desired to sell; that he should stand firm without money. This answer certainly lightened the burden on Conover's heart, and he went flying to other parts of the battlefield to use the money where it would do the most good. The ring having failed to get up a contest in Brevard county, by any Republican, A. D. Johnson was brought forth to contest the seat of Robert A. Harden, Democrat. Both these men were Democrats, but the ring had made a bargain with Johnson that they would seat him if he would promise to vote for Osborn. Johnson promised to do this, and so they attempted to seat him. It will be seen that they desired to unseat six legally elected members and put in one white man as an Indian, which would give the ring seven votes for Osborn independent of the five votes from Leon and two from Columbia county who would not be brought to Osborn's support. The ring, after being forced to the conclusion that they could not capture the chairman of the Committee on Privileges and Elections, called a meeting in the

City Hotel, at which M. L. Stearns presided. At this meeting it was decided that all the members of the ring should vote for James D. Westcott, jr. for Senator, under the understanding with Westcott that if elected they who voted for him should have the offices—in other words the bargain was that the Osborn conspirators should control the Federal offices. By some means this news was communicated to Capt. Charles E. Dyke, then editor of the *Floridian*. The news was brought to Dyke by one of the Democratic members, who thought this a good thing. Dyke went to work to prevent the consummation of this bargain for the reason, he said, that it would be a dangerous thing to have a smart man like Westcott go to the United States Senate in the interest of a corrupt ring. Those Republicans who had sworn vengeance against Osborn had made up their minds to vote for William D. Bloxham before they would see Westcott elected by the ring, and Bloxham would have been elected had it not been for Dyke, who used his influence in favor of Conover. When Dyke came to Conover's rescue he had given up the fight for himself, but was trying to hold his friends together to get them off his hands to the highest bidder. His colored friends did not propose to be disposed of in that way, and so they had a talk with Bloxham, and without any promises from him promised to vote for him if so casting their votes would elect him. This proposition was made to Bloxham the night previous to the election. Dyke's work had been so thoroughly cemented the night before, and the colored brother, who had made all he could out of Osborn and the whole concern, had become weary of the nightly whisky, oyster, and cigar festivities, brought the contest to a close on the 31st day of January, after a struggle of eleven days, during which time there had been twenty-one ballots. The last day of the voting for Senator the members of the ring became greatly excited, and every exertion was made by them to prevent the election. Just before the voting commenced one of them rushed to W. G. Stewart, one of the members from Leon county, and crowded an envelope filled with money into his hand and requested him to use it as he pleased. Stewart, being one of those members who would not take money for his vote, undertook to hand it back to him, but he would not receive it.

Stewart threw the envelope on the ground, whereupon the briber told him he was a crazy man, picked up the envelope and put it in his pocket. Proctor, who had appropriated seven hundred dollars of Osborn's money, learning of the desire of this briber to give away money, requested Stewart to inform him that he, Proctor, would take all the money he had to give away; but Proctor's light for Osborn had been hid under a bushel and could not be trusted further. The joint session met at the usual hour, and it was evident to every one that some great catastrophe was to take place, as the ring men and anti-ring men were now at swords points. The first conflict of words was indulged in by Chadwick, of Putnam, white carpetbagger, and W. G. Stewart, colored, of Leon. Chadwick was denouncing the colored men who were voting with the Democrats for Conover, and Stewart in return denounced him for a nigger-hating —— —— —— On this day there were five ballots taken, some member of the ring moving to adjourn at the close of every ballot; but the joint assembly refused to adjourn. On the fifth ballot John R. Scott, of Duval, who had also worked Osborn's pocket for all it was worth, now rose and denounced Osborn and his ring followers and exposed in the open Assembly the bargain between Westcott and the ring. Horatio Jenkins, on the part of the ring, defended Osborn and the combination which they had entered into, and reminded the Democrats that this was (meaning Scott) part of the Chinese thunder from the Constitutional Convention of 1868, and intimated that the election of Conover meant negro supremacy. Scott was applauded by the anti-ring men and Democrats, which showed that the death knell of the ring had been sounded, while Jenkins drove the remaining colored members who had previously opposed Conover to his support. This was amidst the calling of the roll, and the greatest excitement prevailed, and when tally keepers of the Osborn-Westcott combination perceived that Conover had received the necessaay number of votes, their pencils fell from their hands as though they had a paralytic stroke. M. L. Stearns, now Lieutenant-Governor, who by virtue of his office presided over the joint assembly, now undertook to use his official power to cheat the representatives of the people out of their victory over the ring. Senator John A. Henderson, who had not voted for Conover, waited to hear what Stearns had to say. Stearns then said that there was some mistake, and suggested a re-call of the roll, while members of the ring began to move around among the members for the purpose of bribery, if possible. Senator Henderson arose and said: "This man has been fairly elected, and I demand fair play." Stearns soon saw what would follow, and declared Conover elected Senator. When the result of the vote was declared the scene in the joint assembly was indescribable; anti-ring Republicans and Democrats who had voted against Westcott could be seen and heard shouting and shaking hands over their victory, while the members of the ring, both in and out of the Legislature, seemed awe-stricken and utterly demoralized. This ended the Senatorial contest in Florida in the year 1873. It will be seen that nineteen colored members could not be controlled by the carpetbaggers to support Westcott, and voted for Conover. The remaining six of the twenty-five colored members voted scattering.—See Journal of Joint Assembly, 1873, page 132.

After the election of Senator the members of the ring, for the sole purpose of crippling Conover's influence at Washington, and not for the purpose of purifying elections of any kind—for they were utterly incapable of that—had a resolution adopted by the Assembly to investigate the reports of bribery of members in voting for United States Senator. They attempted to pack the committee by having it elected, thinking they might be successful in bribing colored members enough to enable them to so shape the report as not to implicate the bribed members, while it should work to the injury of Conover. There is no doubt that Conover did use some money to secure his election, but the real wholesale bribery was carried on under the auspices of the members of the ring. Chadwick, of Putnam, carpetbagger, who had voted for the iron-handed Bisbee for United States Senator, but who was ready to vote for Westcott whenever his vote would elect, was put forward to get this resolution through. The anti-ring members and the Democrats at once saw the dodge, and united to elect a committee who would expose all persons on whom they could get any clue who had attempted or had been successful in offering or guilty of receiving a bribe. M. W. Downie, a striker for General Sanford, appeared before the committee and testified that Dockray had given Conover money at different times, which Conover had spent in the Senatorial contest; at the time Westcott and the ring were making their greatest fight Conover had gotten from Dockray eight hundred dollars, which Conover divided into one hundred and one hundred and fifty dollar packages and put these packages of money into envelopes to give to members of the Legislature to prevent them from voting for Westcott. When Dockray was called he admitted having loaned Conover money, but he did not seem to know how much. He said Conover put the money in three or four packages and put it in envelopes, and that he remarked to him at the time that he hoped Westcott would be defeated. When Conover was called he said that he had been in the habit of lending money to members of the Legislature while he was State Treasurer, and he had loaned some money to members of the Legislature at this session. The committee being convinced that it was useless to undertake to prove bribery by bribe-givers and bribe-takers, reported that they could find no sufficient testimony upon which to spot the guilty parties.

The assembly, forced through the clamoring of the people, passed a resolution relative to the disposition of the four millions of bonds issued in aid of the J., P., & M., railroad. Attorney-General William Archer Cocke sent the following communication to the Govenor, who forwarded the same to each House of the Legislature:

"Having observed in the proceedings of the House of Representatives that a resolution of inquiry relative to the four millions of state bonds issued in aid of the Jacksonville, Pensacola & Mobile Railroad Company has been referred to the House Committee on Railroads, I desire to lay before your Excellency matters which have come to my knowledge, from sources deemed to be reliable, relative to the disposition made and proposed to be made of such bonds, which in my opinion, show that immediate action is needed on the part of the government of the State to protect its interest, and to prevent, if possible, the entire loss of the funds provided by law in aid of the railroad. I send herewith a newspaper which contains an account stated to have been made by S. W. Hopkins & Co., of New York, which account, I am informed, contains in many respects correct statements of payments made by said firm, by order of officers of the railroad company, from money received by Hopkins & Co. from John Collinson, of London, for 2,800 of the State bonds which Hopkins & Co., when acting as agents of the railroad company, sold to him. A portion of the amounts charged in the account, I am informed, has never been paid. I am not, of course, able to state with prescision what were the actual payments made by Hopkins & Co. out of the funds, but to the best of my information it exceeds six hundred thousand dollars. Of this large amount I am satisfied, from examination of the items in the account, not more than one hundred and seventy-five thousand dollars were applied to the equipment, construction or repair of the railroad. A large sum, about three hundred thousand dollars, I am informed was paid to parties from whom Milton S. Littlefield purchased shares of stock in the Florida Central Railroad, and which stock he claims to be his property. About fifty thousand dollars was paid to Aaron Barnett on a contract made with him, by the said Littlefield, relative to the navigation and trade of the Chattahooche river, and for steamboats. Fifty thousand dollars were paid to a certain railroad in North Carolina on account of a large claim made by it against said Littlefield. One hundred and four thousand dollars were paid to J. B. Clarke, the brother-in-law of Littlefield, part of which was on account of a judgement obtained by the United States against the Pensacola and Georgia railroad. Fifty thousand dollars were paid to G. W. Swepson, and about twenty thousand dollars to a Tennessee bank, both of which payments were on account of private transactions of said Littlefield. I have specified the foregoing amounts of money misappropriated, basing the statement on particular and reliable information as to the remaining sums charged in the account, whether paid or unpaid. I am informed that there are likewise unjustifiable demands against the board fund, arising out of transactions foreign to the purposes for which the bonds were issued. It will be observed by the Legislature, upon examination of the account, that Hopkins & Co. admit a sale by them of 2,800 bonds. The amount for which they give credit on this account is nine hundred and ninety-seven thousand nine hundred and twenty dollars; the amount stated as received per bond, one hundred pounds sterling; from this was deducted ten pounds per bond for commissions, making on 2,800 bonds twenty-eight thousand pounds sterling—about one hundred and forty thousand dollars. There also was deducted twenty-four pounds per bond—sixty-seven thousand two hundred pounds, about three hundred and forty thousand dollars, which amount was deposited in London to meet the first three instalments of interest. It thus appears from the account, taking the price at which the bonds are stated to have been sold as correct (which will hereafter appear not to be so) that the amount received for 2,800 bonds equalled one million four hundred thousand dollars; and yet the total credit given in the account is nine hundred and ninety-seven thousand nine hundred and twenty dollars; a subtraction of four hundred thousand dollars; equal to thirty-four per cent. of the amount for which the bonds are stated to have been sold. Disastrous as the above transaction may appear, there had taken place another shave by Hopkins & Co. They received, in fact from, Collinson one hundred and thirty-eight pounds sterling per bond, instead of one hundred pounds, equal to one million nine hundred and thirty thousand dollars more than the net amount for which credit was given by them, and five hundred and thirty ahousand dollars more than the sum of money which Hopkins & Co., in the account stated as the net amount received by them for the bonds.

"It will be seen by reference to a letter signed M. S. Littlefield, dated in London, November 14, 1870, that he offered to sell the bonds to Hopkins & Co. for one hundred pounds per bond. They, H. & Co., allege they had a right to credit the bonds in their account at that rate because of this offer, which they assert they accepted and acted on. Collinson states in a bill in chancery, filed by him against Hopkins & Co., that his contract for purchase of the bonds had been already completed when Littlefield wrote the letter above stated; that Littlefield knew the fact; and it also appears, by a sworn statement made by Hopkins & Co., that they did not accept Littlefield's offer until two months after they had made the sale to Collinson.

"Twelve hundred of the four thousand bonds remained in the hands of Hopkins & Co., in October, 1871, and are specified in a deed of trust made by the company to F. H. Flagg and C. L. Chase, and are hereby conveyed in trust to be applied solely to the construction of the unfinished portion of the road. These trustees laid before the members of the Legislature at its last session a letter signed by them, in which they submit extracts from this deed, state the objects of it, and assert that up to that time they had not received any money from the sales of the bonds. This was true at that time. Since then C. L. Chase, one of said trustees, obtained a power of attorney from the officers of the railroad company, and under it placed one hundred and ninety of the bonds in the hands of L. P. Bayne, of New York, giving at same time Hopkins & Co. a release of all liability to the railroad company, as a means of obtaining possession of said bonds, one hundred and eighty-six of which Chase sold to Collinson, and paid to Bayne about one hundred thousand dollars in gold from proceeds, to be credited by Bayne on an account which he sets up against the railroad for damages, amounting to two hundred thousand dollars, for a breach of contract, made by Littlefield with him, by which Bayne was to be employed to sell the bonds. This claim Chase liquidated at one hundred and fifty thousand dollars, and secured to Bayne the one hundred and ninety bonds. Chase, also, as attorney, agreed, in addition to the cash paid to Bayne, to secure him out of the future sales of such of the one thousand two hundred bonds as he might get possession of, a further sum sufficient to make up the amount of one hundred and fifty thousand dollars. Chase, as agent of the road, also agreed to pay Bayne from the sales of the bonds, and from other resources belonging to the railroad, a further sum of one hundred and fifty thousand dollars, which Bayne claimed he had advanced to Littlefield for the purposes of the railroad, and for which he had in possession about four hundred thousand dollars of State bonds, called six per cent. bonds, as collateral, which bonds Bayne has been pressing the Legislature to redeem for several years, and his debt has been represented by those who supported his request, as a debt due by the State for money advanced by Bayne for the benefit of the State. Chase, also, as attorney for the road, agreed with the agents of the Western Division of the Western North Carolina Railroad, to apply two hundred thousand dollars out of the proceeds of the sale of the 1,200 bonds so remaining unsold, whenever payment therefor should be received from Collinson, to pay towards a debt due by Littlefield to said road. The balance of said debt he agreed should be secured and paid by the Jacksonville, Pensacola and Mobile Railroad in like manner as was agreed for the payment to Bayne.

"The debt claimed by the North Carolina Railroad to be due to it by Littlefield, arose out of his connection and that of George W. Swepson with the business of said road. Littlefield has been indicted in North Carolina on account of his acts as President of such road. He was demanded of your predecessor by the Governor of North Carolina, but owing, as I am informed, to certain proceedings in our State courts, he was not delivered up.

"C. L. Chase, acting under the power of attorney, given to him by the Jacksonville, Pensacola and Mobile Railroad, and also in his capacity as trustee under the deed of trust, united in New York in November or December last, with the agents of the North Carolina Railroad, L. P. Bayne and others, and procured and caused to be entered in a court in the City of New York a decree whereby the Jacksonville, Pensacola and Mobile Railroad and the trustees consented that the bonds remaining unsold (except 224 which are to be returned to the State), are to be delivered to Collinson, who is to have the right to buy at any time inside of seven months. If Collinson does purchase, the price of the bonds is to be paid by him to the National Trust Company, of New York City, by it to be kept subject to the said decree, which provides that the money shall be paid out as follows: The North Carolina Railroad is to receive $200,000; L. P. Bayne $60,000; Chase and his company, $80,000; Aaron Barnett $30,000; Calvin Littlefield $25,000; Collinson's lawyer,

Hopkins' lawyer, receiver etc., about $25,000, and sundry other sums are to be paid amounting to more than the sum for which the bonds will sell. I shall be able to lay before you a copy of this decree.

"I am informed that the railroad company has assented to the entry of judgments in Gadsden Circuit Court in favor of Chase and his copartners, who were contractors to construct the road to Mobile, doing business under the style of the Florida Construction Company. The judgment is asserted to be given for money due the company for work done on the road and material furnished. I am assured that of the amount for which judgment was taken more than two-thirds is for money for which the road is not liable, and as to matters disconnected with its construction. I am also informed that Chase received of Bayne nearly forty thousand dollars in connection with the sale of the bonds, and part of the sum of one hundred thousand which Chase secured to Bayne. The Florida Construction Company caused the steamboats which the railroad company owned to be attached in Georgia in a suit based on the said judgment, and the boats were sold for a small sum. The railroad being thereby unable to carry freight on the river, earnings fell short a very large amount of what they should have been. Two other judgments have been obtained in Gadsden county against the railroad, and on the first Monday of January last twenty miles of the road, which had been levied on under executions issued on the several judgments, were sold by the sheriff, and the purchaser is in possession and claims to hold independent and free of the lien of the State adverse thereto. No notice of this illegal sale was given to the State authorities by the railroad company, so far as I am informed, and no application was made to the courts to prevent the sale.

"At the last term of the United States Circuit Court, held in Jacksonville, certain persons, citizens of other States, obtained a decree by the consent and assistance of the President, Milton S. Littlefield, by which the marshal of the Northern District is directed to take possession of that portion of the line of road between Lake City and Quincy, and between Tallahassee and St. Marks, and to sell the same at public outcry to satisfy and pay a sum of four hundred thousand dollars, or thereabouts, being the amount of principal and interest of bonds issued by the Pensacola and Georgia Railroad which was made by the trustees of the internal improvement fund. The holders of these bonds were not paid because the trustees took the check of George W. Swepson as cash, which check has never been paid. At the time when the decree was rendered in the United States Circuit Court, the road was in the hands of a receiver, appointed by the Judge of the Second Judicial circuit, at the suit of certain parties. The suit was afterwards dismissed, and thereupon, by order of the Judge of the State Court, the receiver gave up possession of the road and the United States Marshal took possession of it under the authority of the decree of the United States Circuit Court. A receiver had been in possession of the road under an order made by the Judge of the Fifth circuit of the State, in a suit brought by the trustees of the internal improvement fund, but the Judge of the Second circuit treated the order as null, and put his own receiver in possession, as before stated. I am informed that a sale of the road will be made by the marshal in a few weeks, unless prevented by judicial authority. It is thus apparent that the lien of the State on a large portion of the line of railroad owned by the Jacksonville, Pensacola and Mobile Railroad, is in danger of being rendered insecure, and that the earnings will be applied by those who purchase the road at the sale under the legal proceedings of the State. The entire scheme of railway connection with Mobile will be thus destroyed and the State greatly damaged. This result is not only the consequence of the illegal acts of the officers of the Jacksonville, Pensacola and Mobile Railroad, the result of the gross frauds in respect to the bonds, but has been aided overtly and covertly by the President of the road. That portion of line of the road between Lake City and Jacksonvile is also in the hands of a receiver, and is operated by him as an independent road. This suit in which the receiver was appointed was brought to establish the claim of a party who alleges that he has stock in the corporation by which said part of the line of the Jacksonville, Pensacola and Mobile Railroad was formerly owned, and alleges that the Florida Central Railroad, which was formed by those who purchased said line of road at a sale thereof in 1869, by the trustees, is still the owner thereof, and still in existence and corporation, never was merged in the company called the Jacksonville, Pensacola and Mobile Railroad; that the issuance of the State bonds based on such a line of road was illegal, and that the State has no lien on the road.

"It will be seen that the State is deeply interested in this question. The principal owner of the stock in the Florida Central Road is Milton S. Littlefield. He purchased the greater part of the stock with money which he obtained from Hopkins & Co. out of the proceeds of the sale of the 2,800 State bonds. He has endeavored to keep separate the business accounts of the line formerly owned by the Florida Central Road, and by his votes and that of others he has kept on foot a separate set of officers, such as President and Directors of said Central Road. By the terms of the law under which the State bonds were issued to the Pensacola and Mobile Railroad the road was to pay interest to the State each six months, and the State was to pay interest to the bondholders. The fund provided by law to pay such interest was to be derived from the net earnings of the road. It was asserted by the company that when the road should be repaired, equipped and extended from Quincy to the river—twenty miles—the earnings would be sufficient to pay interest on the four million dollars. The result has been otherwise. The earnings have not increased; the road has been and is out of repair; the rolling stock has run down and been destroyed by reason of the bad condition of the road. The expenses have been great; enormous salaries, utterly beyond the business done, have been paid, and a large amount of the earnings has been spent in litigation and in improper and illegal ways. The extra expenses which have been, by the placing of the road at various times in hands of receivers of courts, should have been avoided. Owing to these causes no interest has been paid by the road to the State to enable it to pay the interest on State bonds. I am assured, however, that all the interest coupons up to this date have been cancelled, and that all will be delivered to the State. I regret, however, to learn that this result has been obtained by appropriating money paid by Collinson for bonds; that already a sum of between four and five hundred thousand dollars has been spent of the bond fund in that way. I respectfully suggest that the Legislature should make provision for the protection of the interests of the State in the public works it has loaned the credit of the State to complete, and to compel those who have fraudulently possessed themselves of money arising from a sale of the bonds to refund it with interest; to defeat the schemes that are on foot to work further wrong and injury to the State, and insure proper application of the proceeds of the bonds and the completion of the important enterprise itself, that adventurers be no longer allowed to make the said public works a means of raising enormous sums of money to be dissipated with reckless profligacy. WILLIAM ARCHER COCKE,

Attorney General.

L. P. Bayne appeared before the Legislature in person at several sessions and attempted to impress upon the minds of the members of that body that the bonds which he held against the State had been issued by the State to raise revenue for the support of the government. His position was that an Act should be passed issuing one million State bonds bearing six per cent. interest, to mature in thirty years. That these bonds were to be sold for not less than seventy-five cents on the dollar, and the first proceeds thereof be applied in taking up or redeeming the bonds held by Bayne from Littlefield. It is evident that Bayne and Littlefield understood each other in this scheme, and had Bayne been successful Littlefield would have shared with him in the spoils. Many of the less informed members of the Legislature, believing Bayne to be an "honest 'Publican from de Norf," favored and voted for his proposition, which they did not understand then, nor do they understand to this day. Some of the influences brought to bear which induced the colored members to vote for the measure were that Bayne had procured the assistance of some of the influential white citizens around Tallahassee to advocate the passage of this measure. The Legislature, however, refused to pass it because Bayne did not pay money enough to the carpet-bag members. Although this glaring fraud was so fully exposed by Hart's Attorney-General, yet no act was passed by the Legislature to recover the money fraudulently expended or appropriated by Littlefield. This was, of course, natural, as Littlefield had so abundantly filled the coffers of the carpet-bag members at the very inception of his fraudulent career in Florida.

In the Senate a concurrent resolution, which originated in the House and passed that body by almost unanimous consent, was now passed, authorizing the appointment of a joint committee of three on the part of the House and two on the part of the Senate to examine and adjust the accounts of ex-Governor Reed, which accounts had been referred to in his last annual message. L. G. Dennis and A. D. McKinnon were appointed on the part of the Senate, and W. F. Green, J. W. Johnson and J. C. Gass on the part of the Assembly. After a thorough investigation the committee, on the 12th day of February, made the following report:

"The undersigned joint committee, appointed to examine and adjust the accounts of ex-Governor Harrison Reed, referred to in his last message, beg leave to report that they have performed that duty and find justly due to Governor Reed the sum of twenty-four thousand dollars for legitimate and necessary expenditures, principally under the Act of the Legislature of August, 1868, which imposed heavy responsibilities for which no adequate means were provided, and rendered necessary by the disorganized and unsettled condition of the State during the first year of his administration. They submit the accompanying bill and unanimously recommend its passage.

(Signed) "L. G. DENNIS,
"Chairman."

In the Senate the bill accompanying the report of the committee to pay the Reed claim, was referred to another committee with Horatio Jenkins, Governor Reed's old enemy, as chairman, and that committee reported back the claim and recommended the passage of the bill to pay it. When the general appropriation bill came up for consideration, L. G. Dennis moved that $24,000 be appropriated for the relief of ex-Governor Harrison Reed, in accordance with the recommendations of report of Joint Special Committee, provided, that the Comptroller shall deduct from this sum any amount which may be found due the State on account of appropriations heretofore made for contingent expenses of the Governor. This amendment was lost by seven to nine. Shortly after a motion was made to reconsider, and still another to lay the motion to reconsider on the table. This motion would have been defeated had it not been for the vote of M. L. Stearns, Lieutenant-Governor. When the vote stood ten for and ten against laying on the table, Stearns, remembering how Governor Reed's friends had charged him with stealing the freedmens' meat and flour, thought this a good opportunity to get even with him, and he therefore gave the casting vote in favor of laying the amendment on the table. This ended the Governor's claim in the Senate. In the Assembly the bill paying Governor Reed's claim came up for consideration, and after several amendments were offered and defeated, it was referred back to the committee with instructions to report at the next meeting of the Legislature. Thus it was that this just claim was defeated. Twenty-four thousand dollars was a small compensation for Governor Reed, who had maintained peace and civil government in the State under the most trying circumstances that had ever occurred in its history. Corrupt men stirring up strife between the races as a cloak with which to hide their corrupt acts from the public gaze of the North; some of the most rabid whites urging their people to open resistance; the carpetbagger, after instigating this teaching, encouraging the freedmen to strike the first blow; the Governor not only expended the small amount of the contingent fund voted him by the Legislature, but the author was personally cognizant of the thousands of dollars which Governor Reed paid from his pocket to maintain peace and order in these most trying days of the State's history. Although Governor Reed left the executive chair a poor man, stripped of nearly all his earthly wealth by means of which he had saved the State and its people thousands, yea, hundreds of thousands of dollars and at the same time prevented the general shedding of innocent blood, yet he had the consolation to know that He who watches over the destiny of all peoples, governments, kingdoms, and principalities, would reward him as one who had deprived himself for the benefit of the many.

At this session of the Legislature there was not that bitterness on the part of the Democrats that had heretofore been exhibited, for the reason that the cause had been removed. Every session of the Legislature before that time had witnessed the unseating of Democratic members who had been fairly elected, which caused a great deal of bad blood. The civil rights bill had passed at this session without any great opposition, the whites knowing that all the negro wanted was fair treatment on railroads and steamboats—for he was not able to eat in the hotels even if he had a desire to do so, and he could not therefore give any trouble. Hart and the ring, anticipating Conover's course as United States Senator, entered into a plot to hold as many of the leading freedmen as possible. Conover not being very popular, it would be necessary for him to appoint more colored men to office than Hart. The ring and Hart were determined to beat both Conover and the negro. The plan was to send to the Senate the names of colored men to fill offices in Democratic counties whenever it could be done without exposing their object. Of course the Democratic Senators would object, and thereupon enough carpetbag Senators would vote with them to defeat the confirmation of the negro, and he having no way of knowing who voted against him, was told that Governor Hart and the ring did all that they could for him and had sent his name to the Senate, but the Democrats had defeated his confirmation. One colored man, whose name was sent up to the Senate from Waukulla County for Tax-Assessor, could scarcely write his name, but he had great influence among the colored brethren and could secure the delegation from that county in political conventions. He was not confirmed, of course, but his name being sent up secured him to the ring for all time to come.

This session of the Legislature was a very disastrous one for the ring. Scarcely had they got over the shock of being routed in the election of Senator before Hamilton Jay, Conover's secretary while Treasurer, was elected State Printer, which took the printing from the ring and placed it in the hands of Charles E. Dyke, who had assisted Conover in his election to the Senate. The Democrats who voted for Conover and the anti-ring Republicans now held a secret meeting for the purpose of laying plans to continue their resistance to the ring for the next four years. At that meeting was Conover, Purman, Dyke, C. H. Pearce and a host of others. The Democrats seemed satisfied with the good intentions of all the Republicans, but it was evident that they had no faith or confidence in Mr. W. J. Purman. It was, however, agreed in that meeting that while the members of each party would retain their principles as such, they would continue to co-operate until the ring and its methods should be utterly swept from power in Florida.

After a session of forty-three days the Legislature adjourned on the 19th day of February, *sine die.*

CHAPTER XVII.

Death of Governor Hart. Stearns Assumes the Reins of Government. He Attempts to Get Rid of Attorney-General Cocke by Stratagem. The Preliminary Party Returning Boards. Stearns Attempts to Tie the Hands of a High Judicial Officer. Freedmen to Support Stearns' So-Called Administration. The Election of Congressmen and Members of the Legislature of 1874. Frauds Committed in the Counties of Leon and Jefferson.

After the adjournment of the Legislature of 1874, Governor Hart was not able to attend to the duties of his office other than to sanction any appointments which Stearns and other carpet-baggers would desire; and while these appointments were supposed to be made by him, yet they were really made by Stearns. Many of the names that had been rejected by the Senate were now again appointed in utter violation of the constitution, notable among which was E. C. Weeks, of Leon County, as Sheriff. Weeks was now appointed Sheriff, which meant a death struggle for the supremacy of the ring in Leon County and a general war in the State to suppress all opposition to this formidable combination.

Governor Hart died in Jacksonville on the 18th of March, 1874, and was given a large and respectable funeral by all classes of citizens. At the news of his death Stearns, although in his proclamation expressing great sorrow at the departure of the deceased Governor, yet the catastrophe so lighted up his path to the United States Senate or to the gubernatorial chair that he could not hide the ecstasy into which he had fallen. In fact, a general rejoicing was indulged in throughout the carpet-bag clan who were friendly to the ring, and social meetings were held at which they renewed the pledge to each other for fraud and plunder. Stearns was the most rotten piece of gubernatorial timber that was ever placed at the helm of government.

Hart had attempted, during his administration, to force Attorney General Cocke to resign his position in the Cabinet, but had not succeeded. Stearns, now finding Cocke, by virtue of his office, a member of the State Returning Board, undertook to get rid of him by stratagem. He had an understanding with all the members of Hart's Cabinet to resign, and present their resignations in a body. This was to be done apparently out of courtesy to the incoming Governor, but the real object was to obtain Cocke's resignation, which would be accepted, while he would refuse to accept the resignations of the others. Everything was made ready to capture this Samson. Cocke had not informed the other members of the Cabinet that he would not be caught in this trap, and it was hopefully expected that he would follow in their wake. When the hour arrived to commence the play Cocke was missing, but the others proceeded to the Executive Chamber and presented their resignations to the chief, who, after looking around for Cocke, delivered a short address, refusing to accept their resignations, which was full of disappointment and distress. The play ended in failure, owing to the absence of the leading performer. The resignation of Jonathan C. Gibbs, who had been appointed by Governor Hart after a hard fight by the colored brother, would have been accepted but for fear of the same power.

Stearns, baffled in the effort to get rid of Cocke, now buckled on his sword for the United States Senatorial contest. He and other leading members of the carpet-bag ring met in Jacksonville and agreed to make a determined fight in all the counties—and especially in the Black Belt counties—to elect members to the Legislature of 1875 who would vote for a Ring carpet-bagger for the next United States Senator. To get Colonel Bisbee's individual support in this fight he was put forward as the candidate of the Ring; but those who belonged to the inner ring, consisting of Martin, Stearns, Wentworth and the "Little Giant," L. G. Dennis, were secretly arranging for the election of Stearns, he agreeing to appoint Wentworth Lieutenant Governor as soon as he should be elected United States Senator.

The Ring had succeeded in every one of the Black Belt counties in establishing county Republican committees in opposition to the regular Republican committees. These committees were even now denominated as the party returning boards of the different counties. These preliminary returning boards, whenever there were not enough Ring supporters in a precinct to bring up a Stearns delegation, would appoint delegates from other precincts to make up the full measure. A convict was as suitable for their purposes as the most honest man. The precinct returning boards, through the instructions from the county returning boards, would commit all frauds necessary to sustain the county returning boards in throwing out any precinct that was not solid for Stearns and the Ring managers. The county returning boards were to superintend, perfect and defend all frauds committed by the Ring, and make all necessary arrangements for taking any case in which the preliminary boards had failed to beat the masses to the State Returning Board, or to the Central Committee, of which Mr. E. M. Cheney was still Chairman. The State Returning Board had a general supervision over all the frauds of these county preliminaries and decided all contests coming up from the counties in favor of the Ring; and the question of right or wrong, of majorities or minorities, found no favor with this corrupt carpet-bag party Returning Board. Another power assumed by this Returning Board was to prepare all the papers and make good all the frauds committed upon the ballot box in the different counties by the Ring, and define the same before the State Board of Canvassers. Whenever opposition in any county was so strong among the freedmen that money and intimidation was not sufficient to remove it the Ring would propose a compromise by having the two committees to meet jointly, and the side that could poll the most votes at the meeting should have the Republican organization of the county. To illustrate their desperate efforts when these committees would meet, the most of whose members were freedmen, the carpetbaggers would take members of the committee into their houses, seat them at their tables for dinner or breakfast, and give them money to come over before the committee took a vote; and when this failed, they would hand the freedman some fine book to read (when perhaps the poor fellow did not know "B from a bull's foot") and tell him to sit awhile in the parlor and enjoy himself; while they would retire, locking the door behind themselves and rush to the committee meeting. The other side in a great state of excitement would hunt diligently for their lost statesman, who could not be found until the committee had accomplished its work and the Ring through fraud and false imprisonment had procured their legal status in the county. Whenever the leading colored men had pluck, they would resist the carpetbag organizations obtained in this way, as was the case in the counties of Leon and Jefferson.

The Ring, in the attempt to capture the Black Belt counties, did not hesitate to resort to anything, however disgraceful it might be. In Duval county they drew the color line on honest Dan McInnis, and circulated among the freedmen the story that McInnis wanted to get up a mulatto church. John R. Scott now played the traitor to McInnis and supported the charge made by the Ring. Joseph E. Lee, who had not been long in the State, had been sent to Jacksonville from Tallahassee by Jonathan C. Gibbs, to A. A. Knight for employment. Lee was from Philadelphia, and knew nothing of the condition of the State and the trouble through which the colored people had passed by reason of carpetbag management. He, too, joined in with the Ring against McInnis, who undoubtedly was one of the most honest and upright colored men that was ever elected to the Legislature in this State. Martin, Stearns and many other leading members of the Ring came to Jacksonville to assist in the fight made on McInnis, and succeeded in beating him in the county convention, and Lee and Scott were nominated for the lower branch of the Legislature. Thus, through falsehood and deception, the man who had been working for the people and against carpetbag treachery was defeated to make place for those whom the Ring managers could control.

Archibald, a carpetbagger who had been appointed Judge of the Fourth Judicial Circuit by a former Governor, had complained that the salary of his office was not sufficient for him to subsist on. Stearns and the Ring managers being very anxious to get rid of W. H. Christy, their old enemy, as Superintendent of Schools in Duval county, and retain Archibald and make a judicial ally of him, called a secret meeting in Jacksonville to take into consideration this important subject. The meeting was attended by Stearns as Governor and other members of the Ring, and a spirited discussion ensued. It was finally decided that Archibald should be appointed Superintendent of Schools in Duval, and Christy removed. The edict went forth, and Archibald was appointed. It happened, however, before Archibald qualified, a question then arose as to whether, under the Constitution, he could hold the office of Judge and that of Superintendent of Schools at the same time.

Archibald, a carpetbagger who had been appointed Judge of the Fourth Judicial Circuit by a former Governor, had complained that the salary of his office was not sufficient for him to subsist on. Stearns and the Ring managers being very anxious to get rid of W. H. Christy, their old enemy, as Superintendent of Schools in Duval county, and retain Archibald and make a judicial ally of him, called a secret meeting in Jacksonville to take into consideration this important subject. This meeting was attended by Stearns as Governor, and other members of the Ring, and a spirited discussion ensued. It was finally decided that Archibald should be appointed Superintendent of Schools in Duval and Christy removed. The edict went forth, and Archibald was appointed. It happened, however, before Archibald qualified, a question arose as to whether, under the Constitution, he could hold the office of Judge and that of Superintendent of Schools at the same time. They cared nothing for the Constitution, but the real question was as to how Randall and Westcott would decide the matter. It was therefore agreed to get the private opinion of the Chief Justice, which was had. He informed them that the very moment Archibald accepted the office of Superintendent of Schools he vacated his office as Judge. A second meeting was called in Jacksonville, which brought Stearns and his ring managers together. At this meeting it was decided that one of Archibald's best friends should be appointed and that Archibald draw the pay and perform the duties of the office. This decree was at once put in execution by the appointment of one Rollins, of Ft. George, in Duval county, as Superintendent, and Archibald drew the pay and performed the duties of the office. This little transaction worked nicely for several months, when there appeared in the political horizon a speck of cloud which kept increasing in size and ugliness until the terror-stricken carpetbaggers were forced to call Rollins to his post. J. W. Bentley, a wealthy Democrat, being a member of the School Board, contended that Rollins, the real Superintendent, could not deputize Archibald to perform his duties. The carpetbaggers, fearing that the matter might be made public, called Rollins to his post. The Judge, however, was paid from the time he was appointed—that is, from the time he was appointed preceding Rollins's appointment. Whether the Judge continued to receive the salary of Superintendent after the storm created by Bentley was over, is not known, but it is presumed that a fair division was made of the salary, as he did not resign the judgeship.

The lines between the Ring and anti-Ring element in the Republican party were now drawn more distinctly than were the lines between the Democratic and Republican parties. Colored men in the Black Belt counties, some of whom could scarcely write their names, had been appointed Justices of the Peace, and were now called upon to use their authority to compel the freedmen to swear allegiance to Stearns. False charges were trumped up and they were carried before these Justices—the Sheriffs in some counties assisting in getting up the charges. The colored defendant was often conveyed to jail secretly, and after being safely lodged in prison would be told by the Sheriff that if he would support Stearns and the Ring he should be set at liberty. We take for illustration the following: In Leon County the opposition to Stearns and the Ring was more powerful than in any other county, for the reason that the colored leaders in opposition to the Ring in that county had more pluck Two young colored men who were natives of the county, had been sent to school in Georgia, and had come back with a fair education. Of course when they came back to the county they had sufficient intelligence to cast their fortunes with the anti-Ring freedmen. They, being natives, had great influence with the freedmen. The Ring discovered this fact, and undertook to buy them off and bring their influence to Stearns. One of these young men, James D. Thompson, now an attorney at law, was paid some fifty dollars to go over to the Ring. He received the money very thankfully, and then went to the livery stable, hired a horse and buggy, and went out to a public meeting where he exposed the Sheriff—Major E. C. Weeks, carpetbagger—who had paid him the money. This action on the part of Thompson had the effect of greatly injuring the Ring in that county. A few days after, Thompson was arrested and lodged in jail by the Sheriff without any complaint having then been made against him. Thompson gave bonds, and was attempting to proceed against the Sheriff for false imprisonment. This was discovered by the Sheriff and Thompson was again arrested, when he then filed a petition before Judge J. D. Westcott, one of the Supreme Judges, for a writ of *habeas corpus*, which was at once granted, and before the Sheriff had time to fix things up Thompson was before the court. The Judge at once inquired into the cause of Thompson's imprisonment, and found that the Sheriff had no commitment or other authority upon which to hold him. In the petition for the writ of *habeas corpus* Thompson had prayed that a summons *duces tecum* be issued to one De Vaughn, a colored Justice of the Peace, to show whether he had issued any warrant against him. De Vaughn made his appearance before Judge Westcott, and he and the Sheriff being separated, and not allowed to hear each other's evidence, De Vaughn swore that he had given the Sheriff a commitment for Thompson on account of an affidavit taken in his court against him, but could not produce the affidavit, nor could he tell the nature of the complaint nor by whom made. The Judge took this testimony in writing. When the Sheriff testified, he stated that De Vaughn had not given him a commitment for Thompson, and that he had arrested Thompson on suspicion. Thompson was discharged, and when the Grand Jury met it happened that a majority of it was composed of Democrats and anti-Ring freedmen. Westcott appeared before the Grand Jury and presented this testimony. De Vaughn was indicted for perjury. When he was arraigned before the court for trial, a jury was impanneled of the most ignorant and dishonest of the colored men, all blacks—in fact, they were picked for their special notoriety in the community as cow, hog and chicken thieves, and kept around the court house and up and down the streets of Tallahassee, whiskied, fed and paid to induce the masses to sustain Stearns and the Ring.

Judge Westcott's testimony against De Vaughn had no more effect upon the minds of this so-called jury than a drop of fresh water would have upon the Atlantic ocean to affect its saltness. De Vaughn was acquitted after the jury had spent some time in room, though during the time spent there they were not deliberating upon the testimony and the law given them by the Court, but deliberating as to who they could get to write their verdict. Finally the Deputy Sheriff wrote the verdict and signed the name of the foreman. This was a grand victory for Stearns—the saving this perjured colored brother from the State prison, and all the cow, hog and chicken thieves throughout the county and State, as the news was conveyed to them, shouted hurrah for Stearns. This is only one imperfect sample (but the imperfection consists in not being able to give the full details of the victory) of the many acts of oppression the people of Florida underwent while passing through the fiery furnace of carpet-bagism.

The Northern machine politicians assert that it was the incompetence and unfaithfulness of the negro voter to the Republican party that brought about the unhealthy condition of things which made the solid South,— it was these and kindred acts of the carpetbaggers which furnish the key to unlock the door that reveals the secrets of the solid South, while these very carpetbaggers were sustained by the Northern machine politicians. From the beginning to the end of Stearns' so-called administration it was contaminated with packed juries for political purposes, and during the last two years of his term it became a patent fact that scarcely a person brought before the courts in the Black Belt counties could be convicted from the fact that the petit juries were mostly composed of the very worst element among the freedmen—that element that made its living by stealing pigs, chickens, cows, and other property from the whites and the more industrious freedmen. When an acquittal could not be had in the most conclusive case of larceny by reason of some honest freedman or some white man on the jury, the thieves on the jury, or those who sympathized with the thief, would cause a mistrial, which, in most cases would end in an acquittal. So far as the juries and the ministerial officers were concerned, the courts for the last two years of Stearns' administration were mere political clubs for the purpose of securing his election. The people, both black and white, became disheartened on account of the loss of Stock through thieft and almost gave up in some sections the industry of stock-raising, which, for some years ruined the Black Belt counties, and brought those who owned the lands in debt, as well as the freedmen, who had to get the landlord or merchant to send off and buy every pound of meat that they ate.

The Congressional delegation, with the exception of Abijah Gilbert, now being against the Ring, they determined to make a desperate fight to secure both Congressmen, the United States Senator, and as many members of the Legislature as possible preparatory to gaining control of the entire Federal patronage, or at least to so cripple Conover as to leave him with no influence with the President. The Democrats nominated Judge Finley in the Second Congressional District, and J. T. Walls completely cleaned out the Ring in that District and was nominated. John A. Henderson then resided in Leon county. The notorious Purman, then a member of Congress from the First Congressional District, was determined to be renominated; but the Ring, with Stearns at its head, could not afford to have him go back to Congress after having betrayed them and gone in with Conover. The returning boards of the party had been instructed in all the counties in this District to send anti-Purman delegates; and whenever they could not get people enough together to hold a convention, they were to appoint delegations and send them up to the District Convention. This was accordingly done. The astute Purman hearing of this fact, so arranged things as to capture the convention, the delegates sent up by the returning boards to the contrary notwithstanding. The convention was called to order and an anti-Ring delegate elected as chairman. A full set of officers was elected, all of whom were anti-Ring, and a committee on credentials appointed. The convention then took a recess to await the report of the committee on credentials. When the convention reassembled it found that the Ring had captured the State Assembly Hall in which they had assembled, and had put a Ring chairman in the place of the one elected by the convention. When the anti-Ring delegates attempted to enter a general mob began. The scene was now indescribable. Knives, pistols, clubs and everything that could be used for head-breaking, were sought after as eagerly as though the life of the seeker depended upon the discovery of the article sought, and this was about the case. The poor ignorant freedmen knocked each other down with clubs and broke each others heads, until there was not left a desk in the Assembly chamber but had lost from one to all its legs to be used upon the heads and bodies of the freedmen in the defence of the most deceptive and corrupt set of men that have ever planted foot on Southern soil. Stearns, being at the head of the government, ordered Purman and his followers from the capitol, and threatened to call out the militia (most of whom were disreputable colored persons lying around to intimidate other freedmen into the support of Stearns) if they should refuse to go. Purman called his convention in the public street and then nominated himself for Congress. The Ring and Stearns had promised to nominate Jonathan C. Gibbs, then in Stearns' Cabinet; but they were afraid to nominate him, as they thought he might be able to whip Purman out of the field and get to Congress, when, remembering how the Ring had treated himself and Governor Reed, this elephant might, with his heavy black foot, be able to crush them worse than Purman could. Robert Meacham, who had always been completely controlled by the Ring, was nominated as the Ring candidate. Mr. Gibbs, who had always opposed Purman and his methods, both in Jackson county and in his former nomination to Congress, was in perfect health before the meeting of the convention and during its sitting. He had just finished delivering a powerful speech against Purman in the Stearns' convention, reacapitulating all his cruelty. He went home and ate a hearty dinner, after which he suddenly died. It was whispered and generally believed that he was poisoned by some of the carpetbaggers, because they dreaded his growing popularity; but whether it was the Ring or Purman wing, was not ascertained. The contest now opened in the Black Belt counties in West and Middle Florida for Ring supremacy. Osborn, and other members of the Ring being interested in the scheme of the Great Southern Railroad, and having hopes that the scheme would be successful, had passed through the Legislature a general bill for the incorporation of railroads and canals. This bill authorized the arrest and imprisonment of any person who allowed stock to walk on any railroad. Martin was Speaker when the bill passed and Stearns presided over the Senate at the same time, and these officers of course signed the bill. The Leon county delegation had always made it a point to vote against all railroad bills that they did not understand, and this was one which they had voted against. They expected a fight with Stearns and the Ring, and saved this little campaign document to be used in the proper time. Purman was hard pushed by the Ring, until the author of this work informed him of this law, which had been voted for by all the members of the Ring in the Legislature; and he at once made use of it in his speeches. He would read the law and then explain it as an act aimed at the freedmen by Stearns and other members of the Ring. At Chattahoochee, in Gadsden county, Stearns and Martin had a cart-load of guns brought to a public meeting to be used against Purman and his followers. They had fed the freedmen on so much bad whisky that they came near getting themselves killed. The freedmen became uncontrollable and commenced shooting indiscriminately in every direction, routing Stearns, Martin and Purman, and running them away from the meeting. Purman returned later in the evening and called a lot of colored women together, and after giving each of them some money, he said to them that he was a good "Publican," and wanted supper; and to further assure them that he was a good "Publican," told them that he did not want to sleep with any white person, but wanted to sleep with the blackest person in the neighborhood. John D. Harris, a Methodist preacher, was along as one of Purman's canvassers, and it looked as though he had been "dipped" three or four times, and so Purman selected him to sleep with. This action on the part of Purman had its desired effect, as most of the freedmen spoke out and declared him to be a good "Publican," and he had no more trouble in that part of the county.

Purman being one of the trained members of the Ring, was confident that fraud at the ballot box would be attempted to defeat him for Congress, so he had himself nominated in Jackson county for the Assembly. This was for a two-fold purpose—first, to make what he could out of the election of U.S. Senator, which was to take place at the coming session. Second, to intimidate Stearns and cause him to desist from opposing him, Stearns fearing that Purman would expose in the Legislature the rottenness of his administration. The fight went on for several weeks, when at length Stearns sued for peace. Meacham was then taken out of the field by Stearns, and Purman was required to pay the war debt, which was estimated at five hundred dollars. Meacham said that as he had been the victim of Stearns' fight and spent his own money, the benefits of the compromise should inure to him. Purman told that he paid the five hundred dollars to Stearns, and Meacham came out minus the five hundred.

Walls, in the Second District, was less fortunate than Purman, as he had a secret enemy to fight. The Ring did not dare to oppose him openly for fear of weakening themselves with the mass of the freedmen; but they worked like heroes to defeat him secretly. The Democrats that year did but very little to carry the First District, but the watchful and still-hunting Finley worked hard for his election in the Second District. For some reason not altogether known, there was a falling off from the Democratic vote in that district, and the canvass did not amount to much more than organizing for 1876. Both Purman and Walls were counted in, while Purman was also elected to the Legislature. The leading colored men in the district did not support Purman because they had any confidence in him, but because he was the strongest man they could confront the Ring with. Had Bloxham been nominated for Congress by the Democrats that year, he would have defeated Purman. Judge Finley contested the seat of Walls and was admitted into Congress. Stearns and the Ring, anticipating that the Legislature would be very close, and knowing that if Leon and Jefferson counties sent up anti-Ring delegations to the Legislature they would be unable to pass plunder legislation, set to work to carry these counties at whatever cost. Thousands of dollars were expended in these counties to defeat the anti-Ring regular Republican tickets, and the whole power of the administration was brought to bear, with now and then a tithe of recognition from the State party returning board, and urging the election of the Ring tickets. The freedmen were told that the Ring was in favor of high taxes upon the lands of the ex-slaveholders so as to compel them to sell these lands cheaply to the freedmen or the State would take the lands for taxes and give them out to the freedmen. They would tell the freedmen that the anti-Ring members of the party were in favor of low taxes, so that the whites could hold the land and rent them to the colored people at high prices. While the better informed freedmen paid no attention to this demagogism, there were quite a number of the more ignorant class who believed these sayings were righteous and that Stearns and the Ring were good 'Publicans, as they wanted to give the colored brother land. The whites in these counties seeing the great disadvantages under which the anti-Ring nominees were laboring, refused to put a legislative ticket in the field, and advised the Democrats in Leon county to vote for the anti-Ring Republican ticket. Stearns soon learned what had taken place, and called his Ring followers together at Jacksonville. In the caucus it was decided, if the anti-Ring ticket had any show of election, fraud upon the ballot box should be resorted to as it was at Yellow Bluff. It was also decreed that the County Commissioners in these counties should appoint none but Ring inspectors at the ballot boxes in these counties, except now and then a representative of the Democratic party to keep down suspicion. This order was carried out to the letter; inspectors were appointed in the largest colored precincts with instructions to return the vote for the Ring candidates. In Leon county the notorious Joseph Bowes and De Leon, ballot-box stuffers of the very highest type, were selected as inspectors of the two largest precincts in the county. C. H. Walton, editor of the *Tallahassee Sentinel*, which was one of the leading papers in the support of Stearns' so-called administration, was on the Board of County Commissioners in Leon county, and was the chief manipulator in securing the appointment of Bowes and DeLeon as inspectors of election. These two worthies, who were aware that the whites would be on the watch for them, proceeded to the polling places over night in order to get what freedmen they could, by giving them whisky and money, to give countenance to the fraud. De

Leon was so closely watched at his precinct by the whites that he could do nothing. Bowes was more successful. At his precinct the Democratic inspector did not arrive until after the polls were opened, and before opening the polls he stuffed three hundred fraudulent tickets into the box, and these tickets were counted for the Ring legislative ticket, and yet the precinct was carried against them. Both Leon and Jefferson gave large majorities against the Ring, and anti-Ring delegations were elected. When news reached Stearns that the Ring had been defeated in these counties he became wrathful with his manipulators and sleep left his eyes, until a plan was devised to change this most damaging result. Another council was called, this time in the Executive office, and there it was determined to instruct the legal County Returning Boards to throw out sufficient precincts in each of the counties to show majorities for the Ring candidates. In Leon county DeLeon, who had failed to commit fraud at the Miccosukie precinct, made affidavit that some illegal votes were polled at that precinct. Though the affidavit did not state who voted illegally nor for what candidate these illegal votes were cast, the precinct was thrown out by the Board, which consisted of Major E. C. Weeks, Sheriff; a so-called Justice of the Peace, Samuel Snowden, colored, appointed for the purpose, and Samuel Walker, County Judge, who voted No. Sufficient precincts were thrown out in Jefferson county to secure the election of the Ring candidates. Geo. W. Witherspoon, headed the anti-Ring ticket in Jefferson county, and the author of this work headed the anti-Ring ticket in Leon county for the Senate. There was no Senator to be elected in Jefferson county, and Witherspoon headed the ticket for the Assembly. Stearns and the Ring were now happy, and thought the war was over.

As soon as these so-called canvassers adjourned *sine die*, counsel was employed by Wallace and Witherspoon to compel an honest canvass of the votes. Judge R. B. Hilton, Democrat, was employed by the anti-Ring members in Leon county, T. F. Clark, Esq., and   Whitfield, of Jefferson county, Democrats, were employed by Witherspoon. These gentlemen proceeded by a writ of mandamus against these Boards of Canvassers, and Judge P. W. White, of the Second Judicial Circuit, who had been appointed by Governor Reed, granted a peremptory writ ordering the Board to count the votes as returned, and forward the same to the State Returning Board. At one time they hesitated to obey the order of the Judge, for the reason that they thought if they were ordered to prison it would not really be confinement. The sheriffs of Leon and Jefferson counties were Ring carpetbaggers, but the Judge intimated to some of their friends that should they disobey his order he intended sending them down into Wakulla county for imprisonment, where the "Crackers" were waiting with their mouths open to take them in. The order was then obeyed without a murmur, and a second return was sent up to the State Board of Canvassers. Stearns was still determined to continue the counting out process. The whites in Leon county now became incensed at the action of the Governor and his Ring managers, and loudly denounced these repeated attempts at fraud. The anti-Ring freedmen had a consultation with some of the whites, at which the freedmen came to the determination that it was their duty to adopt the shot-gun policy against those who should undertake to hold a seat in the Legislature to which they were not elected. It was there solemnly agreed that if John N. Stokes was counted in as Senator the anti-Ring freedmen were to walk into the Senate chamber and kill him in his seat. The same judgment that was to be visited on Stokes was to be visited on the other members holding seats by fraud. Great excitement prevailed throughout the two counties that had been cheated out of their just representation, and if it had been persisted in, would have caused a general uprising of the anti-Ring freedmen, and with the whites as auxiliaries, bloodshed would have been certain, with Stearns as the first victim. Some of the Conover carpet-baggers who had been informed what would certainly take place made haste to inform Stearns of what would be the certain outcome if the fraud were persisted in, positively stating to him that it could not be consummated without force and violence. On the day of the canvass of the vote by the State Returning Board a large number of the freedmen who supported the Ring, and the anti-Ring freedmen, were present. Many of them from the country brought with them such arms as they could secure, thinking, some of them, that the proceedings under mandamus was a man who was to compel the Board of Canvassers to count the true returns; they declared if "Old man Daniels" did not count in the rightful candidates, he and Stearns should be put to death.

R. B. Hilton, Esq., appeared before the Board and demanded the counting of the returns sent up by the order of Judge White, and proceeded to argue his case. He denounced the action of the County Board of Canvassers for throwing out precincts without the authority of law, and threatened a mandamus to compel the Board to count the true return should they fail to do so. T. F. Clark and Whitfield also appeared and argued the case of Witherspoon. Stearns, in the meantime, fearing the consequences, had instructed the Board to count in the anti-Ring delegations from Leon and Jefferson counties, and sent for the author, and after inquiring what would be the result should the Ring ticket be counted in, admitted the fraud and said it was done without his approval; but his action in keeping these men in office was sufficient testimony of a guilty knowledge without further evidence. He finally wound up by saying:

"The saddest thing under my chin—
The Wallace ticket is counted in."

The Board, after the conclusion of the arguments of counsel, counted the true returns from Jefferson and Leon counties, which elected the anti-Ring delegations. Purman was also counted in as a member of the Assembly from Jackson county.

CHAPTER XVIII.

The Beginning of the End. The Stewart-Sturtevant Contest. Election of United States Senator, and Miscellaneous Subjects.

A week before the meeting of the Legislature of 1875, the leading members of the Ring began to assemble at the capital to look after the interests of their secret candidate for Senator. Nightly caucuses were held in the Executive office, and the counting of noses was gone over every night as to how each Republican member would probably stand on the election of Speaker of the Assembly and President of the Senate. The Democratic leaders also assembled in goodly numbers to look after the interests of their favorite candidates. The attempted frauds by the Carpetbaggers in the counties of Jefferson and Leon was reasonably looked to by the Democrats to give them the organization of both branches of the Legislature and the United States Senator.

The night preceding the meeting of the Legislature a caucus was called by the Ring members for the purpose of organizing the two houses next day. David Montgomery, of Madison county, carpetbagger, was put forth for Speaker, but the colored brothers from Leon and Jefferson, who had been the victims of unsuccessful fraud by the Ring, hesitated to put a man in the chair who would have no scruples in packing a Committee on Privileges and Elections that would oust the two anti-Ring delegations from these counties. The Ring members pretended that the fight was over and that the "lion and the lamb must now lie down together;" but the anti-Ring delegations knew that this meant that the lamb was to lie down in the lion's belly. Three days were spent in the attempt to elect a Speaker, but before the Speaker could be elected a caucus was called of the Democratic, anti-Ring Republican and Independent members. The caucus determined to elect Thomas Hanna, Democratic member from Washington county, as Speaker, the other offices to be divided between the Democrats and the colored men. On the meeting of the Assembly the next day it was evident that the scepter of the Legislature of Florida would in a few minutes pass from the hands of the despoilers and into the hands of those whose interest was inseparable from its soil and whom Stearns afterwards in his message described as being "as loyal and patriotic as any people in the Union." William Watkin Hicks, of Dade county, put forth the name of Mr. Hanna, and Montgomery was his opponent. Hanna was elected by a large majority. The Democrats, true to their promise, then elected, with the assistance of the anti Ring members, H. S. Harmon, colored, Chief Clerk, and James D. Thompson, colored, Sergeant-at-Arms. Nearly all the minor offices were filled by colored men. The colored brother was now even with the Ring for the defeat of Osgood for Speaker in 1874. The election of Hanna utterly demoralized the Ring in the Assembly, and it was unable to muster its forces in sufficient number any more at this session to misrepresent those who had voted for them. In the Senate the struggle for supremacy was a deadly one. By the consent of the Republicans, Senator J. L. Crawford, Democrat, was elected temporarily President. The Senate was composed of twenty-four members, and the Democrats and Republicans had equal numbers. The object of the Republicans in consenting to let Senator Crawford preside as temporary Chairman was that it would silence his vote; but the Doctor decided that he was not Lieutenant-Governor, and as a Senator his vote could not be questioned. Ten days were wasted in the attempt to elect a Republican for President *pro tem.*, during which time Stearns and his Ring managers were holding secret meetings with the Democrats to secure his election to the United States Senate and to have a Democratic President of the Senate during his canvass to secure his election to the Senate, and thus leave the State under a Democratic Governor. There were plans and counter-plans made by the Democrats, who had no faith in Stearns' power as to leaving the State a Democratic Governor. Some of the friends of ex-Governor Walker suggested the plan to elect an anti-Ring colored man President of the Senate. They contended that this would have the effect of bringing to the support of Governor Walker all of the anti-Ring colored members, and at the same time would drive those

Democrats who thought the election of Stearns as Senator would give them the State government from him for fear that a negro might become Governor. There were several caucuses held looking to the consummation of this plan, and the most notable thing in these caucuses was the sentiment of the ex-slaveholders, both in and out of the Senate, that they would rather see an honest ex-slave in the presidential chair of the Senate than to see Stearns go to the United States Senate by their votes, when they believed him to be a party to all the election frauds that had been committed in the State since 1868. The Democratic members from the west were almost unanimous for the election of Stearns, provided they could get the State government. The struggle in the Senate continued until Stearns was assured that he could be elected. A majority of the Democratic members finally consented to the election of Stearns to the United States Senate, leaving them the State government. Stearns immediately called a caucus of all the Republican Senators, to whom he proposed the election of A. L. McCaskill, Democrat, as President *pro tem.* of the Senate. It was then propounded to him by both wings of the Republicans as to whether he was an aspirant for Senator. He solemnly declared that he was not, and that he would not accept if elected. The caucus then adjourned, and within five minutes after its adjournment McCaskill was elected President *pro tem.* of the Senate, all the Republicans voting for him but one, and this was Stearns' henchman Hill, of Gadsden county. The anti-Ring Republicans did not know exactly where they stood, nor did they know where to find Stearns until he delivered his message to the Legislature. Hear him appeal to those "loyal and patriotic people" whom he and his Ring followers had defrauded out of seats in the Legislature for seven years: "It will become your duty, on the second Tuesday after your organization, to proceed, in accordance with an act of Congress and the Constitution of the State, to the choice of a United States Senator for the term commencing the fourth of March next. While I am aware of the great interest felt upon this subject, and fully appreciate the importance of securing an able and upright representative in the councils of the nation, yet I venture the suggestion that the people of the State have greater interest in the home government." He here attempts to impress upon the minds of the Democrats that it was their first duty to get clear of him by electing him to the Senate and leave A. L. McCaskill Governor. Again he attempted to impress upon their minds that should they elect him they would read no "bloody-shirt" speeches from him; nor would he vote for any bill in Congress looking to the protection of all classes of citizens in the State against discrimination on account of color. He says: " Freedom of political opinion and action has been accorded alike to all, and recognized as an essential principle of free government. Equal civil and political rights are denied to none, and the most cordial good will prevails among all classes of our people. We need no Congressional enactments or other interference to secure to any class of our citizens the full enjoyment of their just constitutional rights, since slavery and secession are things of the past, buried beyond the possibility of resurrection; since all the States are restored to their constitutional relations with the general government, and true and lasting peace has come." These utterances of Stearns took very well with Democratic members, who were not aspiring to the United States Senate, but they fell like cold water on the politicians, and though he thought he should certainly pull through, these Democratic aspirants were busy at work to prevent the consummation of this plan. The Democrats now commenced in earnest the memorable struggle to oust Sturtevant, Republican, from the Twenty-first Senatorial District, and seat Stewart, the legally elected member. The following report exhibits the real facts in the case:

Hon. A. L. McCaskill, President of the Senate:

SIR—Pending the investigation of the following preamble and resolution:

WHEREAS, Mr. Sturtevant holds his seat in this Senate as Senator from the Twenty-first District illegally and unjustly; and, whereas, the election returns from Dade and Brevard counties show that a large majority of the votes cast were given for Mr. Israel M. Stewart as Senator, but by partisan trickery and fraud he has been unlawfully deprived of his seat as such Senator, and that Mr. Sturtevant now occupies the seat without right and without a shadow of title; therefore, be it

Resolved, That we declare the seat now occupied by the said Sturtevant to be vacant, and that Israel M. Stewart, the Senator elect, come forward and be sworn in as Senator from the Twenty-first District.

The official opinion of the Attorney-General as to whether there is any law now in force governing contested election cases in this State, was referred to the Committee on Privileges and Elections, and a thorough investigation and consideration of the same resulted in two reports. The majority report fully sustained the Attorney-General's opinion, that is, that the act referred to in Thompson's Digest is now in force in this State, and the report was adopted by the Senate. The adoption of the majority report, however, does not settle the question as to Mr. E. T. Sturtevant's right and title to a seat in this Senate. *Per contra:* the committeee are of the opinion that inasmuch as the returns of Brevard county (one of the counties composing the Twenty-first Senatorial District), have not yet been canvassed and counted by the Board of State Canvassers, his right and title to a seat in this Senate is not touched by the adoption of the majority report. The returns of the Twenty-first Senatoria District must be canvassed and counted by the Board of State Canvassers before "notice" of contest can be legally served. In January, 1873, Mr. Israel M. Stewart petitioned the Senate to canvass and count the returns of Brevard county, and pronounce an enlightened and just judgment thereon; and his petition, by the unanimous consent of the Senate, was referred to the Committee on Privileges and Elections. No legal or other objection was then raised against Mr. Stewart's petition. Mr. Sturtevant did not then raise the question that "notice" of contest was not given, and the legality of his petition to the Senate for a seat as Senator of the Twenty-first Senatorial District was unanimously acknowledged. But the committee, kind to Sturtevant, but cruel to Stewart and the people of the Twenty-first Senatorial District, pocketed the petition. In January, 1874, the following resolution was introduced in the Senate:

Resolved, by the Senate of the State of Florida, That Israel M. Stewart, who was duly elected as Senator from the Twenty-first Senatorial District of said State at the last regular election held in that District in the year A. D. 1872, be now sworn in as Senator from the Twenty-first District of Florida, and that Mr. Sturtevant is hereby declared as not entitled to a seat on this floor.

Mr. Stewart's legal right to contest having been recognized by Mr. Sturtevant and the entire Senate in 1873, could not be denied in 1874. A majority vote of the Senate was Mr. Sturtevant's sheet-anchor of hope, and as a dernier resort to save himself he voted for himself; and notwithstanding Mr. Stewart, in the name of his insulted and outraged constituency, vigorously and persistently demanded his right to a seat as Senator of the Twenty-first Senatorial District from January, 1873, to January, 1875, Mr. Sturtevant now says for the first time that "notice" of contest was not served on him. Inasmuch as Mr. Sturtevant cannot claim protection under the law now in force governing contested election cases in 'his State, the committee report further that at the general election held on the fifth day of November, 1872, in the counties of Dade and Brevard, comprising the Twenty-first Senatorial District, E. T. Sturtevant was a candidate for the office of State Senator in said District; that he was also Judge of the County Court of Dade county; that there was but one precinct in said county; that Judge Sturtevant was made an Inspector at said precinct, and at the close of the election on that day, as Inspector, he and two other Inspectors solemnly certified under oath that the whole number of votes cast for State Senator in Dade county was thirty, of which Israel M. Stewart received sixteen and E. T. Sturtevant fourteen —majority of two for Mr. Stewart. This statement has not been denied at any time or by any person. Subsequently, however, Judge Sturtevant petitioned himself as the clerk of the election and also judge of the County Court, (and, furthermore, a candidate at said election for the Assembly—these two, E. T. Sturtevant and W. H. Gleason, constituting the modest Board of County Commissioners(to set aside his own return under oath as a precinct inspector, and to reject from such return the names of three citizens who had voted for Israel M. Stewart, alleging as a sufficient reason for such rejection that two of them, citizens of foreign birth, were permitted to vote without producing their naturalization papers, and the name of the other did not appear on the registration book. As Judge of the County Court E. T. Sturtevant took the evidence in ex-parte affidavits, and as one of the Board of County Commissioners sat in judgment on his own case, and deliberately declared his return, made under oath, to be illegal, rejected the votes of three citizens, and declared himself to have received a majority of the votes cast in Dade county. These returns were on file in the Secretary of State's office, are in the recollection of many Senators who are present, and are testified to by them. The Constitution of Florida, Article III, reads—"The powers of the Government of the State of Florida shall be divided into three departments: Legislative, Executive and Judicial, and no person properly belonging to one of the departments shall exercise any functions appertaining to either of the others." &c. Now, if Judge Sturtevant properly belonged to the judicial department, and if the function of the legislative department is to judge of the returns and election of its members, then neither as judge nor county canvasser could he make this judgement—that is, rejecting the votes of these citizens and declaring himself to have received a majority of the votes cast in Dade county; nor could the executive department make, nor any act of a previous Legislature be mandatory to a subsequent Legislature as to the force and effect of evidence, either as *prima facie* or conclusive, as to the election of their members; for, as to this, each house is sovereign and absolute and must prescribe its own rules of procedure in judging of the qualifications, elections, and returns of its members. The returns of Brevard county show that the whole number of votes cast for State Senator was sixty-nine, of which Israel M. Stewart received thirty-nine, C. B. Magruder seventeen and James Payne, Sr., thirteen, a majority of nine for Mr. Sturtevant over all the other candidates. Mr. Sturtevant received not a single vote in Brevard county. It is alleged that from accidental or other causes the returns from Brevard county were not received in time for the Board of State Canvassers, and not until after a certificate had been given to Mr. Sturtevant, bottomed on his own certificate of the vote of Dade county, showing a majority of one over Stewart in said county. That the returns of Brevard county were filed with the Board of State Canvassers and subsequently submitted to a committee of the Senate on Privileges and Elections, is within the recollection of many Senators who are present and testified to by them. Also the committee are in possession of a certified copy of the returns on file in the clerk's office of Brevard county. The facts here stated are known to be true by at least one-half of the Senators present; they are proven to a demonstration, beyond all question, have not been denied, and are without just ground of objection. The aggregate number of votes cast for State Senator, in the Twenty-first Senatorial District on the fifth day of November, 1872, foots up thus: For Israel M. Stewart, fifty-two; for C. B. Magruder, seventeen; for E. T. Sturtevant fourteen, and for James Payne, Sr., thirteen—majority for Stewart thirty-eight over Sturtevant, and of eight over all the other candidates, that is, Magruder, Sturtevant and Paine.

Your committee present this case as one most extraordinary in its various phases of moral turpitude. A just regard for the rights and privileges of the Senate, a decent respect for public opinion, for the offended laws and the principles long established for the government of judicial and legislative procedure demands an unqualified censure by every Senator. The statutes of this State, the rules of every court of law, the customs of every country, and our own natural sense of justice between men—all, all forbid that a man shall be a judge in his own case; yet we have here the legislative power of the Senate held for years by a Senator so-called under a decision made by himself on his own certificate, and kept in the Senate by his own vote, without an election of the people, swearing that he is qualified for the office of Senator under the Constitution, and seemingly without hesitation. In conclusion the Committee recommend the adoption of the following resolution:

Resolved, by the Senate, That E. T. Sturtevant was not elected as Senator of the Twenty-first Senatorial District, and is not entitled to a seat in this Senate, and that Israel M. Stewart was elected as Senator at the regular election held on the fifth day of November, 1872, and that he be now sworn in as Senator of the Twenty-first Senatorial District.

JOHN L. CRAWFORD, Chairman.
A. D. McKINNON.
F. A. HENDRY.

The minority report admits the election of Stewart, but contends that no notice was given to Sturtevant of the contest. The minority report was too barefaced for any decent man to sign, and though the carpet-baggers wrote the report which is signed by Frederick Hill, colored, it is evident that Durkee, carpet-bag Senator from Duval county, refused to sign it because of its admission of fraud and oppression. Hill, therefore, was made the cats-paw for "society carpet-bag gentlemen." When the majority report was read it created a stampede among Republican Senators, and it was some time doubtful whether the Ring members could hold their grip by drawing tightly the party lines. The Democrats resorted to every thing they possibly could which they thought would secure to them that majority of one which they were entitled to. The carpet-baggers and Governor Stearns, on the other hand, brought every thing to bear to retain Sturtevant in his seat. The "Little Giant," L. G. Dennis, was put forward by Stearns as the carpet-bag leader of the Senate for the express purpose of keeping Sturtevant in his seat, and to also make him more influential throughout the State among the freedmen preparatory to leading them to the standard of Stearns in his struggle for the nomination for Governor in 1876, should he miss the United States Senate. Pending the discussion of the report of the committee, sometimes the Democrats would outgeneral the "Little Giant," and he would thereupon order the Republicans to leave the Senate without a quorum. This went on for several days, when the Democrats, getting tired of this fighting and retreat tastics, ordered the Sergeant-at-Arms to take to his assistance two other persons and arrest the absconding members. The Republican members were at the house of a citizen taking dinner when the two assistants came in and seized the worst looking fellow in the crowd. It turned out that the man whom they thought could be easily carried was the worst customer of the lot. This was Parlin, of Escambia county. No sooner had they seized him than he drew an old revolver—about half a yard long it seemed to be—and commenced firing in the direction of the two assistant Sergeant-at-Arms, who returned the fire, but fortunately no one was hurt. The news in a short time was all over town and great excitement prevailed. The "Little Giant" then, to get up a bloody-shirt sensation, in company with three or four of the absconding Senators, marched up and down the streets with revolvers in their hands, cursing Democrats. This pleased some of the more simple of the freedmen on the streets, for they thought that Dennis was a good "Publican." The absconding Senators did not return to the Senate until next morning, when all sorts of resolutions were introduced denouncing the conduct of the assistant Sergeant-at-Arms. After Dennis had exhausted all his parliamentary law and the other Republican members had seen Stearns' giant cleaned up, each Republican member commenced leading himself. Senator McCauley, Democrat, from the Eleventh Senatorial District, had been set upon by the carpet-baggers as an offset to Sturtevant, and every time the question of Sturtevant's right to a seat was called up they would call in question the seat of McCauley. There was no ground whatever upon which to question the right of McCauley to a seat. To put an end to the matter—as no Republican Senator dared to put in Stewart at the peril of his life, the author of this work made the point that neither Sturtevant nor McCauley could vote upon the question, as both were interested that the other should go out. Of course the Chair ruled that McCauley could vote and Sturtevant could not. The Chair was appealed from, and on that appeal involving the question of McCauley's right to vote, he was prevented from voting, and the Chair was not sustained in his ruling. This ended the farce of attempting to get Sturtevant out. The Senators of the previous Senate were responsible for this outrage on a free ballot; and while this Senate was also not blameless, yet they had something behind which they could hide the shame of the crime in the shape of *res judicatia*. There are two acts of mine, committed during these days of reconstruction, which I regret: that of voting to sustain Sturtevant, and voting for Stearns for Governor in 1876.

The Democrats, now baffled in the attempt to oust Sturtevant, turned their undivided attention to the election of U. S. Senator. Some of them still clung to the idea of electing Stearns to the Senate, while the larger number of them, influenced by aspirations for Senatorial honors, vigorously opposed this plan.

The colored brothers now held first class diplomas of a seven years' course of instruction from carpetbag university of bribery and fraud in Florida, and if they did not practice what they had been taught in this school, it was because manly instinct forbade them. General caucuses and demagogue speeches would not bring them, nor could the "corner" caucuses control them. The carpetbag aspirants found it necessary to treat them as they did white carpetbag members of the Legislature—that is, to give champagne and oyster suppers for their entertainment, at which supper the aspirant must be present and partake with his guests, and approach them on the subject of the Senatorship, and those who could be bought got something worth the name of bribe-taking. Although the colored brothers held these diplomas, but a very small minority of them at this session of the legislature availed themselves of the benefits of their education. The Democrats, in the canvass which had just closed, had denounced from the stump the many acts of bribery committed by the Republican members of the Legislature, and it had its effect, at least upon the mind of the average colored member, who now saw that both branches of the Legislature had been lost to the Republicans, which loss was greatly attributed to these acts of bribery. There was a good deal of money spent by different carpetbag aspirants to secure the coveted prize of Senator, but the colored brother made it a business to take what money he could get and all the merchandise the briber could muster up before he was called upon to vote, and then vote against the candidate of the briber. For an illustration: George Witherspoon, colored, was approached by a Jew to vote for Gov. Walker for Senator. This was without Walker's knowledge. This Jew was a great admirer of the ex-Governor, and thought if Witherspoon could be secured that the whole delegation from Jefferson County would follow. The Jew had his doubts about Witherspoon, but promised to pay him five hundred dollars and all the merchandise he needed for his family if he, Witherspoon, would vote for Gov. Walker—the Jew being a merchant at the time. Witherspoon was not the man to let this chance pass, but said he thought the money and goods must be had before voting. The Jew objected to this, and asked W. G. Stewart, who was postmaster at the time, as to whether Witherspoon could be trusted with his five hundred dollars or not. Stewart informed him that he did not care to have anything to do with the affair. The Jew then made Witherspoon swear that he would vote for Gov. Walker when the time arrived, which oath Witherspoon did not hesitate for a moment to take. The money was paid, and Witherspoon also had free access to the store of the Jew, and silks and finery to the amount of several hundred dollars were added to the money consideration for the coveted vote. The Jew was now in great glee and anticipated a splendid success. When the roll was called on the vote for Senator, Witherspoon voted for Samuel Walker, Republican. This startled the Jew, who went inside the bar of the Assembly chamber and requested Witherspoon: "Give me that ting back," meaning the money and goods aforesaid. Witherspoon contended that he had voted for Walker, but the Jew insisted that it was not the Walker agreed upon. Witherspoon, to get rid of him and yet retain the goods and money, in a loud tone of voice threatened to have him arrested for attempted bribery, when the Jew, fearing the consequences, begged him to say no more about the matter and he might have both money and merchandise.

Some of Gov. Walker's friends had secured another Republican vote, as they thought, which would certainly carry the ex-Governor through. This man was Charles Avery, carpetbagger from Leon county. When the roll was called in the joint session Gov. Walker received one majority of all the votes cast— Avery voting for Walker. The Democratic members were so much elated over the election of Walker that they could not remain in their seats, and one of them—Duncan, from Hamilton— ran across the chamber and shook his fist in the face of W. W. Hicks, Independent. The Republicans now began to cry: "Treason!" "Sold out, sold out!" The outcry being against Avery—some swearing that he ought to be killed. Avery, not being strong enough to stand the fire, after the excitement had somewhat abated, arose and informed the presiding officer that his vote was cast for Samuel Walker, Republican. In the meanwhile Governor Walker had been sent for by his friends and informed that he had been elected United States Senator.

The Governor hurried to the scene. He tells us that as he was nearing the Assembly Chamber the sun began to rise higher and higher, and as he turned to walk up the steps to the hall his pathway got brighter until he reached the hall, when he was informed that it was a mistake—he had not been elected. The sun by this time had begun to set, and the elements became darker and darker, until there was not a ray of Senatorial light anywhere around him. The vote cast by Avery was undoubtedly cast for Governor Walker, but he was intimidated into declaring that it was intended for Samuel Walker. Samuel Walker had opposed the election of Avery in the election just closed, and was even a candidate against him for the Assembly.

After the Walker failure the Democrats became very despondent relative to the election of any of the Democratic aspirants, and Stearns was again secretly pushed forward by his friends. By some means not entirely known, Col. Horatio Bisbee had secured the support of most of the Independents, and if Stearns had been true to him he would have been elected. Stearns set apart a day for the election, and the whole power of his rotten administration was to be brought to bear to secure the election of Bisbee, and he held back the appointments in most of the counties to accomplish this end—at any rate, he gave this as his reason for holding them back. All of the members of the Leon county delegation would have voted for Bisbee if Stearns would have agreed to send to the Senate for confirmation anti-Ring officers for that county. This he agreed to do; but feeling confident that this would secure the election of Bisbee and defeat his combination with the Democrats, he refused to carry out his promise before the day arrived for the election, which caused the Leon and Alachua county delegations to vote for some other candidate.

The next attempt to elect a Democrat was made by S. B. Conover, United States Senator. Hon. John A. Henderson, who, when Conover was elected Senator in 1873, and Stearns as Lieutenant-Governor undertook to cheat him in the open joint session out of his election, demanded fair play, was now settled upon by Conover and the Democrats to be elected on a certain day. This movement was only revealed to those Republicans who were to vote for Henderson and to the Democratic members. The plan was that three colored Republicans should be absent when the roll was called in joint session and thus leave the Democrats in the majority, when all of them were to vote for Henderson. Ten minutes before the joint session met the Republican members of the Senate received a note from Judge J. D. Westcott stating that three colored men were out (mentioning their names), and that Henderson would be elected that day. This news was conveyed to all the Republican members of both Houses and to the freedmen on the streets, and a general outcry was made among the faithful to bring back the sheep that were lost. Houses were searched and buggies were sent in every direction, and the cry of treason could be heard from the mouth of every colored brother, who was urged on by the subtle carpetbaggers, all adding fury to the excitement. The three stray sheep, hearing the furious howls of these would-be wolves, soon made their appearance, and were thrown upon the shoulders of the carpetbag shepherds and safely landed in the fold. There was great rejoicing among the ninety-and-nine, and Henderson was defeated.

W. W. Hicks, whose peculiar mission seems to have been to elect Bisbee to the United States Senate—while he was professing to be Independent, and Bisbee was considered by the Democrats to be a very obnoxious partisan—now, maddened at the defeat of Bisbee, arose in the joint session and, after charging bribery to the members of the Legislature, in a very elaborate speech nominated C. W. Jones of Escambia county for Senator. This summersault of Hicks fell flat and Jones fell with it, but only to rise again when the Stearns plan was exposed. The election of Stearns was then thought to be assured, but unfortunately for him the Little Giant was overheard in the darkness of the night explaining to another carpetbagger how the thing was to be done. Stearns was to appoint George E. Wentworth, carpetbagger of Escambia county, Lieutenant-Governor on the day he, Stearns, was elected Governor. Wentworth would take possession of the Executive office as soon as Stearns was elected, when he was to hand in his resignation of the office of Governor to Wentworth. The first act of Wentworth in his new capacity was to accept this resignation. This was to be kept secret from the Democrats until Stearns had crossed the Senatorial gulf. The next day this plan became noised abroad among some of the Republicans, but it was doubted by some of the Democrats, who thought they would soon be in possession of this strong carpetbag fortification. Geo. P. Fowler, white Republican, but not a member of the Legislature, proceeded post haste to the boarding-house of that old Democratic veteran, J. L. Crawford, and demanded to see him at once. The doctor hesitated to get out of his bed, as the night was very cold and it was raining, but Fowler said, "I must see you." The doctor's curiosity now being excited, he got up and received the tidings of the messenger. Fowler then informed him that Stearns had appointed Geo. E. Wentworth as Lieutenant-Governor, which appointment was not to be made known until after Stearns was elected United States Senator. He said he got his information as an eye witness, having seen the commission signed by Stearns, and that its authenticity could not be doubted; and urged the doctor to inform all the Democrats of this treason at once. The doctor, in less than an hour after receiving this intelligence, had informed every Democratic member of the Legislature. The Stearns stock from this hour went down to rise no more in the Senatorial market.

The Ring, in the session of 1873, voted for J. D. Westcott upon an agreement of controlling the Federal offices, and was now given an opportunity, by the Leon county delegation, to again vote for him. Westcott, who had been severely criticized by some of the whites for allowing his name to be used by the ring in the previous Senatorial struggle, had alienated himself from them and had gone in with the anti-ring Republicans. Of course the Ring had pledged each other to touch no one for any office who was not allied to them, and the Democrats would not vote for him because they desired that he should remain on the Supreme bench. C. W. Jones now made another attempt. When he had come within one vote of the necessary number, he arose from his seat and addressed the presiding officer of the joint assembly, and said, "that in behalf of fifteen hundred voters whom I have the honor to represent, I cast my vote for C. W. Jones." M. Martin then rose and cast his vote for C. W. Jones," thereby giving him two majority, when Jones withdrew his own vote. The Democrats did not rejoice very much over Jones' election, as he was not their choice. This ended the last circus of carpetbag Senatorial elections in the Florida Legislature, after taking twenty-five ballots.

Stearns, furiously mad on account of his defeat, now turned his whole attention to the gubernatorial nomination of 1876. No Republican could be appointed to office without swearing allegiance to him and his ring. The anti-ring Republicans in the Legislature, anticipating his object, went to work to defeat all nominations sent to the Senate under such contract. Whatever may be said about the white people's unfriendly attitude to the Republican party in the State, they showed a willingness, when such names were sent to the Senate, to vote against their confirmation if it could be proved to them that these appointments were made to suppress the anti-ring freedmen in their attempts to oppose Stearns.

C. H. Walton, editor of the *Tallahassee Sentinel*, after having done all he possibly could to defraud the Leon delegation out of an honest election, now came up for State Printer, and undertook to intimidate this delegation into his support; but the delegation, having already humiliated themselves by voting for carpetbag ring candidates for U. S. Senator, and in the Senate by voting to sustain Sturtevant, had made up their minds to swallow no more of this deadly poison, and voted openly for Charles E. Dyke, Democrat, who had demanded in his paper an honest canvass of the votes in Leon county. The ring howled " Treason," but to no effect.

At this session of the Legislature the amendments proposed by the former Legislature were adopted, among which was the amendment abolishing annual sessions and creating biennial sessions.

The claim of Gov. Reed was again considered by this session of the Senate, and a committee appointed to examine the claim made the following report:

"The Committee on Claims, to whom was referred the claims of ex-Gov. Reed, upon examination of the case, find that it has been passed upon by special committees of two successive sessions of the legislature, and considerable amounts reported due him. They find, also, that there are large amounts alleged to have been paid him on account of the State, which are denied by him; and as grave legal questions are involved in the final adjustment of the accounts, which cannot be determined by your committee, they therefore recommend that the whole matter be referred to the Attorney-General for final adjustment."

A bill was reported for that purpose which was not acted upon at this session. Thus the pioneer of civil government in Florida, and the restorer of peace, was denied justice at the hands of the people's representatives. Nothing was done in the Assembly with regard to this claim.

W. J. Purman, member of Congress, served as a member of this Legislature, and took part in the election of Senator. A resolution was adopted by the Assembly calling upon the Congressional delegation of our sister State, Georgia, to represent Florida in the Congress of the United States, as Conover and Purman were here in Florida in attendance upon the Legislature.

The carpetbaggers, having virtually lost their majority in both branches of the Legislature, and both branches having Democratic presiding officers, were unable to pass plunder bills at this session, and the people breathed pure air. After a session of fifty-two days the two houses akjourned on the 26th of February, *sine die*. This Legislature sounded the death knell of the last carpetbag law-making power in Florida.

The number of representatives in the Legislature who could neither read nor write, during the seven years of carpetbag rule in Florida, was six—four colored men, Republicans, in the Assembly and one in the Senate, and one Democrat in the Assembly, white; and for the benefit of those who contend that the Southern white man cherishes no good will for his black brother, or that "no good thing can come out of Nazareth," it is only necessary to say that the colored men, however illiterate, when they rose to address the presiding officers of either branch of the Legislature, were listened to with marked attention by the Southern whites, even though sometimes their remarks had been taught them by some unprincipled carpetbagger for the purpose of exciting the feelings of the whites against the negro. The same considereation accorded them in the open sessions was maintained in the committee rooms. Not one word of criticism or ridicule was ever heard from one of them. They showed themselves ever ready and willing, when the colored members would listen to them, to instruct them in their legislative duties. Nearly nine-tenths of the bills introduced in the Legislature by the average colored member—outside of plunder bills—were written by Southern white men. The colored men who began to and continued to study professions found a ready friend in the Southern white man, who freely extended the right hand of fellowship to push the ex-slave to the zenith of his profession. Now and then you would run upon some puppy in the shape of a Southern white man whose attainments in his profession were more in the color of his skin and in the fine clothes bought by his parents than in his cranium, who would endeavor to riducule colored professional men who were his superiors in the profession. The carpetbagger, as a general thing, did not believe a negro should aspire to any profession, nor would they give him any instruction as to his profession unless the benefit of it would inure to some carpetbagger in the way of political aggrandizement. From the very inception of reconstruction to this session of the Legislature, whenever a colored man would attempt to express his opinion against the questionable methods of the gang of adventurers who were in possession of the government, he would be whistled at, hissed at, and ridiculed, while on the floor of the legislative hall, and his language criticised, to compel him to desist from opposing them.

CHAPTER XIX.

The Campaign of 1876—Preparation for Fraud. Drew before the Supreme Court. Stearns in Consultation. Drew Inaugurated. The Colored Brother Worth a Promise, but not Worthy to have it Fulfilled. Carpetbag Legacies to the Colored Brother.

In the Spring of 1875 Stearns called the members of the Ring together in Jacksonville, and at that meeting it was determined that he, and no other, should be the next Governor of Florida. W. W. Hicks, who pretended to oppose the Ring as an Independent at the commencement of the Legislature, was appointed by Stearns as Superintendent of Public Instruction of the State. This at once mustered him into the Ring as a leading member. The public schools and school teachers, as far as possible, worked for the nomination and election of the Chief. In the black-belt counties any one could get a certificate to teach school for the colored people who would pledge him or herself to canvass for Stearns in the neighborhood where they were to teach, no matter how illiterate the person might be. In Leon County, where there was the greatest opposition to Stearns, he had appointed the notoriously immoral ballot-box stuffer, Joseph Bowes, as Superintendent of Education. There was no crime so great, no act so low but that he was capable of committing it.

To enable the reader to form an intelligent conception of some of the colored teachers appointed as instructors under the regime of Stearns, the following is given—a sample of what came under our personal observation, in an attempt to instruct the pupils in arithmetic. "What will ten hogsheadsfull of molesses come to at twenty-five dollars a hogshead?" The pupil, who had been taught by better teachers under the administration of Governor Reed, would protest, and inform their professor that the words were "hogshead" and "molasses;" but the professor would scold and storm at them and threaten to punish them by a severe flogging if they did not accept his pronunciation. The pupils would of course have to succumb. After finishing the arithmetic lesson they must next go through the catechism. "Who is the 'Publican Governor of the State of Florida?" Answer—"Governor Starns." "Who made him Governor?" Ans.—"The colored people." "Who is trying to get him out of his seat?" Ans.—"The Democrats, Conover, and some white and black Liberal Republicans." "What should the colored people do with the men who is trying to get Governor Starns out of his seat?" Ans.—"They should kill them." This was done that the patrons, some of whom could read, would be impressed by the expressions of their children, and would be ready to put any one to death who would come out into the country and say anything against Governor Stearns. In many instances this teaching had its effect upon the minds of freedmen. These teachers received from twenty-five to thirty-five dollars per month. The whole public school system was made a powerful auxilliary to the campaign fund of Stearns in the year 1875-6. The State Superintendent, while possessing unquestionable ability relative to the duties of his office, devoted his whole energy and time to the nefarious canvass for the nomination of Stearns to the utter neglect of the education of the masses. The same was true as to the Superintendents of some of the black belt and other counties—organizing political clubs instead of schools.

At the January term of the Supreme Court of the State for 1876, Stearns and the Ring received a terrible black eye at the hands of that court. Stearns attempted to establish the validity of the four millions of bonds issued in aid of the Jacksonville, Pensacola and Mobile Railroad Company. The Ring, after having at a previous session of the Legislature attempted to buy out Holland's claim, now brought suit against him before Judge Archibald, of the Fourth Judicial Circuit, to oust Holland, claiming that he had no title; and to get possession for the State. The validity of these bonds was not discussed by the Supreme Court of the United States in the suit brought then by Colonel Bisbee—who had been employed by Stearns without authority of law—and the Ring thought they had reasonable hopes that our Supreme Court would not dare to decide against their constitutionality. The author of this work, at the session of the Legislature of 1874, anticipating the object of the Ring to get possession of the railroad so as to more completely override the will of the people, had a consultation with Charles E. Dyke, editor of the *Floridian*, as to the propriety of slipping a clause into the amendments to the State Constitution whereby the State would be prohibited from owning stock in railroads. This amendment was introduced and adopted without being noticed by the Ring, and became a part of the Constitution in 1875. The amendment is as follows: "The State shall not become a joint owner or stockholder in any company, association or corporation." The Supreme Court, in rendering its opinion, said: "We hold that the Governor is not authorized to speak for and in the name of the State in this case; that there is no statute or warrant of law which authorizes him to bring this proceeding or set up this claim; that the Governor cannot, by pleading or otherwise, bind the State and fasten on her people obligations for millions of dollars without statutory authority commanding him so to do." . . . . "So here we have the spectacle presented of the people of Florida, by their representatives, impeaching the Governor who issued these bonds, for so doing with intent to violate the Constitution and Act of 1870, and the present Governor, Stearns, employing private counsel and using the name of the State of Florida to fasten on the people this enormous debt, under the pretext that they are protecting the State by assuming an obligation which the State never recognized." The Court, in commenting on the point made by Colonel Bisbee, Stearns' private counsel, that Holland could not raise the point of the unconstitutionality of the bonds, said: "Why? Because our sovereign Lord and King, that is, the present Governor and his private counsel, have seen fit to claim and allege that they, in the name of the State and for the State, are seeking to establish a lien on this property."

One of the points raised by Holland in the Circuit Court was that the plaintiff had no cause of action. This point, with others, had been overruled by the Judge. The Supreme Court, after citing the clause of the Constitution before mentioned, decided that the bonds issued in aid of the Jacksonville, Pensacola and Mobile Railroad were unconstitutional, and that the plaintiff had no cause of action. Justice Westcott, of the Supreme Court, and Judges Goss and Bryson, of the Circuit Court, all Southern men—Bryson and Goss, Republicans, and Westcott, Democrat—adjudicated this important case. [See 15 Fla. Reports, page 455.] Stearns was one of the leading impeachers, and this action on his part is only further evidence of the utter fallacy of the several attempts to impeach Governor Reed.

The attempt to saddle the four millions of bonds on the State, by the Governor, who should have used his official power in its interest, was a powerful campaign document placed in the hands of the Democrats in the canvass of this year and added many votes to that party. Stearns, although defeated in this scheme, did not relax his efforts to secure his nomination. The Stearns managers had, pending this suit, promised some of the freedmen to make them conductors and baggage masters in the event that it was successful. These men, now seeing no hope of the promises being carried out, were rather left in condition to be captured by the anti-ring Republicans. Stearns, to offset this tendency, now for the first time informed them what he knew about certain lands around Lake Jackson, in Leon county. He had for several years been United States Surveyor-General, and had discovered fractional pieces of Government lands around this lake that had been occupied for a number of years by the white planters whose lands were adjoining. W. U. Saunders, who had been temporarily mustered into the ring, was employed to bring this matter to the attention of the freedmen in the name of Stearns, and while Saunders would make good fees in securing entries for them, he could also be able to raise Stearns in the estimaation of the freedmen, many of whom entered these lands, paying enormous fees to Saunders, and forcibly took possession of them only to be ousted, which was done by proceedings for forcible entry. Saunders informed them that all the lands and large plantations around Lake Jackson were Government land, and if Stearns was elected he would see to it that they would get them all. This was a convincing argument, and many of the freedmen deserted the anti-ring Republicans and went in for Stearns "to get land."

The so-called Central Committee of the Republican party called themselves together in the latter part of the Spring of 1876 for the purpose of calling a State convention to nominate a candidate for Governor and appoint delegates to the National Republican Convention. The Ring, knowing that a large majority of the Republicans of the State was opposed to their man Stearns, were at a loss as to where to hold the Convention so as to better intimidate and terrorize the delegates who should come to the convention against Stearns, "for their name was legion." At the suggestion of Stearns it was agreed to hold this convention at Madison, the home of the carpet-baggers Eagan and Montgomery, who were really complete masters of the freedmen, and could make some of them do anything—as in the case of Montgomery, who, it was reported and generally believed, while he was tax collector of the county became a defaulter for several thousands of dollars and then induced some of the freedmen to set fire to the court-house and thus destroy the tax records. From the issuance of the call for the convention until and during its riotous session, whisky was the strongest argument used to demoralize the colored people, with now and then a little money thrown in to keep up the hired loafers who did nothing but follow up white carpet-bag ballot-box stuffers and halloo themselves hoarse for Stearns. The school teachers of the type mentioned in this chapter, at the command of the preliminary fraudulent county returning boards, and all the county officers were in attendance at the precinct meeting and County Conventions interfering with and disturbing the proceedings in riotous manner in the interest of Stearns. Through all these outrageous exertions four-fifths of the delegates sent to the convention were opposed to the nomination of Stearns, and these delegates could not be bought, although repeated attempts were made to buy enough of them to secure his nomination. This failing, on the part of the State Fraudulent Returning Board, or Central Committee, of which Mr. E. M. Cheney was Chairman, through the direct order of Stearns, arrogated to themselves the right to say who were the legal delegates to the convention. This Committee, a majority of whose members were under the the thumb of the Ring, actually took the place of the convention, and decided the eligibility of the delegates, and without regard to decency or justice, excluded every delegation that they had any idea would oppose Stearns. In fact, the colored people in the Black Belt Counties who had sent up delegations solidly against Stearns were as comcompletely disfranchised as they were before being allowed to vote by the National Government; and if the colored people had known then that Democratic success in the State would be no worse than it has? proved, they would have dragged that Committee from their hiding place (for they were locked up in a room) and hanged them to the first limb of a tree accessible and then voted the Democratic State ticket.

One of the most amusing incidents that happened during this mob was that Stearns desired to find out whether Conover had much money to use in his canvas in case the delegates who were turned out of the convention should nominate him as against Stearns. He did not want the nomination if Conover had plenty of money, for the reason that he would not be able to buy him out of the field before the day of election. W. H. LeCain, carpetbagger, a member of this Central Committee and a professional ballot-box stuffer, was sent to Conover as a spy. He pretended that he would vote to let in the legal delegations if Conover would give him several thousand dollars. Conover had between five and six hundred dollars in greenbacks, but told LeCain to come back in the evening, when he would have plenty of money. He was staying with a wealthy citizen of Madison, and as soon as LeCain departed he sent out and had this money exchanged for dollars and half dollars in silver, and put it into a shot bag. When LeCain returned in the evening Conover drew his bag on him and gave him to understand that this was a bag of gold, at the same time exhibiting several gold pieces in his hand. He told LeCain if he would vote to put in the legal delegations he could have it all, amounting to five thousand dollars. LeCain wanted to see "the pig in the bag," which the astute Conover refused, but he said: "You can get it all." LeCain returned to Stearns with the news of the scarcity of money with Conover. Stearns was then willing to take the nomination, feeling certain of being able to buy Conover off the field before the election.

The freedmen had been ordered in from the country, and large numbers from the slums of the different counties and cities of the State, armed with such weapons as were obtainable, now pervaded the city under the influence of bad whiskey, ready to fight for the despot Stearns, and this so-called convention must therefore go down to posterity as nothing less than a raging mob, with the Governor of the State and four members of his Cabinet, McLin, Cowgill, Eagan and Hicks, as the leaders. One person was shot and several wounded by the mob, which lasted several days, and when the legally elected delegates became fully convinced that they could not be heard in the Stearns convention they organized an open air convention and nominated S. B. Conover, of Leon county, for Governor, and Josiah A. Lee, of Sumter county, for Lieutenant-Governor, and a full set of delegates to the National Convention. Stearns, after a hard fight even with the delegates of his own choice, was nominated for Governor. David Montgomery, of Madison county, was nominated for Lieutenant-Governor. The Stearns mob then elected delegates to the National Convention, but unfortunately for them they very unwisely excluded the colored brother from the list of delegates. The Conover convention headed its delegation— one-half of which was colored—with ex-Governor Harrison Reed. J. Willis Menard was also chosen as one of the colored delegates. This delegation was admitted to seats in the National Convention, while the mob delegation was sent back to Florida in disgrace—that is to say, any other set of human beings would have considered it a disgrace, but it had apparently no effect upon these heartless plunderers.

The delegation to the National Convention returned to the State, and Conover, who had been recognized by that body as the Republican nominee, brought with him a letter from the Republican National Committee recognizing him as the regular nominee of the party and advising Stearns to retire from the field. In the meantime the Congressional District Conventions had been called—one to meet in Tallahassee and the other in Jacksonville, and Stearns had his managers at work in the several counties buying up the delegates, in order to get himself indorsed by these bodies as the regular nominee of the party.

Conover delivered the letter brought by him from the National Committee to Stearns, who paid no attention to it, as he was confident that all was well. When the convention of the First District was organized as opposed Conover man was elected chairman. It was soon learned, however, that Stearns had secured him by unfair means. This man was R. H. Dennis, colored, of Escambia county. The skirmishing had not proceeded far before George Washington Witherspoon, colored—whom Stearns had attempted to defraud out of a seat in the Legislature in 1875, and one of the delegates who had been disfranchised at Madison—arose and declared for Stearns. Of course every one knew what carried George to that side. Before the vote was put, the author of this work warned the convention that if Stearns was endorsed he would be defeated; nevertheless, he was endorsed by the convention, after which W. J. Purman was nominated for Congress, and the convention adjourned.

In the Second District John R. Scott, of Duval, was one of the aspirants for the Congressional nomination, and he had a very strong following. W. H. Sampson, who was Scott's personal and political friend, advised him not to accept the nomination, but to give his support to some one who would be friendly to him, and suggested that he should see Colonel Bisbee, which Scott did. He proposed, if Bisbee would secure to himself or his friend the collectorship of customs at Jacksonville, he would, when the convention met, go in for the Colonel for the Congressional nomination and advise his friends to do so also. Bisbee agreed to this. He then turned to Sampson and desired to know what he wanted. Sampson replied that he wanted nothing. Colonel Bisbee then said that in case he was nominated and elected, anything he could do for him would be done with pleasure—and thus the bargain was confirmed. We shall see further on in this chapter whether the colored brother was "worth a promise" or not.

The District Convention met in Jacksonville. Stearns having been endorsed in the First District, many of the Republicans having come to the conclusion the party was on its last legs, went in and endorsed him here also. Gen. J. T. Walls was an aspirant for a third nomination, but Scott, true to his promise to

Colonel Bisbee, threw his influence to his support, and the Colonel was nominated. The Conover State ticket still remained in the field, and the Democrats saw nothing ahead but success. The Democratic State Convention was called to meet at Quincy. Everything was cut and dried for the nomination of Geo. F. Drew, of Madison. Some of the Democrats were opposed to the nomination of Drew, for the reason, as they said, that he had blown both hot and cold during the rebellion. This opposition was overcome by the promise of some of Drew's friends that he would put ten thousand dollars into the State canvass. Drew was nominated as a conservative Democrat, and Noble A. Hull, of Orange county, was nominated for Lieutenant-Governor. R. H. M. Davidson was nominated for Congress in the First District, and Jesse J. Finley received that nomination in the Second District. Conover being financially embarrassed, was unable to make a canvass, and informed Charles E. Dyke that he would have to withdraw from the field unless the Democrats would furnish him sufficient money for the expenses of the campaign. Dyke, remembering the promises of Drew's friends, left Tallahassee in haste and went in search of the millionaire. Drew—unlike the self-sacrificing Bloxham, willing to gives his few thousands for the redemption of his people—would not recognize the promise, and refused to entertain Dykes' proposition to give Conover sufficient money to make his canvass. Things began to look very gloomy for Conover, and to mislead Stearns and compel him to make some effort to get him to withdraw, he issued a public circular to his friends disclosing his determination to remain in the field until the day of election. This circular had the desired effect. A private consultation was had between Stearns and Conover, and an agreement was entered into that, in consideration of twelve or fifteen hundred dollars, Conover should withdraw and advise his friends to to support Stearns. The money was paid, and Conover withdrew, but he did not carry out one very important part of the bargain, namely, "advise his friends to support Stearns." In fact, he could not, with any show of decency, ask his friends to vote for Stearns. If the Ring had suffered Conover to be the regular nominee of the party he would have been elected by a good majority, but the Democrats would have secured both branches of the Legislature. Conover would have secured enough fair-minded Democrats to give his administration a fair trial. Had Governor Reed, in 1872, resorted to one-fifth of the dirty work of which Stearns was guilty, he would have been renominated and elected Governor.

Each party now had their candidates fairly before the people for their inspection. The Democrats went into the canvass with candidates whose integrity and honesty could not be attacked by the Republicans, except that Drew's Union record was secretly assailed by Purman in a circular signed "A True Democrat." On the other hand, the Republicans witnessed the spectacle of their candidate for Governor being charged with stealing the meat and flour given by the government as a charitable contribution to helpless men, women and children, who had just emerged from two hundred years of slavery, many of whom were clad in rags; the second man on their ticket, Daniel Montgomery, publicly charged with arson; the third man on the ticket, W. J. Purman, burdened with the crime of causing the slaughter of the innocent victims of the Jackson county troubles; and the fourth man on the ticket, Col. Horatio Bisbee, having arrested Democratic members of the Legislature on trumped up charges, in order to give the carpetbaggers a majority, and further, with attempting through the agency of Stearns of attempting to fasten the illegal four millions of bonds upon the State. The Colonel had for several years been United States District Attorney, during which time these acts were committed, and the Democrats laid them at his door; and he did not then, nor will he ever explain them to the satisfaction of the Southern people.

Stearns and his helpers went forth to fill their appointments, as planned by the State Central Committee. They had not been in the field long before they became convinced from the outlook that Stearns would be repudiated at the polls. When he returned to Tallahassee after filling his first appointment, he called a meeting of his intimate ring friends and informed them of the outlook. At this meeting it was decreed by McLin, Eagan, Martin, Montgomery, L. G. Dennis, Cheney, and a number of other leading lights, that Stearns should be counted in, whether he received sufficient votes or not. Col. William M. Saunders, colored, was designated to encourage the colored voters, many of whom were doubtful of Stearns' election, and were ready to turn over to the opposition. The author of this work was not present at this meeting, but obtained his information as to the intention of Stearns and his managers from Saunders; and, judging from their subsequent acts, such a decree was issued. Many schemes were contrived at the Executive office to put Stearns in as Governor, and among the most notable were the following : First: That the ring county officers, whose duty it was to appoint the inspectors of election, should appoint only those as Republican inspectors who would commit all the fraud that possibly could be committed at the ballot box in favor of Stearns. Second: In large Democratic precincts where the ring inspectors would be watched so closely that they could not commit fraud, gross irregularities were to be committed, so that the precinct could be thrown out by the board of county canvassers. Third: In Democratic counties having a full set of Republican officers, or a majority of the board of canvassers, Democratic precincts were to be thrown out on account of these irregularities if the people would submit to it without violence. Fourth: If the throwing-out process raised too much excitement, these irregularities were to be sent up to the State Returning Board, while the action of the county board was to be sent immediately to E. M. Cheney, chairman of the fraudulent returning board of the party at Jacksonville, who would prepare the papers for the final count. Fifth: In the black belt counties general repeating was to be resorted to by the freedmen, and if detected, Stearns, the Governor-elect, would protect them. The 'plans were so systematically laid that those leading colored men who had heretofore been lukewarm toward Stearns, now came to the conclusion that he would be the next Governor in spite of all opposition. The repeating part of the game, in Leon county, was placed by Stearns in the hands of W. U. Saunders, concerning whom we shall give more light hereafter. These rules were laid down by experts who had no difficulty in enforcing their strict enforcement. It will be noticed that the species of fraud contemplated in this election was of about the same order as those practiced in the election of 1870, mentioned in the ninth chapter, when Bloxham ran for Lieutenant-Governor, with the addition of repeating. The Democrats had now commenced the canvass in earnest. Judge R. B. Hilton, Democratic candidate for Presidential elector, and Wilkinson Call, commenced the canvass in the west, and when they had proceeded as far as Leon county the Judge discovered that he needed funds; and as the millionaire Drew had not come up to the promises of his friends, the Judge found it necessary to mortgage sufficient property to B. C. Lewis & Sons to raise six hundred dollars for the purpose of defraying his expenses. This done, he proceeded with the canvass. The theme of his argument was high taxes and carpet-bag misrule, which awakened those Democrats, Northern settlers and honest colored men who had heretofore turned a deaf ear to Democratic arguments. The great orator, Senator Ben Hill, of Georgia, was called over to "Macedonia to help them." Hill addressed a large concourse of both colors in Jefferson County, and if there was any doubt about the solidity of the whites it was dispelled after this speech. He also made many converts among the colored men. The seat of war was in Leon County, where Rev. W. G. Stewart, colored, had, before Conover withdrew, denounced Stearns from the stump in the most severe terms for stealing the freedman's meat and flour. Stewart had lived several years in Quincy, and had learned the whole history of the matter. Bloxham, who had often heard Stewart arraign Stearns for this crime, was always on hand at the Republican meetings to remind the people of what Stewart had said, and gave us so much trouble that we devised a plan to dodge him. We ceased announcing our meetings by posters, and instead sent men around on horseback to give the necessary notice two or three hours before the time of speaking. By this means we got clear of Bloxham at our meetings. At these meetings the people would be instructed not to go out to hear Bloxham, but for our lives we could not keep the black brother away from the silver-tongued orator. We would go to a precinct and get the brother all right for Stearns, and would report that all was well; but when we would hear from that precinct again Bloxham had been there and taken him back. This thing continued until the day of election. At one of the Democratic demonstrations in Tallahassee, Stearns' managers, for the purpose of getting United States troops into the State, undertook to create a disturbance. The colored people were in town in large numbers, and of course fearful of Democratic ascendency, were much excited. Bowes, the Superintendent of Public Schools, instructed the colored people to interfere with the Democratic procession, and if it had not been for the intervention of the author and W. G. Stewart perhaps hundreds of innocent people would have been sent to untimely graves. This was towards the end of the contest, and the average white man had "blood in his eyes." Two weeks before election the colored brothers in every precinct were notified by Saunders, Bowes, and other leaders that, unless they voted as many times as they could on the day of election they would be put back into slavery. This trick had a great deal of weight with some of the colored men who, while hating Stearns, were afraid to trust the Democrats. The author of this work and W. G. Stewart advised the colored people to each cast one vote for Stearns, and if such votes would not elect him let him be defeated.

One of the most daring acts of oppression during this campaign was the conduct of Stearns in Manatee county. Capt. John F. Bartholf, Republican, Clerk of Court in this County, resigned the position on account of sickness. He sent his resignation immediately to the Governor, and with it the name of a man whom he recommended as his successor. This was in time to have the clerk appointed before the time for the appointment of inspectors and the making other necessary arrangements for conducting the election had passed. Stearns received the resignation and the name of the man recommended; but now was the opportunity to silence a whole Democratic county, for to have no clerk made it impossible to have an election, and so he absolutely refused to make any appointment. On the day of election the white citizens of the county showed themselves equal to the occasion. They organized in each precinct a Board of Inspectors and secured such papers as were necsesary, polled the full Democratic vote and sent the returns to the State Board of Canvassers. In Leon county, on the day of election, the whites worked industriously among the colored men and secured at least four hundred votes for the Democratic ticket, nine-tenths of whom were not coerced, but cast their votes against Stearns because they were disgusted with his methods.

The colored brothers, now following the instructions given them by Stearns through Saunders, began to vote early and often. From the Georgia line to the capital was a distance of twenty miles, with three or four precincts between those points. They started early in the morning and voted at every precinct on that line of march to the capital, and each time the same man would vote under an assumed name. It can be fairly estimated that at least five hundred votes were secured in Leon county alone by this method. How much of this repeating was done in other parts of the State we shall not attempt to say; but this was a general order to be observed throughout the State, when it could be done without detection. The counties were not then divided into precincts as they are now, and therefore the voter could cast his ballot any where in the county. At one of the Lake Jackson polls, where Stearns had worked up considerable influence through his Government land information, the handy Superintendent, Joseph Bowes, had camped all night, carrying with him a cart load of rifles. He had notified the colored people to meet him out there, which was done. He informed them that Governor Stearns had sent the rifles out there for their protection. On the contrary, the guns were carried out for his protection in case the whites should detect him in his contemplated frauds. Bowes had prepared in the office of the Tallahassee *Sentinel*, the official organ of the Governor, several hundred tickets with the names of the Republican candidates printed in very small type. The tickets were about an inch and a half long by an inch wide. He opened the polls on the morning of election, before the hour designated, and before the whites arrived and deposited in the box as many of these tickets as he desired. When the whites arrived they felt confiden that something was wrong, but what it was they could not exactly tell, but at the close of the polls, when the ballot box was opened the secret was revealed. Several hundred of these "little jokers" bounced out and were counted just as though they had been honestly voted. The whites protested against counting them, but Bowes and the balance of the board said that they were in the box and must be counted. A large majority was by this means sent in for Stearns, from this poll, and Bowes was lionized by the Governor and his managers for this heroic act.

Before the polls closed on the day of election the Stearns managers sent up the cry of fraud, and commenced to send messages to different parts of the State to make good the frauds and irregularities committed under their instructions, and turn them to the injury of the Democratic candidates. United States troops were sent down to insure a fair count, closely followed by the "visiting Statesmen." There have been many things said throughout the country about a bargain between the Democrats and Republicans, with reference to the State being given to Drew, the Democratic nominee for Governor, and to Hayes, the Republican nominee for President. The facts are these: The Tilden managers from the North, Sellers and Biddle, were simply caught in the trap that Stearns had set for them. The Stearns managers commenced filing affidavits before the Board of Canvassers, and Sellers and Biddle insisted that the Democrats should do the same. Judge Hilton, N. L. Campbell and George P. Raney became disgusted with these know-alls, and contended that the powers of the board were purely ministerial; but as these gentlemen were from New York, and were sent by Tilden, their judgment prevailed. Hayes was more fortunate than Tilden, as he had the Governor at his back, as well as a majority of the canvassing board. From abroad were General Barlow, William E. Chandler, Gen. Lew Wallace, Governor Noyes and others, all managers on behalf of Hayes. This board, waiting for affidavits from some of the counties, the returns from which had not been sufficiently doctored, delayed the commencement of the canvass. The Tilden managers, not knowing what the Hayes managers meant, applied to the Judge of the Second Judicial Circuit, P. W. White, for a mandamus commanding the board to commence the canvass. Pending the consideration of the petition, the board commenced the canvass, and the proceedings under the petition were discontinued. The board decided that it had power to hear evidence as to the legality or illegality of votes cast in a county, and to add to or exclude votes from the returns sent up by the county boards of canvassers. During the canvass, which lasted several days, the little band of conspirators could be seen at night hovering around Stearns in his room at the City Hotel, relating to him what they intended to do in the final result. The Democratic lawyers were wasting time and breath when they undertook to argue a point before the two so-called Republican members of the board unless their argument would keep on the fraud inaugurated. Just before the final result it seems that something broke loose among the conspirators, and it was whispered around that one of them, Cowgill, was about to cave. Whether this was true or not we are not able to say; but the Hon. W. E. Chandler was much excited about something, and wanted a thousand dollars at once, and M. Martin, carpetbagger from Gadsden county, gave him the money. How much more was raised we never learned. Shortly after this money was given the excitement ceased. In order to keep down any excitement and to commit Attorney-General Cocke to the process of excluding votes, the conspirators agreed to take up Clay county, where twenty-nine votes were rejected by the Board of County Canvassers which were cast for Drew, and six votes were rejected that were cast for Stearns. These votes were now added to the respective candidates, the Attorney-General voting with the conspirators for their restoration. Some of the Democratic managers thought this a very impartial beginning, and were jubilant at the result; but Judge Hilton, who sat in the Amen corner of the Democratic party, thought it boded no good for the final result, and gave them Lochiel's warning. They next came to Manatee county, and here the real intention of the conspirators was made apparent. The board rejected the whole vote of this county upon the ground that it appeared in evidence that there were such irregularities and fraud in the conduct of the election in receiving votes of persons not registered, and on account of there being no registration, and consequently no legal list of qualified voters, no designation of voting places, and no notice of election. Cocke, the Attorney-General, now began to vote "No." In Hamilton county a Democratic precinct was deducted from the returns upon the grounds of violation of the election law and of fraud. Five votes were deducted from the returns of Hernando county upon the ground that they were illegally cast. Five hundred and fifty-seven votes were deducted from the returns of Jackson county upon the ground of fraud and irregularity. When Leon county was reached the Democrats showed conclusively that the ballot box at Lake Jackson precinct had been stuffed with the "little jokers," and moved to throw it out, but the conspirators voted No. Two votes, however, were deducted upon the ground that they were illegally cast. From Jefferson county's returns sixty-one votes were deducted upon the ground that they were fraudulently cast. Seven votes were deducted from the Orange county return upon the ground that they were illegally cast. From the returns of Monroe county the vote of a whole precinct was deducted upon the ground of irregularity and fraud. Judge Cocke, not to be inconsistent, voted with the conspirators, except upon the rejection of Manatee, Monroe, Hamilton and Jackson counties. Thus it was that nine-tenths of the irregularities committed were in Democratic counties, and were the work of officers appointed by Stearns for that very purpose, and of which he and his managers reaped the benefit. A majority of four hundred and ninety-seven for Drew was turned into four hundred and fifty-eight for Stearns. A majority of ninety-three for Tilden was turned into nine hundred and twenty-eight for Hayes. The board having completed its dishonest work, adjourned without delay. If the Tilden managers had let this board go on and make their canvass, and had then applied to the Supreme Court for a mandamus to compel them to count the returns as sent up by the county boards of canvassers, Tilden would have received, what he was really entitled to, the electoral vote of Florida.

The conspirators were now happy in anticipation of the returns of both masters, Stearns and Hayes. McLin, one of the conspirators, and one of the then editors of the Tallahassee *Sentinel*, came out in a long editorial declaring that one of the fixed things of the times was that Stearns would be the Governor of Florida for the next four years.

The visiting statesmen returned to the North and the Florida lawyers now began to set up shop for themselves. R. B. Hilton, N. L. Campbell and Geo. P. Raney, on the 13th day of December filed in the Supreme Court a petition for a writ of mandamus, and entered a motion for an alternative writ to be issued according to the prayer of the petition, which asked that the Board of State Canvassers be compelled to reassemble and canvass the returns as sent up by the County Boards of Canvassers or show cause why they should not do so. The alternative writ was issued, and Stearns employed J. P. C. Emmons, who had been so successful in Gov. Reed's case, to defend his title before the court. The board, in their first answer, raised the question of jurisdiction of the court, which answer was afterwards amended showing upon what grounds the votes from the several returns were not counted as sent up. The counsel of Drew demurred to the answer of the respondent. The demurrer was sustained by the court and a peremptory writ was issued, commanding the board to count the votes from the face of the returns. Of course there is no answer to any such writ, but the conspirators undertook to trifle with the court and filed a protest instead of executing its mandate. The court then intimated clearly to the conspirators what they might expect if its mandate was not immediately obeyed. The conspirators, viewing the iron bars of the prison house in fear and trembling, with weeping eyes returned and made the canvass. The second canvass gave Drew 195 majority over Stearns, and the Hayes electors 214 over Tilden. The board in this canvass threw out the returns from Clay county so as to save the Hayes electors. Cocke, the Attorney-General, submitted a protest to the court against the throwing out of Clay county. The board did not recanvass the vote for Congressmen. Purman had been counted in by 295 majority, and Bisbee by 141 majority. Bisbee retained his seat but Purman was ousted. As there was nothing before the court but the prayer of the relator to have the vote for Governor canvassed, the court struck from the return to its order all that related to the canvass of votes other than those for Governor, saying: that because the respondents had encumbered the records of the court with unnecessary matter, in which the court was not concerned, they do pay the cost of the proceeding.

Stearns, looking back over the hard labor of his plundering career, and seeing that the packing of juries, the prostitution of the public schools, the disfranchising of whole counties, mob conventions, planned irregularities in elections, the public money expended to get posession of railroads, and the wholesale stuffing of ballot boxes had availed nothing, still was loath to give up the Government when he was actually in sight of the promised land. He called a consultation of the Ring chiefs at the City Hotel and required to know from them whether they would support him should he maintain that he was Governor, the decision of the Supreme Court to the contrary notwithstanding. With one voice they all answered yea! The understanding was that all the colored people in the surrounding country should be notified that Stearns would be inaugurated on the day set apart by the constitution, and they were notified accordingly. Some of the carpetbaggers doubted the propriety o fdefying a Republican Supreme Court, but the "Little Giant" declared if Stearns did not hold on to the Government he would kill him. The day before Drew was to be inaugurated Stearns saw many strange faces in Tallahassee among the whites, and he began to grow pale and talk weak. The "Little Giant" now seeing that Stearns was about to yield up the ghost, went out and filled himself with the red beverage of hell and came to the hotel to murder him, and he would have attempted to do so, if he had not been locked in a room and detained until he fell asleep. In the meantime the whites had made great preparations for the inauguration of Drew. Early the next morning Drew and Stearns were seen coming out of a house together, as though they had been holding a long consultation. The whites were on hand from Georgia and from all parts of the State in large numbers, and the confiding freedmen came also to see the inauguration of Stearns. Drew seems to have made it all right with Stearns or Stearns with Drew; and Stearns procured a team and drove into the country while Drew was inaugurated.

The whites had stationed in an old cotton storehouse close by the capital, between three and five hundred men, armed with repeating rifles, with the intention of slaughtering the men who might attempt to inaugurate the defeated candidate. Everything, however, passed off quietly, and the new Governor was inaugurated amidst the shouts of thousands of glad-hearted people, both white and black, who now boasted that their votes had done the work. Thus ended the eight years of carpetbag famine and pestilence.

The Democrats, as soon as the Legislature was organized in 1887, passed a law for the organization of a new Board of Canvassers, consisting of Democrats, and caused a recanvass of the electoral vote of the State as sent up by the Republican County Boards, which showed that Tilden had carried the State by ninety-three majority. The certificate of this result was sent, one to the President of the United States Senate, and one to the Speaker of the House of Representatives.

Horatio Bisbee, now snugly seated in Congress for two years, put there through the influence and labor of the indefaitgable Scott—was looked upon as being above any political turpitude toward his black brother. He was now put in a position to use the great traits which he was supposed to possess, and to remember the promises made to his colored benefactor, but before the cock crowed thrice he had denied Scott. Gen. Hopkins. of Jacksonville, a Democrat, was appointed Collector of Customs without the knowledge or indorsement of Scott, and was confirmed. Elder Sampson, who had been with Scott when the bargain was made, and to whom the Colonel had also offered service, chanced to have his son Walter at Washington learning the trade of type-setting. He thought this an excellent chance to have the Colonel do something for him, and accordingly advised his son to request his aid in procuring a situation in the Government printing office. Walter made the request, but was put off from time to time with the request to "call again," until, as he said, his shoes, his patience and his money became exhausted, and he gave up the pursuit. Some time after Congress had adjourned the Colonel came back to Jacksonville, and Sampson somewhat astonished at his conduct, called upon him to know why the promise had not been fulfilled. The Colonel replied that if Scott's name had been sent to the Senate his incompetency would have defeated his confirmation. "But," said Sampson, "Colonel, was that the understanding?" The Colonel, not caring to hear any more about the promise, said abruptly—"Oh h——l, I have something else to attend to," and then quietly strode away.

Although the carpet-bag Government was overthrown in 1876, a certain property was bequeathed to the colored people by the carpet-baggers which has been and still is to a certain extent very damaging and burdensome to them. They left upon the minds of thousands of our people the impression that the drunkard, the thief or the most ignorant were as fit to represent them in the government as the most intelligent and upright men of the race. They impressed upon the minds of thousands of our people the idea that the great privilege of the suffrage is a purchasable merchandise; that political meetings and conventions must be run and controlled by mobs, so that peaceable and intelligent men should not have a hearing in them; that the best way to accumulate money and acquire an education was to spend their time in gossipping in politics. The demoralization in which our people were left by the carpet-baggers is gradually being wiped out by the labors of the best men and women and by the colored press of the State. Our people are becoming fully awakened to the necessity of the proper education of their children. The greater portion of them, who heretofore spent their time in going around electioneering for the purpose of pulling carpet-baggers into office to the neglect of legitimate and profitable occupation, now turn their attention to acquiring property and education. From reliable statistics it appears that they have accumulated, since emancipation, two millions of dollars of property. In all the professions, trades and occupations it is admitted both by our friends and our foes that our progress is satisfactory, and in many instances wonderful. While our people were much excited and dissatisfied with the Democratic ascendency in the State government in 1876, and while in some localities they were the victims of some injustice under Democratic rule, still it has proved a blessing in disguise. The future is full of hope. Prejudice on account of color is passing away, and the negro has experienced his worst day in this State. But there is one pillar under the right-hand corner of this great edifice of progress that is full of decay and which threatens its destruction. It is the greatest enemy of our people, and must be met and destroyed. Whence comes this threatened danger? Strange, but nevertheless true, it proceeds from the house of God, and its name is Immorality—Licentiousness. Numbers of immoral and ignorant men have invaded the pulpits of our churches and are using the livery of Heaven to serve the devil in. In some of the church denominations the Board of Examination of candidates to preach are in no better standing as to morality and education than are the candidates, and therefore, often, unfit candidates have no trouble in procuring a license to preach. In many instances these disciples of Satan are frequenters of bar-rooms, and their conduct is no better than the lowest class that frequents such places. These men have in times past been guilty of every wrong that can be committed against innocence and virtue, and have violated every moral law and obligation. It will require energetic work and patient teaching to put up the bars against them. We have as good and virtuous men and women among us as are to be found anywhere in the world; and these the subject of this part of this chapter will not affect, other than to cause them to put forth greater efforts to stamp out this curse from among us. As a general rule contagious diseases breaking out in a community have their origin in the most filthy portions of that community, and if not stamped out at once, they penetrate to the cleanest dwellings and attack the learned and wealthy as well as those living in the slums. If we will apply this rule to the malady of immorality among our people, we may be profited in every effort that is made to stamp it out. Immorality is one of the worst enemies to the negro's intellectual and material progress.

THE END.

APPENDIX.

APPENDIX A.

CONSTITUTION OF FLORIDA, 1868.

We, the people of the State of Florida, by our delegates in convention assembled, in order to secure to ourselves and our posterity the enjoyment of all the rights of life, liberty and property, and the pursuit of happiness, do mutually agree, each with the other, to form the following constitution and form of government in and for said State.

ARTICLE I.

SECTION 1. We do declare that all citizens, subjects and people of this State are by birthright free and equal, entitled to equal rights and privileges under the Constitution and laws of the United States.

SEC. 2. No law shall be made that in spirit or intent recognizes any right of property in man, nor shall slavery or involuntary servitude exist in any form except as punishment for crime after due conviction in courts of law.

SEC. 3. That all political power is inherent in the people, and all free governments are founded on their authority and established for their benefit, therefore, they have at all times an inalienable and indefeasible right to alter or abolish their form of government in such manner as they may deem expedient.

SEC. 4. That all men have a natural and inalienable right to worship A mighty God according to the dictates of their own conscience, and that no preference shall ever be given by law to any religious establishment or mode of worship in the State.

SEC. 5. That no property qualification for eligibility to office, or for the right of suffrage, shall ever be required in this State.

SEC. 6. That every citizen may freely speak, write, and publish his sentiments on all subjects, being responsible for the abuse of that liberty; and no law shall be passed to curtail, abridge, or retain the liberty of speech or of the press.

SEC. 7. That the right of trial by jury shall forever remain inviolate.

SEC. 8. That the people shall be secure in their persons, houses, papers and possessions, from unreasonable seizures and searches; and that no warrant to search any place, or seize any person or thing, shall issue without describing the place to be searched, and the person or thing to be seized as nearly as may be, nor without probable cause supported by oath or affirmation.

SEC. 9. That no person shall be taken, imprisoned, or disseized of his freehold, liberties, or privileges, or outlawed, or exiled, or in any manner destroyed or deprived of his life, liberty, or property, but by law of the land.

SEC. 10. That courts shall be open, and every person for an injury done him in his lands, goods, person, or reputation, shall have remedy by due course of law, and right and justice administered without sale, denial, or delay.

SEC. 11. That in all criminal prosecutions the accused hath a right to be heard by himself or his counsel, or both; to demand the nature and cause of the accusation; to be confronted with the witnesses against him; to have compulsory process for obtaining witnesses in his favor; and in all prosecutions by indictment or presentment a speedy and public trial by an impartial jury of the county or district where the offence was committed, and shall not be compelled to give evidence against himself.

SEC. 12. That all persons shall be bailable by sufficient securities, unless in capital offences where the proof is evident or the presumption is strong; and the *habeas corpus* act shall not be suspended unless when in case of rebellion or invasion the public safety may require it.

SEC. 13 That excessive bail shall in no case be required; nor shall excessive fines be imposed; nor shall cruel or unusual punishment be inflicted.

SEC. 14. That no person shall for the same offence be twice put in jeopardy of life and limb.

SEC. 15. That private property shall not be taken or applied to public use unless just compensation be first made therefor.

SEC. 16. That in all prosecutions and indictments for libel the truth may be given in evidence, and if it shall appear to the jury that the libel is true, and published with good motives and for justifiable ends, that the truth shall be a justification, and the jury shall be the judges of the law and facts.

SEC. 17. That no person shall be put to answer any criminal charge but by presentment, indictmet or impeachment; but the Legislature may provide for the trial of persons without presentment or indictment for crimes below felony.

SEC. 18. That no conviction shall work corruption of blood or forfeiture of estate.

SEC. 19. That retrospective laws punishing acts committed

before the existence of such laws, and by them only declared penal or criminal, are oppressive, unjust, and incompatible with liberty, wherefore no *ex post facto* law shall ever be made.

Sec 20. That no law impairing the obligation of contracts shall be passed.

Sec. 21. That the people shall have a right in a peaceable manner to assemble together to consult for the common good, and to apply to those invested with the powers of government for redress of grievances or other proper purposes, by petition, address, or remonstrance.

Sec. 22. That no soldier, in time of peace, shall be quartered in any house without the consent of the owner; nor in time of war but in a manner prescribed by law.

Sec. 23. That no standing army shall be kept up without the consent of the Legislature, and the military shall be in strict subordination to the civil power.

Sec. 24 That perpetuities and monopolies are contrary to the genius of a free people and ought not to be allowed.

Sec. 25 That no hereditary emoluments, privileges, or honors, shall be granted or conferred in this State.

Sec. 26. That a frequent recurrence to fundamental principles is absolutely necessary to preserve the blessings of liberty.

Sec. 27. That this State has no right to sever its relations to the Federal Union, or to pass any law in derogation of the paramount allegiance of the citizens of this State to the Government of the United States.

Sec. 28. That, to guard against transgressions upon the rights of the people, we declare that everything in this article is excepted out of the general powers of government, and shall forever remain inviolate, and all laws contrary thereto, or to the following provisions, shall be void.

ARTICLE II.

DISTRIBUTIVE POWERS OF THE GOVERNMENT.

Section 1. The powers of the Government of the State of Florida shall be divided into three distinct departments, and each of them confided to a separate body, to wit: those which are legislative to one, those which are executive to another, and those which are judicial to another.

Sec. 2. No person or collection of persons,' being one of these departments, shall exercise any powers properly belonging to either of the others, except in the instance expressly provided in this constitution.

ARTICLE III.

EXECUTIVE DEPARTMENT.

SETION 1. The supreme executive power of the State shall be vested in a Governor, who shall be commander-in-chief of the army and navy of the State, and the militia, except when called into actual service of the United States.

SEC. 2. He shall be elected for four years, and remain in office until his successor is chosen. He shall be a natural-born citizen of the United States, and shall be at least thirty years of age. He shall have been a resident of this State at the adoption of this Constitution, or for three years next preceding his election. He shall hold no other office under the State or the United States while exercising the office of Governor.

SEC. 3. He may require information in writing from the officers of the executive department upon any subject relating to their respective duties.

SEC. 4. He may, on extraordinary occasions, convene the Legislature by proclamation, and shall, at the commencement of every session, communicate in writing such information as he may possess in reference to the condition of the State, and recommend such measures as he may deem expedient.

SEC. 5. In all cases of disagreement between the two houses in respect to the time of adjournment, he may adjourn the Legislature to such a time as he may think proper, not beyond its regular meeting.

SEC. 6. He shall have power to remit fines and forfeitures, pardon, reprieve, and commute, after conviction, for all offences except treason and cases of impeachment, subject to such regulations as may be prescribed by law.

SEC. 7. There shall be a seal of the State, which shall be kept by the Governor, and used by him officially, which shall be the great seal of the State.

SEC. 8. There shall also be a Lieutenant-Governor, who shall be an advisory officer of the Governor, and shall be chosen at the same time, and possess the same qualifications as the Governor, and who shall, in case of a vacancy by death, resignation, or otherwise, in the office of Governor, exercise all the power and authority belonging to that office. He shall be *ex-officio* President of the Senate during the sessions of the General Assembly, but, except in case of a tie, shall have no vote.

SEC. 9. There shall also be chosen, at the same time and place, and for the same period, a Secretary of State, Treasurer, Auditor, Attorney-General, Adjutant-General, Superintendent of Public Instruction, Commissioner of Emigration, and

Register of Public Lands. Any vacancy in the offices named in this and the preceding section occurring by death, resignation, or otherwise, to be filled by appointment of the Governor, with consent of the Senate, and holding the offices until the next general election.

SEC. 10. The returns of every election for the officers named in this section shall be sealed up and transmitted to the seat of government by the returning officer, directed to the presiding officer of the Senate, who, during the first week of the session, shall open and publish the same in the presence of a majority of the members of the General Assembly. The person having the highest number of votes shall be declared duly elected. But, if two or more shall be highest and equal in votes for the same office, one of them shall be chosen by the joint vote of both houses. Contested elections for executive officers shall be determined by both houses of the General Assembly, in such manner as shall be prescribed by law.

SEC. 11. The executive officers named in this article shall receive for compensation such sums per annum, payable quarter-annually, not less than the following: Governor, five thousand dollars; Lieutenant-Governor, four thousand dollars; Secretary of State, three thousand five hundred dollars; Treasurer, three thousand five hundred dollars; Auditor, three thousand five hundred dollars; Attorney General, three thousand dollars; Adjutant General, three thousand five hundred dollars; Superintendent of Public Instruction, three thousand five hundred dollars; Register of Public Lands, three thousand dollars; which sum shall not be increased nor diminished during the term for which they were elected.

SEC. 12. All commissions shall be in the name and by authority of the State of Florida, be sealed with the State seal, and signed by the Governor, and attested by the Secretary of State.

SEC. 13. Every bill which shall have passed both houses of the General Assembly shall be presented to the Governor. If he approve, he shall sign it, but if not, he shall return it with his objections to the house in which it shall have originated, who shall enter the objections at large upon the journals, and proceed to reconsider it; and if, upon such reconsideration, two-thirds of the whole number voting shall agree to pass the bill, it shall be sent, with the objections, to the other house, by which it shall be reconsidered; and, if approved by two thirds of the whole number voting, it shall become a law. And if any bill shall not be returned by the Governor within five days, (Sundays excepted,) after its having been presented to him, the same shall become a law; unless the General Assembly, by their adjournment, prevent its return, in which case it shall not become a law. The same rule as in this section shall apply to every order, resolution, or vote, to which the concurrence of both houses may be necessary.

ARTICLE IV.

LEGISLATIVE DEPARTMENT.

SECTION 1. The legislative power of this State shall be vested in two distinct branches, the one to be styled the Senate, the other the House of Representatives, and both the General Assembly of the State of Florida, and the style of laws shall be, "Be it enacted by the Senate and House of Representatives of the State of Florida in General Assembly convened."

SEC. 2. The members of the House of Representatives shall be chosen by the qualified voters and shall serve for the term of two years from the day of the general election and no longer. And the sessions of the General Assembly shall be annual, and commence on the second Tuesday of December in each year, until otherwise directed by law.

SEC. 3 The Representatives shall be chosen every two years on the Tuesday next after the first Monday in November until otherwise directed by law.

SEC. 4. No person shall be a Representative unless he be a citizen of the United States, and shall have been a resident of the State at the time of the adoption of this Constitution, or for two years next preceding his election, and the last six months thereof a resident of the county in which he shall be chosen, and shall have attained the age of twenty-one years.

SEC. 5. The Senators shall be chosen by the qualified electors for the term of four years, at the same time, in the same manner, and in the same place where they vote for members of the House of Representatives; and no person shall be a Senator unless he be a citizen of the United States, and shall have been a resident of this State at the time of the adoption of this Constitution, or for two years next preceding his election, and the last six months thereof a resident of the district or county in which he shall be chosen, and shall have attained the age of twenty-five years.

SEC. 6. The House of Representatives, when assembled, shall choose a speaker and its other officers, and the Senate its other officers, and in the absence of the Lieutenant-Governor a President *pro tempore*, and each house shall be judge of the qualifications, elections, and returns of its members; but a contested election shall be determined in such a manner as shall be directed by law.

SEC. 7. A majority of each house shall constitute a quorum to do business, but a smaller number may adjourn from day to day, and compel the attendance of absent members in such manner and under such penalties as each house may prescribe.

SEC. 8. Each house may determine the rules of its own proceedings, punish its members for disorderly behavior, and with the consent of two-thirds expel a member, but not a second time for the same cause

SEC. 9. Each house, during the session, may punish by imprisonment any person not a member for disrespectful or disorderly behavior in its presence, for obstructing any of its proceedings, provided such imprisonment shall not extend beyond the end of the session.

SEC. 10. Each house shall keep a journal of its proceedings, and cause the same to be published immediately after its adjournment; and the yeas and nays of the members of each house shall be taken and entered upon the journals upon the final passage of every bill, and may by any two members be required upon any other question, and any member of either house shall have liberty to dissent from or protest against any act or resolution which he may think injurious to the public or an individual, and have the reasons of his dissent entered on the journals.

SEC. 11. Senators and Representatives shall in all cases, except treason, felony or breach of peace, be privileged from arrest during the session of the General Assembly, and in going to or returning from the same, allowing one day for every twenty miles such member may reside from the place at which the General Assembly is convened, and for any speech or debate in either house they shall not be questioned in any other place.

SEC. 12. The General Assembly shall make provision by law for filling vacancies that may occur in either house, by death, resignation, or otherwise, of any of its members.

SEC. 13. The doors of each house shall be open when in legislative session, except on such occasions as, in the opinion of the house, the public safety may imperiously require secrecy.

SEC. 14. Neither house shall, without the consent of the other, adjourn for more than three days, nor to any other place than that in which they may be sitting.

SEC. 15. Bills may originate in either house of the General Assembly; and all bills passed by one house may be discussed, amended or rejected by the other; but no bill shall have the force of law until on three several days it be read in each house, and time for discussion being allowed thereon, unless, in case of emergency, four-fifths of the house in which the same shall be pending may deem it expedient to dispense with the rule; and every bill having passed both houses shall be signed by the Speaker and President of their respective houses.

SEC. 16. Each member of the General Assembly shall receive from the public treasury such compensation for his services as may be fixed by law, but no increase of compensation shall take effect during the term for which the Representatives were elected when such law passed.

SEC. 17. The session of the General Assembly shall not extend in duration over sixty days, unless it be deemed expedient by a concurrent majority of two-thirds of the members of each house; and no member shall receive pay from the State for his services after the expiration of ninety days continuously, from the commencement of the session.

SEC. 18. The General Assembly shall by, law, authorize the Circuit Court to grant licenses for building toll-bridges, and to establish ferries, and to regulate the tolls for both; to construct dams across streams not navigated: to ascertain and declare what streams are navigable, but no special law for such purpose shall be made.

SEC. 19 The General Assembly shall pass a general law prescribing the manner in which the names of persons might be changed, but no special law for such purpose shall be passed; and no law shall be made allowing minors to contract or manage their estates.

SEC. 20. The General Assembly shall pass a general law for the incorporation of towns, religious, literary, scientific, benevolent, military, and other associations, not commercial, industrial or financial; but no special act incorporating any such association shall be passed.

SEC. 21. No act incorporating any railroad, banking, insurance, commercial or financial corporation shall be introduced into the General Assembly, unless the person or persons applying for such corporation shall have deposited with the Treasurer the sum of one hundred dollars as a bonus to the State.

SEC. 22. Officers shall be removed from office for incapacity, misconduct, or neglect of duty in such manner as may be provided by law, when no mode of trial or removal is provided in this Constitution. It shall be the duty of the General Assembly to pass a homestead law, by which any public lands belonging to the State may be disposed of to actual settlers at a nominal price.

ARTICLE V.

JUDICIAL DEPARTMENT.

SECTION 1. The judicial powers of this State, both as to matters of law and equity shall be vested in a Supreme

Court, Court of Chancery, Circuit Courts, County Courts, and Justices of the Peace, and such Corporation Courts as the General Assembly may establish; but no Corporation Court shall have criminal jurisdiction in capital cases, nor shall courts have civil jurisdiction above the sum of two hundred dollars.

SUPREME COURT.

SEC. 2. The Supreme Court, except in cases otherwise directed in this Constitution, shall have appellate jurisdiction only, which shall be co-extensive with the State, under such restrictions and regulations, not repugnant to this Constitution, as may from time to time be prescribed by law: *Provided*, said courts shall always have power to issue writs of injunction, mandamus, quo warranto, habeas corpus, and such other and remedial writs as may be necessary to give it a general superintendence and control of all other courts.

SEC. 3. The Supreme Court shall consist of three Justices, one of whom shall be a Chief Justice, and shall be holden at such times and places as may be prescribed by law. The Justices of the Supreme, and Judges of the Circuit Court shall be appointed by the Governor, by and with the advice and consent of the Senate, and the Justices of the Supreme Court shall hold their office from the date of their appointment and confirmation for the space of nine years, unless sooner removed as herein prescribed.

SEC. 4. No man shall be eligible as Justice of the Supreme Court unless he be a citizen of the State at the time of the adoption of this Constitution: *Provided*, That from the date of five years after the adoption of this Constitution no man shall be eligible as Justice of the Supreme Court unless he shall have resided in this State five years next preceding the date of his appointment and confirmation, and shall have practiced law in the courts of chancery and common law of this State two years next preceding his appointment and confirmation.

SEC. 5. The Justices of the Supreme Court shall receive such compensation for their services not less than four thousand dollars to each Justice per annum, as may be fixed by law, which shall not be diminished during their continuance in office, but said Justices shall receive no fees, perquisites of office, nor hold any office of profit under the United States, or any other power.

SEC. 6. There shall be appointed by the Justices of the Supreme Court a clerk whose duties shall be prescribed by law: *Provided*, The General Assembly shall have power to provide for the appointment of a reporter, whose duties shall be prescribed by law.

CIRCUIT COURTS.

SEC. 7. The State shall be divided into convenient circuits: and for each circuit there shall be a Judge who shall, after his appointment and confirmation, reside in the circuit for which he has been appointed, and shall receive for his services a salary not less than three thousand five hundred dollars per annum; but said Judges shall receive no fees, perquisites of office, nor hold any other office of profit under the State, the United States or any other power.

SEC. 8. The Circuit Courts shall have original jurisdiction in all matters, civil and criminal, not otherwise excepted in this Constitution; and, until the General Assembly shall establish separate courts of chancery, the Circuit Courts shall have jurisdiction in all chancery cases, under such rules and regulations as may be prescribed by law.

SEC. 9. A Circuit Court shall be held in such counties, and at such times, and places therein, as may be prescribed by law; and the Judges of the several Circuit Courts may hold courts for each other, either for the entire circuit or a portion thereof; and they shall do so when required by order of the Governor, or the Chief Justice of the Supreme Court; and they may exercise jurisdiction in cases of writs of habeas corpus in any judicial circuit in which the Judge may happen to be at the time the case arises.

SEC. 10. The General Assembly shall have power to establish and organize a separate court or courts of original equity in jurisdiction.

SEC. 11. The same qualification, and none other shall be required for eligibility for office for the Judges of the Circuit Courts and Chancellors as are now required by this Constitution for Justices of the Supreme Court, and they shall hold their office for the space of six years from the date of their appointment and confirmation.

SEC. 12. There shall be appointed for each county in this State, by the Judge of the Circuit Court thereof, a clerk, whose duty shall be prescribed by law, and who shall hold his office four years unless otherwise directed by law.

SEC. 13. There shall be appointed by the Governor, by and with the advice and consent of the Senate, for each county, in this State, a Judge of the County Court, whose duty shall be to take probate of wills, to grant letters testamentary of administration and guardianship, to attend to the settlement of the estates of decedents and minors, and to discharge the duties usually appertaining to courts, of ordinary and such other duties as may be required by law, and exercise such criminal jurisdiction not to extend to crimes of as high grade as felony, and such civil jurisdiction not to extend to amounts over five hundred dollars, as may be prescribed by law, which County Court shall be subject to the direction of the Circuit Court by appeal.

SEC. 14. The Judge of the County Court shall have power to appoint a Clerk in certain counties, to be specified by law, who shall receive such compensation in fees as may be prescribed by law. The Judges of the County Court shall receive such compensation for their services as may be prescribed by law; provided, the General Assembly shall fix the pay of said Judges according to the number of inhabitants in the county in which they may preside.

SEC. 15. A competent number of Justices of the Peace shall, from time to time, be appointed by the Governor, who shall hold their offices for four years from the time of their appointment, and shall exercise such jurisdiction, criminal and civil, with the right of appeal, as may be prescribed by law.

SEC. 16. The Justices of the Supreme Court, and the Judges of the Circuit Court, shall not be removed from office during the term for which they may have been appointed and confirmed, except for wilful neglect of duty or reasonable cause, (which shall not be sufficient ground for impeachment,) for which the Governor may remove any of them, on the address of two-thirds of the General Assembly: *Provided, however,* That the cause or causes shall be notified to the justice or judge so intended to be removed, and shall be admitted to a hearing in his own defence before any vote for such removal shall pass; and, in such case, the vote shall be taken by yeas and nays and entered on the journals of each house, respectively; and, in cases of appointment to fill a vacancy in said offices, the person so appointed shall only hold office for the unexpired term of his predecessor.

SEC. 17. Whenever a vacancy shall occur, either in the Supreme, Circuit, or Chancery, or County Courts, or in the office of Justice of the Peace, or any other office provided for in this article of the Constitution, such vacancy shall be supplied by the power having, in this article of the Constitution, the appointment of said officer, and shall be for only the unexpired term made vacant; but it shall not be competent for the Governor to fill a vacancy in the Supreme, Chancery, or Circuit Courts, except by and with the advice and consent of the Senate: provided, the Governor may fill such vacancy during the recess of the General Assembly, which shall be valid until confirmed or rejected by the Senate.

SEC. 18. All officers provided for in this article of the Constitution, whose removal has not been herein prescribed, may be removed for misbehavior, or other reasonable cause, by the power having their appointment; but no such officer shall be removed, except for wilful neglect of duty, or a violation of the criminal law of the State.

SEC. 19. The Justices of the Supreme Court, Judges of the Circuit Court, and Justices of the Peace, shall, by virtue of their offices, be conservators of the peace throughout the State.

SEC. 20. The style of all process shall be "the State of Florida," and all criminal prosecution shall be carried on in the name of the State, and all indictments shall conclude against the peace and dignity of the same.

SEC. 21. There shall be one Solicitor for each circuit, who shall receive his appointment from the Judge presiding over the circuit for which he shall be appointed, and hold his office for the same term as the Judge of the Circuit Court.

SEC. 22. No Justice of the Supreme Court shall sit as a Judge, or take part in the Appellate Court, in the trial or hearing of any case which he shall have decided in the court below.

SEC. 23. The General Assembly shall have power to establish in each county a Board of County Commissioners, for the regulation of county business therein.

SEC. 24. No duty, not judicial, shall be imposed by law upon the Justices of the Supreme Court, Chancellors, or Judges of the Circuit Courts of this State, except in cases otherwise provided for in this Constitution.

SEC. 25. It shall be the duty of the Governor to appoint for each county in this State one Sheriff, and a number of constables, to be fixed by law, whose duties shall be prescribed by the General Assembly.

ARTICLE VI.

SUFFRAGE AND ELIGIBILITY.

SECTION 1. All elections by the people shall be by ballot, and all voters shall be registered at least one day before the election.

SEC. 2. General elections shall be held biennially on the Tuesday next after the first Monday in November, and the term of service of State and county officers elect shall commence on the third Tuesday of December following.

SEC. 3. Every male person of twenty-one years and upwards who shall have been a bona fide resident of this State at the time of the adoption of this Constitution, or a bona fide resident of this State for six months next preceding the election, and a bona fide resident of the county in which he offers to vote, for thirty days next preceding the election, and who shall not have held any office, civil or military, under the United States, or under any State, and afterwards engaged in insurrection or rebellion against the United States, or given aid or comfort to the enemies thereof, and who shall, before registering, take and subscribe the following oath, shall be deemed a qualified voter at any public election in this State:

I, —— ——, do solemnly swear (or affirm) that I am twenty-one years of age; that I am a citizen of the State of Florida; that I have resided in said State —— months next preceding this day; —— days in this county next preceding this day; that I have never held any office of honor or trust, civil or military, under the United States, or under any State, and afterwards engaged in insurrection or rebellion against the United States, or given any aid or comfort to the enemies thereof; that I will faithfully support the Constitution and laws of the United States, and the Constitution and laws of Florida, and will, to the best of my ability, encourage others so to do; that I will not in any way or manner injure, or countenance in others any attempt to injure, any person or persons on account of past or present support of the Government of the United States; and that I will not deprive or attempt to deprive any person or persons of any civil or political right on account of race, or color, or previous condition, or for affiliation with any political party, which right may be enjoyed by any other class of men: so help me God.

But the General Assembly may remove the disability imposed on account of participation in the rebellion by a two-thirds vote of each house.

Sec. 4. It shall be the duty of the General Assembly to provide, from time to time, for the registration of all persons qualified by this article as electors.

Sec. 5. It shall be the duty of the General Assembly to enact adequate laws, giving protection against the evils arising from the use and sale of intoxicating liquors at elections.

Sec. 6. Returns of elections for all civil officers elected by the people, who are to be commissioned by the Governor, and also for the members of the General Assembly, shall be made to the Secretary of State.

Sec. 7. No person who may hereafter be a collector or holder of public moneys shall have a seat in either house of the General Assembly, or be eligible to any office of trust or profit under this State until he shall have accounted for and paid into the treasury all sums of which he may be accountable.

Sec. 9. No Senator or Representative shall, during the term for which he shall have been elected, be appointed to any civil office of profit under this State which shall have been created, or the emolument of which shall have been increased, during such term, except such office as may be filled by election by the people.

SEC. 10. All civil officers of the State at large shall reside within the State, and all district or county officers within their respective districts or counties, and shall keep their respective offices at such places therein as may be required by law.

SEC. 11. Every person shall be disqualified from serving as Governor, Senator, Representative, or from holding any other office of honor or profit in this State for the term for which he shall have been elected, who shall have been convicted of having given or offered any bribe to procure his election.

SEC. 12. It shall be the duty of the General Assembly to regulate by law in what cases and what deductions from the salaries of public officers should be made for any neglect of duty in their official capacity.

SEC. 13. No member of Congress, or person holding or exercising any office of profit under the United States, or any foreign power, shall be eligible as a member of the General Assembly of this State, or hold or exercise any office of profit under the State.

SEC. 14. The General Assembly shall by law provide for the appointment or election, and removal from office, of all officers, civil and military in this State, not provided for in this constituton.

SEC. 15. The power of impeachment shall be vested in the House of Representatives.

SEC. 16. All impeachments shall be tried by the Senate; when sitting for that purpose the Senators shall be upon oath or affirmation; and no person shall be convicted without the concurrence of two-thirds of the members present.

SEC. 17. The Governor and all civil officers shall be liable to impeachment for any misdemeanor in office, but judgment in such cases shall not extend further than to removal from office and disqualification to hold any office of honor, trust or profit under this State; but the parties nevertheless shall be liable to indictment, trial and punishment, according to law.

ARTICLE VII.

MILITIA.

SECTION 1. It shall be the duty of the General Assembly to provide for the organization of the militia of the State, and officers therein shall be appointed under such rules as the General Assembly may direct.

SEC. 2. No commission shall be vacated except by a sentence of a court martial or upon resignation accepted by the Governor.

ARTICLE VIII.

TAXATION AND REVENUE.

SECTION 1. The General Assembly shall devise and adopt a system of revenue, having regard to an equal and uniform mode of taxation throughout the State.

SEC. 2. No other or greater amount of tax or revenue shall at any time be levied than may be required for the necessary expenses of the Government.

SEC. 3. No money shall be drawn from the Treasury but in consequence of an appropriation by law, and a regular statement of the receipts and expenditures of all public money shall be published and promulgated annually with the laws of the General Assembly.

SEC. 4. The General Assembly shall have power to authorize the several counties and incorporated towns in this State to impose taxes for county and corporation purposes, respectively, and all property shall be taxed upon the principles established in regard to State taxation.

SEC. 5. The General Assembly shall have power to authorize the levying of a capitation taxation tax not exceeding one dollar upon each voter in any one year, the same to be used exclusively for school purposes.

SEC. 6. It shall be the duty of the Governor to appoint for each county in this State one Assessor and Collector of Taxes, whose duties shall be prescribed by law, who shall hold his office for two years from the time of his appointment, but may be removed in the manner prescribed in the Constitution for the removal of Justices of the Peace.

ARTICLE IX.

CENSUS AND APPORTIONMENT.

SECTION 1. The General Assembly shall, in the year one thousand eight hundred and seventy-five, and every tenth year thereafter, cause an enumeration to be made of all the inhabitants of the State; and they shall then proceed to apportion the Representatives and Senators among the different counties, according to such enumeration, on the ratio of population as near as may be, and which rates shall not be changed until a new census shall have been taken.

SEC. 2. When any Senatorial or Representative district shall be composed of two or more counties, the counties of which such district consists shall not be entirely separated by any county belonging to another district, and no county shall be divided in forming districts.

SEC. 3. No county now organized shall be divided into new counties, so as to reduce the inhabitants of either below the rates of representation.

SEC. 4. The several counties of this State shall be entitled to the following representatives, viz: Escambia, two; Santa Rosa, one; Walton, one; Washington and Holmes, one; Jackson, four; Calhoun and Franklin, one; Gadsden and Liberty, four; Wakulla, one; Leon, seven; Jefferson, five; Madison, four; Taylor and Lafayette, one; Hamilton, one; Suwanee, one; Columbia, two; Baker and Bradford, one; Nassau, one; Duval, two; Clay, St. Johns and Putnam, two; Alachua and Levy, four; Marion, five; Hernando and Sumter, one; Orange, Volusia, Brevard and Dade, one; Hillsborough, Polk and Manatee, one; Monroe, one. The several counties of this State shall be entitled to the following Senators: Escambia, one; Santa Rosa, Walton and Holmes, one; Jackson, Washington, and Calhoun. two; Gadsden, Liberty and Franklin, two; Leon and Wakulla, four; Jefferson and Taylor, three; Madison and Hamilton, three; Suwanee and Columbia, one; Baker and Nassau, one; Duval, one; Clay, St. Johns and Putnam, one; Bradford, Alachua and Lafayette, two; Marion and Levy, two; Hernando, Sumter, Orange, Volusia, Brevard and Dade, one; Hillsborough, Polk, Manatee and Monroe, one.

ARTICLE X.

EDUCATION.

SECTION 1. It shall be the duty of the General Assembly to provide a liberal system of free schools, to be under the supervision of the school commission of the State.

SEC. 2. The proceeds of all public lands for the use of schools and seminaries of learnings shall be and remain a perpetual fund, the interest of which, together with all moneys accrued from any other source applicable to the same object, shall be inviolably appropriated to the use of schools and seminaries of learning, respectively, and to no other purpose.

SEC. 3. The General Assembly shall take such measures as may be necessary to preserve from waste or damage all public lands so granted and appropriated for the purpose of education.

SEC. 4. The General Assembly of this State shall forever be

prohibited from making any distinctions in schools, seminaries and colleges based upon caste, color or birth.

SEC. 5. The General Assembly shall have power to establish an agricultural college at the earliest possible moment.

ARTICLE XI.

PUBLIC DOMAIN.

SECTION 1. It shall be the duty of the General Assembly to provide for the prevention of waste and damage of the public lands that have been or may hereafter be ceded to the State of Florida. and it may pass laws for the sale of any part or portion thereof, and in such cases provide for the safety, security and appropriation of the proceeds.

SEC. 2. A liberal 'system of internal improvements, being essential to the development of the resources of the State, shall be encouraged by the Government of this State; and it shall be the duty of the General Assembly, as soon as practicable, to ascertain by law proper objects for the extension of internal improvements, in relation to roads, canals and navigable streams, and to provide for a suitable application of such funds as may have been or may hereafter be appropriated by said General Assembly for such improvements.

SEC. 3. The General Assembly may create internal improvement districts, composed of one or more counties, and may grant a right to the citizens thereof to tax themselves for their improvements. Said internal improvement districts, when created, shall have the right to select Commissioners, shall have power to appoint officers, fix their pay, regulate all matters relative to the improvements of their districts, provided such improvements will not conflict with the general laws of the State.

SEC. 4. The General Assembly may grant aid to said districts out of the funds arising from the swamp and overflowed lands granted to the State by the United States for that purpose, or otherwise.

SEC. 5. The General Assembly may at any time cede to the United States Government a sufficient parcel or fraction of land for the purpose of coast defence and other national purposes.

ARTICLE XII.

BOUNDARIES.

SECTION 1. The boundaries of the State of Florida shall be as follows: Commencing at the mouth of the river Perdito; from thence up the middle of said river to where it intersects the south boundary line of the State of Alabama and the thirty-first degree of north latitude; then due east to the Chattahoochie river; then down the middle of said river to its confluence with the Flint river; from thence direct to the head of the Saint Mary's river; thence down the middle of said river to the Atlantic ocean; thence southwardly to the Gulf of Florida and Gulf of Mexico; thence northwardly and westwardly, including all islands within five leagues of this, to the beginning.

ARTICLE XIII.

CORPORATIONS.

SECTION 1. Corporations may be formed under general laws for municipal, religious, literary, scientific, benevolent, military and other associations, not commercial, industrial or financial, but no special act incorporating any such association shall be passed. All general laws and special acts passed pursuant to this section may be altered, amended or repealed.

SEC. 2. Dues from corporations shall be secured by such individual liabilities of the corporators or other means as may be prescribed by law.

SEC. 3. Each stockholder in any corporation shall be liable to the amount of the stock held or owned by him.

SEC. 4. The property of corporations, now existing or hereafter created, shall forever be subject to taxation the same as property of individuals, except corporations for educational and charitable purposes.

SEC. 5. No right of way shall be appropriated to the use of any corporation until full compensation therefor be first made in money or secured by a deposit of money to the owner, irrespective of any benefit from any improvement proposed by such corporation, which compensation shall be ascertained by a jury of twelve men in a court of record, as shall be prescribed by law.

SEC. 6. The General Assembly shall not have power to establish or incorporate any bank, banking company or moneyed institution for the purpose of issuing bills of credit, or bills payable to order or bearer, except under the conditions prescribed in this Constitution.

SEC. 7. No bank shall be established otherwise than under a general banking law, as provided in the first section of this article.

SEC. 8. The General Assembly may enact a general banking law, which law shall provide for the registry and countersigning, by the Governor of the State, of all paper credit designed to be created as money; and for ample collateral security convertible into specie, or the redemption of the same in gold or silver, shall be required, and such collateral security shall be under the control of such officer or officers as may be prescribed by law.

SEC. 9. All bills or notes issued as money shall be at all times redeemable in gold or silver, and no law shall be passed sanctioning directly or indirectly the suspension, by any bank or banking company, of specie payments.

SEC. 10. Holders of bank notes shall be entitled, in case of insolvency, to preference of payment over all other creditors.

SEC. 11. Every bank or banking company shall be required to cease all banking operations within twenty years from the time of its organization, and promptly thereafter to close its business.

SEC. 12. No bank shall receive, directly or indirectly, a greater rate of interest than shall be allowed by law to individuals lending money.

SEC. 13. The State shall not be a stockholder in any bank, nor shall the credit of the State ever be given or lent to any banking company, association or corporation, except for the purpose of expediting the construction of railroads or works of internal improvement within this State, and the credit of this State shall in no case be given or lent without the approval of both houses of the General Assembly.

SEC. 14. All corporations shall have the right to sue, and shall be subject to be sued, in all courts in like cases as natural persons.

SEC. 15. It shall be the duty of the General Assembly to provide for the organization of cities and incorporated towns, and to restrict their power of taxation, assessments and contracting of debts.

ARTICLE XIV.

INDUSTRIAL RESOURCES.

SECTION 1. A bureau of industrial resources shall be estabslihed, to be under the management of the Commissioner of Emigration, who shall be elected at the first general election, and shall hold his office for the term of four years.

SEC. 2. The Commissioner of Industrial Resources shall colect and condense statistical information concerning the productive industries of the State; and make or cause to be made, at careful, accurate, and thorough report upon the agriculture and geology of the State, and annually report such additions as the progress of scientific development and extended explorations may require. He shall, from time to time, disseminate among the people of the State such knowledge as he may deem important concerning improved machinery and production, and for the promotion of their agricultural, manufacturing, and mining interests; and shall send out to the people of the United States and foreign countries such reports concerning the industrial resources of Florida as may best make known the advantages offered by the State to emigrants; and shall perform such other dutiesas the General Assembly may require.

SEC. 3. It shall be the duty of the General Assembly, at the first session after the adoption of this Constitution, to pass such laws and regulations as may be necessary for the government and protection of this bureau, and also to fix and provide for the compensation of the Commissioner.

SEC. 4. This bureau shall be located, and the Commissioner shall reside at the capital of the State; and he shall annually make a written or printed report to the Governor of the State, to be laid before the General Assembly at each session.

SEC. 5. In case of the death, removal, or resignation of the Commissioner, the Governor, with the approval of the Senate, shall have power to appoint a Commissioner for the unexpired term.

ARTICLE XV.

ELIGIBILITY AND TENURE OF OFFICE.

SECTION 1. All officers of this State, civil and military, before they enter upon the execution of the duties of their respective offices, shall take and subscribe the following oath: I do solemnly swear (or affirm) that I have never voluntarily borne arms against the United States since I have been a citizen thereof; that I have voluntarily given no aid, countenance, or encouragement, to persons engaged in armed hostility thereto; that I have neither sought, nor accepted, nor attempted to exercise any authority, or pretended authority, in hostility to the United States; that I have not yielded voluntary support to any pretended government, authority, power, or constitution within the United States, hostile or inimical thereto; and I do further swear (or affirm) that I will, to the best of my ability and knowledge, support and defend the Constitution of the United States, and of the State of Florida, against all enemies, foreign and domestic; that I will bear true faith and allegiance to the same; that I take this obligation freely, without any mental reservation or purpose of evasion; and that I will faithfully discharge the duties of the office on which I am about to enter: so help me God. Any person who shall falsely take this oath shall be deemed guilty of perjury, and on conviction thereof, in addition to the penalties which may by law be prescribed for that offence, shall be deprived of his office, and rendered forever incapable of holding any office in this State; but the General Assembly may, on the recommendation of the Governor, by a vote of two-thirds of each house, remove the disability imposed in this article for aiding or countenancing the rebellion.

ARTICLE XVI.

AMENDMENTS AND REVISION.

SECTION 1. No part of this Constitution shall be altered except by a convention duly elected.

SEC. 2. No convention of the people shall be called unless by the concurrence of two-thirds of all the members of each house of the General Assembly, made known by the passing of a bill, which shall be read three times on three several days in each house.

SEC. 3. Whenever a convention shall be called proclamation of an election for delegates shall be made by the Governor at least thirty days before the day of election. Every county and Senatorial district shall be entitled to as many delegates as it has Representatives in the General Assembly. The same qualifications shall be required in delegates and electors that are required in members of the General Assembly, and voters for the same, respectively, and the election of delegates to a convention, and the returns of such election, shall be held and made in the manner prescribed by law for regulating elections for members of the General Assembly; but the convention shall judge of the qualifications of its own members.

ARTICLE XVII.

SEAT OF GOVERNMENT.

SECTION 1. The seat of government shall be, and remain permanent, at the city of Tallahassee, until otherwise provided for by the action of a convention of the people of the State.

ARTICLE XVIII.

GENERAL POWERS.

SECTION 1. The jurors of this State shall be citizens of the United States, possessed of such qualifications as may be prescribed by law.

SEC. 2. Treason against the State shall consist only in levying war against it or the United States, or in adhering to its enemies, giving them aid and comfort. No person shall be convicted of treason unless on the testimony of two witnesses to the same overt act, or his confession in open court.

SEC. 3. Divorces from the bonds of matrimony shall not be allowed but by the judgment of a court, as shall be prescribed by law.

SEC. 4. The General Assembly shall declare by law what parts of the common law and what parts of the civil law, not inconsistent with this Constitution, shall be in force in this State.

SEC. 5. The oath of office directed to be taken under this Constitution may be administered by any Judge or Justice of the Peace in the State of Florida, until otherwise provided by law.

SEC. 6. In all actions of law, civil and criminal, every citizen of this State shall be equally competent to give evidence, under such rules and regulations as may be prescribed by the General Assembly.

SEC. 7. No person shall be capable of holding or being elected to any post of honor, profit, trust, or emolument, civil or military, legislative, executive or judicial, under the government of this State, who shall hereafter fight a duel, or send or accept a challenge to fight a duel, the probable issue of which may be the death of the challenger or challenged, or shall be a second to either party, or who shall in any manner aid or assist in such a duel, or shall be knowingly the bearer of such a challenge, or acceptance, whether the same occur or be committed in or out of the State; but the legal disability shall not occur until after the trial and conviction according to due form of law.

ARTICLE XIX.

SCHEDULE AND ORDINANCE.

SECTION 1. All laws of the State, passed and in operation before the assembling of this Convention, not repugnant to the Constitution of this State and the Constitution of the United States, and acts of Congress of the United States, and the ordinances of this Convention, shall be valid and remain of full force and effect until amended, changed or repealed by the General Assembly. All writs, actions, prosecutions, judgments and decrees of the courts of this State, all executions and sales made thereunder, and all acts, orders and proceedings of the Judges of Probate, and of executors, administrators, guardians and trustees, provided they were in conformity to the laws passed and to the Constitution of the State and the United States, the acts of Congress, and not repugnant to the ordinances of this Convention, shall be as valid as if made under the usual and ordinary legislation of the country.

SEC. 2. All fines, penalties, forfeitures, obligations and escheats heretofore accruing to the State of Florida, and not made unlawful by the Constitution of this State, and the Constitution of the United States, and the acts of Congress, and the ordinances of this Convention, shall continue to accrue to the use of the State.

SEC. 3. All recognizances heretofore taken shall remain valid, and all bonds executed to the Governor of the State of Florida, either before or since the first day of January, 1861, or to any other officer of the State in his official capacity, shall be of full force and virtue for the uses therein respectively expressed, and may be sued for and recovered accordingly; and all criminal prosecutions and penal actions which have arisen may be prosecuted to judgment and execution in the name of the State, not repugnant to the Constitution of this State, the Constitution of the United States, the acts of Congress of the United States, and the ordinances of this Convention.

Done in open convention. In witness, the undersigned, the President of said Convention and delegates present, representing the people of Florida, do hereby sign our names this the eighth day of February, Anno Domini eighteen hundred and sixty-eight, and of the independence of the United States the ninety-third; and the Secretary of the Convention doth countersign the same.

D. RICHARDS, *President.*

A. G. Bass,
William Bradwell,
Andrew Shuler,
Green Davidson,
Fred Hill,
John N. Krimminger,
Joseph E. Oates,
Charles H. Pearce,
John Wyatt,
Josiah T. Walls,
Wm. U. Saunders.

Liberty Billings,
Wm. R. Cone,
Jesse H. Goss,
Jonathan C. Gibbs,
Major Johnson,
R. Meacham,
Anthony Mills,
Alexander Chandler,
Eldridge L. Ware.
O. B. Armstrong,

[General Orders No. 110.]

HEADQUARTERS THIRD MILITARY DISTRICT,
(GEORGIA, ALABAMA AND FLORIDA,)
Atlanta, Georgia, December 28, 1867:

Whereas, by General Orders No. 74, from these headquarters, dated October 5, 1867, an election was ordered to be held in the State of Florida, on the fourteenth, fifteenth and sixteenth days of November, 1867, at which election, in pursuance of an act of Congress entitled "An act to provide for the more efficient government of the rebel States," and the acts supplementary thereto, the registered voters of said State might vote "for a convention" or "against a convention," and for delegates to constitute the convention in case a majority of the votes given on that question should be for a convention, and in case a majority of all the registered voters should have voted on the question of a convention;

And, whereas, at an election held in pursuance of said orders, and in conformity to said acts, there were polled on the question of a convention votes to the number of fourteen thousand five hundred and three (14,503), being more than one-half of twenty-seven thousand one hundred and seventy-two (27,172), the whole number of registered voters in said State; and of the whole number of votes polled on the question of a convention, fourteen thousand three hundred (14,300), being a majority of the same, were cast for a convention.

And, whereas, at said election the following named persons were elected as delegates to said Convention from the respective election districts in which they were so chosen:

From the first election district—George W. Walker, George J. Alden, Lyman W. Rowley.

From the second election district—John L. Campbell.

From the third election district—W. J. Purman, L. C. Armistead, E. Fortune, H. Bryan.

From the fourth election district—D. Richards, W. U. Saunders, Frederick Hill.

From the fifth election district—J. W. Childs.

From the sixth election district—T. W. Osborne, Joseph E. Oates, C. H. Pearce, John Wyatt, Green Davidson, O. B. Armstrong.

From the seventh election district—John W. Powell, A. G. Bass, Robert Meacham, Antony Mills.

From the eighth election district—Roland T. Rombauer, Major Johnson, William R. Cone.

From the ninth election district—Thomas Urquhart, Andrew Shuler.

From the tenth election district—J. N. Krimminger.

From the eleventh election district—Horatio Jenkins, jr., Wm. K. Cessna, Josiah T. Walls.

From the twelfth election district—S. B. Conover, Auburn Erwin.

From the thirteenth election district—B. M. McRae.

From the fourteenth election district—L. Billings, N. C. Dennett, William Bradwell, J. C. Gibbs.
From the fifteenth election district—J. H. Goss, A. Chandler, W. Rogers, D. House.
From the sixteenth election district—Samuel J. Pearce.
From the seventeenth election district—C. R. Mobley.
From the eighteenth election district—David Mizell.
From the Nineteenth election district—Eldridge L. Ware.

It is ordered that the persons above named do meet in convention at Tallahassee, Florida, at the Capitol, on Monday, the twentieth (20th) day of January, 1868, and proceed to frame a constitution and civil government for the State of Florida, according to the provisions of the acts above referred to, and that when the same shall have been so framed the said constitution be submitted for ratification to the registered voters of said State, as further required by law.

JOHN POPE,
Brevet Major-General Commanding.

Official:

CHARLES F. LARRABEE,
*Brevet Captain United States Army,
Acting Assistant Adjutant-General, District of Florida.*

TALLAHASSEE, FLA., February 15, 1868.

DEAR SIR: The Constitutional Convention for the State of Florida adjourned on last Saturday to meet again to-day, in the hall of the House of Representatives, at 10 o'clock A. M.

In the meantime I learn that parties broke into the said hall at midnight and formed there an organization assuming to be a Constitutional Convention, and now refuse to surrender possession of said hall.

As the said pretended convention, now in possession of the hall, is an illegal and revolutionary organization, tending to impede, if not defeat, reconstruction in this State, and that the legally organized body may assemble without a collision and, perhaps, serious consequences, I most respectfully ask you, as the highest civil executive officer in our State, to cause to be arrested and removed from the capital Horatio Jenkins, the pretended President of the said pretended convention; Sherman Conant, the pretended Secretary; M. Martin, the pretended Sergeant-at-arms, and all other persons who now prevent, or threaten to prevent, the officers of the regularly organized Constitutional Convention entering upon the discharge of their official duties in said hall.

You are also requested to cause to be arrested at once O. B. Hart, T. W. Osborne, C. R. Mobley, S. B. Conover, J. W.

Purman, and C. M. Hamilton as leading conspirators in disturbing the public peace and inciting to riot, and for illegally attempting to obstruct and defeat reconstruction, and remove them from said hall and capital.

I am yours most respectfully,

D. RICHARDS,
President of Constitutional Convention, Florida.

HON. DAVID S. WALKER.

EXECUTIVE DEPARTMENT,
TALLAHASSEE, FLA., February 15, 1868.

SIR: Your communication of this instant is received.

I cannot comply with your request. The gentlemen now occupying the Representative hall claim that they are the majority of the convention, and are entitled to seats upon the floor. I learn from the gentleman now occupying the President's chair that a majority of the members of the convention have elected him President, and that every member of the convention have elected him President, and that every member of the convention is at liberty to go into the hall and occupy his seat if he desires to do so. It is clearly not for me to determine whether yourself or General Jenkins is the rightful President of the convention.

For the purpose of preserving the peace I shall feel it my duty to use all the power I can command to prevent a collision by the attempt of either party forcibly to eject the other from the hall.

Earnestly hoping that all the members of the convention will meet together and harmonize, I am yours most respectfully,

D. S. WALKER, *Governor, etc.*

HON. D. RICHARDS.

TALLAHASSEE, FLA., February 15, 1868.

DEAR SIR: The enclosed is a copy of the request made on Governor David S. Walker, the chief executive civil officer in our State, and he declines to take any action thereon. You, therefore, as commander of the military at this place, are respectfully requested to promptly arrest and remove from the hall and the capital all parties who offer or encourage any opposition to the legally constituted officers of the Constitutional Convention of Florida entering upon the discharge of their duties in the hall

of the capital. And you are especially requested to arrest and remove from the capital those persons named in communication to Governor Walker.
>Respectfully yours,
>D. RICHARDS,
>*President of Constitutional Convention, Florida.*

COLONEL F. F. FLINT,
Commanding Post at Tallahassee.

>HEADQUARTERS POST OF TALLAHASSEE, FLA.,
>February 15, 1868.

SIR: I have the honor to acknowledge the receipt of your note of this date enclosing copy of a communication from you to Governor Walker, also of this date, and in reply have to inform you that I must decline to comply with your request.

I am, sir, very respectfully, your obedient servant,
>F. F. FLINT,
>*Lieutenant-Colonel 7th United States Infantry, Commanding.*

MR. D. RICHARDS, *Tallahassee, Fla.*

>TALLAHASSEE, FLA., February 17, 1868.

DEAR SIR: As President of the Constitutional Convention of Florida I feel it necessary to endeavor to enter upon the discharge of my duties at the earliest practicable moment after the forcible opposition is withdrawn from the hall in which we were to meet. As you indicated to our committee to-day that the organization now in possession of the hall "had no legal status, nor could get one," I can see no reason why the regularly organized convention should not be permitted to assemble to-morrow morning at the regular hour of meeting. Would be very glad to know your wishes on the subject.
>Most respectfully yours,
>D. RICHARDS,
>*President of Convention.*

MAJOR-GENERAL GEORGE G. MEADE,
Commanding Third Military District.

The undersigned, being a majority of the delegates to the Constitutional Convention of the State of Florida, hereby assent and agree to the following propositions:

1. Richards to resign.
2. Jenkins to resign.

Both to hand their written resignations to Secretary S. Conant.

3. S. Conant, Secretary, to call convention to order, and perform the duties of temporary chairman.

4. Election of President.

Billings, Saunders, Pierce, and Richards to take their seats and vote on the question.

5. The whole convention to abide by action of majority on all and every question.

HORATIO JENKINS, Jr., *President.*
C. R. MOBLEY,
T. W. OSBORNE,
O. B. HART,
  Committee.

TALLAHASSEE, FLORIDA,
February 18, 1886.

DEAR SIR: I enclose you herewith a proposition received this morning from that portion of the convention organized under the presidency of Mr. Jenkins. I have already advised you that I am satisfied, from the information obtained here, that it is entirely impracticable for you to obtain the quorum, twenty-four, necessary to give validity to the acts of the body over which you preside, and which up to February 1, the date of the withdrawal of the members, I consider as the regular organization.

The withdrawal of these members, and the accession to their numbers sufficient to give them twenty-five elected members and their organization and refusal to return to your body or harmonize, except upon the terms here indicated, satisfy me that either the convention must be broken up, or must be reorganized so as to permit the majority to have its rightful influence. Under these circumstances, I feel it my duty to appeal to your desire not to obstruct the discharge of the duties assigned to the convention, and deeming the enclosed proposition a reasonable compromise, to urge you to conform to it, with a view of harmonizing the unfortunate difficulties that have arisen, and thus restore peace and tranquility to the whole body.

Very respectfully, your obedient servant,
GEORGE G. MEADE,
Maj. Gen. U. S. Army, Commanding Third Military District.
D. RICHARDS,
President Constitutional Convention.

APPENDIX B.

LAST CONSTITUTION FRAMED AFTER A NEW CONVENTION WAS ORGANIZED.

Constitution of the State of Florida, framed by a convention of the people assembled at Tallahassee, on the 20th day of January 1868.

PREAMBLE.

We, the people of the State of Florida, grateful to Almighty God for our freedom, in order to secure its blessings and form a more perfect government, insuring domestic tranquility, maintaining public order, perpetuating liberty, and guaranteeing equal civil and political rights to all, do establish this Constitution.

ARTICLE I.

DECLARATION OF RIGHTS.

SECTION 1. All men are by nature free and equal, and have certain inalienable rights, among which are those of enjoying and defending life and liberty, acquiring, possessing, and protecting property, and pursuing and obtaining safety and happiness.

SEC. 2. All political power is inherent in the people. Government is instituted for the protection, security, and benefit of its citizens, and they have the right to alter or amend the same whenever the public good may require it; but the paramount allegiance of every citizen is due to the Federal Government, and no power exists with the people of this State to dissolve its connection therewith.

SEC. 3. This State shall ever remain a member of the American Union, the people thereof a part of the American nation, and any attempt from whatever source, or upon whatever pretence, to dissolve said Union, or to sever said nation, shall be resisted with the whole power of the State.

SEC. 4. The right of trial by jury shall be secured to all and remain inviolate forever; but in all civil cases a jury trial may be waived by the parties in the manner to be prescribed by law.

SEC. 5. The free exercise and enjoyment of religious profession and worship shall forever be allowed in this State, and no person shall be rendered incompetent as a witness on account of his religious opinions; but the liberty of conscience hereby secured shall not be so construed as to justify licentiousness or practices subversive of the peace and safety of the State.

SEC. 6. The privilege of the writ of habeas corpus shall not be suspended, unless when, in case of invasion or rebellion, the public safety may require its suspension.

SEC. 7. Excessive bail shall not be required, nor excessive fines imposed, nor cruel or unusual punishment be inflicted, nor shall witnesses be unreasonably detained.

SEC. 8. All persons shall be bailable by sufficient sureties, unless for capital offences, when the proof is evident the presumption great.

SEC. 9. No person shall be tried for a capital or otherwise infamous crime, except in cases of impeachment, and in cases of the militia when in active service in time of war, or which the State may keep, with the consent of Congress, in time of peace, and in cases of petit larceny, made under the regulation of the Legislature, unless on presentment and indictment by a grand jury; and in any trial by any court the party accused shall be allowed to appear and defend in person, and with counsel, as in civil actions. No person shall be subject to be twice put in jeopardy for the same offence, nor shall be compelled in any criminal case to be a witness against himself, nor be deprived of life, liberty, or property without due process of law; nor shall private property be taken without just compensation.

SEC. 10. Every citizen may fully speak and write his sentiments on all subjects, being responsible for the abuse of that right, and no law shall be passed to restrain or abridge the liberty of speech or the press. In all criminal prosecutions and civil actions for libel, the truth may be given in evidence to the jury, and if it shall appear that the matter charged as libellous is true, but was published from good motives, the party shall be acquitted or exonerated.

SEC. 11. The people shall have the right to assemble together to consult for the common good, to instruct their representatives, and to petition the Legislature for redress of grievance.

SEC. 12. All laws of a general nature shall have a uniform operation.

SEC. 13. The military shall be subordinate to the civil power.

SEC. 15. No soldier shall, in time of peace, be quartered in any house, except with the consent of the owner, nor in time of war, except in manner prescribed by law.

SEC. 15. Representatives shall be apportioned according to population, as well as may be, but no county shall have more than four representatives and less than one representative in the assembly.

SEC. 16. No person shall be imprisoned for debt except in case of fraud.

SEC. 17. No bill of attainder, or *ex post facto* law, impairing the obligations of contracts, shall ever be passed.

SEC. 18. Foreigners who are, or who may hereafter become, bona fide residents of the State, shall enjoy the same rights in respect to possession, enjoyment, and inheritance of property as native-born citizens.

SEC. 19. Neither slavery or involuntary servitude, unless for the punishment of crime, shall ever be tolerated in this State.

SEC. 20. The right of the people to be secure in either person, houses, papers, and effects, against unreasonable seizures and searches, shall not be violated, and no warrants issued but in probable cause; supported by oath or affirmation, particularly describing the place or places to be searched, and the person or persons, and thing or things to be seized.

SEC. 21. Treason against the State shall consist only in levying war against it, adhering to its enemies, or giving them aid and comfort; and no person shall be convicted of treason unless on the testimony of two witnesses to the overt act or confession in open court. This enunciation of rights shall not be construed to impair or deny others retained by the people.

SEC. 22. The people shall have the right to bear arms in defence of themselves and of the lawful authority of the State.

SEC. 23. No preference can be given by law to any church, sect or mode of worship.

ARTICLE II.

BOUNDARIES

The boundaries of the State of Florida shall be as follows. Commencing at the mouth of the River Perdido; from thence up the middle of said river to where it intersects the south boundary line of the State of Alabama on the thirty-first degree of north latitude; thence due east to the Chattahoochee river; thence down the middle of said river to its confluence with the Flint river; from thence straight to the head of the St. Mary's river; thence down the middle of said river to the Atlantic Ocean; thence southeastwardly along the coast to the edge of the Gulf stream; thence southwestwardly along the edge of the Gulf stream and Florida reefs to and including the Tortugas islands; thence northwestwardly to a point five leagues from the main land; thence northwestwardly from the shore, including all islands, to a point five leagues due south from the middle of the mouth of Perdido river; thence to the place of beginning.

ARTICLE III.

SEAT OF GOVERNMENT.

The seat of government shall be and remain permanent at the city of Tallahassee, in the county of Leon, until otherwise located by a majority vote of the Legislature, and by a majority vote of the people.

ARTICLE IV.

DISTRIBUTION OF POWER.

The powers of the government of the State of Florida shall be divided into three departments, to wit: Legislative, Executive and Judicial. No person properly belonging to one of the departments shall exercise any functions appertaining to either of the others, except in those cases expressly provided for by this Constitution.

ARTICLE V.

LEGISLATIVE DEPARTMENT.

SECTION 1. The Legislative authority of this State shall be vested in a Senate and Assembly, which shall be designated "the Legislature of the State of Florida," and the sessions thereof shall be held at the seat of government of the State.

SEC. 2. The sessions of the Legislature shall be annual; the first session on the second Monday of June, A. D. 1886, and thereafter on the first Tuesday after the first Monday of January, commencing in the year A. D. 1869. The Governor may, in the *interim*, convene the Legislature in extra session by his proclamation.

SEC. 3 The members of the Assembly shall be chosen bienially; those of the first Legislature on the first Monday, Tuesday and Wednesday of May A. D. 1868, and thereafter on the first Tuesday after the first Monday of November commencing with the year A. D. 1870.

SEC. 4. Senators shall be chosen for the term of four years, at the same time and place as members of the Assembly: *Provided*, That the Senators elected at the first election from the Senatorial districts shall vacate their seats at the expiration of two years, and thereafter all Senators shall be elected for the term of four years, so that one-half of the whole number shall be elected bienially.

SEC. 5. Senators and members of the Assembly shall be duly qualified electors in the respective counties and districts which they represent.

SEC. 6. Each house shall judge of the qualifications, elections and returns of its own members; choose its own officers, except the President of the Senate, determine the rules of its proceedings, and may punish its members for disorderly conduct and with the concurrence of two-thirds of all the members present, expel a member.

SEC. 7. Either house during the session, may punish by imprisonment any person, not a member, who shall have been guilty of disorderly or contemptuous conduct in its presence; but such imprisonment shall not extend beyond final adjournment of the session.

SEC. 8. A majority of each house shall constitute a quorum to do business: but a smaller number may adjourn from day to day and may compel the presence of absent members in such manner and under such penalties as each house may prescribe.

SEC. 9. Any person who shall be convicted of embezzlement or defalcation of the funds of this State, or of having given or offered a bribe to secure his election or appointment to office, or of having received a bribe to aid in the procurement of office for any other person, shall be disqualified from holding any office of honor, profit, or trust in the State; and the Legislature shall, as soon as praticable, provide by law for the punishment of each embezzlement, defalcation, or bribery as a felony.

SEC. 10. Each house shall keep a journal of its own proceedings, which shall be published, and the yeas and nays of the members of either house on any question shall, at the desire of any three members present, be entered on the journal.

SEC. 11. The doors of each house shall be kept open during its session, except the Senate while sitting in executive session; and neither shall, without the consent of the other, adjourn for more than three days, or to any other town than that in which they may be holding their session.

SEC. 12. Any bill may orginate in either house of the Legislature and after being passed in one house may be amended in the other.

SEC. 13. The enacting clause of every law shall be as follows: "The people of the State of Florida, represented in Senate and Assembly, do enact as follows:"

SEC 24. Each law enacted in the Legislature shall embrace

but one subject, and matters properly connected therewith, which subject shall be briefly expressed in the title; and no law shall be amended or revised by reference to its title only, but in such case, the act as revised, or section as amended, shall be re-enacted and published at length.

SEC. 15. Every bill shall be read by sections in three several ways in each house, unless, in case of emergency, two-thirds of the house where such bill may be pending shall deem it expedient to dispense with this rule; but the reading of a bill by sections on its final passage, shall in no case be dispensed with; and the vote on the final passage of every bill, or joint resolution, shall be taken by yeas and nays, to be entered in the journal of each house, and a majority of the members present in each house shall be necessary to pass every bill or joint resolution, and all bills or joint resolutions so passed shall be signed by the presiding officers of the respective houses; and by the Secretary of the Senate and Clerk of the Assembly.

SEC. 16. No money shall be drawn from the treasury except by appropriation made by law, and accurate statements of the receipts and expenditures of the public money shall be attached to and published with the laws passed at every regular session of the Legislature.

SEC. 17. The Legislature shall not pass special or local laws in any of the following enumerated cases, that is to say: regulating the jurisdiction and duties of any class of officers, or for the punishment of crime or misdemeanor; regulating the practices of courts of justice; providing for changing venue of civil and criminal cases; granting divorces; changing the names of persons; vacating roads, town plats, streets, alleys and public squares; summoning and empanelling grand and petit juries, and providing for their compensation; regulating county, township, and municipal business; regulating the election of county, township and municipal officers; for the assessment and collection of taxes for State, county and municipal purposes; providing for opening and conducting elections for State, county and municipal officers, and designating the places of voting; providing for the sale of real estate belonging to minors or other persons laboring under legal disabilities; regulating the fees of officers.

SEC. 18. In all cases enumerated in the preceding section, and in all other cases where general law can be made applicable, all laws shall be general and of uniform operation throughout the State.

SEC. 19. Provision may be made by general law for bringing suit against the State as to all liabilities now existing or hereafter originating.

SEC. 20. Lotteries are hereby prohibited in this State.

SEC. 21. The Legislature shall establish a uniform system of county, township and municipal government.

SEC. 22. The Legislature shall provide by general law for incorporating such municipal, educational, agricultural, mechanical, mining and other useful companies or associations as may be deemed necessary.

SEC. 23. Laws shall be passed regulating elections, and prohibiting, under adequate penalties, all undue influence, thereon from power, bribery, tumult, or other improper practice.

SEC. 24. Regular sessions of the Legislature may extend to sixty days, but any special session convened by the Governor shall not exceed twenty days.

SEC. 25. All property, both real and personal, of the wife, owned by her before marriage, or acquired afterward by gift, devise, descent or purchase shall be her separate property, and not liable for the debts of her husband.

SEC. 26. The Legislature shall provide for the election by the people, or appointment by the Governor, of all State, county or municipal officers not otherwise provided for by this Constitution, and fix by law their duties and compensation.

SEC. 27. Every bill which may have passed the Legislature shall, before becoming a law, be presented to the Governor; if he approves it he shall sign it, but if not, he shall return it with his objections to the house in which it originated, which house shall cause such objections to be entered upon its journals, and proceed to reconsider it; if after such reconsideration it shall pass both houses by a two-thirds vote of the members present, which vote shall be entered on the journal of each house, it shall become a law. If any bill shall not be returned within five days (Sundays excepted) after it shall have been presented to the Governor, the same shall be a law, in like manner as if he had signed it. If the Legislature by its final adjournment prevent such action, such bill shall be a law, unless the Governor, within ten days next after the adjournment, shall file such bill with his objections thereto in the office of the Secretary of State, who shall lay the same before the Legislature at its next session, and if the same shall receive two-thirds of the votes present it shall become a law.

SEC. 28. The Assembly shall have the sole power of impeachment, but a vote of two-thirds of all the members present shall be required to impeach any officer; and all impeachments shall be tried by the Senate when sitting for that purpose. The Senators shall be upon oath or affirmation, and no person shall be convicted without the concurrence of two-thirds of the Senators present.

The Chief Justice shall preside at all trials by impeachment, except in the trial of the Chief Justice, when the Lieutenant Governor shall preside.

The Governor, Lieutenant Governor, members of the Cabinet, Justices of the Supreme Court and Judges of the Circuit Court, shall be liable to impeachment for any misdemeanor in office; but judgment in such cases shall extend only to removal from office and disqualification to hold any office of honor, trust, or profit under the State: but the party convicted or acquitted shall, nevertheless, be liable to indictment, trial and punishment according to law. All other officers who shall have been appointed to office by the Governor, and by and with the consent of the Senate, may be removed from office upon the recommendation of the Governor and consent of the Senate, but they shall nevertheless be liable to indictment, trial and punishment according to law for any misdemeanor in office; all other civil officers shall be tried for misdemeanors in office in such manner as the Legislature may provide.

SEC. 29. The Legislature shall elect United States Senators in the manner prescribed by the Congress of the United States, and by this Constitution.

SEC. 30. Laws making appropriation for the salaries of public officers and other current expenses of the State shall contain provisions on no other subject.

ARTICLE VI.

EXECUTIVE DEPARTMENT.

SECTION 1. The supreme executive power of the State shall be vested in a Chief Magistrate, who shall be styled the Governor of Florida.

SEC. 2. The Governor shall be elected by the qualified electors at the same time and places of voting for the members of the Legislature, and shall hold his office for four years from the time of his installation: *Provided*, That the term of the first Governor elected under this Constitution shall expire at the opening of the regular session of the Legislature of A. D. 1873, and until his successor shall be qualified. He shall take the oath of office prescribed for all State officers.

SEC. 3. No person shall be eligible to the office of Governor who is not a qualified elector, and who has not been nine years a citizen of the United States, and three years of the State of Florida, next preceding the time of his election.

SEC. 4. The Governor shall be commander-in-chief of the military forces of the State, except when they shall be called into the service of the United States.

SEC. 5. He shall transact all executive business with the officers of the Government, civil and military, and may require information in writing from the officers of the administrative department upon any subject relating to the duties of their respective offices.

SEC. 6. He shall see that the laws are faithfully executed.

SEC. 7. When any office, from any cause, shall become vacant, and no mode is provided by this Constitution or by the laws of the State for filling such vacancy, the Governor shall have the power to fill such vacancy by granting a commission which shall expire at the next election.

SEC. 8. The Governor may, on extraordinary occasions, convene the Legislature by proclamation, and shall state to both houses, when organized, the purpose for which they have been convened, and the Legislature then shall transact no legislative business except that for which they are specially convened, or such other legislative business as the Governor may call to the attention of the Legislature while in session, except by the unanimous consent of both houses.

SEC. 9. He shall communicate by message to the Legislature at each regular session the condition of the State, and recommend such measures as he may deem expedient.

SEC. 10. In case of a disagreement between the two houses with respect to the time of adjournment, the Governor shall have power to adjourn the Legislature to such a time as he may think proper, provided it is not beyond the time fixed for the meeting of the next Legislature.

SEC. 11. The Governor shall have power to suspend the collection of fines and forfeitures, and grant reprieves for a period not exceeding sixty days, dating from the time of conviction, for all offences except in cases of impeachment. Upon conviction for treason, he shall have power to suspend the execution of sentence until the case shall be reported to the Legislature at its next session, when the Legislature shall either pardon, direct the execution of the sentence, or grant a further reprieve; and if the Legislature shall fail or refuse to make final disposition of such case, the sentence shall be enforced at such time and place as the Governor may by his order direct. The Governor shall communicate to the Legislature at the beginning of every session every case of fine or forfeiture remitted or reprieved, pardon or commutation granted, stating the name of the convict, the crime for which he was convicted, the sentence, its date, and the date of its remission, commutation, pardon, or reprieve.

SEC. 12. The Governor, Justice of the Supreme Court and Attorney-General, or a major part of them, of whom the Governor shall be one, may, upon such conditions and with such limitations and restrictions as they may deem proper, remit fines and forfeitures, commute punishments, and grant pardon after conviction, in all cases except treason and impeachments, subject to such regulations as may be provided by law relative to the manner of applying for pardons.

SEC. 13. The grants and commissions shall be in the name and under the authority of the State of Florida, sealed by the great seal of the State, signed by the Governor, and countersigned by the Secretary of State.

SEC. 14. A Lieutenant-Governor shall be elected at the same time and place, and in the same manner as the Governor, whose term of office and eligibility shall also be the same. He shall be President of the Senate, but shall have only a casting vote therein. If during a vacancy of the office of Governor the Lieutenant-Governor shall be impeached, displaced, resign, die, or become incapable of performing the duties of his office, or be absent from the State, the president *pro tempore* of the Senate shall act as Governor until the office be filled or the disability cease.

SEC. 15. In the case of the impeachment of the Governor, or his removal from office, death, inability to discharge his official duties, or resignation, the power and duties of the office shall devolve upon the Lieutenant-Governor for the residue of the term, or until the disability shall cease; but the Governor shall not, without the consent of the Legislature, be out of the State in time of war.

SEC. 16. The Governor may at any time require the opinion of the Justices of the Supreme Court as to the interpretation of any portion of this Constitution, or upon any point of law, and the Supreme Court shall render such opinion in writing.

SEC. 17. The Governor shall be assisted by a cabinet of administrative officers, consisting of a Secretary of State, Attorney General, Comptroller, Treasurer, Surveyor General, Superintendent of Public Instruction, Adjutant-General, and Commissioner of Immigration. Such officers shall be appointed by the Governor, and confirmed by the Senate, and shall hold their offices the same time as the Governor, or until their successors shall be qualified.

SEC. 18. The Governor shall, by and with the consent of the Senate, appoint all commissioned officers of the State militia.

SEC. 19. The Governor shall appoint, by and with the consent of the Senate, in each county, an Assessor of taxes and Collector of Revenue, whose duties shall be prescribed by law, and who shall hold their offices for two years, and be subject to removal upon the recommendation of the Governor and consent of the Senate. The Governor shall appoint in each county a

County Treasurer, County Surveyor, Superintendent of Common Schools, and five County Commissioners, each of whom shall hold his office for two years, the duties of which shall be prescribed by law. Such officers shall be subject to removal by the Governor, when in his judgment the public welfare will be advanced thereby: *Provided*, No officer shall be removed except for wilful neglect of duty, or a violation of the criminal laws of the State, or for incompetency.

SEC. 20. The Governor and Cabinet shall constitute a Board of Commissioners of State Institutions, which board shall have supervision of all matters connected therewith, in such manner as shall be prescribed by law.

SEC. 21. The Governor shall have power, in cases of insurrection or rebellion, to suspend the writ of *habeas corpus* within the State.

ARTICLE VII.

JUDICIAL DEPARTMENT.

SECTION 1. The judicial power of the State shall be vested in a Supreme Court, Circuit Courts, County Courts, and Justices of the Peace.

SEC. 2. The style of all process shall be, "The State of Florida," and all prosecutions shall be conducted in the name and by the authority of the same.

SEC. 3. The Supreme Court shall consist of a Chief Justice and two Associate Justices, who shall hold their offices for life, or during good behavior. They shall be appointed by the Governor and confirmed by the Senate.

SEC. 4. The majority of the Justices of the Supreme Court shall constitute a quorum for the transaction of all business. The Supreme Court shall hold three terms each year, in the Supreme Court room at the seat of government. Such terms shall commence on the Second Tuesday of October, January, and April, respectively.

SEC. 5. The Supreme Court shall have appellate jurisdiction in all cases in equity, also in all cases of law in which is involved the title to or right of possession of real estate or the legality of any tax, impost, assessment, toll, or municipal fine, or in which the demand or the value of the property in controversy exceeds 300 dollars, also in all other civil cases not included in the general subdivisions of law and equity; also in all questions of law alone, in all criminal cases in which the offences charged amount to felony. The court shall have power to issue writs of *man-*

damus, certiorari, prohibition, *quo warranto, habeas corpus,* and also all writs necessary or proper to the complete exercise of its appellate jurisdiction.

Each of the Justices shall have the power to issue writs of *habeas corpus* to any part of the State, upon petition by or on behalf of any person held in actual custody, and may make such writs returnable before himself or the Supreme Court, or before any Circuit Court in the State, or before any judge of said courts.

SEC. 6. The Supreme Court shall appoint a Clerk of the Supreme Court, who shall have his office at the Capitol, and shall be Librarian of the of the Supreme Court library; he shall hold his office until his successor is appointed and qualified.

SEC. 7. There shall be seven Circuit Judges appointed by the Governor and confirmed by the Senate, who shall hold their office for eight years. The State shall be divided into seven judicial districts, the limits of which are defined in this Constitution, and one judge shall be assigned to each circuit. Such judge shall hold two terms of his court in each county within his circuit, each year, at such times and places as shall be prescribed by law. The Chief Justice may, in his discretion, order a temporary exchange of circuits by the respective judges, or any judge to hold one or more terms in any other circuit than that to which he is assigned. The Judge shall reside in the circuit to whtch he is assigned.

SEC. 8. The Circuit Courts in their several Judicial Courts shall have original jurisdiction in all cases of equity; also in all cases at law which involve the title or the right of posession to, or the posession of, or the boundaries of real property; of the legality of any tax, impost, or assessment, toll, or municipal fine, and in all other cases in which the demand or the value of property in controversy exceeds three hundred dollars, and of the action of forcible entry and unlawful detainer, and also in all criminal cases amounting to felony. They shall have final appellate jurisdiction in all civil cases arising in the County Court in which the amount of controversy is one hundred dollars and upwards and in all cases of misdemeanor. The Circuit Courts and the Judges thereof shall have power to issue writs of mandamus, injunction, quo warranto, certiorari, and all other writs proper and necessary to the complete exercise of their jurisdiction, and also shall have power to issue writs of habeas corpus on petition by or on behalf of any person held in actual custody in their respective circuits.

SEC. 9. There shall be a County Court organized in each county. The Governor shall appoint a County Judge for each county, who shall be confirmed by the Senate, and such Judge shall hold his office for four years from the date of his commission, or until his successor is appointed and qualified.

SEC. 10. The County Court shall be a court of oyer and terminer.

SEC. 11. The County Court shall have jurisdiction of all misdemeanors and all civil cases where the amount in controversey does not exceed three hundred dollars; and its jurisdiction shall be final in all civil cases where the amount in controversey does not exceed one hundred dollars; but in no case shall the County Court have jurisdiction when the title or boundaries of real estate is in controversey, or where the jurisdiction will conflict with that of the several Courts of Record; but they may have coextensive jurisdiction with the Circuit Courts in cases of forcible entry and unlawful detention of real estate, subject to appeal to the Circuit Court. The County Court shall have full surrogate or probate powers, but subject to appeal. Provision shall be made by law for all other powers, duties and responsibilities of the County Courts and Judges. There shall be a regular trial term of the County Courts six times in each year, at such times and places as may be prescribed by law.

SEC. 12. The grand and petit jurors shall be taken from the registered votes of the respective counties.

SEC. 13. In all trials, civil and criminal, in the Circuit and County Courts, the evidence shall be reduced to writing by the clerk of the court or his deputy, under control of the court; and every witness after his examination shall have done, shall be at liberty to correct the evidence he has given, and afterwards shall sign the same; such evidence shall be filed in the office of the clerk, with the papers in the case.

SEC. 14. All pleas shall be sworn to either by the parties or their attorneys.

SEC. 15. The Governor shall appoint as many Justices of the Peace as he may deem necessary. Justices of the Peace shall have criminal jurisdiction and civil jurisdiction not to exceed fifty dollars, but this shall not extend to the trial of any person for misdemeanor or crime. The duties of Justice of the Peace shall be fixed by law. Justices of the Peace shall hold their offices during good behavior, subject to removals by the Governor at his own discretion.

SEC. 16. The Legislature may establish courts for municipal purposes only in incorporated towns and cities. All laws for the organization or government of Municipal Courts shall be general in their provisions, and be equally applicable to the Municipal Courts of all incorporated towns and cities.

SEC. 17. Any civil cause may be tried before a practicing attorney as referee upon the application of the parties, and an order from the court in whose jurisdiction the case may be authorizing such trial and appointing such referee. Such referee shall keep a complete record of the case, including the evidence taken, and such record shall be filed with the papers in the case in the office of the clerk, subject to an appeal in the manner prescribed by law.

Sec. 18. No other courts than those herein specified shall be organized in this State.

Sec. 19. The Governor by and with the advice of the Senate shall appoint a State attorney in each judicial circuit, whose duties shall be prescribed by law. He shall hold his office for four years from the date of his commission, and until his successor shall be appointed and qualified. The Governor, by and with the advice and consent of the Senate, shall appoint a Sheriff and Blerk of the Circuit Court, who shall also be Clerk of the County Court and Board of County Commissioners, Recorder, and ex-offico Auditor of the county, each of whom shall hold his office for four years. Their duties shall be prescribed by law.

Sec. 20. A constable shall be elected by the registered voters in each county for every two hundred (200) registered voters; but each county shall be entitled to at least two constables, and no county shall have more than twelve constables. They shall perform such duties under such instructions as shall be prescribed by law.

Sec. 21. Attorneys at law, who have been admitted to practice sn any court of record in any State in the Union, or to any United States court, shall be admitted to practice in any court of this State on producing evidence of having been so admitted.

ARTICLE VIII.

ADMINISTRATIVE DEPARTMENT.

Section 1. There shall be a cabinet of administrative officers, consisting of a Secretary of State, Attorney General. Comptroller. Treasurer, Surveyor General, and Superintendent of Public Instruction, Adjutant General, and Commissioner of Immigration, who shall assist the Governor in the performance of his duties.

Sec 2. The Secretary of State shall keep the records of official acts of the Legislature and executive departments of the governments, and shall, when required, lay the same, and all matters relative thereto, before either branch of the Legislature, and shall be the custodian of the great seal of the State.

SEC. 3. The Attorney General shall be the legal adviser of the Governor and of each of the Cabinet officers, and shall perform such other legal duties as the Governor may direct, or as may be provided by law. He shall be reporter for the Supreme Court.

SEC. 4. The Treasurer shall receive and keep all funds, bonds, or other securities, in such manner as may be provided by law, and shall disburse no funds, bonds or other securities, except upon the order of the Comptroller, countersigned by the Governor in such manner as shall be prescribed by law.

SEC. 5. The duties of the Comptroller shall be prescribed by law.

SEC. 6. The Surveyor General shall have the administrative supervision of all matters pertaining to the public lands, under such regulations as shall be prescribed by law.

SEC. 7. The Superintendent of Public Instruction shall have the administrative supervision of all matters pertaining to public instruction; the supervision of buildings devoted to educational purposes, and the libraries belonging to the university and the common schools. He shall organize an historical bureau for the purposes of accumulating such matter and information as may be necessary for compiling the history of the State. He shall also establish a cabinet of minerals and other natural productions.

SEC. 8. The Adjutant General shall, under the orders of the Governor, have the administrative supervision of the military department, and the supervision of the State prison, and of the quarantine of the coast, in such manner as shall be prescribed by law.

SEC. 9. The Commissioner of Immigration shall organize a Bureau of Immigration for the purposes of furnishing information and for the encouragement of immigration. The office of Commissioner of Immigration shall expire at the end of fifteen years from the ratification of this constitution, but the Legislature shall have power to continue it by law.

SEC. 10. Each officer of the cabinet shall make a full report of his official acts, of the receipts and expenditures of his office, and of the requirements of the same, to the Governor, at the beginning of each regular session of the Legislature, or whenever the Governor shall require it. Such reports shall be laid before the Legislature by the Governor at the beginning of each regular session thereof. Either house of the Legislature may at any time call upon any cabinet officer for information required by it.

ARTICLE IX.

EDUCATION.

SECTION 1. It is the paramount duty of the State to make ample provision for the education of all the children residing within its borders, without distinction or preference.

SEC. 2. The Legislature shall provide a uniform system of common schools and a university, and shall provide for the liberal maintenance of the same. Instruction in them shall be free.

SEC. 3. There shall be a Superintendent of Public Instruction, whose term of office shall be four years, and until the appointment and qualification of his successor. He shall have general supervision of the educational interests of the State. His duties shall be prescribed by law.

SEC. 4. The common school fund, the interest of which shall be exclusively applied to the support and maintenance of common schools and purchase of suitable libraries and apparatus therefor, shall be derived from the following sources:

The proceeds of all lands that have been or may hereafter be granted to the State by the United States for educational purposes. Donations by individuals for educational purposes. Appropriations by the State. The proceeds of lands or other property which may accrue to the State by escheat to forfeiture. The proceeds of all property granted to the State, when the purpose of such grant shall not be specified. All moneys which may be paid as an exemption from military duty. All fines collected under the penal laws of this State. Such portion of the *per capita* tax as may be prescribed by law for educational purposes. Twenty-five per centum of the sales of public lands which are now or hereafter may be owned by the State.

SEC. 5. A special tax of not less than one mill on the dollar of all taxable property in the State, in addition to the other means provided, shall be levied and apportioned annually for the support and maintenance of common schools.

SEC. 6. The principal of the common school fund shall remain sacred and inviolate.

SEC. 7. Provision shall be made by law for the distribution of the common school fund among the several counties of the State in proportion to the number of children residing therein between the ages of four and twenty-one years.

SEC. 8. Each county shall be required to raise annually by tax, for the support of common schools therein, a sum not less than one-half the amount apportional to each county for that year from the income of the common school fund. Any school district neglecting to establish and maintain for at least three months in each year such school or schools as may be provided by law for such district shall forfeit its portion of the common school fund during such neglect.

SEC. 9. The Superintendent of Public Instruction, Secretary of State, and Attorney-General, shall constitute a body corporate to be known as the Board of Education of Florida. The Superintendent of Public Instruction shall be President thereof. The duties of the Board of Education shall be prescribed by the Legislature.

ARTICLE X.

HOMESTEAD.

SECTION 1. A homestead, to the extent of one hundred and sixty acres of land, or the half of one acre within the limits of any incorporated city or town, owned by the head of a family, residing in this State, together with one thousand dollars in value of personal property, and the improvements on the real estate, shall be exempted from forced sale under any process of law, and the real estate shall not be alienable without the joint consent of husband and wife, when that relation exists. But no property shall be exempt from sale for taxes, or for the payment of obligations contracted for the purchase of said premises, or for the erection of improvements thereon, or for house, field or other labor performed on the same. The exemption herein provided for in a city or town shall not extend to more improvements or buildings than the residence and business houses of the owner.

SEC. 2. In addition to the exemption provided for in the first section of this article, there shall be and remain exempt from sale by any legal process in this State, to the head of a family residing in this State, such property as he or she may select to the amount of one thousand dollars: said exemption in this section shall only prevent the sale of property in cases where the debt was contracted, liability incurred, or judgment obtained before the 10th day of May, A. D. 1865. Nothing herein contained shall be construed as to exempt any property from sale for payment of the purchase-money of the same, or for the payment of taxes or labor.

SEC. 3. The exemptions provided for in sections one and two of this article shall accrue to the heirs of the party having enjoyed or taken the benefit of such exemption, and the exemption provided for in section one of this article shall apply to all debts except as specified in said section, no matter when or where the debt was contracted or liability incurred.

ARTICLE XI.

PUBLIC INSTITUTIONS.

Section 1. Institutions for the benefit of the insane, blind and deaf, and such other benevolent institutions as the public good may require, shall be fostered and supported by the State, subject to such regulations as may be provided by law.

Sec. 2. A state prison shall be established and maintained in such a manner as may be fixed by law. Provision may be made by law for the establishment and maintenance of a House of Refuge for juvenile offenders, and the Legislature shall have power to establish a home and workhouse for common vagrants.

Sec. 3. The respective courts of the State shall provide in the manner fixed by law for those of the inhabitants who by reason of age, infirmity, or misfortunes, may have claims upon the aid and sympathy of society.

ARTICLE XII.

MILITIA.

Section 1. All able-bodied male inhabitants of the State, between the ages of eighteen and forty-five years, who are citizens of the United States, or have declared their intention to become citizens thereof, shall constitute the militia of the State, but no male citizen of whatever religious creed or opinion shall be exempt from military duty except upon such conditions as may be prescribed by law.

Sec. 2. The Legislature shall provide by law for organizing and disciplining the militia of the State, for the encouragement of volunteer corps, the safe keeping of the public arms, and for a guard for the State prison.

Sec. 3. The Adjutant General shall have the grade of Major General. The Governor, by and with the consent of the Senate, shall appoint two Major Generals and four Brigadier Generals of militia; they shall take rank according to the date of their commissions. The officers and soldiers of the State militia, when uniformed, shall wear the uniform prescribed for the United States Army.

Sec. 4. The Governor shall have power to call out the militia to preserve the public peace, to execute the laws of the State, and to suppress insurrection or repel invasion.

ARTICLE XIII.

TAXATION AND FINANCE.

Section 1. The Legislature shall provide for a uniform and equal rate of taxation, and shall prescribe such regulations as shall secure a just valuation of all property, both real and personal, excepting such property as may be exempt by law for municipal, educational, literary, scientific, religious, or charitable purposes.

SEC. 2. The Legislature shall provide for raising revenue sufficient to defray the expenses of the State for each fiscal year, and also a sufficient sum to pay the principal and interest of the existing indebtedness of the State.

SEC. 3. No tax shall be levied except in pursuance of law.

SEC. 4. No moneys shall be drawn from the Treasury except in pursuance of appropriation made by law.

SEC. 5. An accurate statement of the receipts and expenditures of the public moneys shall be published with the laws of each regular session of the Legislature.

SEC. 6. The Legislature shall authorize the several counties and incorporated towns in the State to impose taxes for county and incorporation purposes, and for no other purpose, and all property shall be taxed upon the principle established for State taxation. The Legislature may also provide for levying a specific capitation tax on licenses. But the capitation tax shall not exceed one dollar per annum for all purposes, excepting for State, county, or municipal taxes.

SEC. 7. The Legislature shall have power to provide for issuing State bonds bearing interest, for securing the debt of the State, and for the erection of State buildings, support of State institutions, and perfecting public works.

SEC. 8. No tax shall be levied upon persons for the benefit of any chartered company of the State, or for paying the interest on any bonds issued by said chartered companies, counties, or corporations, for the above-mentioned purposes, and any laws to the contrary are hereby declared null and void.

ARTICLE XIV.

CENSUS AND APPORTIONMENT.

The Legislature shall, in the year one thousand eight hundred and seventy-five, and every tenth year thereafter, cause an enumeration to be made of all the inhabitants of the State; and they shall then proceed to apportion the representation among the different counties, giving to each county one representative at large, and one additional to every one thousand registered votes therein, but no county shall be entitled to more than four representatives.

The Legislature shall also, after every such enumeration, proceed to fix by law the number of Senators which shall constitute the Senate of Florida, and which shall never be less than one-fourth, nor more than one-half of the whole number of the Assembly. When any Senatorial district shall be composed of two or more counties, the counties of which such district consists shall not be entirely separated by any county belonging to another district, and no county shall be divided in forming a district, and all counties shall remain as now organized unless changed by a two-thirds vote of both houses of the Legislature.

ARTICLE XV.

SUFFRAGE AND ELIGIBILITY.

SECTION 1. Every male person of the age of twenty-one years and upwards, of whatever race, color, nationality, or previous condition, or who shall, at the time of offering to vote, be a citizen of the United States, or who shall have declared his intention to become such in conformity to the laws of the United States, and who shall have resided and had his habitation, domicil, home, and place of permanent abode in Florida for one year, and in the county for six months, next preceding the election at which he shall offer to vote, shall in such county be deemed a qualified elector at all elections under this Constitution. Every elector shall, at the time of his registration, take and subscribe to the following oath:

I, ———, do solemnly swear that I will support, protect, and defend the Constitution and Government of the United States, and the Constitution and Government of Florida, against all enemies, foreign or domestic; that I will bear true faith, loyalty, and allegiance to the same, any ordinances or resolution of any State Convention or legislation to the contrary notwithstanding, so help me God.

SEC. 2. No person under guardianship, *non compos mentis*, or insane, shall be qualified to vote at any election unless restored to civil rights.

SEC. 3. At any election at which a citizen or subject of any foreign country shall offer to vote, under the provisions of this Constitution, he shall present to the persons lawfully authorized to conduct and supervise such election a duly sealed and certified copy of his declaration of intention; otherwise he shall not be allowed to vote; and any naturalized citizen offering to vote, shall produce before said persons, lawfully authorized to conduct and supervise the election, his certificate of naturalization, or a duly sealed and certified copy thereof; otherwise he shall not be permitted to vote.

SEC. 4. The Legislature shall have power and shall enact

the necessary laws to exclude from every office of honor, power, trust or profit, civil or military, within the State, and from the right of suffrage, all persons convicted of bribery, perjury, larceny, or of infamous crime, or who shall make or become, directly or indirectly, interested in any bet or wager, the result of which shall depend upon any election; or who shall hereafter fight a duel, or send or accept a challenge to fight, or who shall be a second to either party, or be the bearer of such challenge or acceptance; but the legal disability shall not accrue until after trial and conviction by due form of law.

SEC. 5. In all elections by the Legislature the vote shall be *viva voce*, and in all elections by the people the vote shall be by ballot.

SEC. 6. The Legislature at its first session after the ratification of this Constitution, shall by law provide for the registration, by the Clerks of the Circuit Court in each county, of all the legally qualified voters in such county, and for the returns of elections; and shall also provide that after the completion, from time to time, of such registration, no person not duly registered according to law shall be allowed to vote.

SEC. 7. The Legislature shall enact laws requiring educational qualifications for electors after the year one thousand eight hundred and eighty, but no such laws shall be made applicable to any elector who may have registered or voted at any election previous thereto.

ARTICLE XVI.

SCHEDULE.

SECTION 1. That all ordinances and resolutions heretofore passed by any convention of the people, and all acts and resolutions of the Legislature conflicting or inconsistent with the Constitution of the United States and the statutes thereof, and with this constitution, and in derogation of the existence or position of the State as one of the States of the United States of America, are hereby declared null and void, and of no effect.

SEC. 2. That all acts and resolutions of the General Assembly, and all official acts of the civil officers of the State, not inconsistent with the provisions of the Constitution and statutes of the United States, or with the Constitution, or with any ordinance or resolution adopted by the convention, and which have not been, and are not by this constitution, annulled, are in force, and shall be considered and esteemed as the laws of the State until such acts or resolutions shall be repealed by the Legislature of the State or this convention.

Sec. 3. All laws of the State passed by the so-called General Assembly since the 10th day of January, A. D. 1868, not conflicting with the word and spirit of the Constitution and laws of the United States, or with this constitution, shall be valid; all writs, acts, proceedings, judgments, and decrees of the so-called courts of the State, when actual service was made, as the defendant, all executions and sales made thereunder, and all acts, orders and proceedings of the Judges of Probate, and of executors, administrators, guardians, and trustees, provided they were in conformity with the laws then in force, and did not conflict with the Constitution and the laws of the United States and this constitution, shall be valid; the sales of the property or effects of deceased persons shall not prevent the widow from claiming said property in kind, in whosoever hands the same may be found, where the sale had not been made for the purpose of paying the debts of deceased, and where other than lawful money of the United States was obtained for said property.

Nothing herein contained shall be so construed as to make any one who was an officer of any court, or who acted under the authority of any court individually liable, provided they acted strictly in accordance with what was then considered the law of the State, and not conflicting with the laws and Constitution of the United States.

All fines, penalties, forfeitures, obligations, and escheats heretofore accruing to the State of Florida shall continue to accrue to the use of the State.

All recognizances heretofore taken shall remain valid, and all bonds executed to the Governor of the State of Florida, either before or since the 10th day of January, A. D. 1861, or to any other officer of the State, in his official capacity, shall be of full force and virtue, for the uses therein respectively expressed, and may be sued for and recovered accordingly, unless they were contrary to the laws of the United States or this constitution, or to any ordinance or resolution adopted by the convention; also all criminal prosecutions which have arisen may be prosecuted to judgment and execution in the name of the State.

All actions at law or suits in chancery, or any proceedings pending in the courts of this State, either prior to or subsequent to the 10th day of January, A. D. 1861, shall continue in all respects valid, and may be prosecuted to judgment and decree.

All judgments and decrees rendered in civil causes in any of the courts of the State during the period of time above specified, are hereby declared of full force, validity, and effect, provided that unless otherwise provided in this constitution, the statute of limitation shall not be pleaded upon any claim in the hands of any person for the period of time between the

10th day of January, A. D., 1861, and the 25th day of October, A. D., 1865, whether proceedings at law had been commenced before the 25th day of October, 1865, or not; provided further, that all claims of widows, minors, and decendents, which were not barred by the statutesof this State, on the 10th day of January, A. D., 1861, shall be considered good and valid for the period of two years for the ratification of this constitution.

SEC. 4. That State treasury notes, all bonds issued, and all other liabilities contracted by the State of Florida, or any county or city thereof, on and after the 16th day of January, A. D., 1861, and before the 26th day of Obtober, A. D., 1865, except such liabilities as may be due to the seminary or school fund, be and are declared null and void, and the Legislature shall have no power to provide for the payment of the same or any part thereof, but this shall not be construed so as to invalidate any authorized liabilities of the State contracted prior to the 10th day of January A. D., 1861, or subsequent to the 25th day of October, A. D., 1865.

SEC. 5. No money shall ever be appropriated by this State to reimburse purchasers of United States land who purchased the same of the State of Florida.

SEC. 6. All proceedings, decisions, or actions accomplished by civil or military officers acting under authority of the United States subsequent to the 10th day of January, 1861, and prior to the final restoration of the State to the government of the United States, are hereby declared valid, and shall not be subject to adjudication in the courts of this State; nor shall any person acting in the capacity of a soldier or officer of the United States, civil or military, be subject to arrest for any act performed by him pursuant to authorized instruction from his superior officers during the period of time above designated.

SEC. 7. That in all cases where judgments have been obtained against citizens of the State after the 10th day of January, 1861, previous to the 25th day of October, 1865, and where actual service was not made on the person of any department. Such defendant, not served with process, may appear in court within one year after the adoption of this constitution, and make oath that injustice has been done and that he or she has a good and valid defence, and upon making such oath and filing said defence the proceedings in the judgment shall cease until the defence is heard.

ARTICLE XVII.

MISCELLANEOUS.

SECTION 1. Any person debarred from holding office in the State of Florida by the third section of the fourteenth article of the proposed amendment to the Constitution of the United States, which is as follows:

"No person shall be a Senator or Represenative in Congress, or elector of President or Vice-President, or hold any office, civil or military, under the United States or under any State, who, having previously taken an oath as a member of Congress, or as an officer of the United States, or as a member of any State Legislature, or as an executive or judicial officer of any State, to support the Constitution of the United States, shall have engaged in insurrection or rebellion against the same, or given aid and comfort to enemies thereof. But Congress may, by a vote of two-thirds of each house, remove such disability," is hereby debarred from holding office in this State: *Provided*, That whenever such disability from holding office shall be removed from any person by the Congress of the United States, the removal of such disability shall also apply to this State, and such person shall be restored, in all respects, to the rights of citizenship as herein provided for electors.

SEC. 2. Any person elected to the Senate of the United States by the Legislature of this State, or any person elected by the people, or appointed to office by the Governor of the State, or by any officer of the State, under the provisions of the Constitution adopted by the convention of the people, convened on the 25th day of October, 1865, shall not be empowered to hold such office after the same position or office shall have been filled by election or appointment under the provisions of this Constitution. *Provided*, That all officers holding office under the provisions of the Constitution adopted the 25th day of October, A. D. 1856, and not provided for in this Constitution, shall continue to hold their respective offices, and discharge the duties thereof, until the Governor shall, by his proclamation, declare such offices vacant.

SEC. 3. The several judicial circuits of the Circuit Courts, shall be as follows: The first judicial circuits shall be composed of the counties of Escambia, Santa Rosa, Walton, Holmes, Washington and Jackson; the 2d judicial circuit shall be composed of the counties of Gadsden, Liberty, Calhoun, Franklin, Leon, Wakulla and Jefferson; the 3d judicial circuit shall be composed of the counties of Madison, Taylor, Lafayette, Hamilton, Suwanee and Columbia; the 4th judicial circuit shall be composed of the counties of Nassau, Duval, Baker, Bradford, Clay and St. Johns; the 5th judicial circuit shall be composed of the counties of Putnam, Alachua, Levy, Marion and Sumpter; the 6th judicial circuit shall be composed of the counties of Hernando, Hillsborough, Manatee, Polk and Monroe; the 7th judicial circuit shall be composed of the counties of Volusia, Brevard, Orange and Dade.

Sec. 4. The salary of the Governor of the State shall be $5,000 per annum; that of the Chief Justice shall be $4,500; that of each Associate Justice shall be $4,000; that of each Judge of the Circuit Court shall be $3,500; that of the Lieutenant-Governor shall be $2,500; that of each Cabinet officer shall be $3,000. The pay of the members of the Senate and House of Bepresentatives shall be $500 per annum, and in addition thereto ten cents per miles for each mile traveled from their respective places of residence to the capital, and the same to return. But such distances shall be estimated by the shortest general public thoroughfare. All other officers of the State shall be paid by fees as per diem fixed by law.

Sec. 5. The Legislature shall appropriate $2,000 each year for the purchase of such books for the Supreme Court library as the said Court shall direct.

Sec. 6. The salary of each officer shall be payable quarterly upon his own requisition.

Sec. 7. The tribe of Indians located in the southern portion of the State, and known as the Seminole Indians, shall be entitled to one member in each house of the Legislature. Such members shall have all the rights, privileges and remuneration as other members of the Legislature. Such members shall be elected by the members of their tribe, in the manner prescribed for all elections by this Constitution. The tribe shall be represented only by a member of the same, and in no case by a white man : *Provided*, That the representatives of the Seminole Indians shall not be a bar to the representative of any county by the citizens thereof.

Sec. 8. The Legislature may at any time impose such tax on the Indians as they may deem proper; and such imposition of tax shall constitute the Indians citizens, and they shall thenceforward be entitled to all the priviliges of other citizens, and thereafter be barred of special representation.

Sec. 9. In addition to other crimes and misdemeanors for which an officer may be impeached and tried, shall be included drunkenness and other dissipations; incompetency, malfeasance in office, gambling or any conduct detrimental to good morals, shall be considered sufficient cause for impeachment and conviction. Any officer when impeached by the Assembly shall be deemed under arrest, and shall be disqualified from performing any of the duties of his office until acquitted by the Senate. But any officer so impeached and in arrest may demand his trial by the Senate within ten days from the date of his impeachment.

SEC. 10. The following shall be the oath of office for each officer in the State, including members of the Legislature: "I do solemnly swear that I will support, protect and defend the Constitution and Government of the United States, and of the State of Florida, against all enemies, domestic or foreign, and that I will bear true faith, loyalty and allegiance to the same, and that I am entitled to hold office under this Constitution. That I will well and faithfully perform all the duties of the office of ———, which I am about to enter: so help me God."

SEC. 11. The Legislature may provide for the donation of the public lands to actual settlers. But such donation shall not exceed one hundred and sixty acres to any one person.

SEC. 12. All county officers shall hold their respective offices at the county seats of their counties.

SEC. 13. The Legislature shall provide for the speedy publication of all statutes and laws of general nature. All decisions of the Supreme Court, and all laws and judicial decisions shall be for free publication by any person. But no judgment of the Supreme Court shall take effect and be operative until the opinion of the court in such a case shall be filed with the clerk of said court.

SEC. 14. The Legislature shall not create any office, the term of which shall be longer than four years.

SEC. 15. The Governor, Cabinet and Supreme Court shall keep their offices at the seat of Government. But in case of invasion or violent epidemics, the Governor may direct that the offices of the Government shall be removed temporarily to some other place. The session of the Legislature may be adjourned for the same cause to some other place; but in such case of removal, all the Departments of the Government shall be removed to one place. But such removal shall not continue longer than the necessity for the same shall continue.

SEC. 16. A plurality of votes given at an election by the people shall constitute a choice when not otherwise provided for by this Constitution.

SEC. 17. The term of the State officers elected at the first election under this Constitution, not otherwise provided for, shall continue until the first Tuesday of January, A. D. 1873, and until the installation of their successors, excepting the members of the Legislature.

SEC. 18. Each county and incorporated city shall make pro-

JOHNATHAN C. GIBBS.

vision for the support of its own officers, subject to such regulations as may be prescribed by law. Each county shall make provision for building a court-house and jail, and for keeping the same in good repair.

SEC. 19. If at the meeting of the Senate at any session the Lieutenant-Governor has not qualified or is not present, the Senate shall elect one of its members as temporary President before proceeding to other business.

SEC. 20. The Legislature shall at the first session adopt a seal for the State, and such seal shall be the size of the American silver dollar. But said seal shall not again be changed after its adoption by the Legislature; and the Governor shall, by his proclamation, announce that the said seal has become the great seal of the State.

SEC. 21. The Governor, Lieutenant-Governor, and all the State officers elected by the people shall be installed on the first day of the meeting of the Legislature, and immediately assume the duties of their respective offices.

SEC. 22. The Governor and Lieutenant Governor shall have been, before their election to office, nine years a citizen of the United States, and three years a citizen of the State. All other officers shall have been one year a citizen of the State, and six months a citizen of the county from which they are elected or appointed. No person shall be eligible to any office unless he be a registered voter.

SEC. 23. The Governor or any State officer is hereby prohibited from giving certificates of election or other credentials to any person as having been elected to the House of Representatives of the United States Congress, or the United States Senate, who has not been two years a citizen of the State, and nine years a citizen of the United States, and a registered voter.

SEC. 24. The property of all corporations, whether heretofore or hereafter incorporated, shall be subject to taxation, unless such corporatian be for religious, educational, or charitable purposes.

SEC. 25. All bills, bonds, notes, and evidences of debt outstanding and unpaid, given for or in consideration of bonds or treasury notes of the so-called Confederate States, or notes and bonds of this State paid and redeemable in the bonds and notes of the Confederate States, are hereby declared null and void, and no action shall be maintained thereon in the courts of this State.

SEC. 26. It shall be the duty of the courts to consider that there is a failure of consideration, and it shall be so held by the courts of this State, upon all deeds or bills of sale given for slaves with covenant or warranty of title or soundness, or both; upon all bills, bonds, notes, or other evidences of debt, given for or in consideration of slaves, which are now outstanding and unpaid, and no action shall be maintained thereon; and all judgments and decrees rendered in any of the courts of this State since the 10th of January, A. D. 1861, upon all deeds or bills of sale, or upon any bond, bill, note, or other evidence of debt based upon the sale or purchase of slaves, are hereby declared set aside, and the plea of failure of consideration shall be held a good defence in all actions to said suit: and that when money was due previous to the 10th day of January, 1861, and slaves were given in consideration for such money, those shall be deemed a failure of consideration for the debt: *Provided*, That settlements and compromises of such transactions made by the parties thereto shall be respected.

SEC. 27. All persons who, as alien enemies under the sequestration act of the so-called Confederate Congress, and now resident of the State, had property sequestered and sold by any person acting under a law of the so-called Confederate States, or the State of Florida, subsequent to the 10th of January, A. D. 1861, and prior to the 1st of January, 1865, shall be empowered to file a bill in equity in the Circuit Court of the State, and shall be entitled to obtain judgment against the State for all damages sustained by said sale and detention of property. The court shall estimate the damages upon the assessed valuation of the property in question in the year A. D. 1870, with interest, at six per cent. from the time the owner was deprived of the same. But all judgments against the State shall be paid only in certificates of indebtedness, redeemable in State lands. Said certificates shall be issued by the Governor, countersigned by the Secretary of State and by the Comptroller, upon the decree of the court. Oral testimony shall be sufficient to establish the fact of a sale having been made.

SEC. 28. There shall be no civil or political distinction in this State on account of race, color, or previous condition of servitude, and the Legislature shall have no power to prohibit by law any class of persons on account of race, color, or previous condition of servitude, to vote or hold any office, beyond the conditions prescribed by this constituion.

SEC. 29. The apportionment for the Assembly shall be as follows: Escambia, two; Santa Rosa, one; Walton, one; Holmes, one; Washington, one; Jackson, three; Calhoun, one; Gadsden, two; Franklin, one; Liberty, one; Wakulla, one; Leon, four; Jefferson, three; Madison, two; Taylor, one; Hamilton, one; Suwanee, one; Lafayette, one; Alachua, two; Columbia, two;

Baker, one; Bradford. one; Nassau, one; Duval, two; Clay, one; St. John's, one; Putnam, one; Marion, two; Levy, one; Volusia, one; Orange, one; Brevard, one; Dade, one; Hillsborough, one; Hernando, one; Sumter, one; Polk, one; Manatee, one; and Monroe, one. There shall be twenty-four senatorial districts, which shall be as follows, and shall be known by their respective numbers from one to twenty-four inclusive. The first senatorial district shall be composed of Escambia county; the second, of Santa Rosa and Walton; the third, of Jackson; the fourth, of Volusia and Washington; the fifth, of Calhoun and Franklin; the sixth, of Gadsden; the seventh, of Liberty and Wakulla; the eighth, of Leon; the ninth of Jefferson; the tenth, of Madison; the eleventh. of Hamilton and Suwanee; the twelfth, of Lafayette and Taylor; the thirteenth, of Alabhua and Levy; the foureenth, of Columbia; the fifteenth. of Bradford and Clay; the sixteenth. of Baker and Nassau; the seventeenth. of St. John's and Putnam; the eighteenth, of Duval; the nineteenth, of Marion; the twentieth, of Volusia and Orange; the twenty-first. of Dade and Brevard; the twenty-second, of Hillsborough and Hernando; the twenty-third, of Sumter and Polk; the twenty-fourth, of Manatee and Monroe: and each senatorial district shall be entitled to one Senator.

SEC. 30. No person shall ever be appointed a Judge of the Supreme Court or Circuit Court who is not 25 years of age and practicing attorney.

SEC. 31. The Legislature shall, as soon as convenient, adopt a State emblem having the design of the great seal of the State impressed upon a white ground of six feet six inches fly and six feet deep.

ARTICLE XVIII.

AMENDMENTS.

Any amendment or amendments to this Constitution may be proposed in either branch of the Legislature; and if the same shall be agreed upon by a two-thirds vote of all the members elected to each of the two houses, such proposed amendment or amendments shall be entered on their respective journals, with the yeas and nays thereon, and referred to the Legislature then next to be chosen, and shall be published for three months next preceding the time of making such choice; and if, in the Legislature next chosen as aforesaid, such proposed amendment or amendments shall be agreed to by a two-thirds vote of all the members elected to each house, then it should be the duty of the Legislature to submit such proposed amendment or amendments to the people in such manner and at such time as the Legislature may prescribe; and if the people shall approve and ratify such amendment or amendments by a majority of the electors qualified to vote for members of the Legislature voting thereon, such amendment or amendments shall become a part of the Constitution.

SEC. 2. If at any time the Legislature, by a vote of a majority of all the members elected to each of the two houses, shall determine that it is necessary to cause a revision of this entire Constitution, such determination shall be entered on their respective journals, with the yeas and nays thereon, and referred to the Legislature then next to be chosen, and shall be published for three months next preceding the time of making such choice.

And if in the Legislature next chosen aforesaid such proposed revision shall be agreed to by a majority of all the members elected to each house, then it shall be the duty of the Legislature to recommend to the electors of the next election for members of the Legislature to vote for or against a convention; and if it shall appear that a majority of the electors voting at such election shall have voted in favor of calling a convention, the Legislature shall, at its next session, provide by law for a convention, to be holden within six months after the passage of such law, and such convention shall consist of a number of members not less than both branches of the Legislature.

In determiniug what is a majority of the electors voting at such election, reference shall be had to the highest number of votes cast at such election for the candidates for any office or on any question.

APPENDIX C.

FLORIDA.

MESSAGE FROM THE PRESIDENT OF THE UNITED STATES,

Transmitting papers relating to proceedings in the State of Florida.— May 29, 1868—Referred to the Committee on Reconstruction and ordered to be printed.

To the Senate and House of Representatives:

I transmit to Congress the accompanying documents, which are the only papers that have been submitted to me relating to the proceedings to which they refer in the State of Florida.

ANDREW JOHNSON.

Washington, D. C., May 27, 1868.

WASHINGTON, D. C., May 27, 1868.

SIR: In compliance with a provision of an Act of the United States Congress, entitled "An Act supplementary to an Act to provide a more efficient government in the rebel States," I have the honor, as President of the Constitutional Convention of the State of Florida, herewith to transmit to you a copy of the Constitution framed and adopted by the convention, and ratified by the people of Florida at a duly authorized election held on the 4th, 5th and 6th instant.

I am, sir, with great respect, your obedient servant,

HORATIO JENKINS, JR.,
President of the Constitutional Convention, State of Florida.

His Excellency, ANDREW JOHNSON,
President of the United States.

CONSTITUTION OF THE STATE OF FLORIDA.

PREAMBLE.

We, the people of the State of Florida, grateful to Almighty God for our freedom, in order to secure its blessings and form a more perfect government, insuring domestic tranquillity, maintaining public order, perpetuating liberty and guaranteeing equal civil and political rights to all, do establish this Constitution.

DECLARATION OF RIGHTS.

SECTION 1. All men are by nature free and equal, and have certain inalienable rights, among which are those of enjoying and defending life and liberty, acquiring, possessing and protecting property, and pursuing and obtaining safety and happiness.

SEC. 2. All political power is inherent in the people. Government is instituted for the protection, security and benefit of its citizens; and they have the right to alter or amend the same whenever the public good may require it, but the paramount allegiance of every citizen is due to the Federal Government, and no power exists with the people of this State to dissolve its connection therewith.

SEC. 3. This State shall ever remain a member of the American Union; the people thereof a part of the American nation; and any attempt from whatever source, or upon whatever pretence, to dissolve said Union, or to sever said nation, shall be resisted with the whole power of the State.

SEC. 4. The right of trial by jury shall be secured to all, and remain inviolate forever; but in all civil cases a jury trial may be waived by the parties, in the manner to be prescribed by law.

SEC. 5. The free exercise and enjoyment of all religious profession and worship shall forever be allowed in this State, and no person shall be rendered incompetent as a witness on account of his religious opinions; but the liberty of conscience hereby secured shall not be so construed as to justify licentiousness, or practices subversive of the peace and safety of the State.

SEC. 6. The privilege of the writ of habeas corpus shall not be suspended, unless when in case of invasion or rebellion the public safety may require its suspension.

SEC. 7. Excessive bail shall not be required, nor excessive fines imposed, nor cruel or unusual punishments inflicted, nor shall witnesses be unreasonably detained.

SEC. 8. All persons shall be bailable by sufficient sureties, unless for capital offences when the proof is evident or the presumption great.

SEC. 9. No person shall be tried for a capital or otherwise infamous crime, except in cases of impeachment, and in cases of the militia when in active service in time of war, or in which the State may keep, with the consent of Congress, in time of peace, and in cases of petit larceny under the regulation of the Legislature, unless on presentment and indictment by a grand jury; and in any trial by any court the party accused shall be allowed to appear and defend in person and with counsel, as in civil actions. No person shall be subject to be twice put in jeopardy for the same offence, nor shall be compelled in any criminal case to be a witness against himself, nor be deprived of life, liberty or property without due process of law; nor shall private property be taken without just compensation.

SEC. 10. Every citizen may fully speak and write his sentiments on all subjects, being responsible for the abuse of that right, and no law shall be passed to restrain or abridge the liberty of speech or the press. In all criminal prosecutions and civil actions for libel the truth may be given in evidence to the jury, and if it shall appear that the matter charged as libellous is true, but was published for good motives, the party shall be acquitted or exonerated.

SEC. 11. The people shall have the right to assemble together, to consult for the common good, to instruct their representatives, and to petition the Legislature for a redress of grievances.

SEC. 12. All laws of a general nature shall have a uniform operation.

SEC. 13. The military shall be subordinate to civil power.

SEC. 14. No soldier shall, in time of peace, be quartered in any house except with the consent of the owners, nor in time of war, except in manner prescribed by law.

SEC. 15. Representatives shall be apportioned according to population, as well as may be, but no county shall have more than four Representatives or less than one Representative in the Assembly.

SEC. 16. No person shall be imprisoned for debt, except in case of fraud.

SEC. 17. No bill of attainder, or ex post facto law, or laws impairing the obligations of contracts shall ever be passed.

Foreigners who are, or who may hereafter become, bona fide residents of the State, shall enjoy the same rights in respect to posession, enjoyment and inheritance of property as native born citizens.

SEC. 19. Neither slavery nor involuntary servitude, unless for the punishment of crime, shall ever be tolerated in this State.

SEC. 20. The rights of the people to be secure in their

persons, houses and effects, against unreasonable seizures and searches, shall not be violated; and no warrants issued but in probable cause, supported by oath or affirmation particularly describing the place or places to be searched, and the person or persons and thing or things to be seized.

SEC. 21. Treason against the State shall consist only in levying war against it, adhering to its enemies, or giving them aid and comfort; and no person shall be convicted of treason unless on the testimony of two witnesses to the same covert act or confession in open court.

SEC. 22. The people shall have the right to bear arms in defence of themselves and of the lawful authority of the State.

SEC. 23. No preference can be given by law to any church, sect or mode of worship.

SEC. 24. This enunciation of rights shall not be construed to impair or deny others retained by the people.

ARTICLE I.

BOUNDARIES.

The boundaries of the State of Florida shall be as follows: Commencing at the mouth of the river Perdido; from thence up the middle of said river to where it intersects the south boundary line of the State of Alabama and the thirty-first degree of north latitude; thence due east to the Chattahoochee river; thence down the middle of said river to its confluence with the Flint river; from thence straight to the head of the St. Mary's river; thence down the middle of said river to the Atlantic Ocean; thence southeastwardly along the coast to the edge of the Gulf Stream; thence southwestwardly along the edge of the Gulf Stream, and Florida reefs to and including the Tortugas islands; thence northeastwardly to a point three leagues from the main land; thence northwestwardly three leagues from the land to a point west of the mouth of the Perdido river; thence to the place of beginning.

ARTICLE II.

SEAT OF GOVERNMENT.

The seat of government shall be and remain permanent at the city of Tallahassee, in the county of Leon, until otherwise located by the majority vote of the people.

ARTICLE III.

DISTRIBUTION OF POWERS.

The powers of the government of the State of Florida shall be divided into three departments, to wit: legislative, executive, and judicial, and no person properly belonging to one of the departments shall exercise any functions appertaining to either of the others, except in those cases expressly provided for by this Constitution.

ARTICLE IV.

LEGISLATIVE DEPARTMENT.

SEC. 1 The legislative authority of this State shall be vested in a Senate and Assembly, which shall be designated the "Legislature of the State of Florida," and the sessions thereof shall be held at the seat of government of the State.

SEC. 2 The sessions of the Legislature shall be annual, the first sessions on the second Monday of June, A. D. 1868, and thereafter on the first Tuesday after the first Monday of January, commencing in the year A. D. 1869. The Governor may in the interim convene the same in extra session by his proclamation.

SEC. 3. The members of the Assembly shall be chosen biennially, those of the first Legislature on the first Monday, Tuesday and Wednesday of May, A. D. 1868, and thereafter on the first Tuesday after the first Monday of November commencing with the year A. D. 1870.

SEC. 4. Senators shall be chosen for the term of four years, at the same time and place as members of the Assembly: *Provided*, That the Senators elected at the first election from the senatorial districts designated by even numbers shall vacate their seats at the expiration of two years, and thereafter all Senators shall be elected for the term of four years, so that one-half of the whole number shall be elected biennially.

SEC 5. Senators and members of the Assembly shall be duly qualified electors in the respective counties and districts which they represent.

SEC. 6. Each house shall judge of the qualifications, elections and returns of its own members, choose its own officers, except the President of the Senate, determine the rules of its proceedings, and may punish its members for disorderly conduct, and, with the concurrence of two-thirds of all the members present, expel a member.

SEC. 7. Either house, during the session, may punish by

imprisonment any person not a member who shall have been guilty of disorderly or contemptuous conduct in its presence, but such imprisonment shall not extend beyond the final adjournment of the session.

SEC. 8. A majority of each house shall constitute a quorum to do business, but a smaller number may adjourn from day to day, and may compel the presence of absent members, in such manner and under such penalties as each house may prescribe.

SEC. 9. Any person who shall be convicted of embezzlement or defalcation of the funds of the State, or of having given or offered a bribe to secure his election or appointment to office, or of having received a bribe to aid in the procurement of office for any other person, shall be disqualified from holding any office of honor, profit or trust in the State; and the Legislature shall, as soon as practicable, provide by law for the punishment of such embezzlement, defalcation, or bribery, as a felony

SEC. 10. Each house shall keep a journal of its own proceedings, which shall be published, and the yeas and nays of the members of either house on any question shall, at the desire of any three members present, be entered on the journal.

SEC. 11. The doors of each house shall be kept open during its session, except the Senate while sitting in executive session, and neither shall, without the consent of the other, adjourn for more than three days, or to any other town than that in which they may be holding their session.

SEC. 12. Any bill may orginate in either house of the Legislature, and after being passed in one house may be amended in the other.

SEC. 13. The enacting clause of every law shall be as follows: "The people of the State of Florida, represented in Senate and Assembly, do enact as follows:"

SEC. 14. Each law enacted in the Legislature shall embrace but one subject and matter properly connected therewith, which subject shall be briefly expressed in the title, and no law shall be amended or revised by reference to its title only, but in such case the Act as revised, or section as amended, shall be re-enacted and published at length.

SEC. 15. Every bill shall be read by sections on three several days in each house, unless in case of emergency two-thirds of the house where such bill may be pending shall deem it expedient to dispense with this rule; but the reading of a bill by sections on its final passage shall in no case be dispensed with; and the vote on the final passage of every bill or joint resolution shall be taken by yeas and nays, to be entered on the journal of each house, and a majority of the members present in each house shall be necessary to pass every bill or joint resolution; and all bills or joint resolutions so passed shall be signed by the presiding officers of the respective houses, and by the Secretary of the Senate and Clerk of the Assembly.

SEC. 16. No money shall be drawn from the Treasury except by appropriation made by law, and accurate statements of the receipts and expenditures of the public money shall be attached to and published with the laws passed at every regular session of the Legislature.

SEC. 17. The Legislature shall not pass special or local laws in any of the following enumerated cases: That is to say, regulating the jurisdiction and duties of any class of officers, or for the punishment of crime or misdemeanor; regulating the practices of courts of justice; providing for changing venue of civil and criminal cases; granting divorces; changing the names of persons; vacating roads, town plats, streets, alleys and public squares; summoning and impanelling grand and petit juries and providing for their compensation; regulating county, township and municipal business; regu'ating the election of county, township and municipal officers: for the assessment and collection of taxes for State, county and municipal purposes; providing for opening and conducting elections for State, county and municipal officers, and designating the places of voting; providing for the sale of real estate belonging to minors or other persons laboring under legal disabilities; regulating the fees of officers.

SEC. 18. In all cases enumerated in the preceding section, and in all cases where general law can be made applicable, all laws shall be general and of uniform operation throughout the State.

SEC. 19. Provision may be made by general law for bringing suit against the State as to all liabilities now existing or hereafter originating.

SEC. 20. Lotteries are hereby prohibited in this State.

SEC. 21. The Legislature shall establish a uniform system of county, township and municipal government.

SEC. 22. The Legislature shall provide by general law for incorporating such municipal, educational, agricultural, mechanical, mining and other useful companies or association as may be deemed necessary.

SEC. 23. No person who is not a qualified elector of this State, or any person who shall have been convicted of bribery, forgery, perjury, larceny or other high crime, unless restored to civil rights, shall be permitted to serve on juries.

SEC. 24. Laws shall be passed regulating elections and prohibiting, under adequate penalties, all undue influence thereon from power, bribery, tumult or other improper practice.

Sec. 25. Regular sessions of the Legislature may extend to sixty days; but any special session convened by the Governor shall not exceed twenty days.

Sec. 26. All property, both real and personal, of the wife owned by her before marriage or acquired afterward by gift, devise, descent or purchase, shall be her separate property and not liable for the debts of her husband.

Sec. 27. The Legislature shall provide for the election by the people or appointment by the Governor of all State, county or municipal officers not otherwise provided for by this Constitution, and fix by law their duties and compensation.

Sec. 28. Every bill which may have passed the Legislature shall, before becoming a law, be presented to the Governor. If he approves it he shall sign it; but if not, he shall return it with his objections to the house in which it originated, which house shall cause such objections to be entered upon its journals and proceed to reconsider it. If after such reconsideration it shall pass both houses by a two-thirds vote of the members present, which vote shall be entered upon the journal of each house, it shall become a law. If any bill shall not be returned within five days (Sundays excepted) after it shall have been presented to the Governor, the same shall be a law in like manner as if he had signed it. If the Legislature by its final adjournment prevent such action, such bill shall be a law unless the Governor within ten days next after the adjournment shall file such bill with his objection thereto in the office of the Secretary of State, who shall lay the same before the Legislature at its next session, and if the same shall receive two-thirds of the votes present it shall become a law.

Sec. 29. The Assembly shall have the sole power of impeachment; but a vote of two-thirds of all the members present shall be required to impeach any officer, and all impeachments shall be tried by the Senate. When sitting for that purpose the Senators shall be upon oath or affirmation, and no person shall be convicted without the concurrence of two-thirds of the Senators present. The Chief Justice shall preside at all trials by impeachment, except in the trial of the Chief Justice, when the Lieutenant-Governor shall preside. The Governor, Lieutenant-Governor, members of the Cabinet, Justices of the Supreme Court and Judges of the Circuit Court, shall be liable to impeachment for any misdemeanor in office; but judgment in such cases shall extend only to removal from office and disqualification to hold any office of honor, trust, or profit under the State; but the party convicted or acquitted shall, nevertheless, be liable to indictment, trial and punishment according to law. All other officers who shall have been appointed to office by the Governor, and by and with the consent of the Senate, may be removed from office upon the recommendation of the Governor and consent of the Senate, but they shall nevertheless be liable to indictment, trial and punishment according to law for any misdemeanor in office; all other civil officers shall be tried for misdemeanors in office in such manner as the Legislature may provide.

SEC. 29. Laws making appropriation for the salaries of public officers and other current expenses of the State shall contain provisions on no other subject.

SEC. 30. The Legislature shall elect United States Senators in the manner prescribed by the Congress of the United States, and by this Constitution.

ARTICLE V.

EXECUTIVE DEPARTMENT.

SECTION 1. The supreme executive power of the State shall be vested in a Chief Magistrate, who shall be styled the Governor of Florida.

SEC. 2. The Governor shall be elected by the qualified electors at the time and places of voting for the members of the Legislature, and shall hold his office for four years from the time of his installment: *Provided*, That the term of the first Governor elected under this Constitution shall expire at the opening of the regular session of the Legislature of A. D. 1873, and until his successor shall be qualified. He shall take the oath of office prescribed for all State officers.

SEC. 3. No person shall be eligible to the office of Governor who is not a qualified elector, and who has not been nine years a citizen of the United States, and three years of the State of Florida, next preceding the time of his election.

SEC 4. The Governor shall be commander-in-chief of the military forces of the State, except when they shall be called into the service of the United States.

SEC. 5. He shall transact all executive business with the officers of the Government, civil and military, and may require information in writing from the officers of the administrative department upon any subject relating to the duties of their respective offices.

SEC. 6. He shall see that the laws are faithfully executed.

SEC. 7. When any office, from any cause, shall become vacant, and no mode is provided by this Constitution or by the laws of the State for filling such vacancy, the Governor shall have the power to fill such vacancy by granting a commission which shall expire at the next election.

SEC. 8. The Governor may, on extraordinary occasions, convene the Legislature by proclamation, and shall state to both houses, when organized, the purpose for which they have been convened, and the Legislature then shall transact no legislative business except that for which they are specially convened, or such other legislative business as the Governor may call to the attention of the Legislature while in session, except by the unanimous consent of both houses.

SEC 9. He shall communicate by message to the Legislature at each regular session the condition of the State, and recommend such measures as he may deem expedient.

SEC. 10. In case of a disagreement between the two houses with respect to the time of adjournment, the Governor shall have power to adjourn the Legislature to such a time as he may think proper, provided it is not beyond the time fixed for the meeting of the next Legislature.

SEC. 11. The Governor shall have power to suspend the collection of fines and forfeitures, and grant reprieves for a period not exceeding sixty days, dating from the time of conviction, for all offences except in cases of impeachment. Upon conviction for treason, he shall have power to suspend the execution of sentence until the case shall be reported to the Legislature at its next session, when the Legislature shall either pardon, direct the execution of the sentence, or grant a further reprieve; and if the Legislature shall fail or refuse to make final disposition of such case, the sentence shall be enforced at such time and place as the Governor may by his order direct. The Governor shall communicate to the Legislature at the beginning of every session every case of fine or forfeiture remitted or reprieved, pardon or commutation granted, stating the name of the convict, the crime for which he was convicted, the sentence, its date, and the date of its remission, commutation, pardon, or reprieve.

SEC. 12. The Governor, Justices of the Supreme Court and Attorney-General, or a major part of them, of whom the Governor shall be one, may, upon such conditions and with such limitations and restrictions as they may deem proper, remit fines and forfeitures, commute punishments, and grant pardons after conviction in all cases except treason and impeachment, subject to such regulations as may be provided by law relative to the manner of applying for pardons.

SEC. 13. The grants and commissions shall be in the name and under the authority of the State of Florida, sealed by the great seal of the State, signed by the Governor and countersigned by the Secretary of State.

SEC. 14. A Lieutenant Governor shall be elected at the same time and places and in the same manner as the Governor, whose term of office and eligibility shall also be the same. He shall be the President of the Senate, but shall have only a casting vote therein. If, during a vacancy of the office of Governor, the Lieutenant Governor shall be impeached, displaced, resign, die or become incapable of performing the duties of his office, or be absent from the State, the President pro tempore of the Senate shall act as Governor until the office be filled or the disability cease.

SEC. 15. In the case of the impeachment of the Governor, or his removal from office, death, inability to discharge his official duties, or resignation, the power and duties of the office shall devolve upon the Lieutenant Governor for the residue of the term, or until the disability shall cease: but the Governor shall not, without the consent of the Legislature, be out of the State in time of war.

SEC. 16. The Governor may at any time require the opinion of the Justices of the Supreme Court as to the interpretation of any portion of this Constitution, or upon any point of law, and the Supreme Court shall render such opinion in writing.

SEC. 17. The Governor shall be assisted by a cabinet of administrative officers, consisting of a Secretary of State, Attorney General, Comptroller, Treasurer, Surveyor General, Superintendent of Public Instruction, Adjutant General and Commissioner of Immigration. Such officers shall be appointed by the Governor and confirmed by the Senate, and shall hold their offices the same time as the Governor, or until their successors shall be qualified.

SEC. 18. The Governor shall, by and with the consent of the Senate, appoint all commissioned officers of the State militia.

SEC. 19. The Governor shall appoint, by and with the consent of the Senate, in each county an assessor of taxes and collector of revenue, whose duties shall be prescribed by law, and who shall hold their offices for two years and be subject to removal upon the recommendation of the Governor and consent of the Senate. The Governor shall appoint in each county a County Treasurer, County Surveyor, Superintendent of Common Schools, and five County Commissioners, each of whom shall hold his office for two years, and the duties of each shall be prescribed by law. Such officers shall be subject to removal by the Governor when in his judgment the public welfare will be advanced thereby: *Provided*, No officer shall be removed except for wilful neglect of duty, or a violation of the criminal laws of the State, or for incompetency.

SEC. 20. The Governor and cabinet shall constitute a Board of Commissioners of State institutions, which board shall have supervision of all matters connected therewith, in such manner as shall be prescribed by law.

SEC. 21. The Governor shall have power, in cases of insurrection or rebellion, to suspend the writ of habeas corpus within the State.

ARTICLE VI.

JUDICIAL DEPARTMENT.

SECTION 1. The judicial power of the State shall be vested in a Supreme Court, Circuit Courts, County Courts and Justices of the Peace.

SEC. 2. The style of all process shall be "The State of Florida," and all prosecutions shall be conducted in the name and by the authority of the same.

SEC. 3. The Supreme Court shall consist of a Chief Justice and two Asspciate Justices, who shall hold their offices for life, or during good behavior. They shall be appointed by the Governor and confirmed by the Senate.

SEC. 4. The majority of the Justices of the Supreme Court shall constitute a quorum for the transaction of all business. The Supreme Court shall hold three terms each year in the Supreme Court room at the seat of government. Such terms shall commence on the second Tuesday of October, January and April respectively.

SEC. 5. The Supreme Court shall have appellate jurisdiction in all cases in equity, also in all cases of law in which is involved the title to, or right of, possession of real estate, or the legality of any tax, impost, assessment, toll, or municipal fine. or in which the demand or the value of the property in controversy exceeds three hundred dollars, also, in all other civil cases not included in the general subdivisions of law and equity; also, in all questions of law alone; in all criminal cases in which the offences charged amount to felony. The Court shall have power to issue writs of mandamus, certiorari prohibition, quo warranto, habeas corpus, and also writs necessary or proper to the complete exercise of its appellate jurisdiction. Each of the Justices shall have the power to issue writs of habeas corpus to any part of the State upon petition by, or on behalf of any person held in actual custody, and may make such writs returnable before himself or the Supreme Court, or before any Circuit Court in the State, or before any Judge of said courts.

SEC. 6. The Supreme Court shall appoint a Clerk of the Supreme Court, who shall have his office at the capitol, and shall be Librarian of the Supreme Court library. He shall hold his office until his successor is appointed and qualified.

SEC. 7. There shall be seven Circuit Judges appointed by the Governor and confirmed by the Senate, who shall hold their office for eight years. The State shall be divided into seven judicial districts, the limits of which are defined in this constitution, and one Judge shall be assigned to each circuit. Such Judge shall hold two terms of his court in each county within his circuit, each year, at such times and places as shall be prescribed by law. The Chief Justice may, in his discretion, order a temporary exchange of circuits by the respective Judges, or any Judge, to hold one or more terms in any other circuit than that to which he is assigned. The Judge shall reside in the circuit to which he is assigned.

SEC. 8. The Circuit Courts in the several judicial circuits shall have original jurisdiction in all cases of equity, also in all cases at law which involve the title or right of possession to, or the possession of, or the boundaries of real property: of the legality of any tax, impost, assessment, toll, or municipal fine, and in all other cases in which the demand or the value of property in controversy exceeds three hundred dollars, and of the action of forcible entry and unlawful detainer, and also in all criminal cases amounting to felony. They shall have final appellate jurisdiction in all civil cases arising in the County Court in which the amount in controversy is one hundred dollars and upwards, and in all cases of misdemeanor. The Circuit Courts and the Judges thereof shall have power to issue writs of mandamus, injunction, quo warranto, certiorari, and all other writs proper and necessary to the complete exercise of their jurisdicsion, and also shall have power to issue writs of habeas corpus on petition by or on behalf of any person held in actual custody in their respective circuits.

SEC. 9. There shall be a County Court organized in each county. The Governor shall appoint a County Judge for each county, who shall be confirmed by the Senate, and such Judge shall hold his office for four years from the date of his commission, or until his successor is appointed and qualified.

SEC. 10. The County Court shall be a Court of Oyer and Terminer.

SEC. 11. The County Court shall have jurisdiction of all misdemeanors and all civil cases, where the amount in controversy does not exceed three hundred dollars; but in no case shall the County Court have jurisdiction when the title or boundaries of real estate is in controversy, or where the jurisdiction will conflict with that of the several Courts of Records; but they may have coextensive jurisdiction with the Circuit Courts in cases of forcible entry and unlawful detention of real estate, subject to appeal to the Circuit Court. The County Court shall have full surrogate or probate powers, but subject to appeal. Provision shall be made by law for all other powers, duties, and responsibilities of the County Courts and Judges. There shall be a regular trial term of the County Courts six times in each year, at such times and places as may be prescribed by law.

SEC. 12. Grand and petit jurors shall be taken from the registered voters of respective counties.

SEC. 13. In all trials, civil and criminal, in the Circuit and County Courts, the evidence shall be reduced to writing by the Clerk of the Court or his deputy under the control of the Court; and every witness, after his examination shall have closed, shall be at liberty to correct the evidence he has given, and afterward shall sign the same; such evidence shall be filed in the office of the Clerk with the papers in the case.

SEC. 14. All pleas shall be sworn to either by the parties or their attorneys.

SEC. 15. The Governor shall appoint as many Justices of the Peace as he may deem necessary. Justices of the Peace shall have criminal jurisdiction and civil jurisdiction not to exceed fifty dollars, but this shall not extend to the trial of any person for misdemeanor or crime. The duties of Justices of the Peace shall be fixed by law. Justices of the Peace shall hold their offices during good behavior, subject to removal by the Governor at his own discretion.

SEC. 16. The Legislature may establish Courts for municipal purposes only, in incorporated towns and cities. All laws for the organization or government of Municipal Courts shall be general in their provisions, and be equally applicable to the Municipal Courts of all incorporated towns and cities.

SEC. 17. Any civil cause may be tried before a practicing attorney as referee upon the application of the parties, and an order from the Court in whose jurisdiction the case may be, authorizing such trial and appointing such referee. Such referee shall keep a complete record of the case, including the evidence taken, and such record shall be filed with the papers in the case in the office of the Clerk, and such cause shall be subject to an appeal in the manner prescribed by law.

SEC. 18. No other Courts than those herein specified shall be organized in this State.

SEC. 19. The Governor, by and with the advice and consent of the Senate, shall appoint a State Attorney in each judicial circuit, whose duties shall be prescribed by law. He shall hold his office for four years from the date of his commission, and until his successor shall be appointed and qualified.

The Governor, by and with the advice and consent of the Senate, shall appoint in each county a Sheriff and Clerk of the Circuit Court, who shall also be Clerk of the County Court and Board of County Commissioners, Recorder, and ex-officio Auditor of the county, each of whom shall hold his office for four years. Their duties shall be prescribed by law.

SEC. 20. A constable shall be elected by the registered voters in each county for every two hundred (200) registered voters; but each county shall be entitled to at least two constables; and no county shall have more than twelve constables. They shall perform such duties and under such instructions as shall be prescribed by law.

SEC. 21. Attorneys-at-law, who have been admitted to practice in any Court of Record in any State of the Union, or to any United States Court, shall be admitted to practice in any Court of this State on producing evidence of having been so admitted.

ARTICLE VII.

ADMINISTRATIVE DEPARTMENT.

SECTION 1. There shall be a cabinet of administrative officers, consisting of a Secretary of State, Attorney-General, Comptroller, Treasurer, Surveyor-General, Superintendent of Public Instruction, Adjutant-General, and Commissioner of Immigration, who shall assist the Governor in the performance of his duties.

SEC. 2. The Secretary of State shall keep the records of official acts of the Legislature and executive department of the government, and shall, when required, lay the same and all matters relative thereto before either branch of the Legislature, and shall be the custodian of the great seal of the State.

SEC. 3. The Attorney-General shall be a legal adviser of the Governor and of each of the Cabinet officers, and shall perform such other legal duties as the Governor may direct, or as may be provided by law. He shall be reporter for the Supreme Court.

SEC. 4. The Treasurer shall receive and keep all funds, bonds or other securities in such manner as may be provided by law, and shall disburse no funds, bonds or other securities except upon the order of the Comptroller, countersigned by the Governor, in such manner as shall be prescribed by law.

SEC. 5. The duties of the Comptroller shall be prescribed by law.

SEC. 6. The Surveyor-General shall have the administrative

supervision of all matters pertaining to the public lands, under such regulations as shall be prescribed by law.

SEC. 7. The Superintendent of Public Instruction shall have the administrative supervision of all matters pertaining to public instruction; the supervision of buildings devoted to educational purposes, and the libraries belonging to the university and common schools. He shall organize a historical bureau for the purposes of accumulating such matter and information as may be necessary for compiling and perfecting the history of the State. He shall also establish a cabinet of minerals and other natural productions.

SEC. 8. The Adjutant-General shall, under the orders of the Governor, have the administrative supervision of the Military Department and the supervision of the State prison, and of the quarantine of the coast, in such manner as shall be prescribed by law.

SEC. 9. The Commissioner of Immigration shall organize a Bureau of Immigration for the purposes of furnishing information, and for the encouragement of immigration. The office of Commissioner of Immigration shall expire at the end of 15 years from the ratification of this Constitution, but the Legislature shall have the power to continue it by law.

SEC. 10. Each officer of the Cabinet shall make a full report of his official acts, of the receipts and expenditures of his office, and of the requirements of the same, to the Governor at the beginning of each regular session of the Legislature, or whenever the Governor shall require it. Such reports shall be laid before the Legislature by the Governor, at the beginning of each regular session thereof. Either House of the Legislature may, at any time, call upon any Cabinet officer for any information required by it.

ARTICLE VIII.

EDUCATION.

SECTION 1. It is the paramount duty of the State to make ample provision for the education of all the children residing within its borders, without distinction or preference.

SEC. 2. The Legislature shall provide a uniform system of common schools, and a university, and shall provide for the liberal maintenance of the same. Instruction in them shall be free.

SEC. 3. There shall be a Superintendent of Public Instruction, whose term of office shall be four years, and until the appointment and qualification of his successor. He shall have general supervision of the educational interests of the State. His duties shall be prescribed by law.

SEC. 4. The common school fund, the interest of which shall be exclusively applied to the support and maintenance of common schools, and purchase of suitable libraries and apparatus therefor, shall be derived from the following sources: the proceeds of all lands that have been or may hereafter be granted to the State by the United States for educational purposes; donations by individuals for educational purposes; appropriations by the State; the proceeds of lands or other property which may accrue to the State by escheat or forfeiture; the proceeds of all property granted to the State, when the purpose of such grant shall not be specified; all moneys which may be paid as an exemption from military duty; all fines collected under the penal laws of this State; such portion of the per capita tax as may be prescribed by law for educational purposes; 25 per centum of the sales of public lands which are now or which hereafter may be owned by the State.

SEC. 5. A special tax of not less than one mill on the dollar of all taxable property in the State, in addition to the other means provided, shall be levied and apportioned annually for the support and maintenance of common schools.

SEC. 6. The principal of the common school fund shall remain sacred and inviolate.

SEC. 7. Provision shall be made by law for the distribution of the common school fund, among the several counties of the State, in proportion to the number of children residing therein, between the ages of 4 and 21 years.

SEC. 8. Each county shall be required to raise annually by tax, for the support of common schools therein, a sum not less than one-half of the amount apportioned to each county for that year from the income of the common school fund. Any school district neglecting to establish and maintain for at least three months in each year such school or schools as may be provided by law for such district, shall forfeit its portion of the common school fund during such neglect.

SEC. 9. The Superintendent of Public Instruction, Secretary of State, and Attorney-General shall constitute a body corporate to be known as the Board of Education of Florida. The Superintendent of Public Instruction shall be the President thereof. The duties of the Board of Education shall be prescribed by the Legislature.

ARTICLE IX.

HOMESTEAD.

SECTION 1. A homestead, to the extent of 160 acres of land, or the half of one acre, within the limits of any incorporated city or town, owned by the head of a family residing in this State, together with $1,000 worth of personal property, and the improvements on the real estate, shall be exempted from forced sale under any process of law, and the real estate shall not be alienable without the joint consent of husband and wife, when that relation exists. But no property shall be exempt from sale for taxes, or for the payment of obligations contracted for the purchase of said premises, or for the action of improvements thereon, or for house, field or other labor performed on the same. The exemption herein provided for in a city or town shall not extend to more improvements or buildings than the residence and business house of the owner.

SEC. 2. In addition to the exemption provided for in the first section of this article, there shall be and remain exempt from sale, by any legal process in the State, to the head of a family residing in this State, such property as he or she may select, to the amount of $1,000; said exemption in this section shall only prevent the sale of property in cases where the debt was contracted, liability incurred, or judgment obtained before the 10th day of May, A. D. 1865. Nothing herein contained shall be so construed as to exempt any property from sale for payment of the purchase money of the same, or for the payment of taxes or labor.

SEC. 3. The exemption provided for in sections one and two of this article shall accrue to the heirs of the party having enjoyed or taken the benefit of such exemption, and the exemption provided for in section one of this article shall apply to all debts, except as specified in said section, no matter when or where the debt was contracted or liability incurred.

ARTICLE X.

PUBLIC INSTITUTIONS.

SECTION 1. Institutions for the benefit of the insane, blind and deaf, and such other benevolent institutions as the public good may require, shall be fostered and supported by the State, subject to such regulations as may be provided by law.

SEC. 2. A State prison shall be established and maintained in such manner as may be fixed by law. Provisions may be made by law for the establishment and maintenance of a house of refuge for juvenile offenders, and the Legislature shall have power to establish a home and workhouse for common vagrants.

SEC. 3. The respective counties of the State shall provide in the manner fixed by law for those of the inhabitants who by reason of age, infirmity or misfortunes, may have claims upon the aid and sympathy of society.

ARTICLE XI.

MILITIA.

SECTION 1. All able bodied male inhabitants of this State between the ages of 18 and 45 years, who are citizens of the United States, or have declared their intentions to become citizens thereof, shall constitute the militia of the State, but no male citizen, of whatever religious creed or opinion, shall be exempt from military duty, except upon such conditions as may be prescribed by law.

SEC. 2. The Legislature shall provide by law for organizing and disciplining the militia of the State for the encouragement of volunteer corps, the safe keeping of the public arms, and for a guard for the State prison.

SEC. 3. The Adjutant-General shall have the grade of Major-General. The Governor, by and with the consent of the Senate, shall appoint two Major-Generals and four Brigadier Generals of militia. They shall take rank according to date of their commissions. The officers and soldiers of the State militia, when uniformed, shall wear the uniform prescribed for the United States army.

SEC. 4. The Governor shall have power to call out the militia to preserve the public peace, to execute the laws of the State, and to suppress insurrection or repel invasion.

ARTICLE XII.

TAXATION AND FINANCE.

SECTION 1. The Legislature shall provide for a uniform and equal rate of taxation, and shall prescribe such regulations as shall secure a just valuation of all property, both real and personal, excepting such property as may be exempted by law for municipal, educational, literary, scientific, religious or charitable purposes.

SEC. 2. The Legislature shall provide for raising revenue sufficient to defray the expenses of the State for each fiscal year, and also a sufficient sum to pay the principal and interest of the existing indebtedness of the State.

Sec. 3. No tax shall be levied, except in pursuance of law.

Sec. 4. No moneys shall be drawn from the treasury, except in pursuance of appropriations made by law.

Sec. 5. An accurate statement of the receipts and expenditures of the public moneys shall be published with the laws of each regular session of the Legislature.

Sec. 6. The Legislature shall authorize the several counties and incorporated towns in the State to impose taxes for county and corporation purposes, and for no other purpose, and all property shall be taxed upon the principle established for State taxation. The Legislature may also provide for levying a special capitation tax and tax on licenses. But the capitation tax shall not exceed $1 per annum for all purposes, either for State, county or municipal taxes.

Sec. 7. The Legislature shall have power to provide for issuing State bonds bearing interest, for securing the debt of the State, and for the erection of State buildings, support of State institutions and perfecting public works.

Sec. 8. No tax shall be levied upon persons for the benefit of any chartered company of the State, or for paying the interest on any bonds issued by said chartered companies, or by counties, or by corporations, for the above mentioned purposes.

ARTICLE XIII.

CENSUS AND APPOINTMENT.

Section 1. The Legislature shall in the year 1875, and every tenth year thereafter, cause an enumeration to be made of all the inhabitants of the State, and they shall then proceed to apportion the representation among the different counties, giving to each county one reprepresentative at large, and one additional to every 1,000 registered voters therein, but no county shall be entitled to more than four representatives.

Sec. 2. The Legislature shall, also, after every such enumeration, proceed to fix by law the number of Senators which shall constitute the Senate of Florida, and which shall never be less than one-fourth, nor more than one-half of the whole number of the Assembly. When any Senatorial district shall be composed of two or more counties, the counties of which such district consists shall not be entirely separated by any county belonging to another district, and all counties shall remain as now organized unless changed by a two-thirds vote of both houses of the Legislature.

ARTICLE XIV.

SUFFRAGE AND ELIGIBILITY.

Section 1. Every male person of the age of twenty-one years and upwards, of whatever race, color, nationality or previous condition, or who shall at the time of offering to vote be a citizen of the United States, or who shall have declared his intentions to become such in conformity to the laws of the United States, and who shall have resided and had his habitation, domicile, home and place of permanent abode in Florida for one year, and in the county for six months, next preceding the election at which he shall offer to vote, shall be deemed a qualified elector at all elections under this constitution. Every elector shall, at the time of his registration, take and subscribe to the following oath: I, —————, do solemnly swear that I will support, protect and defend the Constitution and Government of the United States, and the Constitution and Government of the State of Florida, against all enemies, foreign or domestic; that I will bear true faith, loyalty and allegiance to the same, any ordinances or resolutions of any State Convention or Legislature to the contrary notwithstanding: so help me God.

Sec. 2. No person under guardianship, non compos mentis or insane, shall be qualified to vote at any election, nor shall any person convicted of felony be qualified to vote at any election unless restored to civil rights.

Sec. 3. At any election at which a citizen or subject of any foreign country shall offer to vote, under the provisions of this Constitution, he shall present to the persons lawfully authorized to conduct and supervise such election a duly sealed and certified copy of his declaration of intention; otherwise he shall not be allowed to vote; and any naturalized citizen offering to vote shall produce before said persons lawfully authorized to conduct and supervise the election, his certificate of naturalization, or a duly sealed and certified copy thereof; otherwise he shall not be permitted to vote.

Sec. 4. The Legislature shall have power and shall enact the necessary laws to exclude from every office of honor, power, trust or profit, civil or military, within the State, and from the right of suffrage, all persons convicted of bribery, perjury, larceny, or of infamous crime, or who shall make or send or accept a challenge to fight, or who shall be a second to either party, or be the bearer of such challenge or acceptance; but the legal disability shall not accrue until after trial and conviction by due form of law.

Sec. 5. In all elections by the Legislature the vote shall be viva voce, and in all elections by the people the vote shall be by ballot.

SEC. 6. The Legislature at its first session after the ratification of this Constitution shall, by law, provide for the registration by the Clerk of the Circuit Court in each county of all the legally qualified voters in such county, and for the returns of elections ; and shall also provide that after the completion, from time to time, of such registration, no person not duly registered according to law shall be allowed to vote.

SEC. 7. The Legislature shall enact laws requiring educational qualifications for electors after the year one thousand eight hundred and eighty, but no such laws shall be made applicable to any elector who may have registered or voted at any elections previous thereto.

ARTICLE XV.

SCHEDULE.

SECTION 1. That all ordinances and resolutions heretofore passed by any convention of the people, and all Acts and resolutions of the Legislature conflicting or inconsistent with the Constitution of the United States and the statutes thereof, and with this Constitution, and in derogation of the existence or position of the State as one of the States of the United States of America, are hereby declared null and void, and of no effect.

SEC. 2. That all Acts and resolutions of the General Assembly, and all official Acts of the civil officers of the State, not inconsistent with the provisions of the Constitution and statutes of the United States, or with this Constitution, or with any ordinance or resolution adopted by this convention, and which have not been and are not by this Constitution annulled, are in force, and shall be considered and esteemed as the laws of the State until such Acts or resolutions shall be repealed by the Legislature of the State or this convention.

SEC. 3. All laws of the State passed by the so-called General Assembly since the 10th day of January, A. D. 1861, not conflicting with the word or spirit of the Constitution and laws of the United States, or with this Constitution, shall be valid. All writs, acts, proceedings, judgments and decrees of the so-called courts of the State, where actual service was made on the defendant : all executions and sales made thereunder, and all acts, orders and proceedings of the Judges of Probate, and of executors, administrators, guardians and trustees, provided they were in conformity with the laws then in force, and did not conflict with the Constitution and laws of the United States and this

Constitution, shall be valid. The sales of the property or effects of deceased persons shall not prevent the widow from claiming said property in kind, in whosesoever hands the same may be found, when the sale had not been made for the purpose of paying the debts of the deceased, and where other than lawful money of the United States was obtained for said property. Nothing herein contained shall be so construed as to make any one who, as an officer of any court, or who acted under the authority of any court, individually liable, provided they acted strictly in accordance with what was then considered the law of the State, and not conflicting with the Constitution and laws of the United States. All fines, penalties, forfeitures, obligations and escheats heretofore accruing to the State of Florida shall continue to accrue to the use of the State. All recognizances heretofore taken shall remain valid, and all bonds executed to the Governor of the State of Florida, either before or since the 10th day of January, A. D. 1861, or to any other officer of the State in his official capacity, shall be of full force and virtue for the uses therein respectively expressed, and may be sued for and recovered accordingly, unless they were contrary to the laws of the United States or to this Constitution, or to any ordinance or resolution adopted by the convention; also all criminal prosecutions which have arisen may be prosecuted to judgment and execution in the name of the State. All actions at law or suits in chancery, or any proceedings pending in the courts of this State either prior to or subsequent to the 10th day of January, A. D. 1861, shall continue in all respects valid, and may be prosecuted to judgment and decree. All judgments and decrees rendered in civil causes in any of the courts of the State during the period of time above specified are hereby declared of full force, validity and effect: *Provided*, That unless otherwise provided in this Constitution the statute of limitation shall not be pleaded upon any claim in the hands of any person for the period of time between the 10th day of January, A. D. 1861, and the 25th day of October, A. D. 1865, whether proceedings of law had been commenced before the 25th day of October, 1865, or not: *Provided, further*, That all claims of widows, minors and decedents which were not barred by the statutes of this State on the 10th day of January, A. D. 1861, shall be considered good and valid for the period of two years from the ratification of this Constitution.

Sec. 4. That State treasury notes, all bonds issued, and all other liabilities contracted by the State of Florida or any county or city thereof, on and after the 10th day of January, A. D. 1861, and before the 25th day of October, A. D. 1865, except such liabilities as may be due to the seminary or school fund, be and are declared null and void, and the Legislature shall have no power to provide for the payment of the same or any part thereof; but this shall not be construed so as to invalidate any authorized liabilities of the State, contracted prior to the 10th day of January, A. D. 1861, or subsequent to the 25th day of October, A. D. 1865.

SEC. 5. No money shall ever be appropriated by this State to reimburse purchasers of United States land who purchased the same of the State of Florida.

SEC. 6. All proceedings, decisions or actions accomplished by civil or military officers acting under authority of the United States subsequent to the 10th day of January, 1861, and prior to the final restoration of the State to the government of the United States, are hereby declared valid, and shall not be subject to adjudication in the courts of this State; nor shall any person acting in the capacity of a soldier or officer of the United States, civil or military, be subject to arrest for any act performed by him, pursuant to authorized instructions from his superior officers during the period of time above designated.

SEC. 7. That in all cases where judgments have been obtained against citizens of the State after the tenth day of January, eighteen hundred and sixty-one, previous to the twenty-fifth day of October, eighteen hundred and sixty-five, and where actual service was not made on the person of any defendant, such defendant not served with process may appear in court within one year after the adoption of this Constitution, and make oath that injustice has been done and that he or she has a good and valid defence, stating the defence, and upon making such oath, and filing said defence, the proceedings on the judgment shall cease until the defence is heard.

ARTICLE XVI.

MISCELLANEOUS.

SECTION 1. Any person debarred from holding office in the State of Florida by the third section of the fourteenth article of the proposed amendment to the Constitution of the United States, which is as follows: "No person shall be Senator or representative in Congress, or elector of President, or Vice-President, or hold any office, civil or military, under the United States, or under any State, who, having previously taken an oath as a member of Congress, or as an officer of the United States, or as a member of any State Legislature, or as an executive or judicial officer of any State, to support the Constitution of the United States, shall have engaged in insurrection or rebellion against the same or given aid and comfort to the enemies thereof. But Congress may, by a vote of two-thirds of each house, remove such disability," is hereby debarred from holding office in this State: *Provided*, That whenever such disability from holding office shall be removed from any person by the Congress of the United States, the removal of such disability shall also apply to this State, and such person shall be restored in all respects to the rights of citizenship as herein provided for electors.

SEC. 2. Any person elected to the Senate of the United States by the Legislature of this State, or any person elected by the people, or appointed to office by the Governor of the State, or by any officer of the State, under the provison of the Constitution adopted by the convention of the people, convened on the 25th day of October, 1865, shall not be empowered to hold such office after the same position or office shall have been filled by election or appointment under the provisions of this Constitution: *Provided*, That all officers holding office under the provisions of the Constitution adopted the 25th day of October, A. D. 1865, and not provided for in this Constitution, shall continue to hold their respective offices, and discharge the duties thereof, until the Governor shall by his proclamation, declare such offices vacant.

SEC. 3. The several judicial circuits of the Circuit Courts shall be as follows: The first judicial circuit shall be composed of the counties of Escambia. Santa Rosa, Walton, Holmes, Washington and Jackson; the second judicial circuit shall be composed of the counties of Gadsden, Liberty, Calhoun, Franklin, Wakulla, and Jefferson; the third judicial circuit shall be composed of the counties of Madison, Taylor, Lafayette, Hamilton, Suwannee and Columbia; the fourth judicial circuit shall be composed of the counties of Nassau, Duval, Baker, Bradford, Clay and St. John's; the fifth judicial circuit shall be composed of the counties of Putnam, Alachua, Levy, Marion and Sumter; the sixth judicial circuit shall be composed of the counties of Hernando, Hillsborough, Manatee, Polk and Monroe; the seventh judicial circuit shall be composed of the counties of Volusia, Brevard, Orange and Dade.

SEC. 4. The salary of the Governor of the State shall be five thousand dollars per annum; that of the Chief Justice shall be four thousand five hundred dollars; that of each Associate Justice shall be four thousand dollars; that of each Judge of the Circuit Court shall be three thousand five hundred dollars; that of the Lieutenant Governor shall be two thousand five hundred dollars; that of each cabinet officer shall be three thousand dollars; the pay of the members of the Senate and House of

Representatives shall be five hundred dollars per annum, and in addition thereto ten cents per mile for each mile traveled from their respective places of residence to the capital, and the same to return; but such distances shall be estimated by the shortest general thoroughfare. All other officers of the State shall be paid by fees, or per diem, fixed by law.

SEC. 5. The Legislature shall appropriate two thousand dollars each year for the purchase of such books for the Supreme Court library as the said court shall direct.

SEC. 6. The salary of each officer shall be payable quarterly, upon his own requisition.

SEC. 7. The tribe of Indians located in the southern portion of the State and known as the Seminole Indians, shall be entitled to one member in each house of the Legislature. Such member shall have all the rights, privileges and remuneration as other members of the Legislature. Such members shall be elected by the members of their tribe, in the manner prescribed for all elections by this Constitution. The tribe shall be represented only by a member of the same, and in no case by a white man: *Provided*, That the representative of the Seminole Indians shall not be a bar to the representation of any county by the citizens thereof.

SEC. 8. The Legislature may at any time impose such tax on the Indians as it may deem proper; and such imposition of tax shall constitute the Indians citizens, and they shall thenceforward be entitled to all the privileges of other citizens, and thereafter be barred of special representation.

SEC. 9. In addition to other crimes and misdemeanors for which an officer may be impeached and tried, shall be included drukenness and other dissipation, incompetency, malfeasance in office, gambling, or any conduct detrimental to good morals, shall be considered sufficient cause for impeachment and conviction. Any officer when impeached by the Assembly, shall be deemed under arrest, and shall be disqualified from performing any of the duties of his office until acquittal by the Senate. But any officer so impeached and in arrest may demand his trial by the Senate within one year from the date of his impeachment.

SEC. 10. The following shall be the oath of office for each officer in the State, including members of the Legislature: "I do solemnly swear that I will support, protect, and defend the Constitution and government of the United States, and of the State of Florida, against all enemies, domestic or foreign, and that I will bear true faith, loyalty, and allegiance to the same, and that I am entitled to hold office under this Constitution. That I will well and faithfully perform all the duties of the office of ―――, on which I am about to enter: so help me God."

Sec. 11. The Legislature may provide for the donation of the public lands to actual settlers. But such donation shall not exceed one hundred and sixty acres of land to any one person.

Sec. 12. All county officers shall hold their respective offices at the county seats of their counties.

Sec. 13. The Legislature shall provide for the speedy publication of all statutes and laws of a general nature. All decisions of the Supreme Court and all laws and judicial decisions shall be free for publication by any person. But no judgment of the Supreme Court shall take effect and be operative until the opinion of the court in such case shall be filed with the Clerk of of said court.

Sec. 14. The Legislature shall not create any office the term of which shall be longer than four years.

Sec. 15. The Governor, Cabinet, and Supreme Court shall keep their offices at the seat of government. But in case of invasion or violent epidemics the Governor may direct that the offices of the government shall be removed temporarily to some other place; but in such case of removal all the departments of the government shall be removed to one place. But such removal shall not continue longer than necessity for the same shall continue.

Sec 16. A plurality of votes given at any election by the people shall constitute a choice, when not otherwise provided by this Constitution.

Sec. 17. The term of State officers elected at the first election under this Constitution, not otherwise provided for, shall continue until the first Tuesday of January, A. D. 1873, and until the installation of their successsors, excepting the members of the Legislature.

Sec. 18. Each county and incorporated city shall make provision for the support of its own officers, subject to such regulations as may be prescribed by law. Each county shall make provision for building a court-house and jail, and for keeping the same in good repair.

Sec. 19. If at the meeting of the Senate at any session, the Lieutenaut-Governor has not been qualified, or is not present, the Senate shall elect one of its members as temporary President before proceeding to other business.

Sec. 20. The Legislature shall at its first session adopt a a seal for the State, and such seal shall be of the size of the American silver dollar. But said seal shall not again be changed after its adoption by the Legislature; and the Governor shall, by his proclamation, announce that said seal has become the great seal of the State.

Sec. 21. The Governor, Lieutenant-Governor, and all the

State officers elected by the people, shall be installed on the first day of the meeting of the Legislature, and immediately assume the duties of their respective offices.

Sec. 22. The Governor and Lieutenant-Governor shall have been before their election to office nine years citizens of the United States, and three years citizens of the State. All other officers shall have been one year citizens of the State, and six months citizens of the county from which they are elected or appointed. No person shall be eligible to any office unless he be a registered voter.

Sec. 23. The Governor or any State officer is hereby prohibited from giving certificates of election or other credentials to any person as having been elected to the House of Representatives of the United States Congress, or the United States Senate, who has not been two years a citizen of the State, and nine years a citizen of the United States, and a registered voter.

Sec. 24. The property of all corporations, whether heretofore, or hereafter incorporated, shall be subject to taxation, unless such corporation be for religious, educational, or charitable purposes.

Sec. 25. All bills, bonds, notes, or evidences of debt outstanding and unpaid, given for or in consideration of bonds or treasury notes of the so-called Confederate States, or notes and bonds of this state paid and redeemable in the bonds and notes of the Confederate States, are hereby declared null and void, and no action shall be maintained thereon in the courts of this State.

Sec. 26. It shall be the duty of the courts to consider that there is a failure of consideration, and it shall be so held by the courts of this State, upon all deeds or bills of sale given for slaves with covenant or warranty of title or soundness, or both: upon all bonds, notes, or other evidences of debt, given for or in consideration of slaves, which are now outstanding and unpaid, and no action shall be maintained thereon: and all judgements and decrees rendered in any of the courts of this State since the 10th day of January, A. D., 1861, upon all deeds or bills of sale, or upon any bond, bill, note, or other evidence of debt based upon the sale or purchase of slaves, are hereby declared set aside, and the plea of failure of consideration shall be held a good defence in all actions to said suit: and when money was due previous to the 10th day of January, 1861, and slaves were given in consideration for such money, there shall be deemed a failure of consideration for the debt: *Provided*, That settlements and compromises made by the parties thereto shall be respected.

Sec. 27. All persons who as alien enemies under the sequestration act of the so-called Confederate Congress, and now resident of the State, had property sequestered and sold by any person acting under a law of the so-called Confederate States, or the State of Florida, subsequent to the 10th day of January, A. D., 1861, and prior to the 1st day of May, 1865, shall be empowered to file a bill in equity in the Circuit Court of the State, and shall be entitled to obtain judgment against the State for all damages sustained by said sale and detention of property. The court shall estimate the damages upon the assessed valuation of the property in question in the year A. D., 1860, with interest at six per cent. from the time the owner was deprived of the same. But all judgments against the State shall be paid only in certificates of indebtedness redeemable in State lands. Said certificates shall be issued by the Governor, countersigned by the Secretary of State and by the Comptroller upon the decree of the court. Oral testimony shall be sufficient to establish a sale having been made.

SEC. 28. There shall be no civil or political distinction in this State on account of race, color, or previous condition of servitude, and the Legislature shall have no power to prohibit by law any class of persons on account of race, color, or previous condition of servitude, to vote or hold any office, beyond the conditions prescribed by this Constitution.

SEC. 29. The apportionment for the Assembly shall be as follows: Escambia, two; Santa Rosa, one; Walton, one; Holmes, one; Washington, one; Jackson, three; Calhoun, one; Gadsden, two; Franklin, one; Liberty, one; Wakulla, one; Leon, four; Jefferson, three; Madison, two; Taylor, one; Hamilton, one; Suwannee, one; Layayette, one; Alachua, two; Columbia, two; Baker, one; Bradford, one; Nassau, one; Duval, two; Clay, one; St. John's one; Putnam, one; Marion, two; Levy, one; Volusia, one; one; Orange, one; Brevard, one; Dade, one; Hillsborough, one; Hernando, one; Sumpter, one; Polk, one; Manatee, one; and Monroe, one. There shall be twenty-four senatorial districts, which shall be as follows, and shall be known by their respective numbers from one to twenty-four inclusive. The first senatorial district shall be composed of Escambia county, the second of Santa Rosa and Walton, the third of Jackson, the fourth of Holmes and Washington, the fifth of Calhoun and Franklin, the sixth of Gadsden, the seventh of Liberty and Wakulla, the eighth of Leon, the ninth of Jefferson, the tenth of Madison, the eleventh of Hamilton and Suwannee, the twelfth of Lafayette and Taylor, the thirteenth of Alachua and Levy, the fourteenth of Columbia, the fifteenth of Bradford and Clay, the sixteenth of Baker and Nassau, the seventeenth of St. John's and Putnam, the eighteenth of Duval, the nineteenth of Marion, the twentieth of Volusia and Orange, the twenty-first of Dade and Brevard, the twenty-second of Hillsborough and Hernando, the twenty-third of Sumter and Polk, the twenty-fourth of Manatee and Monroe, and each senatorial district shall be entitled to one Senator.

SEC. 30. No person shall ever be appointed a Judge of the Supreme or Circuit Court who is not twenty-five years of age and a practicing attorney in this State.

SEC. 31. The Legislature shall as soon as convenient adopt a State emblem, having the design of the great seal of the State impressed upon a white ground of six feet six inches fly and six feet deep.

ARTICLE XVII

AMENDMENTS.

SECTION 1. Any amendment or amendments to this Constitution may be proposed in either branch of the Legislature, and if the same shall be agreed upon by a two-thirds vote of all the members elected to each of the two houses, such proposed amendment or amendments shall be entered on their respective journals, with the yeas and nays thereon, and referred to the Legislature then next to be chosen, and shall be published for three months next preceding the time of making such choice, and if, in the Legislature next chosen as aforesaid, such proposed amendment or amendments shall be agreed to by two-thirds vote of all the members elected to each house, then it shall be the duty of the Legislature to submit such proposed amendment or amendments to the people in such manner and at such a time as the Legislature may prescribe, and if the people shall approve and ratify such amendment or amendments by a majority of the electors qualified to vote for members of the Legislature voting thereon, such amendment or amendments shall become a part of the constitution.

SEC. 2. If at any time the Legislature, by a vote of a majority of all the members elected to each of the two houses, shall determine that it is necessary to cause a revision of this entire constitution, such determination shall be entered on their respective journals, with the yeas and nays thereon, and referred to the Legislature then next to be chosen, and shall be published for three months next preceding the time of making such choice. And if the Legislature next chosen aforesaid such proposed revision shall be agreed by a majority of all the members elected to each house, then it shall be the duty of the Legislature to recommend to the electors of the next election for members of Legislature to vote for or against a convention; and if it shall appear that a majority of the electors voting at such election shall have voted in favor of calling a convention, the Legislature shall, at its next session, provide by law for a convention to be holden within six months after the passage of such law, and such convention shall consist of a number of members not less than both branches of the Legislature. In determining what is a majority of the electors voting at such election, reference shall be had to the highest number of votes cast at such election for the candidates for any office or on any question.

Done in open convention. In witness whereof, we, the undersigned delegates, representing the people of Florida, in convention assembled, do hereunto affix our name this the twenty-fifth day of February, anno Domini one thousand eight hundred and sixty-eight, and of the independence of the United States the ninety-second, and the secretary doth countersign the same.

HORATIO JENKINS, JR., *President*.
S. CONANT, *Secretary*.

Countersigned by—

George J. Alden.
Lyman W. Rowley.
J. W. Butler.
John L. Campbell.
W. J. Purman.
L. C. Armistead.
E. Fortune.
H. Bryan.
M. L. Stearns.
J. E. A. Davidson.
Frederick Hill.
J. W. Childs.
T. W. Osborn.
Joseph E. Oats.
Richard Wells.
Green Davidson.
O. B. Armstrong.
John Wyatt.
John W. Powell.
Robert Meacham.
Anthony Mills.
A. G. Bass.

Roland T. Rombauer.
Major Johnson.
William R. Cone.
Thomas Urquhart.
Andrew Shuler.
J. N. Krimminger.
William K. Cessna.
Josiah T. Walls.
S. B. Conover.
Auburn Erwin.
B. McRae.
A. B. Hart.
N. C. Dennett.
William Bradwell.
J. C. Gibbs.
J. H. Goss.
A. Chandler.
W Rogers.
Samuel J. Pearce.
C. R. Mobley.
David Mizell.
E. L. Ware.

I, Sherman Conant, secretary of the said convention, do hereby certify that the foregoing is a true copy of the constitution adopted on the 25th day of February, A D., 1868.

SHERMAN CONANT, *Secretary*.

APPENDIX D.

FLORIDA POLITICAL FRAUDS.

The following correspondence between Mr. George Couch, of the State of New York, who, with his family, spent last winter and spring in Tallahassee, and Mr. Hilton, of this city, speaks for itself:

CANANDAIGUA, October 6, 1876.

Judge Hilton, Tallahassee, Fla.:

DEAR SIR—I learned while at Florida that in your Governor's election, when Bloxham run, that it turned out at or nearly the close of the time of the expiration of office, that Bloxham was fairly elected but was cheated out of the office through fraudulent returns. I wish you would write out the facts relating to this and send them to me immediately in a statement that I can vouch for. I want to show some of the croakers that the frauds practiced South come from a different side of the house than what they preach. Please answer by return mail.

GEORGE COUCH.

TALLAHASSEE, October 12, 1876.

George Couch, Esq., Canandaigua, N. Y.:

DEAR SIR—To your note of the 6th inst., received this morning, I reply at once.

The facts of the case to which you refer are these: At the election held in this State, November 8, 1870, W. D. Bloxham, Esq., was candidate for the office, not of Governor, but Lieutenant-Governor; Mr. Niblack being at the same election candidate for the office of Representative in Congress—Florida then compsising but one Congressional District. Both were Democrats, and both were elected. Their opponents were Samuel T. Day, for the office of Lieutenant-Governor, and Mr. Josiah T. Walls (colored) for Congressman, Republicans; and they, though neither of them received as many votes as his Democratic competitor, were declared by the State Canvassing Board elected. The Canvassing Board consisted at the time of Jonathan C. Gibbs (colored), Secretary of State, Sherman Conant, Attorney-General (and at the same time Deputy U. S. Marshal), both Republicans, and R. H. Gamble, an old Line Whig, who dissented from the action of a majority of the Board.

The Board were able to perpetrate this outrage by suppressing and refusing to canvass and count the returns from nine counties, in which Bloxham received a majority of 678 votes, and in which Niblack received a still larger majority.

As counsel for Mr. Bloxham, I thereupon applied to the Supreme Court of the State (our highest judicial tribunal), for an *order* (known in law as a writ of *mandamus*), to compel the Board to include in the canvass the rejected returns, and as a result to declare Bloxham elected, and to award him a certificate of his election. The petition praying for the *mandamus* set forth fully the facts of the case—that the election had been held—that Bloxham was a candidate—that he possessed the legal qualifications for the office—that he had received a majority of the votes cast, but was wrongfully denied a certificate of his election by the refusal of the Board to canvass and count the votes cast in the nine counties above mentioned. None of these facts were denied by the counsel for the Board in the arguments before the court on the question of granting the peremptory writ. The objection made was that the court had no jurisdiction of the case, and for that reason should not make the order. But the authorities furnished by the decisions of other judicial tribunals (particularly of the Supreme Court of Iowa), were so directly in point that our court was compelled to decide that it had rightful jurisdiction in the matter. But the court discovered a very nice technical defect in the petition for the *mandamus*, which had not occurred either to the minds of counsel for the Board or to that of counsel for Bloxham, which was this: The petition not only asked that the Board of Canvassers be ordered to count the rejected returns and declare Bloxham elected (which was all right), but that the Secretary of State as the organ of the Board (made so by law), be required to give him a certificate of his election. The court held that inasmuch as the Board had not counted all the the returns and declared Bloxham elected, it had never been the duty of the Secretary to furnish him the certificate; that the petition must therefore be amended by striking out so much as asked that that officer be ordered to give the certificate, and that upon such amendment being made the order requiring the Board to count the rejected returns and declare Bloxham elected, would be granted.

The petition was thereupon amended to meet the views of the court. A few days (perhaps three or four), however, elapsed before the matter could be brought in the court again; and then it was discovered that during the interval a bill had been surreptitiously hurried through the Legislature (in which body, by reason of the rejection of the returns from the eight counties, the Republicans had secured a majority) and had become a law by the approval of the Governor, whereby the State Canvassing Board had been abolished, so that, as the court held, there could be no further legal proceedings against them to compel them to do their duty. Thus (as far as I am aware), by an unprecedented legislative outrage, judicial proceedings instituted in the name of the State, to secure for one of her citizens the office to which a majority of the people had elected him, were summarily arrested.

If you have access to any lawyer's library containing the Florida Reports you will find the case published in the 13 volume, Florida Reports, commencing at page 55, where all the facts are given. The title of the case is "The State of Florida *ex rel.*" Wm. D. Bloxham vs. Jonathan C. Gibbs, Secretary of State, *et al.*" Thus thwarted in the prosecution of his legal rights through the summary and expeditious process of *mandamus* by the intervention of the Legislature, nothing was left for Bloxham but to institute in the same court tedious proceedings by an action at law against his competitor to recover the office. In these proceedings, involving great expense and delays, he was finally successful, and by the unanimous judgment of a court, two-thirds of whose members were Republican in politics, he obtained a decision awarding him the office to which the people had more than eighteen months previous elected him. This second case, for some reason which we are left to conjecture, has not gone into the Florida Reports, but I send you a certified copy of the judgment rendered, taken from the records.

As regards Judge Niblack, elected to Congress at the same time that Mr. Bloxham was elected Lieutenant-Governor, and defrauded of a certificate of his election in the same way, what of him? I answer, after a contest before the House of Representatives at Washington, he finally suceeded in ousting Walls, who had usurped the seat for *twenty-three months*. This tardy act of justice he obtained at the hands of members of Congress two-thirds of whom were Republican. I may add that in the election of 1874, the same gentleman, Mr. Walls, was again a candidate for Congress, Judge Finley being his Democratic opponent. Again he obtained a certificate of election to a seat to which he appears not to have been entitled; and again the House of Representatives (this time Democratic) after a much shorter contest, however, required him to give place to his Democratic opponent.

One thing I have not mentioned in connection with the State Canvassing Board who perpetrated the fraud of which Bloxham and Niblack and the people who elected them were the victims. That is this: Sherman Conant, U. S. Deputy Marshal and now holding the office of Marshal, was not Attorney-General and thus a member of the State Canvassing Board at the time of that election. The then Attorney-General resigned between the date of the election and the day when the election returns were canvassed. He resigned, it is believed, rather than be a party to the fraud which the Republican managers required at the hands of the Board. Marshal Conant was appointed to the vacant office of Attorney-General, and thus one of the Board of Canvassers (still, however, retaining his Federal office) because his reputation as a ballot-box stuffer, established at the election for Governor in 1868, showed that there was no political job unworthy of his hands. As I have said, he is still United States Marshal.

It was during his reign when it was necessary, in 1871, at the meeting of the Legislature, for the Republicans to obtain control of the Senate, that two Democratic Senators were arrested here at the capital and taken off 165 miles to Jacksonville (although Tallahassee was and is one of the places fixed by law for holding the U. S. Court). They were kept at Jacksonville on a trumped up charge of crime, for which neither of them was ever tried, *until the Radicals, by ousting members entitled to seats and putting in their places men having no claim to membership*, obtained a working majority of both branches of the Legislature. Under the same reign, too, it was that a few days before the Tallahassee municipal election in 1871, at which it was thought the vote between parties would be very close, a number of our prominent citizens, all Democrats, were taken to Jacksonville, at the expense of the United States Government, as witnesses, summoned to go before the U. S Grand Jury, not one of whom was, after getting there, called upon to testify.

In view of outrages like these, the recital of which would fill not a letter but a volume, which we have suffered at the hands of our carpet-bag officials, both State and Federal—(our Legislature has been largely controlled by Federal office holders also members of that body), you need not be surprised to hear that the people of Florida are looking with aching eyes and yearning hearts for the man, be he Tilden or Hayes, who is to give us Civil Service Reform. Only this, however, I add: as Conant & Co. are the agencies by which the reform is expected to be accomplished here, in the event of the election of Governor Hayes, and as they are the parties to be reformed by their own expulsion from office, we are not sanguine as to the success of the reform promised us by the Northern supporters of the Republican Presidential candidate. "Can Beelzebub cast out devils?" or will he if he can?

Very truly your friend,
R. B. HILTON.

APPENDIX E.

TALLAHASSEE, FLA., Jan. 31, 1887.

Hon. Harrison Reed, Jacksonville, Fla.:

DEAR SIR—I am engaged in writing up the history of the reconstruction of this State, and as you were the centre of attraction in this theatre, please give me correct information on the following points, which were commonly rumored over the State while you were Governor: Was there any attempt made by Purman, Stearns & Co. to do violence to you while Governor in order to get you out of the way at all hazards? Did you ever overhear any of this gang at any place plotting to put you to death? If so, please state their names and the circumstances. This information will be thankfully received by me.

Yours truly,

JOHN WALLACE.

SOUTH JACKSONVILLE, Feb. 9, 1887.

Hon. John Wallace:

DEAR SIR—In reply to the enquiries of your letter of 31st ult., I regret to say that at various periods during my official term as Governor attempts were made by persons holding Federal offices, by procurement of Senator Osborn, to compel me to surrender my office; but I was not personally cognizant of any intended violence other than that which attended the attempt to forcibly install Lieutenant-Governor Gleason as Governor. On that occasion a conspiracy was formed by Osborn and his military satraps and the Richards-Billings faction, to depose me by violence and take possession of the capitol. This was within a few months after my inauguration, in consequence of my refusal to obey their dictation to "vandalize the State," to quote the expression of Osborn, in my exercise of the appointing power. It embraced all the prominent Federal office-holders in the State, from the marshal down, most of whom were in the Legislature, subject to orders from Osborn under penalty of removal. This conspiracy was defeated only through the vigilance of Adjutant-General Carse, aided by the faithful and incorruptible Sheriff Munger, of Leon county, sustained by leading citizens.

On that occasion the capitol was under siege, and for forty-six days and nights was guarded by an armed force of volunteers under General Carse. By way of intimidation signal rockets were sent up during the night from the City Hotel, where the revolutionists had their headquarters, and my boarding-house was frequently disturbed on stormy nights by the firing of guns and pistols in close proximity. These measures not securing the desired effect, a plan was devised to take me from my room by night and secretly dispose of me, while arousing the North by the charge that a Republican Governor had been assassinated by "rebel Ku-Klux;" and this was only frustrated by its discovery to General Carse, to whose vigilance on that occasion I owe my life.

At a later period I was advised by letter of a meeting of three of the conspirators at a room in the City Hotel, at which it was agreed that I should be violently disposed of. Purman was not of the alleged two, but Stearns was, and the other two were Federal office-holders who were conspicuous in the three subsequent attempts at my impeachment which dishonored the Republican name and overthrew the Republican party in the State.

Soon after this alleged meeting at the City Hotel, the notorious Luke Lott, of Calhoun county, appeared in Tallahassee for the avowed purpose to assassinate me, and was only prevented by my temporary absence, and through the intervention of Governor Bloxham, who learned his mission and persuaded him to abandon it.

I received repeated anonymous threats, and wherever I went on official or private business I was followed by Osborn's spies and emissaries, and on one occasion was arrested in New York at 4 o'clock in the afternoon, on criminal charges framed in Washington, and sworn to by a man I had never seen, admitted to be wholly false, for the sole purpose of compelling my confinement to Ludlow Street Jail over Sunday. It was supposed that at that late hour I could not obtain legal assistance, but, fortunately, Lieutenant-Governor

Woodford was found, and immediately successfully interfered in my behalf.

When I assumed the prerogatives of my office, after the dissolution of the court convened for my impeachment, the infamous Lieutenant-Governor Day publicly offered a reward for my head, and, with the approval of a Republican gathering at Jacksonville, threatened to hang me in she Capitol Square if caught in Tallahassee.

Subsequently, when Day was ousted as Lieutenant-Governor by the court and Bloxham declared elected, I received from Washington, marked "Important" and headed "Strictly Private," a letter from a prominent representative of Osborn & Stearns' Great Southern Railway Swindle, a letter of which the following is a true copy:

WASHINGTON, D. C., June 2nd., 1872.

Hon. H. Reed:

DEAR GOVERNOR—I deem it my duty to put you in possession of some important information I came across this morning when I went to breakfast at the Ebbitt House. I was called one side by a prominent Georgia Democrat with whom I became acquainted two years ago at Atlanta, and whom I served by helping him in a measure he had before Governor Bullock for his approval. This gentleman asked me if I was a friend of Governor Reed, and if I had any interest in you personally? I replied, of course I had, and, as he knew, was largely interested in railroad matters. He then asked me if I had seen the Press dispatches in the morning paper? I replied I had not yet read the papers, when he called my attention to the dispatch saying Bloxham was sworn in as Lieutenant-Governor. He said he was anxious to put me on my guard and to give me some very valuable information for my own benefit, but I must pledge that I would in no way divulge or in any way let the knowledge out to any other person. I gave him a promise which I do not think I am now breaking by revealing this conversation to *you.* This man says that certain Georgia, Alabama and Florida Democrats were here and had had a secret caucus, and that it had been determined that Reed should not be in the way of the election this fall, and that Bloxham now being in the succession and

Georgia and Alabama being Democratic, that Florida must be so, even to the sacrifice of Reed, who should be put under the ground if he did not quietly give way to them. He advised me to make friends with Bloxham, and he and Governor Smith would help me through with my road. I asked him if he was in earnest, and he said most emphatically, "By God, old Reed will not be alive three months if he don't surrender. We now have a chance, and we shall not let it slip—we are bound to have Florida from the Republicans, cost what it may, and the only thing now in the way is Reed." I put the question to him in half a dozen different ways "how they intended to get control, and he replied each time in the same manner. They now had the State and Reed must bite the dust or surrender. I then asked him to give me the names of the parties in this move, and he replied: "You did me a favor in Atlanta two years ago; I now do you one telling you how to secure your railroad interests in both States, but you ask me more than I will tell when you ask for names." This is all I could get, and give it to you as I got it, believing, as I do, every word of it. I have done only for you what I believe you would have done for me, and if I have done you a service I shall be glad.

  I am, yours very respectfully,

L. Box 183, Washington, D. C.

  It would take reams of paper to give you all the details of the conspiracy to subvert the State government to corrupt purposes and involve the State in dishonor for the benefit of an army of "bummers" and political adventurers who fastened upon the Freedman's Bureau to debauch the freedmen for personal aggrandizement. Suffice it that the conspirators were thwarted and, with a few exceptions, have gone hence, leaving the State to their political opponents, who are doing their best to render Republican administration respectable in comparison.

    Very truly, your obedient servant,
      HARRISON REED.

www.ingramcontent.com/pod-product-compliance
Lightning Source LLC
Chambersburg PA
CBHW022141300426
44115CB00006B/284